A TASTE OF POWER

ELAINE BROWN

A TASTE OF POWER

A Black Woman's Story

PANTHEON BOOKS   NEW YORK

Library of Congress Cataloging-in-Publication Data

Brown, Elaine, 1943–
    A taste of power / Elaine Brown.
        p. cm.
    ISBN 0-679-41944-6
    1. Brown, Elaine, 1943–   . 2. Black Panther Party—Biography.   3. Afro-Americans-Biography. 4. Black power—United States. I. Title.
    E185.97.B866A3   1992
    973'.049607302—dc20
    [B]   91-15579
                                                                                              CIP

Manufactured in the United States of America
First Edition

For Ericka Suzanne Brown
Thank you for your gift of life

CONTENTS

ACKNOWLEDGMENTS

Though the writing of this book required eight years of my life to complete, I was not alone. I was bolstered by a small and special community of people, whom I wish to acknowledge:

SUZANNE DE PASSE, who made me believe I had a story worth telling and that I was worthy of telling it.

CALVIN HERNTON, who patiently gave me the tools of his artistry, and challenged me tenderly to be true to the word and find the true words.

KAY LEVATTER, my psychotherapist for seven years, who guided me carefully through the valley of the past.

AMANDA URBAN, my literary agent, who started with me and stayed with me because she believed in me.

LINDA HEALEY, my editor, whose pen was at once healing and merciful.

PIERRE ELBY, whose love over the past years gave me the spirit to see this through and whose support gave me the strength to do it.

DOROTHY CLARK, my mother, who gave me something more than I recognized when I set about this writing: the ability to write.

INTRODUCTION

This is a chronicle of the life of a black woman-child in America. It is my life.

Reflected here is life as I lived it, my thoughts and feelings as I remember them. Here, too, are my personal exchanges with others. In reconstructing them, I have relied on my knowledge of opinions held, and my recollection of articulated ideas and very specific words in their context.

Memory seems a fragile spirit. It may be a river of reality that gathers dreams and desires and change in its flow. Nevertheless, I have tried to be faithful to both fact and feeling.

A
TASTE
OF
POWER

CHAPTER 1

ASSUMPTION

"I HAVE ALL THE GUNS AND ALL THE MONEY. I can withstand challenge from without and from within. Am I right, Comrade?"

Larry snapped back his answer to my rhetorical question: "Right on!" His muscular body tilted slightly as he adjusted the .45 automatic pistol under his jacket.

I was standing on the stage, with him at my side. Several of the key Brothers from the security squads were standing just in back of us. To my left I could feel Big Bob, Huey Newton's personal bodyguard, all six feet eight inches and four hundred pounds of him. In front of me, extending all the way to the back of the auditorium, were several hundred other members of the Black Panther Party, a sea of predominantly male faces. They were black men and women from the party's Central Committee and from various local leadership cadres, from the West Side of Chicago, from North Philadelphia, Harlem, New Orleans, Los Angeles, Washington, D.C., and elsewhere. They had come to Oakland this August of 1974 at my command.

I watched them carefully, noting that no one moved in response to my opening remarks. Here I was, a woman, proclaiming supreme power over the most militant organization in America. It felt natural to me. I had spent the last seven years as a dedicated member of the Black Panther Party, the last four at Huey's right hand.

"I haven't called you together to make threats, Comrades," I continued. "I've called this meeting simply to let you know the realities of our situation. The fact is, Comrade Huey is in exile.

The other fact is, I'm taking his place until we make it possible for him to return."

I allowed them a moment to grasp the full meaning of my words.

"I'm telling you this because it's possible some of you may balk at a woman as the leader of the Black Panther Party." I paused and took a deep breath. "If this is your attitude, you'd better get out of the Black Panther Party. Now.

"I'm saying this also because there may be some individuals in our ranks who have private ambitions and, in Comrade Huey's absence, may imagine themselves capable of some kind of coup." I paused again. No one spoke.

Cocking my head to the side, I continued in the manner I knew was required. "If you are such an individual, you'd better *run*—and *fast!* I am, as your chairman, the leader of this party as of this moment. My leadership cannot be challenged. I will lead our party both aboveground and underground. I will lead the party not only in furthering our goals but also in defending the party by any and all means."

They understood. Two months ago I had been named chairman, making me the second-ranking member of the Central Committee. I was then titularly second only to the minister of defense, who was Huey. The reality was that Huey Newton was the absolute leader of the Black Panther Party. I was now his replacement. They understood.

"Together we are going to move this revolution forward by leaps and bounds, though mindful, of course, that we may have to take one step backward in order to take two steps forward. Specifically, as we had begun to do before Comrade Huey's forced exile, we're going to continue the consolidation of our efforts in one city, *this* city. *Oakland* is the birthplace of this party. Oakland will be the birthplace of revolution in the United States. And that will be so despite the pigs. It will be so despite any petty despots who claim to be our comrades. It will be so despite the criticisms of the infantile leftists, who have accomplished nothing. It will be done despite the voodoo drums of the so-called black nationalists."

I watched a few of the Brothers slap their palms together in common recognition. A subdued laughter of agreement rippled through the auditorium. I began to walk up and down the stage, purposely emphasizing my words with the sound of the heels of my black leather boots. I punctuated each sentence with a nod to one or another of the soldiers standing on stage with me, backing me up.

"It will be done because they can exile a revolutionary leader but they cannot exile the revolution. We *will* move forward with due speed!

"I repeat, I have control over all the guns and all the money of this party. There will be no external or internal opposition I will not resist and put down. I will deal resolutely with anyone or anything that stands in the way. So if you don't like it, if you don't like the fact that I am a woman, if you don't like what we're going to do, here is your chance to leave. You'd better leave because you won't be tolerated!"

I gestured toward Larry. "Comrade Larry Henson is our new chief of staff. He is my replacement for June Hilliard, who has been expelled. He followed too closely in the footsteps of the former chairman of our party, Bobby Seale. *Don't be afraid of these changes, Comrades.* After all, change is what we seek. As Chairman Mao said, 'Let a thousand revolutions bloom!' Change is good. We have to welcome change. Those who resist change will be swept away in the irrelevant dust of history!"

There was a loud chorus of "Right on!"

"Together we're going to take this city. We will make it a base of revolution. The pigs will look at us and wonder. They will look at us, but they will be unable to deal with us.

"We're going to set a revolutionary example here. And the example we lay down in Oakland will be the spark that lights the prairie fire. We will carry our torch to another city, and then another. Each time, each place, the people will take their lead from us, the revolutionary vanguard. Just as the people have demanded and institutionalized our Free Breakfast for Children and sickle-cell-anemia programs, they will demand socialized medicine and decent housing. Soon they will begin to take control of their local political machinery. Then they will attack the economic structure in each city. Bit by bit, city by city, they will whittle away at the capitalist foundation. Eventually, a time will come—not in our lifetimes, Comrades—but a time *will* come when the people will understand their power and the pigs' machinery will be unable to accommodate their demands. That is when the people, black people and poor white people and oppressed people all over America, will rise up like a mighty tide and wash clean this beachfront of capitalism and racism, and *make* the revolution!"

They began to applaud loudly, then louder, and then suddenly they were standing. The Sisters *and* the Brothers were on their feet. When the ovation was over and they were seated, I released my pent-up breath and continued. "For now, Comrades, we *must* take the next step. We *must* make Oakland a base camp for revolution. This is why we can have no internal strife. We have to get moving.

"Let's get busy, then, Comrades. Return to your chapters and branches throughout this country with renewed dedication. Soon the Central Committee will be issuing orders and reports regarding the status of each chapter. Many of you and your people will be called back to the base.

"Let us get busy and prepare a place for the return of Comrade Huey. Let us get busy and prepare a place for the introduction of revolution!" I raised my fist in the air and shouted: "All power to the people! Panther power to the vanguard!"

They leaped to their feet, fists raised in salute: "POWER TO THE PEOPLE! POWER TO THE PEOPLE! POWER TO THE PEOPLE!"

The feelings that washed over me as I spoke were baptismal. There was something in that moment that seemed a reparation for all the rage and pain of my life. Ironically, I had come to it from an abysmal hopelessness, experienced less than two weeks before.

Charles Garry, Huey's attorney, and I had been waiting at the Alameda County jail to take Huey home. Gwen, whom Huey had begun referring to as his wife, to my disgust, was also there, waiting. We were watching Huey. He was pacing up and down the holding cell that occupied a corner of the police processing room. He was restlessly enduring the business of being bailed out. I caught a familiar look of arrogant satisfaction on his face. "Fuck Callins," his slight smile said.

Callins was a black tailor who had solicited business from Huey. He wanted to make suits for Huey and certain other Brothers in the party. Callins had, however, refused Huey's request that he discount those suits. Callins had also confronted Huey with his profit problems, and in Huey's own apartment. There had been a bloody fight. Huey had been arrested and charged with pistol-whipping Callins. That had been earlier in the evening. Now we had come to bail Huey out.

While I noted Huey's irreverent attitude about the whole

affair, it occurred to me how little I, too, actually cared about Callins. He was neither a man nor a victim to me. I had come to believe everything would balance out in the revolutionary end. I also knew that being concerned about Callins was too costly, particularly in terms of my position in the party. Yes, I thought, fuck Callins.

On the other hand, I did not feel any urgency about getting Huey released from jail. I needed a rest from him.

To say that I loved Huey, however, even at that moment, would be to say too little. I loved being loved by him. I loved the protection he offered with his powerful arms and fearless dreams. I loved how beautiful he was, sinewy and sultry at once. I loved his genius and his bold uses of it. I loved that he was the vicarious dream of a man that white men hid from themselves, except when he confronted them, their rules, their world. I loved his narrow buttocks and his broad shoulders and his clean skin. I loved being queen in his world, for he had fashioned a new world for those who dared. Yet I had come to hate life with him. His madness had become as full-blown as his genius. The numerous swaggering "dicks" who had challenged the hero to prove his manhood had finally taken their toll. Now he had outdone them all, including himself.

It was taking an inordinate amount of time for the release process to be completed. Garry and Gwen and I passed the hours with irrelevant chatter and frequent glances at the clock on the wall, which was nearing two in the morning. It was uncharacteristic of the Oakland Police Department to trifle with Huey Newton, even though they had once been considered the most brutal police force in California. That was several years before, however—before Huey's trial for the killing of one of their brothers, Officer Frey. The "Free Huey" campaign that had erupted on the heels of that charge had dominated the nation's headlines and had devastated the local police. While Huey became a national hero, the Oakland Police Department became a defeated little army.

When Huey was finally released from the holding cell, I watched him stride across the room in all his late-night beauty. As always, I consciously sensed my first surrender to him. I forgot the recent madness remembering other times. The mild growth on his face stung as he embraced me in the same powerful way he always did. He hugged Garry as Gwen put a jacket around his shoulders. I signaled Gwen to go outside to summon Larry and Big Bob, so they could bring Huey's car to the front of the building.

That was when the Oakland police demonstrated what had taken them so long.

"Mr. Newton, hold it, please," Captain Something-or-Other said, seeming to emerge from thin air. He had two sidekicks with him. Everybody in the station turned to face him, including the other police.

Huey glared at the captain, bracing his body for a fight.

Garry stepped forward protectively. "What do you want? Mr. Newton is very tired. He . . ."

"Mr. Newton, you are under arrest for a violation of the California Penal Code . . . for the attempted murder of . . . on the night of . . ." the captain stated in "police-ese." There was a note lurking in his tone that said this charge was what they had been waiting for ever since Huey had triumphantly slipped from their grasp. The captain's sidekicks clamped handcuffs on the antihero.

The charge concerned the shooting of a seventeen-year-old black girl who was an Oakland streetwalker. She had been shot several days before and was in a coma. The words "attempted murder" erased the smugness from Huey's face. I thought I saw a flash of genuine terror in his eyes. A few seconds later, he looked overwhelmed by hopelessness. It was just before they returned him to the recesses of the police building. There was a hopelessness hanging in the air, too. None of us knew quite what to do next.

When they finally allowed us to see Huey after he was booked again, the terror was gone. He was back in a holding cell, and back to himself. He had obviously made some instant calculations that he would never ride out the storm that would come from the attempted murder charge. He had, I felt, developed a plan to survive it.

"Raise the bail by morning," Huey commanded. He was speaking to me quietly but intensely, having pulled me aside.

I sighed, and spoke carefully, "*Tomorrow* morning, not this morning. I can't possibly . . ."

"Tomorrow, then." He smiled, satisfied. "Tomorrow we can be in paradise."

Garry, smelling a protracted legal battle, with its attendant headlines, eased over to the side of the cell where Huey and I were standing. He whispered legal strategies to Huey's faraway glance. Gwen remained stolidly in place, wearing a strained look of sorrow.

I contemplated how only a week before I had been planning

to leave the party forever. It was just after Huey had done to me what was commonplace inside our dangerous ranks. He struck me. It was a slap in my face after I had made an innocuous remark. Huey had not so much as raised his voice in anger to me prior to that, not even in that last month, when the snares of his madness had left so many others maimed.

We were in his penthouse apartment, where I had gone to tell him something the police-monitored telephone lines should not carry. When I arrived, a Brother was being "disciplined" on a charge of stealing from the party.

I ignored the bloodied face of the thief, as I had learned to do. I had become hardened to such things, like a Green Beret who learns to think nothing of taking a life: after seeing so many training films on brutal killings, he is no longer repulsed by blood or brutality. I ignored the blood streaming from the nose and mouth of the seated suspect as Huey's security people punished him. I noticed only how cold the apartment was. The cold made me ponder the reason why Huey always kept the windows and sliding glass doors of his twenty-fifth-floor penthouse wide open. Sometimes I had the chilling sense that those open windows and doors meant somebody would be tossed off one of the apartment's many balconies. Recently, it had occurred to me more than once that one day it could be me.

Huey stopped interrogating the thief to talk to me. Typically, he was wearing only a pair of pants, no shirt. His body glistened with the sweat of cocaine abuse. He had probably been up for the last forty-eight hours. His strength shone through, nevertheless, still stunning. Perhaps I loved him too much, I thought.

Before I could tell Huey why I had come, he spoke to me in a sort of stage whisper. "Elaine, it's important that you go back to your music. I want you to study music seriously. The party will pay for everything."

His eyes were glazed, and they darted back and forth almost uncontrollably. What he said to me had nothing to do with anything. I tried to hide my bewilderment, my fear.

"Thank you, Huey," I said anxiously, wanting only to get out of there.

He raised his hand suddenly and smacked me across the face. Then, clenching my jaw with one hand, he pulled me near him with his other, our noses almost touching.

In a careful staccato he said, "Don't *ever* thank me. When you thank me, it means you are separate from me, not *with* me."

Within seconds, my mind began to piece together a road map out, away from him and the party. I knew the signals. There had been more than enough. I would simply take my daughter, Ericka, to visit with my mother in Los Angeles, as we had done on numerous occasions. We would slip away. Soon, I decided.

It was only a few days later that Callins was beaten up and Huey was arrested. That had bought me a bit of time to think. Now none of it seemed to matter, for everything seemed over.

With a sense of futility, I gathered the cash and collateral from the party's various bank accounts and properties to pay Huey's second, $80,000 bail. When he was released, I met him at the bail bondsman's office, where he had to sign various forms. Gwen was with him, clinging to his arm. He reached out and hugged me warmly, and whispered into my ear: "Goodbye."

My eyes closed over tears. I might not ever see him again. His resolve to flee was in his embrace. There was no sound Huey could make or word he could speak or feeling he could harbor that I did not understand in my soul.

He would be silent on the details of his departure, a necessary protection for all of us. He would find refuge beyond the United States. Panthers had already done so—in Cuba, in Algeria. The revolutionary Third World would welcome its famous brother from the belly of the beast. He would surely be taking Gwen, whom I considered his little apolitical strumpet and loyal servant. I blinked away my momentary resentment, conscious that I would never last in the role of Huey's woman. She looked into my eyes, and we smiled at each other. Nobody spoke again.

Huey knew what was required for his survival. Damn the party, the politics, the rhetoric, and the dreaded dependency of everyone, including the "masses." He was unburdening himself. He was the parent running away from the child. If he ever returned, he might be forgiven.

For the first few nights after Huey vanished from Oakland, Big Bob, Larry, and I spent most of our time trying to figure out how to handle his absence, in the party and in the press. He was scheduled to make a court appearance in the next two weeks. We debated if we could carry off the folly of Father Divine's people, who had for years convinced his flock, and everyone else, that "Father" was alive though he was really dead. It was during one of those sessions that the whole thing resolved itself. Larry, Bob, and I were sitting in a booth at the Lamp Post, a bar and restaurant the party operated. A telephone call came for me. I went behind the bar to take it. It was Huey.

"Save my party," he commanded. His voice was low, but passionate. "I won't be back. You're the only one who can do it. You are mine. I can't trust anybody else with my party."

"I can't without serious backup," I heard myself say, my tongue dry with both fear and excitement. "You know. The Brothers will never accept it," I continued, turning away from the patrons on the other side of the bar.

"Let me speak to my man," Huey said, referring to Big Bob.

"That won't work," I said quietly, amazing myself with how quickly and emphatically I had responded.

"You decide, then."

"Larry," I whispered.

"Is he there?"

"Yes." I turned and motioned to Larry to come to the bar. I handed him the telephone, indicating who it was. He took it with reverence.

"Yes, sir, Brother," he said into the telephone.

Then: "I hear you, Brother. I guarantee it." Then: "With my life, Comrade. You have my word." He handed the telephone back to me.

"Now will you save my party?" Huey whispered.

"Yes."

It was done. While Huey repaired himself, I would hold and resurrect life from what seemed nearly dead.

As I considered the seriousness of it, I realized I had made the cardinal decision wisely. I needed Larry. "Politics and war are inseparable in a fascist state," the beautiful George Jackson had said. We could have no revolution in the fascist state of America without an army. Our army was presently in disarray. Larry was a general.

It was true that Big Bob had been Huey's bodyguard; and in that, his loyalty to Huey was unfaltering. It was also true that Bob had accepted leadership from a woman, Audrea Jones, when he was in the Boston branch. Bob's physical size, however—six feet eight inches and four hundred pounds—combined with his emotional insecurity about it and his lack of self-discipline, made a volatile concoction. He was simply not the stuff of generals.

In the ensuing week or so, the correctness of my decision was fully borne out. The three of us were constantly together during that time, trying to understand for ourselves the nature of the Black Panther Party that Huey had abandoned.

We decided to postpone the inevitability of holding a general leadership meeting of all our chapters for as long as possible. We had to first shore up the party's operations in Oakland, our national headquarters. Primarily, we concluded, we had to eliminate any potentially negative reaction on the streets to Huey's disappearance. Huey Newton had been an awe-inspiring figure on those streets. News of his absence would create havoc for us.

We began by riding the avenues of Oakland's subcultures every night to inform them that a shift in party leadership would not release them. Homage would still have to be paid. Blacks operating in Oakland—inside or outside the law—knew it was impossible to get around the party. In our revolution, one had, literally, to be part of the solution or part of the problem. No one on the streets of Oakland could withstand being the latter, with or without Huey. That was our nightly message.

We visited a black-owned bar one night and were seated at a table adjacent to one where a notoriously rowdy fellow sat. He immediately launched into a loud conversation among his friends in which he referred to Big Bob as "fat boy." Two women at his table started to snicker. Bob stood up. Larry and I also had to stand. Bob walked over to the man and smacked him with the back of his oversized hand, hurling him across the entire room, over tables and glasses of Scotch and vodka on the rocks. The loudmouth's cohorts jumped up as Larry reached under his jacket for his .45 and I reached into my purse for my snub-nosed .38. We were forced to back out of the place like gangsters in a third-rate movie. That was when I knew that Bob was a monumental miasma I could never have restrained.

My decision to place Larry in the recently vacated slot of chief of staff was eventually validated in other ways. I came to realize, for example, that Larry was more respected by the Brothers in the security squads than any of the other men who had been in positions of leadership—including Huey, whom few of them knew at all. Moreover, Larry showed initiative. It seemed he intuitively developed intelligent plans for the systematization, housing, maintenance, and care of our military inventory, which had been left in disarray since the expulsion of David Hilliard's brother June, the previous chief of staff. Moreover, Larry seemed to know, as much as anyone, including those who had seen combat in Vietnam, how to use the vast array of weapons we found we had.

Every Panther property housed weapons. It was our most basic requirement. Some houses were virtual arsenals. As I began reviewing with Larry and Bob the various operations in the Northern California Bay Area, I was stunned by the magnitude of the party's weaponry.

In Richmond, Berkeley, San Francisco, San Jose, as well as in Oakland and other cities in the area, there were huge stashes. There were literally thousands of weapons. There were large numbers of AR-18 and AR-18–short automatic rifles, .308 scoped rifles, .3030 Winchesters, .375 magnum and other big-game rifles, .30-caliber Garands, M-15s and M-16s and other assorted automatic and semiautomatic rifles, Thompson submachine guns, M-59 Santa Fe Troopers, Boys .55-caliber anti-tank guns, M-60 fully automatic machine guns, innumerable shotguns, and M-79 grenade launchers. There were suitcases, trunkloads, closets full of pistols, such as Astra and Browning 9mms, .45 automatics, .38s, .357 magnums, .41 and .44 magnums. There were boxes and boxes of ammunition, and large supplies of accessories, such as rifle scopes (including some infrareds), silencing devices, tripods, and interchangeable pistol barrels. There were caches of crossbows and arrows, grenades, and miscellaneous explosive materials and devices.

As I watched the adroitness and precision with which Larry organized the Brothers in the security squads to inventory, classify, clean, and relocate every single item, I became more convinced than ever that I had made my first and most important decision correctly.

There were other problems, however, that would have to be resolved before we could make the announcement of Huey's exile and my leadership to the general meeting. Most of them centered on the fact that the Black Panther Party had really been Huey's party all along. I had been too close to him to see that before. Even if Bobby Seale or June or David Hilliard or some other Central Committee member dismissed in the last month or so of rage had been there, it would have been irrelevant. Huey alone had known and controlled all the pieces. He had manipulated the party so that no one person knew everything except himself. Thus, while Larry inventoried weapons and such, I scrambled to locate and review the party's numerous bank accounts and real property and other records, scattered through our national headquarters office and other party offices and facilities.

Finally, I was forced to contemplate the most serious problem, the probability of internal conflict over my leadership. In that connection, I felt Chicago might present a problem. I knew Los Angeles did.

Southern California, where I had joined the party, no longer had an official chapter of the Black Panther Party. Everything in the area was completely underground. That is, the Panthers there had no overt party affiliation. They lived, for all intents and purposes, like ordinary people. However, they warehoused large arsenals of party weapons, with which they secretly bolstered the enforcement of our political will. The leader of that very tough and loyal sector in Southern California was an arrogant madman, with whom I had had a serious confrontation some time before. On smelling Huey's absence, he drove up to Oakland with three of his men and several of his guns, only a week after Huey left.

Like a buzzard, Steve strutted into the Lamp Post without warning. I watched him from a distance. I watched the absurd show of his men removing his coat, ordering his favorite cognac, and inspecting the other patrons for his security. He was my nightmare.

It had come too soon. I knew it was ultimately inescapable, but the test had come too soon. I had no real idea yet whether Larry was capable of loyalty to my leadership, especially when faced with so formidable a pretender as Steve, a Brother, another man.

As we walked over to Steve's table, I breathed deeply and ordered Larry to follow my lead. Larry would, I hoped, follow through.

"So, the Brother is gone," Steve said, a smirk on his lips. He lifted his cognac glass to me in a mock toast as Larry and I slid into the booth next to him.

"We want to talk to you alone, Steve," I said firmly, concealing my trepidation as best I could. I glared at the other L.A. Panthers, who got up.

"Long time, no see, Sister." He smiled, perfect white teeth glistening. He leaned back into the luxurious red leather of the booth, which matched the bar's deep-pile carpeting.

"What're you doing here?" I said. "You're not supposed to come here. And you know it. You have to go."

"I wanted to find out what was happening, Sister. I heard nobody had seen the Servant since he got bailed out," he said, referring to Huey.

"That's not the point, *Brother*," Larry said. "The comrade just told you you can't be here. Get on up."

"Huey made me a don, Brother," he stated with a wave of his hand, as if it held a scepter. "I have my own operation. *Nobody* tells me what to do."

It all happened in a flash. Larry reached under his jacket, simultaneously motioning to the other Brothers in the Lamp Post with a nod. Big Bob came over.

Shoving his .45 under the table toward Steve, Larry spit out, "Naw, *nigger*. You're going to have to be gone. Now! Bury your ass in L.A. Can you dig it?"

"This is bullshit. I want to speak directly to the Servant! Where is he? Or is he really gone?!"

"You're talking to him now, Brother," Larry said. "When you talk to the Sister here, you're talking to Huey Newton."

It could have gotten uglier, but Steve knew. His people knew. Larry had let them know. Steve removed himself and his small entourage from the Lamp Post that night. In a few days, he would slip out of Oakland, back to his underground home in Los Angeles.

That was only part of the madness I had just inherited. The Black Panther Party was the target of the most violent aggression of the police forces of America. Though battered and floundering, it was still breathing fire. It was at once a lion to be tamed and a terrible sword of freedom to be honed. In August 1974, when I assumed leadership, the Black Panther Party was the only armed revolutionary organization operating inside the United States of Amer-' ica.

There were several thousand diehard troops in Oakland and throughout California, and in nearly every state of the Union. There was, of course, our expansive arsenal of weapons, and the clandestine underground operating out of every chapter, Brothers trained in Vietnam and on the wretched streets of America who could and would use violence to carry out our political objectives.

There was nearly a million dollars in our coffers. There was a staggering amount of party-owned real properties, and a massive inventory of supplies and vehicles. There was the income from posh parties and ghetto streets, and the new contributions of the working black community, now aligned more strongly than ever with the goals of the party. There were the financial contributions of party members themselves from earned and other income, and revenue from sales of various items produced by the party, including our newspaper.

There was the party's history of daring and power, which had given rise to its nationwide and international support by millions of blacks and other people. There were the hundreds of thousands of people, black people and Latino people and Asian people and white people, who participated in or benefited from our free-food programs, our free medical clinics and legal-aid programs, our prison programs, our school and education programs, our service programs for seniors and teens and abused children and battered women and homeless people. There were the thousands who participated in our Vietnam veterans' and workers' rights projects. There were the thousands throughout the United States who read our weekly newspaper, through individual, school, and library subscriptions; and the thousands of others who subscribed to our newspaper outside the United States, in China, North Korea, East Germany, Cuba, and elsewhere. There were the numerous Panther support groups formed by whites in the United States and people in Japan, Italy, France, Sweden, Denmark, and other countries, even including Israel. There were our numerous coalitions with progressive organizations inside the United States and revolutionary movements throughout the world, particularly in Africa, both north and south of the Sahara.

As I prepared to make my announcement that afternoon when I formally asserted absolute leadership over the party, I recognized that it was an exhilarating madness I had inherited. The Black Panther Party Huey had left in my charge was still a force to be reckoned with. There was no question in my mind that it had to be saved.

As I began to speak to my comrades, I recommitted myself to pushing forward our struggle for the complete freedom of black people in America. I recommitted my life to the party, to fulfill its purpose of introducing socialist revolution in the United States, whether or not Huey returned. I believed with everything in me that it could be done. I believed with everything in me that I could do it.

CHAPTER 2

YORK STREET

MY MOTHER USED TO TELL ME: "When I was fifteen or sixteen, I had to walk to school, William Penn High. They called it the 'dummies' retreat.' Pearl Bailey walked with us. Now she's big-time. Sometimes after school a bunch of us would go by Pearl's house on the way home, 'cause there were always great big pots of food on the stove there. And I was always hungry. . . . My friends would hide their lunches when I'd come into the school cafeteria 'cause they knew I'd ask them for some. . . . A lot of the times, when Mama didn't have nothing in the house, I'd go down the street and get the stale bread the baker had thrown out. I'd steal it right out of the bakery trash bins, put water on it, mash it up into dough balls, and eat it. . . . I was just like Topsy, you know. I just 'growed.' "

That was my mother's litany. She performed it nearly every day when I was a girl. She would speak to me matter-of-factly, in run-on sentences, while ironing a pretty dress for me or fixing my hair or washing out my undies.

"And your grandmother, Mama, she could never remember to call me Dorothy. She'd say, 'Frances, I mean, Helen, whichever one you are, come over here.' Things like that. And Papa, if I'd ask him if we were gonna get some shoes, he'd say, 'Need some my damn self' . . . I used to wear shoes with cardboard soles, which I had to keep together with safety pins. . . . Once, when we were coming home from school after stopping at Pearl's house, it started to rain. The rain soaked through the cardboard to my feet, and the cheap dye I had used to cover the fading in my dress began to run down my legs, and everybody laughed at me."

Such recitations were constant. They traveled with us on the bus or in the subway, or even into our bed at night, where my mother would embrace me tightly. In the silence of our nights, she would summarize her days: "They treated me like I was nothing. They must think I'm *nothing*. I'm sick and tired of it. I'm sick and tired of everything." There was a terrible life out there, she warned. Only in our room was it safe; only with her.

Early on, I came to appreciate how right my mother was and to understand that the only way to endure the pain that lay ahead, the only way to survive the misery of life, was to try to eke out a few little victories and never hope for more or dare for more. There was misery not only in being poor but everywhere, in everything.

"You know, Elaine, when I was in my early twenties, I used to hang out with a bunch of musicians and artists. And there was this tough saxophone player, Ted Barnett, that I met one day. He played with all the big bands—like Duke Ellington's, the Count's, all of them."

"Like the ones that play at the Pearl Theater, Mommy?"

"Yes, like them. And he . . ."

"What's that funny sound the bands make, Mommy?"

"Oh, it's nothing; probably just the horns with those mutes on. But anyway, Ted and I started going out, and after a while we decided we would get married. I was so happy and excited. What a fool I was! Mmmh! About a month before we were supposed to get married—I had bought my wedding dress already—I saw a friend of ours I hadn't seen in a while. 'Yeah, Dorothy,' he said, 'sure is something 'bout Ted. Up and got married last night. Hey, I thought you and Ted had a thing going.' "

It was not merely sad or painful to my mother that she had lost her fiancé. What was terrible about it to her was that she had not known better than to have fallen in love. She felt she should have remembered what she always told me: "Love is a misunderstanding between two fools."

Life did not seem a terrible affair just because my mother said so. I felt it. I felt it in the very house where I grew up. I felt it outside the house, out on York Street.

York Street was buried in the heart of the black section of North Philadelphia. Its darkness and its smells of industrial dirt and poverty permeated and overwhelmed everything. There were always piles of trash and garbage in the street that never moved except by force of wind, and then only from one side of the street to the other. Overhead utility wires in disrepair ribboned the sky-line. Cavernous sewage drains on the street corners spit forth their stench. Soot languished on the concrete walkways, on the steps and sides of the houses, and even in the air. Rusted streetcar tracks from another time, a time when people who were alive occupied the territory, ran up and down York Street. And there was the nighttime quiet. As the dark approached each night, houses were sealed tight in fear and York Street became overwhelmed by the quiet, a silent voodoo drum, presaging nightly danger, a gang fight, a stabbing, a fire.

Our house at 2051 was indistinguishable from the other gray-ish, two-story, brick row houses on York Street. It was squeezed with the others into our block, a block no different in color from the rest of the neighborhood.

I was most terrified, though, inside 2051. My greatest fear lay waiting for me in "our" room, my mother's and mine. In our room was complete darkness, and the recognition of nothingness, accompanied by the magnified sounds of mice scurrying and hearts beating in fear. Ours was the back room, upstairs. Occu-pying the other rooms along the upstairs hallway were my grand-mother (middle room) and my Aunt Mary (front room). My grandfather slept downstairs, on a divan covered with gray slip-covers; he remained a nebulous figure to me until he died. For me, only three women lived there—and me.

My grandmother was a very light-skinned woman with a white person's facial features and a large bosom. She carried a lot of weight on her short frame and very large feet. She hobbled from the weight when she walked, hobbling and always singing or hum-ming old Baptist hymns learned back in old Virginia and sung now in the First African Baptist Church every Sunday and in our house every single day.

> Be ready when He come
> Be ready when He come
> Be ready when He come
> 'Cause He's comin' again so soon . . .

He was Jesus, my grandmother's protector from the rats and roaches that overran our house. Jesus was her comforter in wash-ing clothes for more than half a century at a scrub board, in cooking meager meals for her nine children, in begging on the street with a cup for money. Jesus insulated her from the insults and blows of my grandfather, to whom she clung to the end. Jesus was the balm for her whole life, the life she hated from its beginning as the child of a white man's rape. Yes, Jesus would come someday and deliver her. Jesus would surely come someday, she said.

"He will take you in His arms, if you been good, and carry you up to heaven," she always told me. "But if you been bad, Satan's gonna get you and take you to hell, and you'll burn forever."

"I've been good, Grandma."

"I know you have, child. But make sure you don't even think an evil thing, 'cause God knows. He'll send the lightning and the thunder. You can't hide from God."

I used to lie in bed at night next to my mother in the darkness of our room and wonder, If God made me, like my grandmother said, who made God? And if somebody made God, who made the one who made God? I would be hurled to a place, and into a feeling, that terrified me. It was a feeling that I was akin to ether, not made of flesh and bone, as though I had no body. I would bolt up in bed to try to force myself back from that distant place, that feeling of nothingness. I would scream out: *"Mama! Mama! It's that feeling!"*

My Aunt Mary barely spoke, because she barely lived. Living was dangerous. She was a beautiful woman, with smooth skin, the texture of which she attributed to Pond's cold cream, and which was the color of Georgia clay. She wore a tight hairstyle, pressed and oiled, very little makeup, and plain clothes. She was impeccably clean and organized. The inside of the chifforobe in her front room was made of cedar, and she kept her few beautiful, plain clothes on proper hangers inside. She washed all her underwear by hand in Ivory Flakes, placing each item carefully in dresser drawers filled with sachets. Aunt Mary did not seem to worry about God, because she lived too carefully to do wrong or to be noticed by God if she did. She went out only to go to work. Every weekday morning, she walked down the 5 A.M. ugliness of our street with her gabardine coat locked around her body, a cloth scarf wrapped about her hair, lunch bag in hand, off to one more day as a wire clipper on the assembly line at RCA Victor in Camden, New Jersey. She had done that for many years, except for the five or six years between the time she was "let go" and "called back" by RCA, during which she "scrubbed white folks' floors."

Mary appeared to be selfish, or maybe just stingy. She was stingy about giving herself over to anything. Whenever she brought home discounted RCA products, such as the new automatic record player that replaced our old Victrola, she placed restrictions on our use of them. Only she, for example, could put records on the machine. Virtually every night we would all gather in the living room to listen to Aunt Mary's Marian Anderson or Harry Belafonte or Eartha Kitt records. At the same time, my grandmother would voraciously read the *Pittsburgh Courier*, the colored people's newspaper, making comments to no one in particular about the achievements and machinations of our race.

"And you see this picture here. Look, Frances—I mean, Dorothy," my grandmother would mumble, without looking up.

My mother would ignore her and sing along with Eartha Kitt: "Santa Baby, I forgot to mention one little thing—a ring."

"Elaine, child, come here. You see this picture. This is Kwame Nkrumah. You know, he's been to this very house. He used to play saxophone with Frances's husband, John. They went to Lincoln University together. Now he's back in Africa, fighting for . . . Lord, colored people sure is killing each other. You see this here. Two boys got stabbed last week. Mary, Mary! Look! One of them was named Lonnie Washington. I wonder, was that Mrs. Washington's boy? It was only two blocks from here . . . Well, well, well. Mr. DeBerry—you know him—he died. Sure was a fine man. Used to work two jobs to take care of his wife." And she would read on, bits and pieces, flipping through the *Courier*'s pages of orange and black print, though nobody really listened.

And there was my mother. The image I had of my mother in those York Street years was of a strong, protective being. Much of her strength was manifested in heavy hands and muscular arms. In general, I thought of my mother as plain, not in an unassuming fashion, but in an unimportant sense. She spent her time on me, doting on me, fixing me up, my hair, my clothes, my shoes; making sure I always looked "right." She would always tell me how beautiful I was, "the most beautiful girl in the world." I was not like the other little colored girls in our neighborhood, she told me. They had skin that was too dark and facial features that were too African and hair that was not "good" like mine.

My mother would escort me to the bathroom at night so that

she could keep the scampering roaches from my feet as they ran for cover when the light was turned on. She bathed me, often in Alaga starch, because my skin was delicate, making sure I was washed thoroughly, especially my private parts. She would curl my hair like Shirley Temple's for Sunday school and press my dresses in the evenings. She bought secret food for me, to save me from the torture of my grandmother's haphazard cooking, making sure I did not have to eat anything I did not want—like the possums my half-Indian grandfather would slay in homage to some tradition, or the ugly fish he would catch and bring home wrapped in newspaper, or the "chitlin' " dinners that were cooked in our house and sold to make money.

We would go to sleep at night, my mother and I, in our back room, and she would hold me and stroke my "beautiful hair" like a lover. She would often read me stories, helping me shut out the eerie sound of the rodent feet scraping the other side of the salmon-colored flowers on the wallpaper that covered our room. She would press me close and remind me that she was the only one who would protect me from the regular assaults of life, from all those who were out to do her and me no good, which seemed to include everyone. A woman who was "nothing" wrapped her strong arms about my skinniness and protected me from unknown, deadly beasts. When she held me, her large breasts were comforting, and sometimes sensual. We were one against the world, she told me, as she recalled her dream to me.

I used to dream—it was before you were born, while I was carrying you—that I had a little girl. The girl in that dream looked just like you. She was about five years old. We were in a garden. And she had on a little apron which was filled with apples. She would come toward me, offering me the apples, saying, "I came to help you, Mommy."

When I was old enough to walk and talk, my mother sent me to a nursery school operated by the Red Feather charity agency. She worked all day pressing clothes, doing "piece work." They made girls' dresses where she worked, and she would press some and also steal some for me, so I would always look pretty.

Once, I visited her "atwork"—that one-word locale for which my mother left me each weekday. It was Christmastime. She held my hand and guided me through rows of sewing machines and cutting boards. She proudly displayed me, her beautiful product. Bits and pieces of cloth and string littered the floors, and it seemed everyone was bending over something or other, unattentive to me or the colored lights of Christmas strewn along the huge pillars that supported the room, which appeared to be the size of an entire square block.

I was surprised when my mother showed me her work area. It was just a big ironing table. I watched her wrap a scarf around her head, covering her hair and forehead. That was to keep the sweat from her eyes, she said. She found her place among what seemed dozens of other black and Puerto Rican women, pressers, who lined the walls of Rosenau's in a row, all wearing head rags, all with their own jugs of ice water sitting on their ironing boards to keep their lungs clean and their bodies from dehydrating. A Puerto Rican named Yolanda had dropped dead at her board no more than a month before, my mother told me. TB, they had said. She was only twenty-six. It seemed over a hundred degrees in there even though it was wintertime.

I watched my mother work. She slammed a hot iron onto a cotton thing of ice-cream colors, and within seconds, a little girl's dress evolved, bearing the "Cinderella" label. She folded the dress and boxed it for shipping to a retail store. She was paid 25 cents for each dozen dresses she pressed, folded, and boxed, she told me. All the ladies in the row were hollering back and forth to each other, while their ironing boards squeaked in accompaniment to the rhythm their tough hands made as they, too, slammed down hot irons, driving them back and forth to make their quotas and more. "Chile, hand me that box . . . Dottie, I'm up to fifteen dresses. Girl, whatchu say . . . Bitch, get your hand out that bin till I get my batch." By the time we left, I felt like crying. I was not sure why.

Since my mother believed I was too precious for either of the public schools in our neighborhood, when I finished nursery school, she signed me up for an experimental elementary school which accepted only "exceptional" children. Besides, the boiler had blown up at nearby Claghorn Elementary, causing nearly one hundred kids to be scalded; and like the other neighborhood school, it had only half-day classes, with sixty kids to a class.

There was a four-year waiting list for the special school. My mother determined, however, that I would go there right away; there would be no waiting list for me. She fired off letters to the school board and made personal appearances at its meetings. She sought out and got support for her cause from locally prominent colored people. Nearly every day, she would call every colored professional she knew of, including our neighborhood doctor, the funeral home director, and the minister at Jones Tabernacle

A.M.E. Church. She would implore them to understand how hard it was for an ordinary working woman like herself to provide anything decent for her child, how hard it was for her to even keep her head above water as a woman alone, and how she really needed their assistance as men of importance. One by one they were pressed into service to call or write the school board in support of my attendance at the school. When she was finished, I was enrolled in the kindergarten class of Thaddeus Stevens School of Practice, right on schedule.

Thirteenth and Spring Garden Street was a strange location for a special school. It was an abandoned, semi-industrial area that bordered downtown Philadelphia. Most of the people who remained when the small factories closed for the evening were Puerto Ricans and gypsies. When I first approached the old gray façade of Thaddeus Stevens, I thought it was a church or perhaps some kind of castle. It was, however, an experimental school for children who were considered very smart. Reading and writing, addition and subtraction, were taught in kindergarten, and all the classes were very small. Most of the children were white, and nobody in the school lived in the neighborhood, except the very few Puerto Ricans.

My kindergarten class of about fifteen was typical. Most of my classmates were white; Jewish, actually. There was one Puerto Rican, two other colored kids, and one Chinese girl. We would sing:

> I am a good American.
> What do you have to be?
> I am a good American.
> Just take a look at me . . .

I liked my class and the songs we sang. I liked our drawings and printed letters pasted on the walls in exhibition of our prodigiousness. I liked the games we played, the naps we took, and our afternoon treat of graham crackers and milk. I became a happy person and forgot the dark feelings of 2051 West York Street for those seven or so hours at Thaddeus Stevens. I forgot, until I noticed a little thing that cast a small shadow on my new life. My lunch bag was different from the other kids'. Mine was a used brown bag from Max's grocery store "up the street," at the corner of 21st and York. It had grease marks on it and numbers written on the side. Some of the numbers were Max's grocery configurations; some were my mother's "numbers" figures.

Every day, including Saturday but not Sunday, my mother played the numbers, a kind of lottery run by Philadelphia's organized criminal syndicate. I used to listen to her on the telephone in the evening.

"Yeah, Ethel, I had the first digit. I had dreamt a 2. I knew fish was 238, but I didn't like a 3 or an 8, even though I dreamt about a fish."

Turning to me: "Elaine, did you dream anything last night?"

"I dreamt about a pig, Mommy."

"A pig? What was he doing?"

"He was gruntin'."

She would look up my dream in *Prince Zolar's Number Book* (the back inside cover of which was inscribed, "Colored People of the world, unite!").

"Pig is 554," she would say into the telephone, scanning the book, "but a gruntin' pig is 617. Still, I like a double for tomorrow. I'm gonna call that nigger and tell him to box 554 for me for a nickel. I like it."

Her hands would hang up the old black dial telephone receiver, with its matted cord, which sat on a table against a wall in our dining room. She would dial the number runner's house and tell him the combinations to play for her the next day. Then she would pick up her school-lined notebook and enter another day's figures into it. There had to be a pattern, and she would find it. She would hit the number one day, she told me. Big, too. She had years of numbers in a collection of those books. She would then compare her number with the predictions on Lady Dale's Number Card. Finally, she would rub some of Lady Dale's Money Drawing Oil on her strong brown hands.

Whenever she had a "thought," or somebody died or was born or went into the hospital, or something unusual occurred, or she had a vivid dream, my mother would find a three-digit number associated with it. She would jot down that number on the first piece of paper she found, including on Max's bags that carried my lunch to school. The other kids had neatly tucked, clean paper bags. I wondered: Didn't their mothers play the numbers? Their sandwiches were different, too, wrapped in cellophane, brand-new and shiny, unlike mine, often wrapped in used waxed paper. But my sandwiches came with the crusts cut off because I hated bread crusts. And I had Welch's grape juice in my thermos instead of that rotten milk. It all began to balance out again, until I went to Barbara Keesal's house.

In the early fall of our second-grade school year, after the celebration of the Jewish holidays of Rosh Hashanah and Yom Kippur, for which our school was necessarily closed, Barbara Keesal invited me to her Halloween party. Barbara was a chubby Jewish girl who seemed to have everything: a perfect red coat, perfect leggings and boots, a perfect lunch box, perfect dresses, and perfect barrettes for her hair. I was thrilled to be invited to her party.

When my mother delivered me to Barbara's door, which was opened by a uniformed maid, many of the other kids were already there. There were rabbits, ghosts, pirates, dancing girls, and now me, a gypsy. We sat at a long table covered with Halloween-motif tablecloth and napkins and laden with lots of party favors and a bounty of candy corn, apples, cider, and potato chips. More food was served to us by yet another maid. There was carpeting on the floors, and there was a huge chandelier which twinkled on our happy occasion. We laughed and laughed and played games and were told scary stories. When I left Barbara Keesal's party, I was actually frightened, frightened to go back to 2051 West York Street.

My mother latched the old brown door at 2051 behind us, closing out the cold October air. Our lungs were immediately filled with escaping coal gas, the blue haze of which enveloped us. As she guided me through the vestibule, I finally saw the darkness which she constantly complained about. The twenty-five-watt bulbs could not begin to illuminate our house. I saw how ugly it was, its squeaky floors covered with cheap linoleum. As we approached the stairs to go up to our room, I remembered how I had fallen down those stairs a year before and knocked out my front teeth.

My mother made me wait at the bottom of the stairwell while she went into the kitchen to get us a drink of water. I did not want cocoa, because I did not want to wait there alone too long, and I certainly never entered the kitchen at night. I dared a peek at my old grandfather sleeping lifelessly on his divan in the adjacent living room. He looked just like a picture of Satan, with his jutting jaw and sharp nose and skeletal body. I could hear my mother rinsing the roach wings from our glasses. I could hear her opening the door to the icebox, the dripping of its icy water into the pan beneath it echoing through the dining room and into the hall where I stood frozen. Now she was closing the door to the shed kitchen, that cold and damp little appendage to our house through which one might exit to a concrete plot called our back yard. I could hear my mother walk past the monstrous wood-burning stove, which always appeared on the verge of collapse from the grease that corroded it or was stuck in a Crisco can on top of it. She was returning, passing the terrible cellar door that always challenged me to look at it or open it or go beyond it, down weak wooden stairs to a cement tomb where rats played in the coal bin and left their droppings on an old baby crib and other relics I had looked at only once.

Why couldn't I live with Barbara Keesal! At least at night.

I tried to stay away from York Street as much as I could after that. I began to spend most of my after-school hours at the home of another Jewish classmate, Arlene Lander. Arlene, like Barbara, was chubby; and because my mother always worried about how skinny I was—for which she forced cod-liver-oil tablets down my throat every morning—I concluded that that was how rich Jewish girls were supposed to be.

Arlene and I would enter her home through her father's store, Lander's Shoes, located in a mostly Jewish neighborhood on the fringes of North Philadelphia. Arlene's father or mother would greet us girls, on our way up to their apartment above the store, with balloons or some other trinket they had on hand in connection with a shoe sale. I would look at all the shoes on the racks and fantasize about how Arlene could have a new pair of shoes every day if she wanted.

Like Barbara Keesal's house, Arlene's apartment was very bright and had carpeting throughout. There were mirrored walls and soft couches and chairs everywhere. Arlene even had her own bedroom. The first thing we would do was head for the kitchen to make snacks for ourselves, even though a housekeeper was there most of the time and Arlene's grandmother was there all the time. Arlene's kitchen was bright and big, and had a refrigerator and no icebox; it also had a gas oven and an electric mixer and an assortment of other fancy automatic things. We would usually make kosher salami or grilled-cheese-and-tomato sandwiches. We would get soft drinks from one of the cases stored in a big closet in the kitchen, fill our glasses with ice cubes from her freezer, and take trays back to Arlene's room, where there was a television set.

Arlene's grandmother would usually come into Arlene's room to visit us. She was a short woman whose hair was bluish-white like my grandmother's. Her nails were always polished, and her wrist was branded with a line of dark and faded numbers. We might be watching the *Howdy Doody* show or something on Arlene's television when her grandmother came in, inevitably pinching my cheeks with her withered hand. She would proclaim, in her broken English, that I had such a *shayne punim*, and how much I looked just like a little Sabra.

My visits to Arlene's house extended the time between the lightness of Thaddeus Stevens and the weight of York Street. I was elevated with happiness each moment I spent with her and her family, no matter my confusion over their strange Jewish ways; reflected, for example, in the time Arlene's grandmother screamed at her and me after we mixed the *milchikeh* with the *flaishikeh*, or the milk with the meat dishes. Arlene and I had washed the plates on which we had earlier had grilled-cheese sandwiches. In Yiddish, Arlene's grandmother cried out that we had put our plates into the wrong kitchen cabinet. It was a violation of Jewish dietary laws that could be corrected, it seemed, only if the tainted plates were destroyed. Following Arlene's lead, I took my dish from the cabinet and smashed it on the floor.

Otherwise, I felt a sense of well-being at Arlene's, content in the traditions of her Jewish home and with my momentary immersion in the life of a people who lived so well. Jewish life was a good life, I decided, now eagerly making dreidels for Hanukkah or lighting the holiday menorah at school, or sitting down to dinner with increasing frequency at Arlene's. Despite my being a *shiksa* (a non-Jewish girl), as well as a *shvartzer* (a colored girl), I ate dinner there even on Shabbat, the traditional Sabbath holiday usually restricted to family or other Orthodox Jews. With the greatest feeling of pride, I would solemnly wait for Arlene's father to don his yarmulke and prayer shawl, as the sun set on Friday evenings, and light the candles on their dinner table. Before we ate, he would bless the challah bread and the other food, pour glasses of Mogen David wine, and keep the faith of their fathers.

Sometime during that period, terrifying thoughts about God began to overtake my nights. I truly believed in God and I prayed. Now, however, I was beginning to wonder more and more who that giant being really was who controlled life. Where was He? How did He decide who lived where and who did what on His earth? My nighttime fits of anxiety became more and more frequent.

Mama, Mama! It's that feeling!

Now, every night, my mother would leap to turn on the lights when I called out and hold me fast until I stopped shaking. Now, every night, I really needed my mother to hold me, as she had always done. She would protect me forever, I tried to believe, as she lay there half awake to listen to me breathe, to listen to whether I was breathing. Soon, however, I began to feel that only daylight could deliver me.

Morning allowed me to escape, up 21st Street to Susquehanna Avenue, to take the bus along "Susque" to Broad Street. Escaping, I would glance out the bus windows to see the candle and trinket stores, the fish markets, and the meat markets with pigs' feet hanging in their windows, the winos still sleeping from the night before. To me, it was a bus ride through a tunnel of desolation.

Most of the time, my mother would take me; sometimes, Aunt Mary. By the third grade, I had to make the daily trek alone.

Alone now, I had also to face the real tunnel, the tunnel of fears that lay at the bottom of the open mouth of the subway entrance of the Susquehanna and Broad subway station. *Yellow-tiled. You'll be getting on at yellow.* Darkness and danger were down there. There was no place to hide there, and no one to hold me. The terrible, multicolored monster-face I always dreamed of lurked down there. I could be swallowed up and hurled around in the darkness down there. Stealthily, I had to walk down the steps, covered with old chewing gum and spit and trash and North Philly soot, to the turnstile to deposit my token, hoping each day the train would come before death did. People got pushed onto the tracks. There were gang fights underground. Urine spotted the walls and permeated the underground tunnel air, making me nauseous. There were strange men who leaned in corners; I had seen one looking at me once while he masturbated. I learned to stand quietly, Aunt Mary style, immobile, feeling I might survive if no one noticed me, with my curly locks and stolen Cinderella dresses.

When the train finally came, I would stand inside, very still, rigid, holding the rail tightly until the train pulled into the Spring Garden station. *Blue-tiled. You get off at blue.* Finally, I could emerge into daylight and seek the familiar warmth of the old gray bricks that formed Thaddeus Stevens School of Practice. I could breathe again, relax, find my seat by the windows, let the sunlight filter through me and daydream aimlessly.

I grew to hate to leave school, no matter the sweet delays at Arlene's. I hated going back to York Street. Our back room was not safe. If my mother could not escape the horrors she told me about, and those that I now saw and sensed myself, she could not protect me and I could never help her. *I came to help you, Mommy.* It was safe only at the Thaddeus Stevens School of Practice. Decent people were there; not just Barbara Keesal or Arlene Lander, but my teachers, who took me to lovely places in their literature and in their music. Mr. Silver was teaching me to read and appreciate poetry.

> The road was a ribbon of moonlight over the purple moor,
> And the highwayman came riding—
>   Riding—riding—
> The highwayman came riding, up to the old inn-door.

And I learned Irish melodies in Mrs. McCullough's cheery classroom.

> When Irish eyes are smilin'
> Sure it's like the morning dew.

There seemed to be a promise at Thaddeus Stevens. It was not in the victory of hitting a number. It was not in the success of stealing a new dress from a dress factory. It was not in a decent piece of meat for dinner or in songs played over a new RCA Victor record player. It was bigger than my mother's arms. It was a promise with wings that would lift me away from York Street forever and plant me in the security of a white world. I saw that promise and knew I had to join those white people.

I could do it, too, I felt. I would simply have to pay close attention to them. I would have to become more like them. They would begin to see me as one of them, and welcome me into their world.

I became a biddable little wretch. I did anything to belong among them, those white children and white teachers. I was the first to offer to beat overchalked erasers or run messages around the school, or answer a question, or clean up after a class party. I jumped at a chance to trade or give away my lunch treats, my Tastykakes or my Welch's grape juice, to my school friends. Soon I was convinced I was actually beginning to join them, leaving York Street behind. It was my secret.

Now I was a colored girl only on York Street, my mother's sweet little colored daughter who had come to help her. But I was fooling her and everybody on York Street. I was fooling everybody, because I was not really colored anymore.

"You know, Elaine, you're not like the other coloreds. You're different. You don't even look like one." My white friends and teachers at Thaddeus Stevens were telling me that all the time.

Eventually, I discovered that my ultimate disguise could be manipulated through words, their words in their voices. I listened to them, paid attention to their grammar, their syntax, their cadence. I learned to speak exactly like white people, learned to enunciate their language, to say "*th*ese" and not "*d*ese," and "he'll be going" rather than "he be goin'."

Finally, I became white. At least until 2:17 P.M., when school was let out, when the bell would toll and the curtain fall and I would be returned by fate through the subway tunnel, down Susquehanna, down 21st Street to 2051 West York Street, and back to being black.

> If you white, you right
> If you yellow, you mellow
> If you brown, stick around
> If you black, git back
> Way back!

Everyone on York Street knew the truth of that rhyme. Everyone understood. Everyone had always known that dark-skinned colored girls with "bad," or kinky, hair were ugly. Everyone had always known that "high-yellow" colored girls with "good," or straight, hair were pretty. The rule was simple: The closer to white, the better. We derided girls who had short "nappy" hair, or thick "liver" lips, or protruding, high behinds, or skin "so black it's blue."

I did not want to get back. Despite that I was, like most girls on York Street, a few shades "too dark," I had "good" hair and white facial features. I was really not like the other colored girls. My mother had told me that. White people were telling me that. I did not belong on York Street. I belonged in their world. I had not only learned to talk white and act white, I could do white things.

I could play classical music. I had started taking piano lessons after my mother read a series of child-rearing books and decided I needed to be well rounded. Every Wednesday after school, from the time I was about six or seven years old, I took a private piano lesson. In my turn I sat in Mrs. Campbell's living room to learn scales and numerous ditties and other pieces, and to complete each year's John Thompson piano book.

All of Mrs. Campbell's other students were considered "siddity" little colored children. That is, they were all not only light-skinned, they lived in Germantown, a very "nice" section of Philadelphia where refined colored people had broken the color line. All the fathers of the other children seemed to be doctors or lawyers. All their mothers were either teachers or, better, housewives. All the boys had names like that uppity, blond-haired Laddie Avery; and all the girls looked like the famous Dr. Simpson's fair-skinned, straight-haired daughter, Betsy. Although I seemed to be the only one of Mrs. Campbell's students who lived in a "bad" neighborhood, I did not mind. In the end, despite the other students' self-serving inquiries as to where I lived—which they already knew—or who my father was—which nobody seemed to know—or what my mother did for a living—which I refused to tell them—despite everything, I was learning to play European classical piano. Eventually, I even became a featured soloist at Mrs. Campbell's annual spring recitals. I could play Beethoven and Chopin and even Liszt.

There were other white things in my repertoire. I was learning ballet. When I started studying piano, I also began taking ballet lessons. My mother would wake me early Saturday mornings during the school year to take me downtown to the Sydney School of Dance, where I would spend several wonderful hours away from York Street. I was happy at Miss Sydney's. A joyful spirit seemed to live among the bars and mirrors and smooth wooden dance floors. Unlike Mrs. Campbell, Sydney King catered to all kinds of little colored kids—mostly girls—from all over Philadelphia, from good neighborhoods and bad ones, who were both dark-complexioned and light. I even loved Miss Sydney's when my mother bought me a foot-long hot dog and a grape soda at our break. There was, of course, the magnificent pleasure of the ballet itself. At the Sydney King early-summer recitals I was transformed into a blue jay and danced to the "Waltz of the Hours," or I danced in sequined splendor in the children's *corps de ballet*, with pink tights and a pink tulle skirt. I even learned to dance on toe.

Moreover, there were my theater excursions. Once a month, after my Saturday ballet lesson, my mother would carry me off to the Academy of Music to see a play performed by the Mae Desmond Children's Theatre Troupe.

Everything considered, I believed I was really becoming white. So much of my life was white, except when I was returned to York Street and somebody like Mary Alice, who lived down the street, snidely "signified" at me, coming home from school or a ballet lesson.

"Look at her!" Mary Alice might whisper loudly to her cronies as I passed by. "She must think she cute. She ain't poot."

I would have to go inside 2051 to change into my black jeans and white bucks and go back out into the street. I would fetch Barbara and Nita, with whom I was best friends forever when I returned to York Street. We did everything together, played the same games, wore the same outfits, and remained the skinniest girls on our block. By fourth grade, Barbara had started attending Thaddeus Stevens, though I felt she was still not really like me, just as Nita was not. Nevertheless, we were inseparable. Barbara lived at 2057 and Nita lived next door to me at 2049 West York Street. I would get Barbara and Nita, and they would put on their black jeans and white bucks, and we would walk down the street three abreast, so nobody could come between us. We might walk right in front of Mary Alice's house, chanting:

> I ain't gon' talk about your mama,
> She's a sweet ole soul.
> She got a ten-ton pussy
> And a rubber asshole.

York Street threw me back, back to the realization that I might not ever really be white. I *would* have to get back. I saw that every time I returned.

When summer rolled around, I lived in turmoil. I had to be on York Street every day, poor and black all day, every day.

In the summers of my preteen years, "me, Barbara, and Nita"—Barbara, Anita, and I in Thaddeus Stevens winters—would go every weekday morning to Vacation Bible School. Replacing Chopin, the ballet, the theater, and Thaddeus Stevens was Bible School. We would sit in the Sunday-school section of Jones Tabernacle A.M.E. Church to learn our Bible lessons. They were parables of Jesus, typed out onto glossy, colored 3 × 5's, as captions to pictures of Jesus, whose hair was long and blond, whose face was white, who wore sandals and a robe and was usually depicted sitting among his flock of white children. Jesus, we learned, could do everything. He could walk on water, raise the dead, and never die.

> Jesus loves me, this I know,
> For the Bible tells me so.
> Little ones to Him belong.
> We are weak, but He is strong.

After those lessons, we would eat peanut-butter-and-jelly sandwiches and drink lemonade. Then Barbara, Nita, and I would walk back home in the afternoon, synchronously stepping military style:

> We are rough!
> We are tough!
> We are the girls
> Who don't take no stuff!

After we arrived home, we would play out on York Street all those hot days. First, we might jump rope double-dutch. Then there would be hand-clapping games. We would form a circle with some of the other girls on the block and begin by clapping our hands back and forth to each other and shaking our little girlish hips in time to our chants:

> Mama in the kitchen,
> Papa in jail,
> Baby 'round the corner
> Hollerin' "pussy for sale."

Or:

> Wild Bill Hickock was a peaceable man,
> He peed out the window on a bald-headed man.
> He came down the steps with his dick in his hand
> And said, "Hold it, motherfucker,
> I'm a peaceable man."

When the setting summer sun announced the end of one more long day on York Street, I felt that I had survived one more nodal point in the demoralizing cycle. Our mothers would call out to us to come inside, to make the valiant attempt at washing away the North Philly dirt that the summer humidity had ground into our skin. We might, just before leaving each other for the night, do one more round of "Hambone." Patting our feet to establish the rhythm, we would slap our chests and knees with our hands, in accompaniment:

> Hambone, Hambone, where you been?
> 'Round the corner, back again.
> Hambone, Hambone, what you see?
> Two black niggers lookin' at me.

CHAPTER 3

"WE ARE THE GIRLS WHO DON'T TAKE NO STUFF"

AT FIRST IT SEEMED A SMALL MIRACLE had occurred when my mother decided to move from York Street, out of the house that was my grandmother's, where we had lived for as long as I could remember.

We were moving into a place of our own, a one-bedroom apartment in the James Weldon Johnson Housing Project, a barrackslike public-housing complex in another part of North Philadelphia, at 25th and Norris streets. It was close enough for me to remain tied to Barbara and Nita but not far enough from York Street.

To my mother, the important thing about our apartment in the Projects was that it had concrete floors and metal doors. They would restrain the entry of rats, roaches, and "niggers," she told me.

Harm was locked out as we were locked inside, alone, together. We seemed also to be locked in even poorer days than on York Street. We often ate hoe cakes or cereal for dinner, except on my mother's paydays, when we would eat out, mostly at the Horn & Hardart Automat. In between paydays, we were often hungry behind our steel doors and concrete walls.

The government's "relief" program for the poor was beneath my mother's dignity. She did not believe in asking anybody for anything, telling me it was better to steal or starve than beg. We did not need anyone at all, including our "newsy" new neighbors, she said, confirming us as one against the world.

On my thirteenth birthday, however, my mother opened the doors to our Projects haven so that I could have a party. All my friends from York Street were invited. My mother bought me the outfit I demanded: a charcoal-gray felt skirt with a pink poodle embroidered on it, a pink blouse, a gray cinch belt, gray suede bucks, and pink knee socks.

Barbara and I went down onto Susquehanna Avenue to buy records for the party with the ten dollars my mother had given me. We bought "Sister Sookie Done Gone" and some "sides" by Hank Ballard and LaVerne Baker. I ended up with a total of ten new records, "78's" and the new, plastic "45's," records of songs made popular on the radio by Georgie Woods, "the man with the goods, coming to you from Phila-ma-del-phi-yea-aah!"

Despite the fact that my cinch belt curled at my now-chubby waist, or that I still wore an undershirt and not a brassiere, or that I did not have my period, I was elated by the prospect of becoming a teenager. I was not only going to be a real teenager, I was going to have a party, and a whole lot of boys were going to be there.

Once a few of my girl friends started arriving, my mother went out. She did it because she trusted me, she said. Most parents would have stayed at home under the circumstances, she reminded me, and plopped themselves into the middle of their kids' parties. After my mother left, Barbara and I substituted the regular light bulbs with the colored ones my mother had bought for the occasion, and put out the hot dogs and potato salad my mother had prepared.

All the "youngbloods" from the "Avenue" arrived in a pack. The Avenue was the street gang that controlled the territory that included 21st and York Streets. They had named the gang after Susquehanna Avenue, the main street running through the territory. Even though I now lived in Norris Street gang territory, I was, in spirit, part of life on York Street, part of the Avenue.

Having survived the dangerous trek into Norris Street territory, the members of the Avenue sauntered into my place wearing their "do-rags," scarves wrapped about their heads to hold their processed hairdos in place. They concealed half-drunk bottles of white port wine and lemon juice concoctions under their coats. Each fellow carried himself with one hand stuffed into his pant pocket, pulling his sharply pressed khaki pants above his ankles, his other hand remaining free to swing back and forth as he walked, leaning to one side. They all wore black nylon "pimp" socks and black leather, ankle-high shoes called "old men's comforts." To me the fellows were, in a word, "cool."

My other girl friends came in small groups, each one making

an entrance. Every girl's hair was freshly "pressed," and most of them had on tight skirts and cinch belts, with bobby socks and loafers, or else bucks and large hoop earrings implanted in their pierced ears. It was going to be the "toughest" party ever, I thought as everyone arrived—not ruined like Barbara's had been a few months before.

We had been in her whitewashed basement, at 2057 West York Street, on New Year's Eve. Everyone was anticipating "French-kissing" at midnight. When the midnight countdown rolled around, Barbara's father—one of the few in the neighborhood—clicked on the turned-out lights from the top of the cellar stairs. Mr. Moses Benjamin Taylor III was a member of the NAACP and a very religious man who everyone knew did not suffer too much foolishness.

Boys quickly tried to hide wine bottles, and girls started straightening their rumpled blouses, somewhat thankful for that reprieve to adjust the tissue stuffed against little breasts.

"All right, boys and girls," Mr. Taylor announced with church propriety as he began walking down the basement stairs, Bible in hand. "Close your eyes and say with me, please: 'Our Father which art in heaven . . .'"

Barbara cried for three solid days after that, for which her mother, Mattie, whipped her good with the cord of an iron. Barbara was inconsolable, however. She vowed to never, ever speak to her father again.

My party would, of course, be different: better. My mother had gone out for the evening, so we could carry on as we wanted. We could smoke our Chesterfields and Camels out in the open, and even sip from the boys' wine bottles. Everybody could "grind" tight, up against the wall, boys' stiff penises pressing against girls' thighs. Boys could even feel girls up and down.

I was a good hostess. After I served the food, I played disc jockey, and even did "the slop" to get everybody started. Then I waited, slow-dance record after slow-dance record. I waited through the Spaniels' "Peace of Mind," through "Cherry Pie," through "Nightowl." I waited for some "do-ragged" boy to tag my hand to dance slow, to grind. It never happened. I was not once asked to slow-dance.

I retired in tears to a concrete corner. From there, I watched Barbara slow-dancing and Nita slow-dancing and everybody else slow-dancing through a haze. In the blur of things, I certainly had no ability to realize that my mother had returned, everybody but

me swooning to the Five Satins crooning "In the Still of the Night."
I certainly did not hear what she was saying to me when she called
out in horror upon entering our bedroom: "Elaine! I said get in
here! Somebody's had sexual intercourse in this bed!"

I walked heavily into the room to listen emotionlessly to whatever diatribe she was about to issue forth. I had had enough for
one evening.

"I'm not going to have it," she shouted at me, standing in
the doorway. "Who did this?!" she demanded, as I tried to figure
out how she could have known such a thing.

"Look at this stain," she continued, pointing to the center of
the disheveled bed. "It's semen! How could you let this happen?
I gave you a party, I bought the food *and* cooked it. And I *trusted*
you! I work like a dog every day to try to give you things and you
let this happen. Look! There's even a pubic hair right here! Look
at it!"

As she spoke, I contemplated what semen might look like,
and tried to imagine somebody really doing "it." I wondered who
had done it when I had not even had one slow-dance.

"I do not appreciate this shit. Not one bit," she went on. "I
want everybody out of this house right now!"

"That sure is cold," I heard some of the boys mumble in the
living room as everyone began easing out the door. I did not care
about any of it, or certainly any of them. I had only one concern:
that I had not once been asked to slow-dance.

Barbara and her cousin Kathy, who lived on 18th Street, and
our other close friend, Carol Hollins, from 20th Street, stayed
behind to help me clean up the mess, to wash the "process" grease
stains off the walls and sweep the concrete floors. They also tried
to help me figure out who had "fucked" in my mother's bed, which
was also mine.

A few months later, I thought it might have been Nita who
had done "it" in our bed. She casually announced to Barbara and
me one day that she was pregnant. I felt betrayed. It was not
because she was pregnant or that she might have been the one
who did it in my bed. It was that she had actually "gone all the
way" and had not told any of us about it.

I wanted to know what it was like: where did the "dick" actually go. She never got around to filling us in, because she was
busy making wedding plans. Nita's mother had recently been born
again as a Jehovah's Witness and had ordained, therefore, that no
child of hers would have any babies out of wedlock. Within a

month or so after Nita's announcement to us, she got married, in what reminded me of a Tom Thumb wedding ceremony, where children play grownups. Nita's pregnancy and forced marriage forced her out of her house, out of junior high, out of York Street, and out of our lives forever at the age of thirteen, gone to dwell in the house of her teenage husband, a member of the Avenue.

With Nita's pronouncement, the first loss of virginity I knew of, the big question of "doing it" began to permeate our daily lives. Then, in midsummer, Carol Hollins forged the next step in our trail.

"Girl, that shit hurt. I bled like a dog," Carol told Barbara and me one summer afternoon when we were sitting around her house.

"But how did you do it? Who with?" Barbara asked boldly.

"You ever hear of 'Snake' from the Valley?" Carol said.

"No, you didn't fuck somebody from the *Valley*, Carol!" I screamed.

It was a violation of gang territorial laws to have any dealings whatsoever with gang members from other territories. After all, despite my own move into Norris Street, we were all Avenue girls. It was important to understand the nuances of North Philly gang life. It was critical to one's survival—a concept that was my standing priority. First of all, gang members were boys. Although there were a few rough groups of girls who might claim to be a gang, girls were, at best, support groups for boys' gangs or, at least, girl friends of gang members.

I had actually heard of only one girls' gang in North Philly. The terrible Toasties were teenage girls who ran around assaulting other girls who had light skin, long hair, or "good" hair, or who wore "six-button bennies," double-breasted coats. Their practice was to surround a girl with long hair and cut it off; or walk past a victim and, with razor blades secreted between their fingers, slap a girl across the face, leaving a bloody opening a lifetime would never close.

The Toasties were extinct as far as we knew by the time we became teenagers. Anyway, none of us—not Barbara, or Nita, or Kathy, or Carol, or I—none of us was or ever had been intimidated by girls on the streets of North Philly. *We are rough! We are tough! We are the girls who don't take no stuff!* Indeed, no matter how white I was at school, I was still of the stuff of York Street and I could deal with any girl on the streets of North Philly. If some tough bitch even looked in my direction with a confrontational attitude, I put on my ugliest ghetto attitude and became the aggressor. I would get directly into her face, ask the bitch who the fuck she was looking at, and drop my fist to my side. No, none of us was afraid of any girl on the streets of North Philly. The boys were another matter.

Boys' gangs literally controlled life in our various North Philly neighborhoods, and most boys claimed gang membership. They walked in packs and generally terrified everybody with their very presence. They boastfully paraded clothing or insignia or tattoos or other symbols of their gang membership. They had to "stand" for their gang at all times, alone or not, inside or outside their territory, the latter being a very dangerous proposition.

A "blood" caught outside his territory was subject to getting shot or stabbed just for being there. Moreover, territory was complicated to comprehend. Since what territory a gang controlled depended on how hard a gang fought to maintain or expand it, its boundaries could shift at any given moment. Some gangs' territories stretched as much as eight square blocks; some, like that of the Avenue, were contained within four square blocks; others, like Camac and Diamond, incorporated only a single street corner. Given the high density of people in our neighborhoods, however, significant numbers of people were affected by gang activity. The gangs stole from people, robbed houses, took over house parties, punished enemies, and, worse, warred. If a gang war was "called" by a "war council," hundreds of gang members from the two opposing gangs would gather in a vacant lot or open area in some designated territory to battle it out with designated weapons until death or the police ended the battle.

There were many rules for girls about how to relate to a gang and its members. One of the most abiding was that girls living in one gang territory did not so much as hold a conversation with a member of another gang. When Carol told us who "broke her cherry," we knew she was flirting with death.

"No, you didn't fuck somebody from the Valley!" Barbara echoed.

"Not only is he in the Valley," Carol continued dramatically, "he's the leader of the Valley!"

Carol was the bravest girl we knew. We waited with open mouths for her to bestow the next morsel on us.

"Yeah, child," she went on, "we 'macked' for a long time."

"Where were you?"

"Right here, in my house," she said, laughing off the riskiness of the whole affair.

We shrieked with responsive laughter and passed around a Chesterfield cigarette, held by a bobby pin.

"He took off my skirt and then he took off his pants."

We were breathless.

"Then he got on top of me and pushed it in. Girl, I cried. I screamed my head off. Then all this blood came out of me."

"Oooh!" we moaned, turning our heads away from Carol in disgust. Barbara and I vowed to *never*, ever do it.

It was an early evening that same summer. We were, as usual, hanging out at Carol's, playing pinochle, listening to records, and eating greasy French fries that came in brown paper bags. I had been in the bathroom of Carol's tenement apartment, which was laid out like a long railroad car. The bathroom was in the very back of the apartment, after the living room, after the kitchen and the two bedrooms. When I returned to the living room, I saw the front door lying flat on the floor. A bunch of boys, drunk young-bloods from the neighborhood, were standing around in Carol's living room. Neither Carol nor Barbara was in sight.

When they had come to the door about a half hour before, I had thought they believed us. They had insisted we were having a party. We had insisted that Carol's mother had not then and would not ever have let her have company in the house when she was not there.

"Yeah," LeVester had responded in that typical tone of disbelief that signaled the quiet preceding a storm, grabbing his boys and going away.

They were "Avenue niggers," however, and we were "Avenue girls." They surely knew we would not lie to them. They had no reason to crash into Carol's apartment, where there really was no party. They had kicked in the door, though, broken it down at its hinges while I was in the bathroom and hadn't heard it happen.

Nathaniel looked at me through red eyes and asked me to dance. I heard Carol outside now, crying her eyes out, Barbara telling her to shut up. I could also hear Carol's "sissified" younger brother chiding her for what was going to happen to her when their mother came home.

"Oh, no thanks, Nathaniel. I've got to go," I said coolly. Bizarrely, I wondered where he had been on the night of my thirteenth birthday party less than six months before.

"Naw, bitch, I wanna dance *now*," he said coldly. In an instant, one of them put a 45 record on Carol's record player. "Oh, What a Night" began playing.

So we danced. We grinded, his penis getting hard against my leg, his breath reeking of Ripple wine and Doublemint gum.

Just as suddenly as the music started, it was halted. At the same time the lights were clicked off. Somebody pushed me over Carol's mother's imitation-French-provincial coffee table onto her plastic-covered couch. There was a lot of shuffling of feet and scrambling, as hands pulled my legs apart and raised my skirt. I twisted my body, which could not resist yielding to the body that was now on top of me. More hands were trying to pull off my panties. For some reason, I could not scream. I thought about how unbelievable it was that I would have to "give it up" in this way, for it was accomplished as far as I was concerned. I silently put up a futile resistance and hoped only that it would not hurt and I would not bleed like a dog.

Out of nowhere, however, the lights clicked on again. The leader among them had done it. He was standing over the lot, telling them to get off me.

"Naw, man, this ain't right," he admonished them. "This is a Avenue bitch. We can't pull no train on no Avenue bitch."

Miraculously, with his words all of them, the eight or nine who were lined up to take their turn with me and the one on top of me, just backed off. It seemed like the parting of the Red Sea. I was free to get up and walk out, though I was still frozen, legs akimbo. As they regrouped, they mumbled that I was a "jive, funky bitch" anyway and that none of them would fuck me with anybody else's dick. Nevertheless, they did not touch me again. I got up, pulled down my skirt, and simply watched them, Fat Man and LeVester and Nathaniel and Cheese and all the rest, walk over Carol's door and file out into the night.

> Come, ye disconsolate
> Where e'er ye languish
> Come to the mercy seat,
> Fervently kneel.
> Here sits the Comforter
> Tenderly saying,

Earth hath no sorrow
That Heav'n cannot heal.

While my relationship with God was unclear, that did not
seem important. I knew, more than ever, by the time we left the
Projects, that I needed God.

My mother did not deal with the dilemma of God in her life.
She believed in God but refused to go to church, considering it a
phony ladies' club. She went to work, she played her numbers,
she braced herself for life's next assault and moved on. Moving
on was quite literal with her. When we had suffered the Projects
for about a year, she moved us into an apartment in an area called
Tioga. It was an area of North Philadelphia that was one step
removed from the abject harshness of York Street and the Projects;
only one little step, though.

There was something heavy about living there. There was a
loneliness there. It was not in the dismal rooms of that one-
bedroom, cold-water flat. It was not in the barren, hardwood floors
or the snapping sound of the many mousetraps my mother set.
It was not in our continued poverty, reflected in the hot plate that
was our stove or the window box that was our refrigerator. There
was even something acceptably familiar in the pounding bass of
the rock-and-roll songs that reverberated in our apartment every
night from the jukebox in the steak shop below us. I realized that
the sadness came from the absence of Barbara and Carol and
Kathy that the distance created—as life had already distanced the
rest of us from Nita. I was drifting away from the anchor of their
friendship in the murkiness of North Philadelphia. *I* was not
tough. *We* were tough.

Whatever my out-of-the-ghetto, white-is-right confusions,
their friendship was home, the place where people wait for you
to return from flights of fancy, no matter how many trips you
take. As white schoolmates had stopped offering me a place in
their sun, however I talked and behaved, I had stopped seeking
it, time and circumstance sending us to our proper corners. Barbara and Carol and Kathy and Nita were what I was, despite what
I did not want to be. I· was them, on the inside, and they had
always been my only happiness.

It was more than dressing alike and sharing hoagies at the
movies and complaints about our mothers and dirty ditties on the
sidewalk and grape sodas and greasy French fries and lies and
truths. It was more than learning to do the "slop" and the "strand"

together, and having fantasy weddings with boys we knew would never marry us. It was more than sneaking a chance to use the telephones in our houses, only to go over the words to the last chorus of the latest rock-and-roll song. It was getting kicked out of the Uptown Theater together at twelve and resisting being held against our will until the paddy wagon came to take us all to the juvenile jail—to which Barbara's father kept Barbara, Nita, and me from going, and where Kathy and Carol spent one night for "disturbing the peace"—and all of us cheering on Kathy, who tore away from a big white cop and almost outran him down Susquehanna Avenue. It was confessing the growth of pubic hair and having or not having periods, and wearing brassieres we did not need, and not being ashamed. It was talking about forming a girls' singing group, and actually trying to form one, and never mentioning that Barbara could not really sing harmony and always mentioning that Carol could not sing at all. It was being each other's secret, secret sisterlike soul who was always there.

Life was stripped down to its essentials now. My mother went to work and I went to school, Cooke Junior High. That was it. The only relief in the routine for me came in the hours between my arrival home from school and mother's from work. They were luxurious hours to me, hours to dream and fantasize beyond the reality of the world, from which I was now beginning to feel more and more isolated.

I had been a kind of recluse for some time, though, when I reflected on it. I was not withdrawn or shy. I was simply not part of any of the worlds in which I lived. I was mostly a disingenuous player. At school, I remained white. On the streets of North Philadelphia, I was black. From time to time, I pretended I belonged with the uppity colored kids at school or piano lessons, though they were always ready to remind me that I was not of their class—as Howardena Pindell's mother had once done. Howardena's mother told her I could not eat dinner at their house again until I acquired better table manners. By the time we reached our last year at Thaddeus Stevens together, Howardena had actually been forbidden by her teacher mother and engineer father to play with me. They thought I was too crude for Howardena, rather like an "urchin," Mrs. Pindell told my mother, who cussed her out for saying so. It became unimportant to me by the time we graduated to Cooke Junior High, for I was beginning to accept a life outside of life. Once my mother and I moved to Tioga, I became committed to living almost exclusively in my own world.

It was my habit, during those after-school hours in Tioga, to put on shows for myself. I would sit down at the piano my mother had bought for me "on time"—years before, after my grandmother had refused to let me play the old upright on York Street whenever I wanted. I would first play classical pieces, imagining I was a concert virtuoso. Then I would play and sing popular rock-and-roll songs. Then I would turn to the pop tunes popularized by Snooky Lanson and Dorothy Collins on *Your Hit Parade: I was dancin' with my darlin' to the Tennessee Waltz.* I might stop after about an hour or so and try to write a poem, conjuring up an image of myself as the colored Emily Dickinson. I usually spent the rest of the time before my mother returned home looking into the mirror, designing hairstyles, and posturing in imitation of some white movie star like Merle Oberon.

During one such time, while I was concocting a most exotic hairstyle in our bedroom, I was distracted by a note peeking out from under the box of tissues on the dresser top. It was to my mother from a Dr. Horace Scott. It was handwritten on expensive stationery. What attracted me was the sight of my name: "I know *Elaine* is very bright . . . I don't think you should discontinue *Elaine's* piano lessons . . ."

I forgot it and continued with my hairstyle, when, as usual, I was shocked to find that so much time had elapsed, my mother would be home soon. I leaped to straighten up the place, stuffing things into drawers I should have put into the dirty clothes hamper or the trash, and hiding the unwashed dishes in the back of the refrigerator my mother had finally gotten from Gimbel's on credit. Typically, I made it under the wire.

My mother's saga of woes would begin upon her entrance. She was no longer a presser in a dress factory. Now she worked as a clerk for the Veterans Administration. It was the same to me—she would complain about everything.

"I'm so tired," she said on entering, walking out of her shoes. "My supervisor had the nerve to raise her voice to me. I started to slap the bitch, but I've got to keep this job till I get enough in my retirement fund."

I listened to what I had come to think of as her daily song of defeat, as she put away a few groceries and started our dinner. I listened half interestedly as she complained about life in general, "niggers" in general, having no money in general, working in general, how hard it was for her and, in general, how much she needed my help and did not need to come home to "those goddamn dirty dishes in the refrigerator" or "any other bullshit whatsoever."

"I work like a dog every day," she chanted, "but you, nobody, nobody appreciates it. And what do I have to show for it? Nothing!"

It was not that I did not hear her or care. It was that I had other concerns. There was my abiding dilemma over being in my colored skin. There were my more immediate concerns over when I would ever get my period and when I would have the stuff to wear a bra, and whether I would find a great love. Of course, I was silent about all of it, considering such discussion with her futile. My mother's refrain was sufficient affirmation that she was powerless to affect the forces that kept both of us wanting. Her sole determination was to survive; mine was to replant my rotten roots. As we silently cleared away the dinner dishes, that thought made her appear so overwhelmingly pathetic to me that I decided to reach out to her with something.

"By the way, Mom, who is Dr. Horace Scott?" I asked, digging out the dishes I had earlier hidden in the back of our new refrigerator.

Dorothy Clark, my mother, had never cried a tear that I knew of. She was a rock, an industrial, working-class rock who could fight a man on his own terms. If she was anything more, she was my sole protector, to whom I had unwittingly pledged life devotion, forsaking all others. She did not cry, not ever, not until I asked her about the note on the dresser from Dr. Horace Scott. She stopped in her tracks, went into the living room, and fell down onto the couch. I followed her.

Sobs burst forth from my mother, about which I was more curious than caring. Sobs emanated from my mother, the rock, the unfeminine workhorse of a woman. In between, she started to talk.

"I knew this would come up someday," she cried, her face buried in her hands. "I don't know how I thought I could keep it from you."

I wondered what it could be as I sat down next to her and somewhat sympathetically tried to caress her. She toughened to my touch, though, rejecting it. The only time she touched me was at night, when she would still hold me until I fell asleep. Tenderness and open affection were phoniness to my mother, displays put on by upper-crust Negroes and white people.

"But who is he?" I asked again, gently.

"He's your father!" she blurted out with a real pain I had never seen in her.

"Oh God! You don't understand," she continued. "We were never married! He was already married when I met him and started seeing him. But he didn't tell me until . . ."

She released pieces of her terrible secret while I pondered the fact that my father was a doctor. I remembered meeting an "Aunt Lenore," a long time ago, it seemed, and I knew that she was not my mother's sister, but I had never thought about why she was referred to as my aunt. I also remembered a mumbling about how funny it was that the family name of both my parents was Brown. Perhaps I overheard this between the time we moved in with my mother's "second" husband, Perry Clark, and that memorable night she chased him out of our life with a butcher knife. I realized, however, that nowhere in my mind, had I really thought about a father; or, if I had, I had presumed he was dead.

My mother was now telling me that my father was alive. My father was alive and was a doctor. I was ecstatic. I began fantasizing about how I would tell my arrogant, rich Jewish girl friends, along with all the Howardenas at Cooke Junior High, that they were not the only ones whose fathers were doctors or lawyers or something. I began to wonder if I would be rich, now that I knew about him. It hardly mattered to me that my parents had not been married. It hardly mattered that I had not known about any of it until that very moment. What mattered was that I had a real and identifiable father, and that he was an important man.

"Don't feel bad, Mom. I don't care if you weren't married. It's all right," I said tenderly.

When she calmed down with bountiful "I'm-so-sorry's," I asked her about the things I really wanted to know.

"When can I meet him? What does he look like? Where does he live?"

"He looks just like you. In fact, you look more like him than me. The son-of-a-bitch finally saw that, after trying to say at first that you might not be his."

She spoke of him with rage, and avoided most of my other inquiries, especially about seeing him. She told me what a dog he was, and how he had never sent her a dime to help with me. She told me that that was why she had been taking him to court every month, even though his powerful friends at the court—colored judges, of whom I had not realized there were any—"400" Negroes, she said, with names like Juanita Kidd Stout and Raymond

Pace Alexander, had conspired against her. He had been able to disregard for years, literally, his child-support payments of fifty dollars a month. She told me how he thought she was nothing, not good enough for him, not like his wife, who was a charter member of the prestigious colored women's club, the Links. She told me how she guessed that I, too, was not good enough for him, because when he found out his wife could not have children, he had adopted a daughter.

I stopped her. "He adopted a daughter?" It was really the only thing that caught my attention in the half hour that had just passed.

"Yes. The bastard! Right after you were born. She's the same age as you."

My father fantasies fizzled. I had only just found out I had a natural, biological father. He was a doctor, and he lived on Lincoln Drive, that most exclusive area in all of Germantown, reserved for newly rich Negroes. In one glorious minute I had found my sweet chariot out of the poverty of my life, and in the next, it seemed to be speeding away.

For that fleeting moment, I had envisioned all the beautiful new clothes I might have, and the trips I might take, and the fine, refined, light-skinned colored boys who would begin to want me now that I, too, was one of the "better" Negroes. I had envisioned a new and wonderful universe opening up for me on my introduction to my father, not at all minding all those years he had not been around, redeemed by the birth of our long-lost relationship.

When my mother told me about his adopted daughter, I felt it was an abominable rejection. My father had not only discarded me, he had given refuge to somebody else's forsaken child. He had put somebody else's homeless child in my house. He had given some other damned daughter all the benefits of my birthright. He had given his name to some other child who had no name. Once again, I felt the doom of a life outside of life, a bastardization of life itself.

That night, my long-ago, nightly questions returned to my mind like faceless apparitions. Who was God, I demanded of the universe. If God made me, I wanted to know, *now*, who made God. I wanted an appeal, to appeal, to repeal God's works, which were not good. I wanted the one who made God, or the one who made the one who made God, to make me over. I wanted to know if my father had been a different man, would the product of him and my mother know that person I now was, and did not want to be. Finally, with more fear and pain than ever, tears and sweat pouring from me, I bolted up in bed and screamed: *"Mama! Mama! It's that feeling!"*

Even if my father had an adopted daughter, I thought in the clear light of the next few weeks, why could I not see him? I made this inquiry of my mother nearly every day. I felt I was, after all, the perfect daughter. I could play the piano and dance on point and eat properly—having studied a book of etiquette after my experiences at Howardena's house. I could speak properly, like white people even—or, when necessary, like any people, having learned how to blend into any arrangement. He was aware of all that, my mother would sadly respond. Indeed, her diligent, lone efforts to refine me had been at his behest over the years. He had pictures of me and had even seen me in person, though it was only at night, while I was sleeping. His family simply would not tolerate open acknowledgment of me.

There was his father, Dr. Emmett Scott, Sr. He had been secretary to Booker T. Washington after Washington founded Tuskegee Institute; later he became a major financial backer of Howard University. In addition, Emmett Scott, Sr., had been appointed a Cabinet advisor to the Secretary of War under President Woodrow Wilson, the first Negro in America to be installed in a presidential Cabinet. There was also Emmett Scott, Jr., an engineer; and Lenore, a teacher; and Clarissa Scott Delaney, a writer; and my father, a neurosurgeon. They were a socially prominent Negro family. They were the kind of Negroes who proclaimed there had never been slaves in their line. They were the kind of Negroes who thought dark-skinned blacks were inferior and light-skinned blacks were "trash," as the obvious products of illicit relations with Caucasians. They were the kind of family who spoke of my existence secretly, in dulcet-toned Southern accents, born in Tuskegee, Alabama, and settled in Washington, D.C. They were the kind of family that could simply ignore my father's moment of indiscretion with the low-class colored girl who was my mother.

Ultimately, I decided I did not want to meet my father. I decided I would meet him only to tell him everything I thought. If he was so ashamed of his bastard daughter he had invented another one, I wished he were dead. If his wealthy, Negro, Washington, D.C.–based family, about which there were various notations in certain Negro history books, did not want to acknowledge his bastard child, I wished they, too, were all dead. No, I thought, I did not ever want to meet my father.

I was finally on my mother's side. She was right. *We* were nothing! I had no business worrying about my color. It was nothing compared to being nothing at all. I had to work, to fight, to become something other than nothing. I had finally learned that, firsthand.

It was with this awareness that I entered the ninth grade at the Philadelphia High School for Girls. I was not the bastard reject of my father, neither black nor white, a faceless, disembodied misfit who had no place of her own. I was my mother's well-rounded, beautiful, perfect daughter, who was outside and above everybody else on the entire, uncaring planet.

The Philadelphia High School for Girls, or Girls High, was the perfect haven for a perfect girl. To attend, one either had to have a high I.Q. or pass an entrance test. I was not required to take the entrance examination. Girls High was located at 17th and Spring Garden streets, just four blocks from the special school I had attended only two years before.

A replicated statue of the *Winged Victory*, or Nike, the Greek goddess of victory, overwhelmed the hallowed entrance hall of Girls High. We entering girls were taught to silently salute her every day, even though her symbolism may have been lost on most freshman psyches. All freshmen were sure of only one thing, that we were the *crème de la crème*, the smartest girls in Philadelphia and among the smartest in the country.

Girls High was, we learned from day one, the first school of higher learning for women in the United States. It was one hundred years old when I entered in 1957, and steeped in a thousand traditions; and I was part of its two hundredth class. It was an elitist center, the purpose of which was to hone its daughters into the world's movers and shakers.

The Gothic structure of Girls High encased marble floors and marble walls. The old marble seemed to echo the footsteps and arcane academic chatter of girls past, joined by our own as we went to and from classes. I was enrolled in Latin, as were many in my class who thought Spanish or French beneath them. We wore understated Ivy League garb, spoke in tight-lipped, nasal "Eastern" tones, and looked down our noses at anybody who was not a student at Girls High, with the exception of the boys at our brother school, Central High. We conjugated verbs and declined nouns in Latin and in English, and gracefully dressed ourselves in prudery and pretension.

I became a solid-A student in Latin and English, maintained a high grade in history and decent grades in math and science. I rarely, if ever, went to gym class, considering it, like typing—which I refused to take—too plebeian. Since Girls High operated on an honor system, it was presumed by my word that I was present in all classes, which satisfied that minor requirement. In any event, by the end of the ninth grade, I had developed such a reputation I would never have been challenged.

I was considered rather arrogant by my peers and somewhat rebellious and argumentative by my teachers. My English teacher went so far as to give me a final grade of B, because she said I did not behave like an A student. Over the year, she argued when I assailed her over the grade, I had called out to speak rather than raising my hand, deferred doing most daily homework in reliance on my final test grade, and questioned nearly every statement she had made. I accepted her argument in the end because her grade did not matter to me. I was moving on course, becoming better than white, soaring above everybody, a superior, singular, independent, unattached being who needed no one, including a father.

I had, however, taken note of his political posters plastered all over Philadelphia during that time. He was running for Congress on the Republican ticket. Waiting for my bus to go to school, I had caught glimpses of his enlarged poster face, distorted by North Philly dirt and graffiti, and by PUSSY and FUCK YOU scrawled across his nose and chin. He was handsome, I saw, without giving thought to him at all. I was passingly sorry when he lost the election, though it, and surely he, meant nothing to me at all, I maintained.

His face in person, on the other hand, was different. It was my face, my eyes, my lips, my nose, the face of my father. I did not know what to call him when he touched me from arm's length for the first time I knew about. He and my mother had arranged it. It was in the beginning of my tenth-grade year at Girls High. He was proud of me, proud of my grades, proud of everything I had become, my mother told me. He wanted to develop a relationship with me, she said.

I had to meet him at his office, a neat, brownstone, two-story structure in a clean pocket of North Philadelphia. No patients were there when I opened the double door, the top half of which was made of stained glass. He opened the door of his inner office as I was about to sit down in the outer one. He was not much taller than I. His brown skin and mine matched. He had some freckles and wavy hair. He was indeed very handsome, I felt, as he finally embraced me.

"Your mother has been telling me everything about you over the years, you know," he said, studying me.

I was speechless, trying to figure out whether I looked like the most beautiful girl in the world to him. Was my tailored clothing proper? I wondered. Could he see that I really did look like him?

"You've grown into quite a young lady," he continued in a rather formal way, showing me to an office chair across from his desk, on which he sat. His suit was brown, accented by his highly polished, expensive-looking brown shoes and stark-white shirt, the cuffs of which bore his initials.

He told me about "our" family, most of which my mother had, of course, already told me. He emphasized how special our bloodline was, pointing out specifically that I was the image of his sister Clarissa, who had been perhaps the very first colored woman to graduate from Wellesley College. I decided that was where I would go to college; it was, after all, among the preferred colleges for Girls High girls. He asked me about my grades, my life in school, my friends. He said other things to which I paid little attention, I was so dazzled by his handsome face and beautiful eyes and smart appearance. Before I left, after about an hour, I let him know that I accepted the secrecy of our meeting, and he let me know we could continue to see each other in this way.

I did not want to return to my mother. I did not want to return to our latest apartment in another part of Tioga, or to our room. I wanted to start over, to start life over with that fine, refined colored man who was my real and only father, who wanted me in his life. I was noncommunicative with my mother that afternoon. I told her nothing about it, not even my impressions. She was incapable of understanding, I felt. She did not really know him, or me. We, my father and I, were alike, I concluded that day. We were one—not my mother and I—but *he* and I.

As I walked from the bus stop to his office for my next visit, about a week later, I determined to convince him to take me into his life on a full-time basis. The details were unclear to me. I imagined we could stay together in a small apartment, probably in Germantown, where I could take care of myself, or something, while he maintained his other life with his wife and adopted daughter on Lincoln Drive. I did not think of my mother at all.

"How does your mother really feel about your seeing me?" he asked early on.

"It doesn't matter, does it?" I responded conspiratorially.

He smiled. I knew he could understand that I would leave her and her lower-class ways and her North Philly attitudes and her numbers and her poverty if he would just say the word. I would leave her for him, forever.

"It has, you know."

I looked bewildered.

"I see she hasn't told you. Of course not. You see, we've always wanted you in our family, but she wouldn't have it."

I remained blank, not comprehending.

"I mean," he continued, "you are, after all, the only child any of us, my brother and sisters, has ever had; and we wanted you to live with your aunt in Chicago, a fine woman, whose husband is a prominent attorney there . . ."

"As my mother and father?"

"Well, yes. But your mother has always stood in the way," he said with little-subdued acrimony. "Now, of course, I'm not sure what we can do. So I just want to see you whenever possible."

"I guess I'd like that, too," I said rather idiotically, wrestling with the shock of everything he had just calmly told me, at once ashamed of my designs to leave my mother and angry with my mother for concealing so much from me.

As he continued speaking, mostly about how much like his family I was, I began to wonder why he had waited so long to see me, to tell me. Then I wondered what he wanted me to do. Then I tried to imagine life with *his* family. Then I wondered what he thought my mother should have done, or been, to me. Then I remembered what my mother had asked me to do.

We had no food and no money, because my mother's payday was on Monday and it was the weekend. She had instructed me, more times than I had listened, to try to get $10 from him.

Nearly an hour had passed. It seemed time to leave.

"By the way," I asked him casually, and somewhat embarrassed, "could you let me have ten dollars for some school books." My mother had told me to make it seem as if the request was for me personally. I smiled at him flirtatiously.

"Is that what your mother told you to ask me?" he said, suddenly very cold.

"Uh n-no," I stuttered.

"You tell your mother if she wants money from me to take

me to court like she does every month. Has the gall to try to get
a bench warrant for my arrest. Every damn month! Tell her don't
ever again send you to get money out of me!"

Tears filled my eyes as they widened with shock and shame.

"But it's only ten dollars, and we need the money for food!"
I cried out, surprising myself.

"That's what *she* says," he responded passionlessly. "She's got
a job. She can handle everything. You just tell her what I said.
And tell her not to try to play games with me anymore!"

I checked my tears and transformed myself. I became a Girls
High girl, or maybe a North Philly girl. "As far as I'm concerned,
you are the one playing games," I stated firmly, looking directly
into his dark brown eyes. "But don't worry about me asking you
for a cent again," I said in my most arrogant tone. "You don't
have to worry about me again!"

I was holding the outer office door open, and he was looking
at me in disbelief.

"As a matter of fact, I don't want to see you again!" I
screamed. "I'd rather see you dead. And when you die, I'll spit
on your grave!" I bellowed, borrowing language from some old
movie, it seemed. I slammed the Dutch door, cracking the stained-
glass mosaic.

It was the last door I would have to close, I thought, as I
walked back to the bus stop, less damaged than determined. My
mother and I, alone, would survive in his world, in "their" world,
whoever they were, and without their help. That weekend, we ate
eggs and hoe cakes with dry eyes and knowing expressions that
we needed no one at all anymore.

My grades improved, but my attitude did not, until I met Frank
Constant, a pretty, light-skinned colored boy who drove a pink-
and-black Ford that was his very own. He lived in a nice part of
Germantown—though it was not the ultimate, Lincoln Drive. I
considered myself the most distinguished fifteen-year-old girl in
all of Philadelphia when Frank asked me to go out on a date
with him.

I had met him at a party Barbara and I had crashed. We had
started doing that after Barbara began attending Germantown
High and found out where the parties were. We did it only for
the pleasure of upsetting the "siddity" Germantown girls, as we
knew everybody in Germantown was scared of anybody who came

from North Philly. Frank was a bonus, a prize I won from them.

His face was cherubic and slightly freckled. Though he was only seventeen, Frank sported a thick reddish-brown mustache that made him even more attractive. He was the finest boy that had ever called my name. I wanted him more than I had imagined I could want anyone in my life.

I had never really gone out on a date with a boy before Frank. The boys I had known were mostly "gang niggers" from the Avenue. They had no money to take a girl out on a date, even if they had had a mind to do so. If I had done anything akin to dating, it had been dancing exclusively with one of them at a North Philly house party and having him walk me home afterward. This was the kind of limited relationship I had had with Dennis Crump, one of the two terrible Crump brothers who were in the upper ranks of the Avenue. Dennis and I used to stand in hallways or on street corners after a party and French-kiss and press our bodies together. Before that, I had kissed a boy called "Genie," a nickname like those of all the rest of the "Avenue niggers," Rat and Icebox and the psychopathic Bo-Peep.

Frank did not seem to mind picking me up at my apartment, though most Germantown boys would not dare to enter North Philly. We began dating, usually going to drive-in movies, where we would make out during the entire film. We sometimes went to Germantown parties, where I thought I had "died and gone to heaven" just being with him, and especially among them. When Frank agreed to be my date at the Girls High junior prom, I felt my life was at noon, the call to coronation.

I had a tantrum over what to wear to the junior prom and, of course, persuaded my mother to spend a fortune on a black peau de soie dress and black peau de soie high heels, beaded at the toe. I thought the traditional yellow or pink organza was for "ordinary" girls. I would wear classic black.

Frank and I double-dated with my classmate Jackie Bishop and her boyfriend, Donald. Jackie was one of the very few other colored girls in my class.

Later, we went to a private, after-prom party in Germantown, ending up in the early-morning hours at my new apartment— also in Germantown, finally. My mother had scraped together the money, the month before, to rent us a cheery little apartment on a quiet street there.

By daybreak, the four of us had polished off a fifth of vodka. Jackie and Donald had spent the hours carrying on on the sofa.

Frank and I had lain on the living-room floor and kissed so much my lips were swollen and my underpants were soaked. I was dizzy from my share of the vodka, but I remembered begging Frank sometime in the night to go all the way. I had literally begged him to take the "pussy" in exchange for his pledge to be mine.

"You're too serious, Elaine. I don't want to hurt you," he had said, rubbing my nipples under my black peau de soie dress. "I don't want to take advantage of you," he concluded, signaling the end of something. He would, though, he assured me, call me before going off to Lincoln University in the next few weeks.

I had begged him. I had even cried.

He left me at daybreak, nevertheless, aroused, disheveled, and crawling back to a guarded life. I never read the one letter he sent me from Lincoln a month later.

I returned to my vault and fastened the latch. That was where I belonged. I had made a mistake. I had let life catch me.

Occupying life was a strategic affair, I saw, one that required new tactics as the sun rose each day. There was scooping up a dead fish from the sea and drinking one's own urine, and hoping the wind did not change, eyes sharp for a shoreline that I could not be sure existed. The mist had cleared, though, and I knew now to keep clear of sparkling things, like pretty colored boys and fatherly horizons.

It was a something-to-do diversion, I thought uninterestedly, when I lost my virginity on the night of my sixteenth birthday, to Frank's best friend, David Valentine. Frank had left him behind, and I soon did too.

It was, in many ways, a relief when, months later, Jackie asked me at school one day if I would be willing to go out with a Jewish boy. He was Donald's best friend at Cheltenham High, she told me. He was interested in meeting a colored girl.

Bob Ludwig came to the door of my little Germantown apartment looking like the Jewish prince that he was. He was six feet tall. His jet-black hair was in stark contrast to his white complexion, and complemented his very blue eyes and the natural blush on his high cheekbones. His navy sport jacket was expensive, its richness set off by the whiteness of his tailored shirt. I had just had my hair cut very short and felt I looked "Paris-chic," or something like that. His face reflected his satisfaction.

He showed me to his brand-new, cream-colored Chrysler Imperial—the top of the line that year, replete with a signature covered tire planted on the outside of the trunk. The interior of his car was a matching cream color, including the plush leather seats. The dashboard explained everything on a small brass plaque fastened there: "To Bob, with love from Mom and Dad." It had been his birthday present.

We went to a drive-in restaurant, ordering the obligatory cheeseburgers and malts from a carhop. Everyone noticed us, I saw, because Bob had the biggest and newest car on the teen roads of that time. Afterward, we went to the Lincoln Drive-In Theater, where we talked a bit. We returned to my house and listened to Johnny Mathis sing "All the Time" and all the other songs that made people fall in love. Bob was seventeen and I was sixteen, and we were soon among those whom Mathis joined together.

Bob called me every day after school. We saw each other every weekend, each time pledging love "until the Twelfth of Never." Soon I was writing songs for Bob: having sometime before abandoned my Emily Dickinson dreams, now I was putting music to my poetry. We talked about black and white things, and Jewish things. I began to practice reciting the words of Ruth: "Whither thou goest, I will go; and where thou lodgest, I will lodge: thy people shall be my people, and thy God my God." We eventually made love on the floor of his grandmother's apartment in Oxford Circle, while she was on vacation in Florida.

Bob's father had a real-estate company which seemed to own or broker all the real property in Oxford Circle. Oxford Circle was a middle-class Jewish area of Philadelphia that was being abandoned by Jews as they became rich, in somewhat the same manner and ratio as they were abandoning Orthodox Judaism for Conservative, and soon for Reform. Bob's family lived in the high-class neighborhood of Cheltenham by then, but they continued to do business and attend synagogue in their old neighborhood of Oxford Circle.

Six months went by before Bob announced that he had not told his father or mother he was dating a colored girl. I actually did not understand his anxiety. I was not only unlike other colored girls, I was not only capable of being white, I could walk, talk, and act like a good Jewish girl. I had even considered converting to Judaism, I told him. I asked him, therefore, why he was telling me such a thing. He dropped it.

It did not come to a head the day he refused to take me to a walk-in movie theater in the downtown area.

"I might see somebody in my family," he had said.

"So what?" I asked, my voice reflecting the Yiddish speech pattern that had passed to him from a European ghetto.

Every Jew in Philadelphia was making a pilgrimage downtown to see the film *Exodus*. The publicity surrounding the showing of the movie was wild, especially since bands of local Nazis were picketing the film (in protest of its depiction of Hitler). I insisted we go. Bob insisted we could not.

Nothing was even said the night he took me to his well-appointed house to hear him play the drums that he had bragged he could play so well. Despite his parents' being out of town, he was so afraid a relative, or even the off-duty maid, might surprise us, he rushed me out the door minutes after we arrived.

It finally happened on a Friday night, in the early hours of Shabbat. It was in Oxford Circle. It was at the stoplight at the corner where his parents' synagogue sat. It was when the upwardly mobile faithful were filing out of the synagogue into the cross-section where Bob's cream-colored Chrysler Imperial had been stopped by a red light.

"Could you duck down," he said to me nervously. "It's my parents' temple." There was panic in his voice now. "If they see the car, they'll see you."

I fell down. I fell down onto the lap of my Jewish prince, who had come, and whom I tried hard not to believe would go. I listened to his heartbeat as it thumped in his stomach and reverberated in the groin that was to have produced my children. He held my hand tightly in his clammy one. His thigh muscle tightened as he shifted his foot from brake to gas pedal. We left the scene with a screech.

I cried for days waiting for Bob to call me, to make it right. He finally telephoned about a week later. He told me he had confessed everything to his mother. She had hoped he would never tell his father, who would, at best, disinherit him. She had vowed they would "sit *shivah*" on him if he continued the relationship. She would perform a variation of the Jewish rite for the loss of a loved one, for one who was dead though living, for a loved one who had violated Jewish law. It seemed dating me was such a violation, a violation he could not commit, he said. Besides, Bob ended, the strain of everything had been too much. He had, at the age of seventeen, developed an ulcer. We would simply have to stop dating. We would probably never be able to see each other again.

I wondered how I could return to the world. But only a few months later, after writing more songs about Bob and crying about Bob, I went to a party at Carol's house. It was at her new house, in a better neighborhood than her old one, bought with her father's insurance payments when his arm was cut off by a factory accident.

My brand-new olive-green trench coat was stolen at Carol's party. That should have sent me home to my mother—as Bob had, as everything did. Instead, I borrowed a jacket from Carol and went off with three girls to another party.

It was in Germantown, in the "lowlife" section, however, in those few blocks controlled by Germantown's only gang, the Pike. The idea of Germantown having a gang was always a joke to those of us from the ghetto. Perhaps that was why I forgot what I should have remembered.

We had taken the bus from Carol's to Germantown Avenue. We had begun walking to the party from there, and had just turned down the little street across from Tony's Steak and Hoagie Shop. None of us had paid much attention to the six or seven young-bloods hanging in front of Tony's. They were now upon us.

"Hey, baby, where y'all goin'?" one of them hollered as they caught up with us halfway down the little street. "Is it a party? Can we come?"

"Well, it's invitational," one of the girls foolishly blurted out.

They grouped around us, not exactly threatening us but blocking our way.

"It's not really a party," I offered quickly. "We're just going to some girl's house to listen to records." I finally remembered what I had forgotten.

"Yeah, well, can we go with you fine things?" said another of them, his do-rag falling over his left eye.

Out of nowhere, the headlights of a car mercifully broke into our strained discourse.

One girl waved to the fellow driving the car. He was alone. He stopped. She seemed to know him only casually. I realized I knew her only casually. He offered her a ride, which she accepted on condition that he take all of us.

When he opened the door to his old two-door Plymouth, the four of us moved carefully toward the car.

"Well, we'll see you fellas later," I said cheerily, trying to dispel the feeling of ugliness that was in the air.

Every one of us knew the rules: a girl could get "jumped on" for not speaking to a fellow on the street when spoken to, much less for trying to be "slick."

"Hold it a minute, baby," one of the do-rags said to me, pulling me back by my arm.

The other girls piled into the Plymouth.

"What's your name?" he asked.

"Kathy," I said, as though my telling him a phony name carried some significance.

"Well, Kathy, ain't you gon' kiss me goodbye?"

The smell of white port wine and lemon juice combined with Doublemint gum on his breath stung my face with a bitter memory. It was as familiar as the smell of his fried hair contained by his do-rag. Memory made the decision. I estimated that I could reach the car faster than having to deal with him. The rest of the girls, two of them crunched into the front seat with the driver, were beckoning to me. I eased over to the Plymouth and bent down to squeeze myself into the back seat. I simultaneously smiled at my street suitor and said, "I've got to catch this ride. I'll see you . . ."

I did not finish.

"Motherfuck you, then, bitch!" he spat out as he kicked one of his old men's comforts into my face. The blow caught me on the chin and knocked me out of the car onto the concrete street.

I was surprised to land alive. In that split second, I noted curiously that I would have thought people whose heads hit concrete with such force died instantly. I thought I heard the tires of the car screech. I had. It was driving away, as more feet fell upon me and the toes of more old men's comforts pounded into my face. It became very silent, like being on a street at two in the morning after a heavy snowfall. I did not hear any voices, and I began not to feel their feet at all.

Sadness filled me. My mind whispered that it was sad that I had lived only sixteen years. It was sad, I felt, that I was going to die. I began to imagine that I had dreamed it all. I began to think that I was in some middle moment between life and death. I was, perhaps, already dead and had only some kind of lingering consciousness, like music that plays on a bit after a radio is turned off. I was an electrical circuit that was not fully broken. I did not feel pain or fear. I just felt sad for the death of me. And I felt happy that it did not hurt, that dying was so easy.

A car motor whirred in the distance. I could hear it. I heard feet scrambling away, away from my face. I heard them running.

"Come on, come on, Elaine!" a voice shrieked at me. I was picked up and tossed into the Plymouth that had returned to get me. My girl friends were screaming and crying. I looked at them in wonderment. I felt I was waking up, or that they were part of my dream.

"Oh, come on, I'm all right," I said calmly.

One girl handed me a mirror as the car careened around a corner.

"Look at your face!" she wailed.

I could hardly see it. My face was covered with blood. It occurred to me then that I did not want to die. Dying would not be easy and sweetly peaceful as I had thought moments before. The back of my head began to throb, and I started to cry. I promised myself that I would get those black motherfuckers, if I lived. I would call Dennis Crump or somebody I knew from the Avenue to get them.

I tried to clean up my face with the tissues one girl handed me as they drove me home.

My mother became hysterical, but then jumped into action, calling a cab and throwing on her clothes at the same time. She rushed me to Jefferson Hospital, where I was born, and where we waited three hours for a young white intern to tell her that my nose was not broken and there was nothing he could do for me. He told her to take me home and give me some aspirin for the pain that was all over me now. It was a Saturday night; they had gunshot wounds and other more serious problems to attend to. My mother refused to leave without calling everybody in sight a rotten, no-good, lying, motherfucking, prejudiced son-of-a-bitch. Defeated, she took me home.

In a moment of obvious insanity, she actually started to telephone my physician father, while I begged her to hang up. She did. We both knew I had no father. She washed my wounds with peroxide and changed the bedclothes. She fluffed up pillows behind my head and held me until I fell asleep.

CHAPTER 4

SOME OTHER LIFE

*Arma virumque cano, Troiae qui primus ab oris
Italiam fato profugus Laviniaque venit . . .*

"I SING of arms and the man," the Roman poet Virgil began his *Aeneid*. We translated his entire epic poem in our twelfth-grade Latin class at Girls High, just one class now, of only eight girls. It was an elitist badge I wore with satisfaction.

There had been two Latin classes of about thirty girls each in the ninth grade. The attrition rate was due to the difficulty of the work. We had read Virgil as well as Ovid and others over those last four years, and we had vigorously competed in Latin projects with the boys at Central High. To our great dismay in twelfth grade, the boys in the Central High Latin class had outdone all our competitive efforts by not only translating the *Aeneid* but rendering their translation into English dactylic hexameter. Nevertheless, we eight girls knew we were among the best in the country in that archaic endeavor, and the best among us was Francine.

Francine Bowden and I had been relatively close during our years at Girls High. Initially, it was because of the alphabetical proximity of our last names. It was also because we were the only two colored girls in our Latin class. We had been the only two in it from the beginning.

Francine was a genius. She was able to sight-read the most difficult poetic passages in our Latin texts with superhuman speed and accuracy. Moreover, she demonstrated the same brilliance in calculus and chemistry and in all her other subjects. Francine, like very few others, had maintained a straight-A average from ninth grade through our year of graduation. Her record was even more outstanding considering that she had carried five instead of the usual four major subjects in her curriculum, an astonishing record, in light of the undeniably insuperable odds she had faced.

After school each day, Francine had had to go back into the bowels of North Philadelphia, where she lived and where, she told me, her family complained about her reading all those books that had nothing to do with getting a real job. She lived in a blighted area generally referred to as "Cross Town," which I determined, on the one or two rare occasions I had been there, was distinguishably worse than any other place in Philadelphia—including York Street. She wore clothing that was clearly secondhand and shoes often held together by pins or staples. Her hair usually looked dirty, and certainly had not had the blessing, as it were, of the weekly hot comb that pressed and straightened most colored girls' natural down. She had almost always eaten lunch alone, by benefit of the school's charitable milk fund.

She had even borne up under the snide insults tossed at her by the "high-yellow," high-browed colored girls at Girls High, running from themselves. She had accepted being left out of the exchanges among the intellectually snobbish white girls, who held white conversations in white cliques. They had made it absolutely clear to Francine—as they had to all us colored girls—that her grades and intellect would not remedy the flaw of her dark skin or dark life. Yet Francine had managed to endure all of it. She had plowed through those four years and emerged intact. Moreover, she was unquestionably the smartest girl in the class.

The aspect of Francine I pondered most, though, was that she was exposed. She had no ballet lessons or good hair or changeable voice behind which to hide. She was me stripped of all façades. She was at once everything of which I was terrified and everything I longed to be. She was poor and black, brilliant and proud.

Francine became the first person about whom I felt a sense of pride. I felt it as strongly as I had felt anything. I was proud of her and proud to know her, even though I shamefully never mustered the courage to come out and offer real friendship to her. No one I knew at Girls High had ever been socially friendly with Francine. All I had done was wield my North Philly toughness for her, to silence the nasty tongues of the other colored girls. I had also regularly hurled Francine's academic statistics into the lily-white faces of all the smart white girls. I had reminded all of them, now buzzing over their acceptances to Vassar or Wellesley as graduation approached, that Francine had been offered no less than ten full scholarships to the best Eastern colleges and universities, including most of the Seven Sisters. She had accepted the scholarship to Temple University only because she could not have afforded even the incidentals at Smith or Radcliffe.

Francine was on my mind as I walked down the aisle of the Girls High auditorium, pristinely outfitted in my requisite white calf-length graduation dress. I thought of it as her day, a day of reckoning and retribution. It would be Francine's day and, however vicariously, mine, too. For Francine was the lost Nita, resurrected; and she was a lost piece of me, and all of us colored girls, it seemed. She had taken our blows and held tight to our dignity. She was *our* Winged Victory.

I looked at Francine when I reached the stage and found my place in the front row of seats with the class geniuses, where she was, of course, seated. Although I had maintained relatively high grades, I was to sit there only because I had to have easy access to the grand piano on stage. I was to accompany the class in its vocal renditions of two traditional anthems.

Most of us ignored the graduation rhetoric. Everyone, especially the front row, was anxious to hear the announcements of the academic prizes. The faculty bestowed appropriate gifts on graduating girls for outstanding achievement in mathematics and science, in foreign languages, in the arts, and even in sports. When Francine was passed over for the calculus prize and then for the trigonometry prize, I became perturbed. When she was passed over for the English prize, I started to become angry, watching white girls in white dresses get out of their seats; watching white girls in the front row hand their bouquets of red roses to their neighbors to accept their prizes with boring little speeches; watching white girls sit down.

The Latin prize was finally announced, which only one of eight of us could possibly receive, which only Francine should have received. Francine was passed over again. It was an outrageous display of racial prejudice—a concept, a reality that was so profound it was not missed even by me, who wanted to be white.

In angry frustration, I held up the graduation exercise. I did petty things, like slowly taking off my bracelet—the wearing of which was *verboten* anyway—before starting the piano accompaniment to each song, and on the second song by refusing to acknowledge the choir director's cue. Though ineffectually trivial, these gestures were grand little moments of menace amid the perfection and whiteness, where even a small splotch in the order was a blight.

At the stuffy graduation luncheon afterward, I boldly smoked cigarettes, one after another with Donna Lowe, the barely colored girl who was my best friend at school, to the great annoyance of the faculty—"Girls, Girls High girls do not smoke," it had been announced time and again. In furtherance of my paltry protest, I talked aloud to Donna, as teachers and students stood before us making teary-eyed speeches, dragging out saccharine anecdotes of our past. In the middle of the principal's address, Donna and I got up and walked out. Before leaving, however, I filed among the luncheon tables to find Francine to say goodbye, ignoring all the other girls I knew. As we could think of nothing else to make our point, Donna and I finished with our after-graduation family formalities and went over to Cherry Hill, New Jersey's Latin Casino supper club, and got drunk on vodka martinis bought for us by men over thirty.

Temple University was considered a mediocre college refuge for a Girls High girl. I was not concerned, however, with Temple's rating among that superficial bunch of girls, particularly since I knew some of them were enrolled in lowly state colleges and a few of them were even preparing to get married, albeit into well-to-do families, and become *Hausfraus* for the rest of their lives. I was even less concerned about my course of study at Temple, since I was attending college only because there was nothing else to do.

Although I was advanced into junior-level English and Latin classes after taking the placement tests at Temple, I discovered I was not so brilliant as to be able to skate through the academic rigors of that university. I had assumed I could operate there with the same arrogant attitude that had taken me through Girls High with a B-plus average. Temple required a routine with which I was unfamiliar. In order to obtain comparable grades, I had to study each night. That represented a conflict. If I studied, I would be like everybody else. It was necessary to be somewhere above everyone or crash to nothingness.

Studying had the additional burden of conflicting with my new schedule. I had begun going out virtually every night alone. I would go to one of the downtown bohemian coffeehouses to listen to beatnik poems and have esoteric conversations with unconventional, free-thinking white people about the meaning of a Jean Genet play or an Ingmar Bergman film.

Going out alone seemed right. Everyone I knew from high

school had another life now, as did my old neighborhood friends. Barbara worked as a secretary and stayed in North Philly most of the time. Nita, and now Kathy, had many children to take care of. Carol Hollins had miraculously been accepted into a state teachers college. In any case, North Philly was behind me, as life seemed behind me more than ahead.

In the past year, my dance card had been filled mostly with boys I could mistreat. There had been Venice, who used to give me lunch money nearly every day in the twelfth grade, and to whose meek request one night that we actually have sex I responded with rolled eyes, a smug laugh, and a simple no, thereby dismissing him from my life. There had been Joe Dixon, who was not so much malleable as he was poor, too poor to go out anywhere. He was, actually, an interesting repast who had introduced me to the sounds of avant-garde jazz and to the deliciousness of lovemaking. As that was the extent of our relationship, that became the extent of him. There was also Melvin, who clung to me for unknown reasons. Sometimes I allowed Melvin to take me to the coffeehouses. I kept Melvin in my life for two reasons: he looked very much like Frank Constant and he had a car. He would drive me to the coffeehouses and wait for me outside while I drank cups of café-au-lait with some white boy, whom I would leave after a while to go off with Melvin. It was, after all, the way to treat all of "them," I had finally learned.

Although I did not make Dean's List or any such thing at Temple, I managed to maintain a decent scholastic average that first semester. It was an impressive achievement, I thought, in light of the long nights I spent in the coffeehouses, and considering that I spent most of my days at Temple reliving those nights and hanging out with my pal Billy James.

Billy was a well-read, well-dressed Negro who had gone to Central High and had lived all his life in Germantown. Billy and I had seen each other around, mostly at the Germantown parties Barbara and I had crashed a lifetime ago. We had instantly latched on to each other at Temple. I had given some thought to contacting Francine, but felt I had nothing to say or, more appropriately, nothing to offer her since she was lost anyway to the premed laboratories at Temple. Billy was my kindred. In no time, we came to be soul mates.

Billy and I had each always felt alienated from everything, we discovered. Unspoken, it was our bond. We had stumbled along different paths to arrive at Temple only to find we were on the same lonely road, bastard children of forceful mothers who had tried to send us where they could not go. The problem was, neither they nor anyone seemed to know where that was. We had survived under the pretense that we were special, knowing that we were simply strange or estranged. Together, though, we convinced everyone at Temple of the former and made ourselves very popular.

We were the best dressed among the few Negroes at Temple, and even among the predominant number of rich Jewish students. We had gone to the best schools and were considered very smart. We were the best dancers and put together routines so exciting people at Temple dances formed a circle around us to watch. Our greatest point of popularity was our sharp wit, expressed usually before small audiences in the common areas of the Temple campus, where we would perch daily and rather loudly exchange satiric commentary about everything under the sun. But we knew. We knew a sense of separation from the mainstream of life, and we knew it had to do mostly with our inability to fit into any mold, anywhere. Billy kept my secret and I kept his, though we never assessed how important it was. We would have fallen in love had we not been so terrified of life. We just held on to each other. That was why Billy was devastated when I told him, in the middle of our second semester, that I was leaving him alone at Temple.

> In Some Other Life
> I could love you dearly.
> In a life without stress
> How our lips could caress
> But I've found that the number's too great
> Of those who would have us wait
> For Some Other Life,
> Some Other Life . . .

I had written those lyrics for him at sixteen, and now he was walking toward me. I was outside Temple University going toward the bus stop. I had not seen or heard from him since the time he told me he had an ulcer at seventeen. He was nineteen now. Bob Ludwig's blue eyes sparkled when we recognized each other; mine filled with tears. I had written all those songs for him and cried over him and vowed revenge on him and longed for him since then.

He had been in New York for the past year, he told me, playing drums in a jazz band in Greenwich Village. He had left his mother's house forever. He had told her before he left that he would love whomever he chose, and damn the inheritance of his father. He told me all the right things, there on the streets of North Philadelphia outside Temple University.

"I have never stopped loving you," he said, as though time had not passed, as though it would be easy to take up where things had died.

He was so beautiful, however. He was so perfect. I agreed to see him that night at his new apartment, ironically located in North Philadelphia, near Temple.

His Ludwig-brand drum set overwhelmed the uncarpeted apartment. He opened a bottle of wine and put Coltrane and Mose Allison on his record player. I tried not to whine about the pain of the past, to act as though I had not missed him. I listened to him tell me how much he wanted to be with me, only me, and wondered how much what he said had to do with his aspiration to be a jazz drummer. I heard him tell me how he no longer cared about color, any color, my color. I heard him swear he would sit *shivah* on his entire family for me.

Two years made me wary of his welcome words. But as I listened to him, his words became the words to all the poems and all the songs I had ever loved. As my head and my heart became filled with the words and the wine, I remembered the biblical refrain of Ruth. He kissed me and I felt I would faint. He fondled me, and the voice of Mathis echoed in my head. When he walked me to his bedroom, I felt a chill. My resentment and anger had not been kissed away. Limply, I sat down on his bed with him and watched him begin to make love to me. Gently, I pulled away from him.

"Let's go to a movie tomorrow," I suggested, quivering, straightening my dress.

He wanted to talk about it in the morning. I told him I would not be staying until morning.

"You think because I'm colored I'm easy," I blurted out, ready to accept the consequences of my words. "You think you can slide back into my life after causing me so much pain and after all this time?"

He swore he had tried to find me. He begged me to consider what he had gone through when he found I had moved with no forwarding address. He screamed at me to, "for God's sake," understand what he was willing to give up for me. He was back in my life to stay, he vowed.

I refused to submit. He delivered his ultimatum. He told me that if I left him that night, he would never call me again. He never did.

I wrote more song-poems about Bob. I cried every day so hard, so unconsolably, for the next several months that my mother began suggesting I see a doctor. In between, I left Billy at Temple University. I had no reason to be there. My counselor at Temple told me, when I announced I was withdrawing, that I would have to pay the two hundred dollars I owed the university before I could get my transcripts, if I wanted them.

I spent the next year abusing Buddy. He was the nice Jewish fellow who owned the wholesale jewelry store at which I bought presents for my new coworkers. I had become the "token," the first and only Negro service representative at the Philadelphia Electric Company. A month after I was hired, I was thrust into the window of the stately main office downtown. I accepted being so displayed because the new position came with a small salary increase, and because I rather relished the image of the company's executives sweating. The newly elected president, John Kennedy, had demanded that private corporations begin integrating their legions of employees with qualified Negroes.

Buddy had asked me for a date every time I had gone to his nearby store to buy a trinket for some Electric Company worker's birthday or baby shower. I had smiled and always refused him; he looked too much like Bob Ludwig to me. When I found out that Buddy owned the jewelry store, I accepted his standing invitation.

I tested him on our very first date. I suggested we have dinner at the most ostentatious place in town. I wanted to go where we would be seen by his people. As he agreed to my suggestion without a second thought, he presented me with a gift of gold jewelry from his store.

During that next year of ostentatious dates, Buddy presented me with numerous other pieces of jewelry. He also took me to New York whenever I decided we needed a change of pace. I had to see Richard Burton play Hamlet in modern clothes, for example, and I just had to be in New York for New Year's Eve.

Buddy also bought me clothes, and paid for a demonstration record he felt I should make of the songs I had written. Finally, he paid to have my front teeth capped—for they had grown in crooked, an ugly residue of York Street. Never once did I really thank him for anything, for which he often stated I was he very personification of the word "bitch." It did not stop him from loving me, though. It also did not stop me from making him pay for more than he knew. I did not even say goodbye to Buddy.

The flight from Philadelphia was perfect. I had sold my piano and piddling stock in the Philadelphia Electric Company to pay for my ticket. I had three hundred dollars left. I was fleeing to California. I was fleeing York Street and Bob and a doctor named Horace Scott, and even my room with my mother. I did it without warning, suddenly, frantically. It was an Icarian escape.

What had really been so terrible in Philadelphia? I thought as the airplane lifted off. It was true there had been the specifics of poverty. I had survived the poverty, however, relatively unscathed, having lived in my maternal cocoon. I had never really been hungry or ill clothed or without a roof over my head. I had even been exposed to some of life's finer offerings. I had certainly not experienced the nightmare of my mother's reality, or my grandmother's. I was a rich little ghetto girl, up from the ashes of my mother's womb.

Why was I flying away, then? There was nothing to run from, except that by the time I had reached the magical age of twenty-one, I still could not go to sleep alone, or without keeping on all the lights and the television. I was terrified of being with myself; I had no self. I was not only terrified of sleeping alone, I was even terrified of being alone when I bathed, the hollow sound of a bathroom always reminding me of my nothingness. Even my own voice frightened me, its true sound distorted by the pitch and inflections of the variegated castes and colors I wore. I realized I was a fragmented being who could not choose a favorite color, much less a lover or a life work. It was not simply black or white. I lived in an amorphous gray. That was why I had to leave Philadelphia. I did not exist in Philadelphia.

"I am because I think I am," my one-time idol Ayn Rand had screamed in her book *Anthem*. I had read every word in every book Ayn Rand ever wrote in the year I was nineteen. Those words, her words, had abated the pounding of lifelong angst, the consciousness of being born without the consciousness of being. After I had hungrily sopped up all of Ayn Rand's tomes, I ran to one of her meetings. It was a gathering of the Dollar Sign Club, an elitist set of people who thought of themselves as "Atlases" who were organizing to shrug. I dragged Billy James with me. We constituted 100 percent of the Negro attendees. Though we were welcomed, we could not accept the ideas embraced by the strange white organisms who sat icily listening to what became clear as Rand's, and her protégé Nathaniel Brandon's, cold and antihuman philosophy. Billy and I ran out of there, with me finally settling on the unsettling idea that there was no philosophy for me.

California offered itself to me. It seemed to present the possibility of creating a life or finding one. It would be mine, and I would slip it on like a glove.

I had told everyone in Philadelphia, including my mother, that I was leaving to try my hand at being a professional songwriter. It was a real consideration, given the nearly three hundred songs I had written by then, mostly maudlin ones about love and other pain.

There was really no particular shape, of course, to the dream California held out. It did hold, however, a rare, sweet memory that had been a summer oasis on two occasions before.

I had gone to California by train the first time. It was with my grandmother, when I was nine years old. The next time, at fourteen, I went alone, on a new prop-jet airplane. It was all done with mirrors as far as I knew, for I never thought about how my mother provided for such trips.

Each time I had stayed at the home of my mother's sister Frances. Frances was the only member of my mother's family to have gone to college—primarily because her older sisters, including my mother, had paved her way with their hard-earned wages. She had finished college, become a teacher, and, best of all, married a nice colored minister. His Presbyterian Church had assigned him early on to parishes in California, first in Oakland, then Pasadena, and eventually in a middle-class Negro area of Los Angeles.

I had become preteen chubby at Frances's house in Pasadena, where there was an abundance of fruit that fell off trees in their yard, and no roach wings in glasses or anywhere at all, and no mice scampering about near one's feet for bits of dropped food. One could eat in California and smell grass in California and even sleep in the dark there.

On my second trip, I experienced an earthquake and the magnificent sequoias. Frances's husband, John Doggett—brother of the famous jazz and blues organist Bill—had been part of a summer church camp that was held in the national park. Once we arrived among the redwoods, I had bowed my head with the Christian gathering, me in homage to a profound sense of belonging. I felt comfortable among those towering trees, my fears subsumed by their constancy and power. I would not be calling Frances this time, but California surely had something for me.

I thought the three hundred dollars I had when the plane landed in Los Angeles would be enough. It was April of 1965, and I had just turned twenty-two years old. In less than a week, I had spent most of my money on rent for an apartment in Hollywood, a fully furnished "single" that fortunately came with a television set.

I had spent the first three days in Los Angeles at an old hotel nearby. I had seen its picture in a brochure. The hotel's photograph was, as might have been expected by anyone but a twenty-two-year-old, quite an exaggeration. That did not matter to me. It was a beginning.

I met an old man who lived at the hotel. He told me he was a film producer and that his name was Lou. I decided he was a kind man because he bought me dinner each of the three nights I stayed at the hotel. Moreover, he promised that he would keep a lookout for a part for me in an upcoming film.

Once I moved into the apartment, I pushed the notion of professional songwriting out of my head and began looking for work. By the end of the first week, I had no job and my money was almost gone. As the due date for my weekly rent approached, a spark of hope came with the ring of my new telephone. It was a woman's husky voice.

"Lou gave me your number and said you might be interested in making some money," the voice said.

I listened without responding.

"Anyway, I have a client I can't see tonight. I have another appointment."

I wondered what kind of client she meant, but remained what I felt was smartly silent.

"You'd be doing me a favor and helping yourself," she continued. "He'll pay four hundred dollars."

"Four hundred dollars for what?" I asked earnestly.

"He has a number of problems and needs someone to make him happy."

He was a "trick," she explained. She told me what to do. I said I would do it.

When he came to the door, she told me, I should say: "You are my slave. You've been disobedient so I'm going to punish you." I should wear black clothing and high-heeled shoes, and have a belt to use on him, because he loved to be beaten. I should also have on hand something called amyl nitrite, a drug contained in a capsule that I should break in half and place under his nose every fifteen minutes or so. She also told me to purchase a very strong perfume and to wear a lot of it.

"Do you think you can handle all that?" she asked.

"Of course," I said, feeling rather shrewd.

I spent thirty dollars of my last forty dollars on the cologne and the amyl nitrite, a powerful prescription drug, I discovered, meant for heart patients. Amazingly, I was able to purchase it without a problem from a nearby drugstore.

When he came to my door, I was surprised to see how well dressed and elegant a white man he was. I just looked at him and forgot my lines.

"Am I your slave?" he asked, once the door was closed. His eyes changed even as he began to speak, as though he were being transformed into some supernatural being.

"Well, yes," I stammered, trying not to snicker.

"I've disobeyed you and I must be punished," he filled in solemnly.

He hurriedly took off his clothes, while I remained, as instructed, in mine: tight black pants, black turtleneck sweater, and high-heeled black shoes. I reeked with the fumes of Prince Matchabelli's Albano.

He threw his huge naked fleshiness onto my convertible bed and begged me to beat him. I grabbed the belt and simply whipped him, as though I had done it before. He lay there whimpering and moaning, while I intermittently popped the amyl nitrite capsules under his nostrils. After nearly two hours, he reached a climax, face down on my sofa bed, his sweaty buttocks locked in ecstasy, facing me.

He sprang up suddenly, a "normal" being. He began chatting with me while I wondered how I should ask him for the money. As he was thanking me profusely, he stopped abruptly, realizing he had left his car parked in a no-parking zone. He jumped into his clothes to run outside to repark his car.

Even when I saw him snatch his watch from my nightstand, I did not understand. It was not until twenty minutes after he closed the door that I felt the humiliation. It had been a joke. *I* had been the "trick." I was not so much humiliated by the act as by my stupidity. I cried for one hour until I slept, sitting up, to avoid his filth, which remained on my bed.

I managed to survive by pawning Buddy's jewelry until I found a job selling books door-to-door. In a few months I left that job, because I could not continue to con people into buying the garbage I was successfully pushing on them as encyclopedia sets. I should have anticipated then that I would find myself with no place to live. Nevertheless, I was unprepared when I was evicted.

I broke down and called my Aunt Frances, making the undesirable connection to Philadelphia. She admonished me for being frivolous, for quitting college, for not saving my money, for getting myself into such a predicament. She told me I could stay with her and her minister husband and their three children in their eighteen-room house for one week, and one week only. I declined her supercilious offer, thinking I would rather turn tricks than live with her and her Christian family. As I was packing up my things to go nowhere, an acid-head hippie I talked to on occasion, who lived nearby, showed up and offered to take me in.

His one-room cottage was at the foot of the Hollywood Hills. It resembled a Victorian parlor. It was a dark place, filled with furniture that appeared to have come from an East European home at the turn of the century. It was cluttered with books and records and plants. It seemed to complement his state of mind, however, a peaceful insanity, which was induced and assisted by his daily ritual of dropping one full capsule of LSD. Bruce Lynn, who had been Bruce Lev and Bruce Levin and Bruce Levinsky, took care of me with a maniacal kindness. He not only provided me with a place to sleep, he fed me, introduced me to the music of Bob Dylan, and turned me onto acid. He also found me a job as a cocktail waitress.

The Pink Pussycat was the hottest spot in West Hollywood. It was one of the numerous strip clubs in the area. Its claim to fame was that its strippers had stage names like Dina Martin or Samantha Davis or Frannie Sinatra. It had become popularized by such foolishness on *The Johnny Carson Show*. Carson, who had just moved his program from New York to L.A., seemed to think the idea of the place was so hilariously Hollywood that he regularly referred to the Pink Pussycat in his nightly monologues. After that, every white businessman from Maine to Iowa who could justify a business trip to Los Angeles made his pilgrimage to Carson's Pink Pussycat.

They came in droves. Besides the strippers onstage and the booze and the scantily clad cocktail waitresses, these pillars of corporate America could stare at Hollywood's rich and famous. Everyone had begun patronizing the place. It was that year's thing to do. Business boomed. Wads of cash traded hands there, much of which stayed in the palms of the flashy waitresses, among whom I had become the one and only Negro.

In merely two weeks, I was taking home nearly a hundred dollars a night in tips. It was in 1965 dollars. It was September and I had not so much as batted one of my new false eyelashes over the recent fire that had been the Watts riots. My focus was on my handsome income, which was rising almost daily.

I was considered exotic by most of the patrons. They would say to me: "Are you from Ethiopia?" or "*Buenas noches, señorita*" or "What island in the Caribbean?" They were merely curious, I knew, about the particulars of my background; for I had learned in a short time that white men far away from home would go very far "to taste brown sugar." That was why Jay Kennedy was so indistinct when we met.

Frank Sinatra was reportedly coming to the first of the two regular shows that night. The gossip in the place was that he wanted to take a look at *his* namesake. Lots of other stars had been there before. Sinatra, however, seemed to command the most respect. I could tell, because Fritz, our gay Austrian maître d', had begun flitting about in a real dither over where Mr. Sinatra would sit and, more significantly, how much money he could demand from customers who wanted to sit near Mr. Sinatra. While the other cocktail waitresses haggled over who would get to serve the Sinatra table, I remained quiet. My assigned tables that night were adjacent to what was to be Sinatra's. I knew, therefore, that I would make a bundle of money. When the doors finally opened, an orderly pandemonium took over.

Toward the end of the show, the platinum-blond waitress who had landed the Sinatra table called me aside.

"Jack wants to see you," she said.

"Jack who, Diane?" I said curtly, imitating her *Guys and Dolls* New York accent.

"Entratter," she finished snidely.

"Who's he, Diane?" I asked, with a sigh.

She raised false platinum-blond eyelashes to heaven and sighed back, "Owns the Sands in Vegas. He's with the Sinatra party."

I threw back my head in victory over the undeclared contest in which we had all taken part. Turning my backside to her tight-lipped expression, I tried to act casual as I strolled over to Sinatra's table.

"Thank you for coming over, ah . . ." a rather large man at the table said to me, standing up and extending his hand.

"Elaine," Harry Schiller, the owner of the club, filled in for him. Harry had brazenly planted himself at their table. I noticed that he was actually licking his greedy lips over how happy he was that "they" had been pleased by at least one of his "whores."

We were Harry and Alice Schiller's whores in many ways. They taught us how to make money for them.

"Girls, if your Heavenly Father hasn't endowed you with large breasts, endow them yourselves," Alice would say to us every night. She would give us such instructions before the club opened, while Harry checked out the bar and cash registers.

"If a customer asks you out," Alice would advise us, "never say yes and never say no."

She insisted only that we push drinks and look beautiful. If anybody wanted to sell a little in between, that was not Alice's business—unless it was to one of the vice cops who frequented the place. That was the essence of the Schiller philosophy. We practiced what they preached.

We learned to take a hotel key pressed into our hands along with a large bill by a customer at the first show and offer it to a customer at the second show for another large bill. We knocked over drinks so a businessman far away from home would be forced to buy more. We let customers tip us for each round of drinks by pushing a bill down our bosoms, if the bill was big enough. Most of us regularly had "dates" after work, which, most of the time, amounted to nothing more than breakfast at Ollie Hammond's. Most of the time. We were definitely Harry's whores when one thought about it.

"How do you do, *Elaine*," Jack Entratter said, introducing himself.

It was hard for me to respond with the same civility, decked out in my merry-widow bra—the top portion of our outfits—the cups of which were stuffed to their outer limits with Pink Pussycat cocktail napkins to create the required cleavage. It was hard for me to feel dignified before those well-dressed men, much less the smiling Sinatra, in the black leotard bottom of the costume that was pulled up between the cheeks of my buttocks, which were thinly veiled by black fishnet pantyhose. It was impossible to muster any semblance of propriety in that uniform, completed by very high-heeled black shoes and a pink ostrich-feather "tail" that wrapped about my hips and swept to the floor.

Nevertheless, I tried to follow Entratter's formal lead, nodding to each of the several men at the table as Entratter introduced him: "Mr. Sinatra . . . Mr. Kennedy . . ."

"We'd like to invite you to a small party at Frank's house tonight, Elaine," Entratter said after the introductions.

I had not had time enough to open my mouth in response when Harry quickly chimed in: "Go on, honey, you can leave now." Then, adding insult to injury, he turned to Sinatra and said, "Sure, Frank, she'll be happy to go."

I rode with Entratter and his girlfriend, Corinne, to Sinatra's house. We swished away from the brassy lights of West Hollywood and out onto Sunset Boulevard's curves into the lushness of Beverly Hills, following Sinatra's car. We turned off Sunset onto Delfern Drive and immediately into the imposing driveway of a virtual mansion. It was a huge white house supported by Corinthian columns right out of the Old South. I walked to the door in wide-eyed wonder.

Sinatra personally fixed drinks for the few of us there and joined us in his huge white living room to talk. At some point, Sinatra and Entratter began to get into a rather boisterous argument. Their voices were an echo to me, however; I could concentrate only on the fact that I was actually sitting in front of Frank Sinatra. Sinatra broke the spell I was under by snatching a huge brass bowl from his coffee table, which was stocked with about two hundred packs of cigarettes, and hurling it at Entratter's head. As blood trickled down Entratter's forehead, Sinatra demanded he pick up the bowl and every "fucking pack of those cigarettes." From my still-distant place, I watched Entratter bend his huge, important-looking, well-dressed form down on both knees. He obediently picked up the bowl and refilled it with every pack of cigarettes that had been thrown at him. Sinatra went upstairs with some girl he had picked up earlier.

Blithely saying good night to Entratter and his girlfriend as they left, I finally realized why I was there. It was because of the old white man sitting on the couch next to me. We were the only two left. There was no party. I was to be the party. I woke up.

Jay Kennedy was talking to me about his latest book, *Favor the Runner*. He had been talking to me all along, it seemed. Now he was talking to me about "my" people, about W. E. B. Du Bois and Martin Luther King, Jr., and Stokely Carmichael. I tried to follow what he was saying, mostly to keep his mind off what I knew was his motivation for having had me brought there. As he was not talking about money, he was not talking about anything. I had learned that much in six months in Hollywood. There was no way to keep up with him, however. He was going too fast, and I knew nothing about "my" people or anything else about which he was speaking. It did occur to me, though, that he knew an awful lot.

It was soon 4 A.M. and all very ridiculous, not the least aspect of which was the fact that I was still bedecked in my Pink Pussycat buffoonery, which had been covered only by the cape I wore back and forth to the club.

"I have a suite here," he said finally. "Why don't you stay till morning. Someone can drive you home then . . . please, I hope you don't misunderstand me; I'll sleep in the living room. You can have the bedroom to yourself."

I was not thinking about the sleeping arrangements at that point. I was contemplating the fact that people had houses in which they also had suites for guests.

I properly uttered, "Well, thank you very much, Jay," wondering if one called fifty-five-year-old men by their first name.

He escorted me upstairs to his suite, gave me a robe, and said good night. I lay awake for nearly an hour, despite my exhaustion. Two weeks before, I had literally had no address. It was quite a giant step to a bed in the house of Frank Sinatra.

It was not until the morning, after a white-uniformed maid, who might have been Swedish, had brought coffee and orange juice to my bedside, and after Sinatra had told me, timidly approaching the top of the house's giant staircase, that his Negro chauffeur, George, would take me home, that I really took note of Jay Kennedy. He greeted me in the foyer as I was about to leave and asked me for my telephone number. He asked if he might call me to have dinner with him before he returned to his home in New York.

His blue eyes were tender and respectful. Despite his age, his physical strength became apparent to me, not only in the strong tufts of stark white hair that clung firmly to his head, but in his solid-steel stance. I said I would love to have dinner with him.

I had never heard of the Beverly Hills Hotel. It was a huge 1920s pink stucco, California thing that seemed to be "the" place among those who knew.

"*Guten Abend*, Mr. Kennedy." The maître d' bowed, and showed us to our table. We drank Piper Heidsieck champagne, bottled in 1952. We ate beluga caviar in the "queen's way," and then cracked crab with a mustard sauce. Our dinner was lamb, served on skewers, with wild rice.

It was in the soft and settled elegance of that room that I saw him for the first time as a man. His blue eyes, the color of the Caribbean, sparkled in the candlelight. They seemed to twinkle because of a wonderful secret only he knew but would reveal if one entered his place. His fleshy oval face was not so handsome as it was beautiful. It was a face that exposed the reality of the rough times along the way, with a humanity gleaming from it so brilliantly my heart trembled. As he came to life before me, I saw a being so filled with the passion of life I, too, began to feel alive. He was at once foreign and familiar, a character in a novel one could have read or a melody one hums on hearing it for the first time.

"Did you go to the March on Washington?" he asked me seriously.

"Well no," I said, as if I had thought about it at all. Outside of the fact that I had not considered any of what was going on in the civil-rights movement pertinent to me, I had been unable to fathom, much less find acceptable to North Philly–trained responses, the nonviolent philosophy of Martin Luther King. It was incomprehensible to me that King's followers would, for the sake of realizing rights guaranteed by the Constitution, nonviolently withstand dog bites and being spat upon and being viciously hosed—as I had seen on the televised news reports—by those who were supposed to protect those rights.

"I helped organize it," he said, shocking me, making me feel instantly guilty about something. "It's a tactic, you know, nonviolence. It's not an end in itself. It's really the only reasonable means by which blacks can fight racism and, eventually, its foundation, capitalism, to be free from oppression. This movement is bringing together the races, the masses of people in this country, on which a more powerful movement can be built to overcome our common enemy, which is not each other."

"You seem to be talking about Communism, though," I ventured, in an attempt to appear knowledgeable. "I don't want to be a Communist," I finished sincerely, noting that he had used the term "black" and not "Negro."

"Communism is only a word, one we've been taught to fear. It's a single, simple word that's invoked every time people attempt to assert their human rights. Working people in this country, including most black people, are the backbone of industry, yet they receive few if any of the benefits produced by their labor. Communism has to do with sharing that wealth . . ."

I began to listen, but, hearing his subtle exegesis, I felt that his conclusions were inconsistent with his reality, with his apparently rich lifestyle. I gave little consideration to how relevant his conversation might be to me.

"But what about you?" I asked. "What has any of this got to do with you?"

"I have some experience with the hardships of life under capitalism in America," he said. "Of course I'm surviving personally, in many ways because I'm a white man. But what kind of a man would I be if I understood what I do and turned my head away. . . . You know, my family was so poor that I was only able to finish the eighth grade. We needed whatever money I could earn, once I was able.

"The streets of New York, where I grew up, were unkind to a young boy. I took any job I could find. I worked ten to twelve hours a day and still couldn't feed myself or help my family. I was often so hungry I had to beg. The more I saw overstuffed people throw food into the garbage bins that waifs like me scavenged to survive, the more I realized that I would never make enough money to live on, because the owners of the places where I worked always took the profits for themselves."

"But how did you survive? How did you learn to write books? What did you . . ."

"Oh, that's enough about me for now"—he smiled—"for that was then. I simply want to gaze upon your sweet face," he said, touching my cheek gently with a strong but smooth-textured hand.

He ordered violins to our table and sang a Russian folk song to me as they played.

The music I heard, though, was not in the old Russian melody he sang, nor in the strings that supported its refrain. It was the sound of his being that was the song that penetrated my soul, like Rachmaninoff or Ravel, evoking a life rhythm in me, a thing I thought I recognized from somewhere long ago.

We were there for hours. We found ourselves the last of the diners. There were moments during the evening we simply looked into each other's eyes. I surrendered to a tenderness in me that had been forsaken and settled down to a comfort I had never known. Before the night ended, I felt I knew what it might be like to truly live.

CHAPTER 5

THE CHILD HAS DIED

BY THE TIME Jay became my life, my mother was preparing to move to Los Angeles to live with me. I had forgotten the conversation she and I had had several months before. I had called for her help somewhere in the frantic moments between the time I was evicted and when I moved in with Bruce Lynn and got the job at the Pink Pussycat. She had found seventy-five dollars to wire me so I would not be homeless. That was all I remembered.

When she called me at my new apartment in Hollywood and told me she had already sold her furniture, given final notice at her job, and was ready to come to L.A., I was actually stunned. After she had wired the money, she had called her sister Frances to curse her out for not providing me a place to live, and had pledged she would move to California to help me. "Anyway, I need a change," she had said, I finally remembered.

I had a place of my own now. I was making so much money at the Pink Pussycat I could pay my monthly rent with two days' tips. And also, there was Jay.

My life was beginning to open and close like a seasonal flower on his comings and goings between Los Angeles and New York. When he was in Los Angeles, I breathed for him. When he was in New York, I held my breath. That was why I forgot about my mother coming to Los Angeles to help me. That was why I forgot my casual agreement that she should uproot her entire life in Philadelphia to make sure I did not die in L.A.

Her feet were so swollen when she arrived in Los Angeles, she could barely wear shoes and could hardly walk at all. Sitting for four days in the cramped conditions of the bus from Philadelphia had done it. She was so frightened of being locked up for hours in an airplane, she had actually taken a bus across country. When the taxi I sent to the Hollywood bus station brought her and her life's possessions to my small apartment, it dawned on me that a tragic mistake had been made. There was really no place for her with me anymore.

She rested for a week or so, to recuperate from the bus ride, before venturing out to find work. During that time, she cooked hot meals for me, to make her "contribution," as she characterized it, in light of the fact that my contribution was cash, all the money I brought home from the Pink Pussycat. When her feet were healed, I took her there.

She did not attempt to hide her disgust when she entered the Pink Pussycat. She was chagrined when I took off my cape, unveiling myself, my bare buttocks and puffed-up breasts. Her eyes filled with incredulity that I, her perfect child, was doing such an imperfect thing. I placed her in a seat in another waitress's section, near the back, and turned away from her as though I had not seen the disappointment on her face. From time to time, I visited her as she sat alone through the two striptease shows, sipping ginger ale, mortified.

She said very little on the way home in the taxi. She tried to introduce the subject of my forgotten songwriting. But when I counted out the $150 in tips I had made that night, and gave her $50 for herself, her attitude about the Pink Pussycat softened, and she completely abandoned her feelings of disappointment when I reminded her that it was there that I had met Jay.

"Oh, that's right. I wouldn't have thought people like that went there," she exclaimed.

I had told her about meeting him. I had not told her about loving him.

"Elaine, you know, this is what you need. This is the answer to everything. Now tell me again about Sinatra's house. I can't believe you were there!"

I wanted to tell her that she did not understand. What was important was our love, the love between Jay and me. He offered me unconditional love, a love I had longed for all my life. That love was supreme, I wanted to say.

"What does he do?" she asked as an afterthought. "I don't think you told me." That he was apparently rich and "in" with Sinatra were all that seemed to matter to her.

"He's a writer—novels and screenplays. He wrote the script for *I'll Cry Tomorrow*. And I think I did tell you." I tried to end the conversation, wishing she had remained in Philadelphia, hoping she would soon find a job and move far away from the world I lived in with my love.

"Where is he now?" she said, initiating another interrogative barrage.

"He's in New York or Connecticut, where he writes," I told her.

At no point did she comment on the thirty-three-year difference in our ages. She made no inquiry about whether I loved him or he loved me. It did not occur to her to ask me if he was married—which he was.

"So, when are you going to see him again?"

I tried to circumvent further discussion by telling her I was tired. "I'll see him when he returns from New York," I finally responded.

"When will that be?" she persisted, following me into the bathroom, where I began to remove my two sets of false eyelashes and the rest of my heavy makeup.

"I really don't know. Our relationship is rather new, so he doesn't explain his comings and goings to me."

When Jay returned a few weeks later, and I told her he and I would be taking a short trip to Las Vegas, she was overjoyed. She was thrilled that her daughter was getting close to such a man, and would gladly tell my employers I was in a hospital or something if they called to question my absence. She nearly jumped out of her skin when I told her we would be the guests of Jack Entratter.

"Now, isn't he the one you said owns the Sands Hotel?"

"Yes, Mama, he's the one," I said, packing my bag.

"Shit! You're in now. This is big time!"

We were treated like royalty from the moment our airplane landed in Las Vegas. A chauffeur picked us up at the gate, and we were taken by limousine to the Sands Hotel.

We drove along a smooth road that had been carved out of the desert, the limousine's tinted windows and air conditioning repelling the glaring sun and the intense, dry heat. Suddenly, we came upon giant buildings alive with millions of flashing lights, even though it was daytime. Like a mirage, the marquee of the Sands filled the limousine window out of which I was looking, agape.

WELCOME TO JACK ENTRATTER'S SANDS HOTEL—STARRING FRANK SINATRA!

We were shown to our suites by a bowing legion of bellhops.

"Get Mr. Kennedy's bags! Escort Mr. Kennedy to his suite!" the bell captain shouted to his men. "Is there anything else we can get for you, Mr. Kennedy?"

We walked through the main casinos, through a multicolored collection of slot machines and roulette tables and hopeful human beings, to a secluded garden area. We were shown to our suites —we had two suites because Jay insisted on maintaining what he thought of as some semblance of propriety. His suite, where we would stay, was a two-room bungalow that opened onto a private patio. We unpacked and made love.

It was unclear to me why we would be staying in Las Vegas for a week or more. Jay did not tell me any details. He said something about talking to Frank about playing a role in a movie based on his book *Favor the Runner*. It was the story of Jay's love-hate relationship with Harry Belafonte, whose manager he had been at one time. That was all he told me. It was all I felt I needed to know.

While Jay attended his meetings during the day, I ravenously read his writings and the other books he had brought for me.

There was a treatise by Spinoza, who seemed to understand too much about everything, and a book by Sartre, who frightened me. I read most of *Steppenwolf*, but Hermann Hesse, like Sartre, confronted me with the absoluteness of human loneliness. I skimmed through a book by the black writer James Baldwin, *The Fire Next Time*. There were also pages of the untitled book on which Jay was currently working, about a United States espionage agent going to China. Jay had been to China, before the Cultural Revolution.

I was cramming as much information as I could into my head to make myself fit for him. I read all day in the sunshine on the patio of Jay's suite. I never went to the casinos. I not only considered it a lowly exercise, I knew it was a futile one—after years of experience with the numbers my mother had played and never really hit big.

On about our third or fourth day there, I decided to take a

break from reading, to get my hair coiffed for him. I called the Sands' beauty salon. The receptionist there told me there were no openings for that afternoon. She suggested I try the small hotel across the street that took the Sands' overflow. That salon told me someone could take me in about fifteen minutes.

"May we help you, miss?" a man standing at the door of the beauty salon across the strip said the minute I stepped up to the doorway.

"I have an appointment to get my hair done," I said, entering the shop.

"I'm afraid there's been a misunderstanding," he replied. "We're booked solid for the rest of the afternoon."

As I looked around the nearly empty shop, I realized I had almost escaped the memory. The rush of blood that comes with humiliation overwhelmed me. I felt dizzy from being slammed so hard against my reality. *If you black, git back, way back.*

"Well, I just called fifteen minutes ago. I'm the one who called from the Sands. I made an appointment," I responded weakly.

"Do you know the name of the person you spoke to?" he asked, looking around the shop with mock concern. The hairdressers standing around shrugged their shoulders, puzzled looks planted on their faces.

Holding my head high to restrain the flow of tears, I turned sharply away from them without speaking another word and walked back to the Sands. I cried the entire hour it took me to wash and style my hair myself.

Though we usually had our dinner in one of the hotel's restaurants, Jay ordered it in our suite that evening. He wanted to be intimate, he said, though his mood was celebratory. Perhaps Sinatra had agreed to star in his film.

"Your hair looks especially beautiful tonight," he said, with what I felt was a psychic irony, as he opened a bottle of champagne.

Tears trickled down my cheeks. I could not speak. When he saw my tears, he came around to my side of the dining table and knelt down beside me. He begged me to tell him what was wrong, pressing me tightly in his arms. I cried out my little story.

As I spoke and he stroked my hair, he began to shake, literally. He was shaking so hard, my body trembled in his embrace.

As he released me and got up, I saw that his face was so red he looked as if he would burst. He snatched up the telephone receiver and demanded to speak to Entratter.

"This will not be tolerated!" he said to me. "I haven't spent all these years of my life fighting . . ." Interrupted, he spoke into the telephone.

"Jack! What son-of-a-bitch owns the—what's the name of the place, darling?—the fucking hotel across the street?!"

He fired out my story with such rage, even I became scared.

"I want something done about it, now!" he finished.

I dried my tears and smiled at him, a comforted child. I was indeed his child. It was a subject we had exhausted already—what the difference in our ages meant, the father-daughter aspect of our love. It did not characterize or interfere with our love, we had declared. It did not define us. For now, though, I was happy as his child.

In a few minutes, Entratter came to our suite.

"I've got the asshole on hold, Jay," Entratter said, bursting through the door and marching to the telephone. "I told them to transfer the call in here."

Entratter picked up the telephone. "Okay, release the call," he said into the receiver. Covering the mouthpiece, he turned to Jay. "I told the shmuck who owns the hotel we'd put him in the Vegas River and close the fucking place down if this wasn't straightened out. I'm waiting for the owner of the beauty shop."

The only thought that went through my mind was whether or not Las Vegas had a river.

"He's on," Entratter said, handing the telephone to Jay.

"Yes, this is Mr. Kennedy. Don't try to explain a fucking thing, because we're going to destroy you . . . Shut up, cocksucker! Just listen! I do not accept your apology. The thing you better do is fucking hope Miss Brown does, you shit!" He slammed down the receiver.

Jay and Entratter whispered in a corner after that, as I watched from the perch in my gilded cage.

I never answered the dozen or more messages from the beauty shop or the hotel across the street sent to my suite over the next few days, each one more desperate than the last. When we left Las Vegas, I had no idea whether or not the beauty salon owner had or would suffer any consequences for the way I had been treated. It did not seem unfathomable. I had learned that Jay was, among a million other things, a deadly serious man. And I knew that I had been a witness to something deadly serious a few nights before—whether or not the rumors were true that Las Vegas was controlled by some kind of criminal syndicate, and whether or not Jay had any link to such a thing. On the airplane back to Los Angeles, I envisioned the owner of the beauty shop begging for mercy before being tossed into the Las Vegas "river."

"I could've died and no one would've known," my mother moaned to me when I arrived home from Las Vegas. Jay had gone back to New York.

He had taken me to Los Angeles and sent me off from the airport in a taxicab. He had then boarded another flight to New York. There was a brownstone in Manhattan. There was also his nearby Connecticut retreat. The brownstone was where his wife lived, and where he could not, he swore. It was all shrouded in non sequiturs. Whatever the reality, he was gone from me, and I was holding my breath.

"I could've died alone in the ten days you were gone," my mother was saying. "The least you could've done was call me once to give me the number where you were in case of an emergency."

"What was wrong, Mom?" I stated flatly.

"What does it matter. I don't like your tone, anyway. The fact is, while you were off on vacation, I was sick as a dog. I had no one to turn to. In fact, a dog would've been better off."

We were standing in the kitchen. I was pouring myself a Coca-Cola. "Mom," I said, ready to spill everything I had ever thought about saying to her, "Mom, today, I think, we're going to have to cut the umbilical cord."

She started to walk away from me, but I persisted, blocking her path in the narrow kitchen, holding the sink on one side and the stove on the other.

"I mean, I'm sorry my father was a bastard. And I'm sorry your father was, at best, a disappointment. And I'm sorry that Ted Barnett left you damn near at the altar. I'm sorry for everything in your life that has brought you so much pain and made you so bitter. But I can't make it up to you. I can't! I can't, I won't be, your life. I can't make my life yours or live your life over for you or be your lifelong mate, or whatever it is you want from me."

"I don't want a goddamned thing from you!" she retorted, ready for the confrontation, as she had been ready for confrontation and pain all her life. "I'm not going to listen to another word of this. I'm too old for this shit. I'll pack my things and get out of your house tonight. I won't be spoken to like this!"

I held on and looked directly at her. For the first time, it seemed, I saw her face. It was a child's face, angular and brown like mine. I had always refused to see that we were alike in any way. She was hard and I was soft. She was not smart and well read like me. We were nothing alike, I had told people, realizing now that we were as we had been—virtually one person. There was more than an umbilical cord to be broken. There was grabbing an identity for myself and letting her go, alone. She was my one and only mother, my rock, whom I really loved. But suddenly I saw that I had to leave her, to climb out of her or cast her out of me.

"No, Mom," I said finally. "Today, you listen to me."

She raised her strong hand as if to strike me. She had never hit me before.

I braced myself. "If you hit me, I'll hit you back," I said, surprising both of us. "You've got to face me this one time. I went to Vegas with a man I love, who loves me. It is my love and my life! And I just want to figure out how to live it. And not on your terms! Love is *not* a misunderstanding between two fools. That's *your* misunderstanding."

For the second time I had ever witnessed it, my mother cried. I had not intended to hurt her. I had simply wanted to be released from a bondage I had not really acknowledged until I started speaking. I had to be released or I would be bound to her forever.

She began looking for a place of her own the next day. There was guilt, though, my guilt.

As I began to help my mother search for an apartment, it all seemed wrong. And Jay was not there to make it right. I wondered if he could make it right. Perhaps my mother and I had to be joined at the hip forever. When my mother found a nice place in another part of Hollywood, *we* moved in. Nothing had changed.

We said nothing about Jay while I waited each time for him to return. Inevitably, he came back. Inevitably, he returned to New York. It was a month-on, month-off affair. I quit my job at the Pink Pussycat, where I had been working for six months. Jay was leaving me enough money to live on while he was away; when he returned, I lived with him. I set my mother aside with the rest of the world.

There was, of course, something familiar in that, in having no relationship to anything. There was something familiar in having no ready reserve of friends. There was still Hallie, a waitress at the Pink Pussycat, with whom the thread of friendship was being broken as the days separated me from that life. Bruce had been eased away as the clinging stress of my one acid trip and the exotica of his daily ones made me want to distance myself from that much enlightenment. Recently, there was Billy James, from Philadelphia, who had moved to California to attend graduate school at UCLA and had called me when he arrived. Despite the fact that Billy reminded me too much of me, I loved to be with him. I might call Billy and take some of the cash Jay left me and take him out to dinner, or dancing at the Whiskey A-Go-Go and P.J.'s. There was no one else.

When Jay returned, we were together twenty-four hours a day, staying either at the Beverly Hills Hotel or at Sinatra's house on Delfern Drive. He wrote, and I read what he wrote or what he suggested might be good to read.

At the Beverly Hills Hotel, we had our breakfast at a white wrought-iron table in the garden of our suite there, Jay explaining things I could never remember one minute later about the flowers and plants that surrounded us. We might have our lunch in the hotel's popular dark-green-carpeted Polo Lounge, me drinking vodka martinis with a cheeseburger, him laughing at me. We always had dinner in the hotel's main dining room, always at the same table, with the same violins.

Sinatra's gargantuan house on Delfern Drive, where we stayed alone when Sinatra was on the road or in one of his other houses, was our cocoon. It was where I wrote songs for Jay, at the white upright piano near the bar off the living room where I had first heard his voice. It was where Jay could write in the sun, in a chaise longue at the pool, or swim for an hour at a time.

After nearly a year, Jay found a small place for us in the Hollywood Hills. When we were together there, Jay spent hours telling me his stories, ideas, information about the world. Then, as always, he taught me.

A collage of data and concepts was being impressed upon me. It was all so fast, so intense, so global, I had neither the time nor the tools to digest or evaluate most of it. I was the perfect student, however. I was willing and capable, attentive and worshipful. I could listen to Jay with ears that were receptive, unthreatening guardians of his seemingly secret treasure trove of information. I never questioned what he knew or how he knew what he told me. I simply believed in him.

During that time, he explained to me the distinction between socialism and communism.

Socialism, he said, was a desirable social arrangement. It was the introduction to the utopian ideal, the world order of no order: communism.

⟍ Under socialism, he said, the state, a true people's government, centralized all the wealth of the land for the purpose of fairly redistributing it to each member of society, according to ability *and* need. Socialism kindled the flame of humanity inside the hearts and minds of human beings, he said, and built the foundation on which the state could wither away completely, to introduce a universal egalitarian arrangement. Then, Jay explained, human beings would be capable of sharing the fruits of the planet equally and beneficially—communally, communistically—not by rule of law, but by obedience to their higher selves.

Conversely, capitalism, Jay said, produced an unjust and inhuman social scheme by promoting private ownership of property, accumulation of personal wealth, profit-driven production, and the exploitation of human beings.

Under a capitalist scheme, men were discouraged from cooperation with each other in favor of competition. Thus, one ruthless man, or a small conglomeration of such men, was encouraged to grab all, or nearly all, of the very land of a nation, all of its waterways, crops, gas and oil and mineral deposits, its communication and transportation networks. Such men then extracted the highest price possible for the use of these things. Capitalism, Jay said, bred the barbarism of Social Darwinism, wherein only the strong survive and the weak are destroyed.

The evil of capitalism was so intrinsic, Jay expounded, that the very essence and quality of human life become contingent on personal wealth. Disregarding human need or knowledge or contribution to society, ethical standards or moral considerations, wealth alone became the single measure of human worth. In a capitalist society like the United States it was inevitable that a few men—and the most ruthless, he reiterated—had ended up controlling life itself. The others, the "weak," the majority, had been forced by the few to battle it out with each other for jobs that offered only wages for their contribution to the development process, wages that determined for their entire lives the quality of those lives, or whether they lived or died.

Moreover, under capitalism, Jay explained, the added social ills of racism, discrimination, and prejudice develop and thrive. Capitalism's dog-eat-dog philosophy generated and cultivated disharmony and distrust among human beings.

Jay seemed to me a hurdy-gurdy man of ideas gone wild,

grinding out more and more, faster and faster. My brain twirled to keep up with his tune.

During that first year we were together, Jay told me something I was reluctant to hear. He taught me to begin to appreciate myself as a black woman.

Perhaps he was talking about how to differentiate between tactics and strategy, both military and political. Perhaps he was discussing Marxism versus Marxism-Leninism versus Stalinism or Maoism. Perhaps he was telling me the strange story about the brutal assassination of Leon Trotsky. Perhaps he was talking about why Hemingway had really committed suicide. Whatever the topic, we were, as was often the case, in bed, drinking champagne and smoking cigarette after cigarette.

I interrupted him to get out of bed to go to the bathroom. I was nude. He commented on the highness of my derriere, how beautiful it was. It was not a compliment to me. I resented his aside. I thought of it as an uncomfortable reminder that I was a Negro, or black, whatever it was—the negative stereotype being that black women's behinds were offensively high, their feet offensively flat, and so forth. Furthermore, I felt I did not have such a feature. I did not mind listening to him discuss the merits of the civil-rights movement or the Black Power Movement, and the like. Issues concerning black people, however, were not personally relevant to me. They were as extraneous to my reality as his stereotyped "compliment."

"You mustn't deny your beauty because 'they' have defined you otherwise," he said, seeing my annoyance over his remark.

I did not respond. I used the toilet and returned to the bed with a sigh, waiting for another lesson; and waiting also to remind him that I could not be so easily classified. I was unique. I was waiting to defend myself and assail him with the charge that that was really why he accepted me, and really why he could love me. I waited, ready to pounce on him.

"You don't understand, darling," he said in his tender, patient tone, which seemed patronizing now. "The African woman's genitals are tucked neatly, sweetly, underneath, and her buttocks are, therefore, high. Not like the European woman's genitals, raised and thrust forward, ass low and flat as a result. Nature accommodated your ancestors and you, keeping your delicate parts away from harm, away from the high grasses through which you had to run.

"To me, my darling, your firm and regal behind is one of

your most beautiful physical attributes, one of your few parts saved from the bastardization of slavery."

He kissed away my tears and filled the silence with the sound of making love to me. I wrote another song for him . . . *And her man took her hand / till the shaking ceased / and she knew she could love / and she knew peace / for the child has died, and the woman found . . .*

That was our life when we were together. We did not discuss what happened when we were apart, any more than we discussed his wife in New York or his daughter, who was only a few years younger than I, or anything else connected to his trips away from L.A., away from me. We would be married someday, we vowed. He promised.

There were other unsaid things in our life. There was what I considered his paranoia. He always checked and double-checked door locks wherever we stayed, never entering a room without opening closets and looking under beds. He even looked a room over for listening devices, and said nothing specific about anything over the telephone. He stayed away from windows and slept so lightly I could not turn over in bed without waking him. Added to that were his cryptic, seemingly paranoid statements, such as his reference one day when he returned to me about how "they" had tried to kill him when he was in Miami. There were his vague references to his work in Spain during the Spanish Civil War and, later, with the U.S. government's Office of Strategic Services, known as the OSS.

Whenever I asked him, on rare occasions, to clarify something regarding his personal life, he usually smiled and told me not to worry about it. When he told me about Spain and the OSS business, though, I felt it was a categorical contradiction, and I told him so. It seemed, I mildly ventured, incompatible with what was obviously his Communist philosophy to have worked with the OSS, the organization he had explained was the forerunner to the post-World War II CIA. Typically, he suggested it was unimportant for the moment.

Of course, I did not know that Jay was a Communist, with or without a capital *C*, any more than I believed he did anything but detest the CIA—and that without regard for the fact that the protagonist of his new novel was a CIA agent. The novel, it seemed to me, had more to do with the hearts of men than with systems. After more than a year of loving him, I realized I was not really sure of anything about him. I was not even sure how he earned all the money he spent. There was more than a wife and a brownstone in New York in Jay's life that was beyond me. What did it matter? I concluded. I was not going anywhere away from him.

The first time we went to San Francisco, we saw Molière's *Tartuffe*, performed by the ACT Repertory Company. Self-conscious over being the only black in the theater, I made sure I laughed in all the appropriate places. I looked down my nose at the white audience during the cocktail breaks between acts and, later, as Jay and I left in the limousine waiting for us outside the theater. We had supper at Eddie's, a dark red, intimate place.

During the day in San Francisco, we drove along the edge of the Bay, our limousine engulfed in cold fog. We would stop and get out to walk awhile, our driver following. We fed seagulls and our fantasies of a perfect future.

One night, we went to Sausalito to listen to Bole Sete from Brazil on bongos. We went to another performance of the ACT Repertory Company, to see Shaw's *Dear Liar*. Afterward, we went back to Eddie's for dinner, our third time. It was becoming *our* restaurant in San Francisco.

A young black fellow opened the limousine door in front of Eddie's that night. He held out his black hand to assist me. I was a cold personage, removed from him as from the rest of the world, draped in my designer minidress and matching cocktail hat of black-and-white tapestry. I pointed the toe of my expensive patent-leather shoe, extending a white-stockinged, thin leg out of the limousine along with my hand, and barely looked at him through my false eyelashes.

I heard him, though, his hand supporting me as I exited the black limousine. I heard him, though he said nothing at all. He called me "bitch." *Whore, dirty, motherfucking bitch. You have the nerve to come here with this old white man in this fancy car trying to pretend you ain't no nigger! Fuck you, bitch!*

My head was throbbing by the time we were seated in Eddie's. Before we ordered dinner, I drank more than half a bottle of Piper Heidsieck, and ate only beluga caviar for dinner. I became dizzy, and remained so for the duration of our stay in San Francisco.

The old dissociative terror returned. In a state of panic one night, I confessed to Jay all my infantile fears about myself, my constant longing for identity, the old "feeling." He knew, of course.

He saw me clinging. He held me tighter than ever in the bleakness of the rest of the days in San Francisco.

After San Francisco, though, after the parking valet at Eddie's, after telling Jay everything, the dissociativeness returned full-blown. *Mama! Mama! It's that feeling!* Even Jay's arms could not steady my heart rate or keep me from begging him to leave the lights on all night, or from bolting up in the middle of the night to force myself back into myself. I had returned to the terror, to my dreaded sense of nonexistence. I could not understand why.

In Tahoe, Jay told me his Einstein story. He had a cabin there on the North Shore. It was a small, two-story thing out of a child's picture book. It was sparsely decorated, in a woodsy way, replete with fireplace and kerosene lamps. The deep winter snow that covered the earth during the times we were there crushed against the cabin's back door, softly locking us in.

Jay had to be in Tahoe for weeks at a time on business. As usual, it was not my business. It was separate from me, a separate entity, a separate life from his "real" life, his past, his work, New York, his daughter, even Sinatra. I was his distant darling, who lived for him and only with him. I had no role in his daily life, as I had none in any life. It was all becoming crystal clear to me in Tahoe, like the quiet of the snow, like the frozen lake outside Jay's cabin door.

But Jay held me in front of the fire at night and during the day on ski lifts to the tops of mountains down which we never skied, and in bed, reassuring me at every step that we would be together forever. He read to me in bed, holding a book with one hand and me with the other, as I turned the pages, shivering under the down comforter. It was at such a moment that he told me his Einstein story.

"You know Albert Einstein was probably autistic," he said, looking up to the ceiling, as though for guidance, keeping me close to his body.

"Artistic?" I asked. His New York accent exposed my ignorance.

"No. *Au*-tistic. He barely spoke a word during the first nine or ten years of his life. He seemed to live in a world closed off from everyone else, including his own parents."

My heartbeat increased.

"His mother and father decided, after years of frustration, to send little Albert away for help, to an asylum."

I began to hyperventilate. He went on as though he did not notice.

"Not many days before Albert was to be sent off, his uncle visited him. His uncle was a mathematician. There was Albert, sitting in a corner in his room, immobile, locked inside himself, dead silent.

"His uncle knelt down next to him and asked, 'How are you today, Albert?' Nothing. No response. Albert's parents started to lift him out of the corner. It was no use, they tried to convince his uncle. The uncle held them off and continued talking to Albert.

" 'Albert, what if I told you that we could call the floor in this room *A*. Then the ceiling could be *B*. This wall would be *C*, that one *D*, then *E* and *F*. You, then, Albert, you could be *G*.'

"A few tears trickled out of the boy's silent eyes. They all saw it. It was a sign that he was alive, connected. His uncle and he became very close after that; and, of course, Albert never went to an asylum."

My own tears were uncontrollable. I did not need to know why Jay knew what he had told me about Albert Einstein. I knew why he had told me. He did know me. He did love me. I was present on the planet—verified and validated by him, through him, because of him, and only with him.

During one of Jay's visits to his "real" world, everything was moved out of our Hollywood Hills place. It would be a more convenient and more comfortable arrangement for him, he explained briefly by telephone, if we would resume our old routine. All of it was only temporary, anyway, in the long run, he added to my silence. None of it was what we wanted. We could talk more about it later, if I wished.

Our world was being disassembled. Actually, that world had been my fantasy, a place that had never really been *ours*. It was not a place where we lived together. It was simply where we stayed together when Jay came to Los Angeles. Perhaps it was like our relationship, I thought, powerless to do anything about any of it. Jay had decided to get that place when he felt being at Sinatra's or the Beverly Hills Hotel was too costly, a double entendre. Now the place in the Hollywood Hills was too costly. It was in his name, of course, a record that could link him to his other life—me. I realized I had never had my own key to the place.

It would be a funny memory when we were free to be to-gether, as we would, he elaborated over dinner at the Beverly Hills Hotel, to my widening eyes, after he returned.

Not much later, I decided to move out of "my" apartment, where my mother also lived. I found a more desirable, or more expensive, place in the Westwood area, the wonderland that se-questered UCLA students and faculty from the rest of Los An-geles. I had taken a clerical job to augment my nonexistent income and fill my days while I waited for Jay to return. My mother, of course, moved to Westwood with me.

I had considered going back to school when Jay glowingly reported to me his daughter's achievements at an Eastern uni-versity. With the expense of her schooling, he could not also pay for mine at that time, he had said, sidestepping the jealousy I expressed by insisting that I, too, needed a college degree. College could not make me any more brilliant than I was, he had said with a smile, offering nothing more.

My mother and I continued to hold superficial conversations, and continued to keep our distance. That had been our pattern since our confrontation over the Las Vegas trip, a long time back, it seemed. She pointedly avoided the subject of Jay with insin-uations that said he was married and would never get divorced. And I conspicuously avoided her, eating out alone most of the time, and spending my time at home singing the songs I had written for Jay at the piano I had bought.

Another black woman lived in our otherwise lily-white build-ing in Westwood. She wore a faddish Afro hairstyle, which fas-cinated me. She often said hello to me on the elevator. I barely muttered a response, swishing the hair of my fashionable "fall," the flowing hair extension I had begun wearing, away from my cheek.

"Is that you I hear playing the piano, Sister?" she asked me one day on our ride up to our respective floors.

A quiver went through me when she spoke to me. I did not feel I was her "sister" by any definition. I was conscious of her meaning, as Jay and I had discussed the new black militancy, which included such personal references—him telling me what an im-portant turning point it was. That was fine for conversations with Jay over dinner, I felt. That was enough.

"Probably," I nodded in response to her question, not looking at her.

"You play beautifully. Sing beautifully, too."

"Well, thank you," I responded, surprised by how happy I was to hear her compliment.

"I don't recognize any of the songs I hear you singing. Do you write them?"

"Ah yes," I answered, looking at her now, taking in her fuzzy hair.

I realized she was the first person my age I had spoken to in a long while, except for the times I saw Billy James.

"My name is Beverlee Bruce," she said, offering her hand.

Beverlee and I became friends, in a manner of speaking. We began having dinner together, and the growing Black Power Movement was the usual topic of discussion, though I felt, and told her I felt, it was meaningless.

"We can no longer accept what Whitey promises," she would intone. "Praying and marching won't get it. We need freedom now. Our brothers, Stokely and Rap, are leading us to a new day."

"Yes," I would retort, "a day of self-destruction," imposing my own translation on one of Jay's analyses.

"Even so," she always pressed on, "we have nothing to lose but our chains."

"But they're all Communists," I would assert, quoting the news of the day, but trying mostly to trap her.

"No, they're not! Those Brothers are nationalists. They're talking about building a black nation."

That concept startled me. What would a black person have to give or give up, I never dared ask Beverlee, to be part of such a black nation?

Beverlee was relentless and too smart for me, armed though I was with Jay's lessons. She spat out to me the words of Malcolm X, Langston Hughes, Ralph Ellison, and Richard Wright. When Jay came to town, however, I could forget her and her smart arguments.

During another of his absences, Beverlee asked me if I would give piano lessons to some girls in Watts who were students in a tutorial program she had organized. It was a field project she had set up in connection with the master's degree in education toward which she was working at UCLA. Rather whimsically, I agreed to do it.

The Jordan Downs Housing Project was a sprawling camp of desolation deep in Watts, the scene, Beverlee reminded me as she drove us there, of the greatest uprising of black people against oppression in our time.

"Yeah. Watts, 1965," Beverlee said dramatically.

It was now 1967, summertime.

As Beverlee's car turned into the entrance of Jordan Downs, I shuddered. It was all too familiar. When we got out of her car, I shuddered again at the starkness of the poverty. The whirring of a nearby industrial motor shook the ground as we walked, though nobody else seemed bothered by it.

I ignored the snide looks I received from the Jordan Downs tenants, who, hanging surreptitiously in doorways, were reviewing my costly minidress, long-haired fall, and expensive leather sandals. Jordan Downs was a virtual replica of the James Weldon Johnson Project, where I had lived behind steel doors a millennium ago.

Beverlee opened the heavy door to the ground-floor apartment she had rented for her program. There were a few rickety chairs inside. Used books sat on a chipped bookcase, next to an old upright piano. There was government-issue, drab paint on the walls and government-issue linoleum cracking on the floor.

Six or eight girls were inside, standing around against the walls. They became wide-eyed when we entered. They were between ten and twelve years old. Beverlee herded them together, like a teacher, to introduce them to me, their new piano instructor.

"This is Miss Brown, girls," she said, somewhat condescendingly, I thought. "She'll be coming every Saturday morning to give you piano lessons. You'll each get a half hour private lesson on alternate Saturdays, and you can practice here during the week. Is that okay?"

"Yes, Miss Bruce," they said obediently.

I remained silent, petrified. There was something in that room more horribly familiar than the bleakness of Jordan Downs. I looked at the girls, their skinny little-girl frames, and winced. I recoiled when I beheld their little faces, the blankness in their eyes. It was a look from long ago I knew well. And I knew them.

They were *me*. It was me I saw. There was my face, my pain, my nothing-little-nigger-girl expression lingering on their faces and in their eyes.

I saw the poverty of our lives, the poverty of little black girls who live on the same planet, in the same world where people, people like me, drank expensive bottles of champagne that clouded the mind with bubbles that obliterated them, us; where men, powerful men, made big decisions about their own lives and footnotes about the lives of them, us, that pushed us back, back into nothing little corners on the outskirts of life.

Though I stood frozen in place, I wanted to turn and run from their mirror. I wanted to scoop them up in my arms and take them away from Jordan Downs and Watts and all that they meant. I wanted to take them somewhere away from watching Mommy get beaten up and beaten down, from looking for Daddy, who was gone and would not return—not ever. I wanted to take them away from wearing somebody else's clothes and wishing for somebody else's life and feeling like nothing at all. I wanted to take them somewhere else, because I knew there *was* somewhere else.

I had had the luxury of sight, while they were doomed to a ghetto myopia so profound they might never see or think or dream, or even know they could see or think or dream. They were doomed to live and die in a piss-poor bastardization of life. They were doomed to never know that living was not hitting a number or stealing a dress or selling chitlin' dinners or drugs, or maybe even their very own bodies, to survive. They were damned to never recover from that terrible joke played on them, on us, by greedy men who had played with and stolen our very lives.

That was it. They needed a life. I needed a life. We needed a world in which to grow, a new and better arrangement where little black girls like us could blossom and live on equal footing with other human beings, not stuffed away in Watts or North Philadelphia, which were the same place.

As I looked at the sweetness of their brown faces, I wanted to hide from them and from all I knew. I stood in a trance, gazing at the worn books white people had charitably tossed to them to soothe their Judaeo-Christian consciences. I stood transfixed by the realization that I could not deliver what they really needed, even if I came to them every day in my minidresses with my piano lessons.

I managed a smile at each one of them, as each girl stood before me saying, "Hello, Miss Brown." Looking into their expectant eyes, I could not open my mouth.

I wanted to fall to my knees and ask them for forgiveness. I wanted to beg them to forgive me, for I had tried to forget. I wanted to beg them to forgive me for leaving them for so long, as I had to now, for I could never go back there again if I wanted to stay sane. I wanted to beg them to be patient with me, for I had to go back there again if I ever wanted to be free of all the pain of my life.

He would take care of everything. I had to talk to him. My heart was bursting when I called New York after that Watts visit. I called his trusted assistant, Eileen, whose number he had given me for emergencies. This was an emergency.

"Jay, spring is gone," I said right off, without any of the amenities, when he called back. "You said we'd be married by spring. You said we'd be in Paris by spring. When are you coming back? I need to see you. Now. Right now," I blurted out. "Jay, are you listening?"

"Yes, darling," he said hesitatingly. It was a horrible hesitation, hesitation from a man who always stood on solid ground. "Yes, darling. I'll be back in a week or so and we can talk then."

"I want to talk now," I demanded. I no longer wanted to be his child, diminished and dismissed until "we" could rationally discuss whatever it was I wanted to discuss.

"All right, fine, Jay. Just tell me now whether or not you intend to marry me."

"Darling, it's very complicated. You know that. You've known it all along. This is simply not a good time or place to discuss it."

"When will a good time come? In another two years? Perhaps four?" I whined.

He stalled. I cried, recognizing that it would never be. I cried words that begged him to understand that I was willing to relinquish my very soul to him if he would say the word. I would be his forever. I would surrender to comfort with him and forget freedom. His god would be my god. I would forget Watts and never go back to any Watts anywhere. We could grow old together and be all that mattered. We could create a world outside of misery. We could live together forever after, playing Cinderella and Prince Charming, daughter and father, lovers, friends, whatever we chose. But he stalled, and I knew it was not possible.

I returned with Beverlee to Jordan Downs for the next several weeks. I bought shiny red-covered Thompson piano primers and got to know the girls more than I wanted to. They expected so little from me, and I gave them less than they deserved. Beverlee scored points in her master's program, and Jay returned.

The Beverly Hills Hotel restaurant was not elegant or beautiful anymore. It was where he lived and I did not and, I had begun to see, could not. Still, I wanted to surrender to him, to remain safe with him. But he hesitated again.

There was the reality of his wife, he reminded me, whom he could not divorce at that time, for financial and other considerations that I did not care to understand. There were other realities that I did not hear him talk about as I drank the last of the Piper Heidsieck.

I became cold to him and tried to tell myself I hated him, he who had been everything, who had saved me from everything, including the fears I had been burdened with by my own mother. He had been a tender daddy and a powerful protector. He had been a patient teacher and a gentle lover.

It was now or never, I told him, all or nothing, simultaneously condemning myself and saving myself. I ignored his tears. I told him it did not matter anymore, because there was no place for me in his world and he did not belong in mine.

"Don't you see, Jay, you were right. It was not my mother or my father. It was not North Philly or Germantown. My pain is not unique. Others, like me, are suffering. There is only one, ultimate source of our suffering—the white man and his greed. The white man has stolen everything from us."

Of course he knew. He had taught me.

"Our Father is not in heaven," I went on. "He is on earth and on the dollar bill, in whom we'd better trust . . . And he's *white*—like you.

"The white man controls what we eat and whether we eat; where we live and how; whether we walk or ride. He is our doctor, our lawyer, our general, our jailor, our administrator, our master.

"Don't you see, Jay, you have been my one and only love, but I can't lie anymore, to you or to me. I can't pretend to be blind to what is so very clear. I can't go on like this any longer . . . *We* can't go on any longer."

Jay's book *The Chairman* was published about a year or so later. It was the one he had been working on while we were together. It was a novel about a white man who is a CIA operative and also a college professor. He is commissioned by the CIA to go into China to gather information about a major biological advance the Chinese have made. The published version had a new chapter.

Before the professor-agent leaves for China, he pays what may be his last visit to the only woman he has ever loved. He may not return from the trip into China. His love is a young black woman. She chain-smokes, plays the piano, and sings original songs, mostly written for him, in throaty renditions. When he visits her in Los Angeles on his way to China, she has changed—does not want to see him, no longer loves him. She has become a Black Power militant, joined some Black Power group. It is an irony he can barely deal with.

In loving her so, for so long, he has taught her everything he knows about the world, the struggles of people, their social and political movements. He has, he realizes, created the very schism that is now between them, one that he knows he can never bridge. In loving him so, she listened too well. She learned too well. Now she must leave him, and his white and powerful world that oppresses her. Now she must leave him when he needs her more than she ever needed him.

CHAPTER 6

GETTING BLACK

TOMMY JACQUETTE WAS the first black man I met. I realized I had known only "niggers" and a few colored fellows. I had heard of black men—men who were loving fathers and caring husbands and strong protectors. I had not really known any.

Tommy was so tall, he almost had to bend down to see me when Beverlee Bruce introduced us.

"This is Brother Jacquette," Beverlee said, adding that he was a Watts uprising warrior. She spoke with a black militant voice inflection, the cadence of which had been set by men like Stokely Carmichael.

"How're you doin', Sister," Jacquette said, reaching out a generous hand to me.

"Fine," I mumbled through lips that could not seem to open. We were standing in the middle of Jordan Downs. Beverlee and I had just left the Saturday tutorial.

Tommy Jacquette was a willow tree adorned by a shirt in a multicolored, geometric African pattern referred to as a dashiki. He had on khaki pants and black combat boots. His voice was deep, resembling the voice of Paul Robeson, whose records had been played on York Street a long time ago. He called me "Sister" so genuinely, so purposefully, it was not an appellation but an affirmation.

"I understand you write songs and poetry, Sister," he continued, turning a second later to give a Black Power handshake to another black fellow.

A number of them gravitated to him, deep in the middle of Jordan Downs, while we spoke. "Right on, Brother," they said

among themselves, to each other, hands touching in a cuplike
fashion, thumbs upward, palm-to-palm.

"Yes, I do write songs," I responded, convinced I would write
something about him. I would write songs about all of them, this
new breed of black men who were exchanging bits of conversation
about plans for the future of black people, about how to help their
Brothers and Sisters.

"You ought to come down to the Black Congress sometime,
Sister. Maybe you could do something for black people. You know,
get involved."

"Yes, maybe," I said as I looked to Beverlee to rescue me.

The Black Congress building might have housed an insurance
company before Watts 1965, as time was marked in black Los
Angeles in 1967. It was deep in the ghetto, at Florence and Broadway, a dismal corner which was not strictly in Watts. It was, however, a corner in the very heart of where the 1965 uprising had
raged, when Watts had really been the entire Los Angeles black
community.

The Congress, as it was called, was an umbrella group, made
up of virtually every black organization in the area. It was administered by an executive committee composed of a representative
of each member organization. The Black Congress was the expression of a collective desire to emphasize the common will and serve
the common interests of black people.

Tommy Jacquette was on the Congress's executive commit-
tee. He represented the Watts Summer Festival Commission,
which had been formed to keep people's consciousness of Watts
alive. There was one woman member, Margaret Wright, who
headed the local branch of the powerful National Welfare Rights
Organization. There was the progressive Black Panther Political
Party, headed by John Floyd. There was the militant Community
Alert Patrol, headed by Ron Wilkins, known as "Brother Crook."
There was the more militant US Organization headed by Ron
Karenga, who was called "Maulana." The executive director of
the Congress was a rather mild-mannered, middle-class man
named Walter Bremond.

Only seconds after our introduction, Walter Bremond urged
me to volunteer to work on the Black Congress's newspaper. Experience was not as important as willingness and commitment to
black people, Bremond responded to my hesitation. It would be
a long ride on the bus from Westwood, I thought.

I wondered what would have happened to the Black Congress's newspaper had Bremond not employed me. The staff numbered two, including me. John Floyd, the more experienced of us, became, by default, the head of the staff. John had a certain charm, despite the fact that his look was a bit too reminiscent of my father. He wore wire-rimmed glasses and carried a briefcase everyday, which contained his pistol. He taught me the language and the ideas of the Movement, that is, the left or militant wing of the black struggle for civil and human rights. He delivered me into the peripheral ranks of that movement.

John Floyd and I wrote copy together, pasted up storyboards, and typed and turned out, in six weeks, the first issue of the Black Congress newspaper. It was called *Harambee*—Swahili for "Let's Pull Together." We also slept together, once. After that, however, John ignored me on a personal level, which I took personally, even though the times had changed and making love had become a thing akin to drinking water.

Over those weeks, I developed a routine. I worked during the day in an office at UCLA and, most evenings and weekends, found my way to Florence and Broadway to work on the newspaper or do whatever else was necessary: type, clean offices, answer telephones. I began writing poems and songs about black men, black people, in between fashioning with John the next issue of *Harambee*, and attending any rally or meeting remotely connected to the struggle.

I did not resist at all when Crook strapped the two bandoliers of shotgun shells around my waist before taking me to the San Diego rally. He also placed two shotguns on the rear floor of his "hoopty," his automobile, in which we would ride to the rally. Guns were the natural accessory of the new black militants, who were determined to claim their manhood "by any means necessary." Crook, who came out of the Slauson gang, was currently head of the Community Alert Patrol, which organized blacks to resist police violence. Sandra Scott, his lady, was to have gone with us to the rally but had become ill. Now just the two of us were riding south on the San Diego Freeway at the maximum speed Crook's 1938 Plymouth, replete with running boards, could muster.

We joined several hundred others who had come to San Diego to support a black U.S. Navy man who was facing a court-martial for having referred to President Johnson as a "warmonger." The reaction of Navy officials to his remark seemed particularly outrageous since thousands of Americans who opposed the Vietnam

War had been defiling the name of the commander in chief of their armed forces.

Crook and I stood together listening to the speeches denouncing "the Man," the white man, who spoke with a forked tongue about freedom.

I thought she was Germanic-looking when she approached us. She had big bones that were a hanger for what seemed her incongruous, Africanesque garb. Angela Davis introduced herself to Crook and me, as people did at such rallies. I had been watching her do the same to others as she moved through the crowd. She smiled a scared smile, a smile with too many teeth, most of which were tobacco-stained. She was with her statuesque sister, a stunning beauty named Fania, who walked so regally one might step aside and bow for her. As Angela was telling us how she had just returned to the United States from studying abroad, in Germany, I was struck by her humble honesty about herself. She did not try to shade her freshman relationship to America's radical movement, which made me feel less intimidated by all the others there, who projected themselves as veterans. We did not talk much, but I watched her, later, conversing in French, of all things, to Karenga, the Maulana from the Black Congress. It was at a house party, a North Philly–like thing, where people could drink cheap wine and dance and talk about who was talking to whom.

Crook left me alone there within minutes of our arrival, going off to take care of some secret, "black male militant" business. I latched on to another L.A. woman, who had a "street" quality with which I felt at home. Everyone else was too "black," dressed up in African costumes and African names. Bobbi Hodges was a uniformly caramel color, rather like Angela, whom she was not like in any other way. I hung on to Bobbi for safety's sake.

The house was filled with members of Karenga's US—as opposed to "them"—Organization, which had a branch in San Diego. Most of them were men, all of whom, like Karenga, were wearing dashikis, dark glasses, and shaved heads. They were a flash of some part of my past. Perhaps they were like Omega Psi Phi fraternity pledges I had seen during my stint with one of them, the one who took my virginity. That sense of *déjà vu* became stronger as I looked at them, taking me back to Germantown and the colored fellows who looked down on girls from North Philly. I stayed close to Bobbi, on a couch in the living room, and observed the house party, chain-smoking.

"You Sisters want to contribute something toward some

food?" a young woman said to Bobbi and me, reaching out a hand that bore rings on all its fingers, like the one in her nose and the ones on many of her sandaled toes. She wore a very short "natural" and a long attitude that shouted how "black" she was, "blacker than black," like the youths in Mao's Cultural Revolution who were "redder than red."

Bobbi gave her three dollars, and I contributed five dollars to the collective pot. Bobbi and I talked about what all young blacks talked about in 1967: the struggle. We discussed freedom and revolution. We seriously pretended that our commitment to that struggle was an old thing, not born the day before yesterday, when some of us were "white," or not really "black."

When the food came, Bobbi and I got up to get into the line that was forming near the kitchen of the house, the owner of which was unknown to us. Another young woman, who might have been twenty-two and who wore a floor-length African to-galike dress, a "gran buba," tapped our shoulders.

"Sisters," she said, "you will have to wait until our Brothers are served. Yeah," she added, validating herself in a clipped meter, "our Brothers are our warriors. Our warriors must be fed first, Sisters."

Her newly styled words only reminded me of words I had heard from "tough" girls in North Philly who had attempted to challenge me with their hostile attitudes.

"Excuse me," I said sarcastically, reaching back in time. "Excuse me, *Sister*. Nobody said anything about 'our warriors' when money was changing hands. I want my food now."

"Yeah," Bobbi chimed in. "I want my three dollars worth of this Kentucky Fried Chicken—now, ain't that 'black.' "

Bobbi and I smirked and stood our ground—until a bald-headed dashiki came over to us, folded his arms across his chest, and explained the "rules" to us in a way we could understand. Sisters, he explained, did not challenge Brothers. Sisters, he said, stood behind their black men, supported their men, and respected them. In essence, he advised us that it was not only "unsisterly" of us to want to eat with our Brothers, it was a sacrilege for which blood could be shed.

Bobbi and I poked out our mouths and returned to the couch with our cigarettes and no Kentucky Fried Chicken. The great Karenga, no longer talking with Angela, sashayed over to us and looked down into our faces.

"How're you beautiful Sisters doing?" he said in a high pitch.

"Is there a problem I can assist you with?" He seemed to have left a rhyme hanging in the air.

"Not really," I said, crossing my legs and blowing a circle of smoke, from practice in my teen years, around his bald head.

He looked like a vanilla-fudge Buddha, waving the smoke away with his pudgy hand and a snicker.

There was just enough chicken for the fifty or so "warriors" to get their fill. There were not enough cigarettes for Bobbi and me. Bobbi left before Crook finally returned in his "hoopty." It was after midnight.

I violated all the "sisterly" rules and launched into Crook about leaving me there for so long. I demanded he grab one of those otherwise useless shotguns and deal with the entire household of Karenga followers. Instead, he laughed his head off, and made me laugh with him, reluctantly. We laughed about it all the way back from San Diego, stopping at his place to make love and avoiding mention of Sandra Scott.

I could barely look Sandra in the eye over those next weeks when we saw each other at the Black Congress. I followed her around, though, because Sandra had a genuinely brilliant mind. She had seemingly read everything, at least everything about political and social movements and revolutions. She was a student at California State University, Los Angeles, and a devotee and protégée of her sociology professor, Harry Truly.

When Sandra introduced me to Harry, it was done with reverence; she referred to him as the brilliant Dr. Truly, or words that conveyed such a feeling. Harry was a small man, a bit like a black leprechaun. He was forming something called the Black Student Alliance.

Harry, I concluded, was something other than brilliant. He was a professor of sociology by day and the architect of a complex scenario for power by night, a scenario that was designed, among other things, to deliver him to the front and center of history. He would ride into history on the waves of the revolution that would rise in the not-too-distant future.

Harry's vision was that the Black Student Alliance, or the Alliance, as he came to call it, would be a revolutionary union of all black student unions in America. Black student unions were beginning to be formed on several college campuses in Southern California, making a spiritual connection to the growing national black student movement. Numerous loosely organized black campus groups had emerged on the East Coast, taking their lead from the activist civil-rights organization SNCC (Student Nonviolent Coordinating Committee) in the South. As Black Power sentiments were beginning to overpower the popular, once-integrated SNCC of Stokely Carmichael and Rap Brown, however, they were also bearing down on the new black students now organizing, particularly those in California, the catchall outpost of new ideas. Indeed, the black student movement was taking a left turn away from concentrating on campus curricula and civil rights. Harry was not alone in seeing that shift, but he was certainly singular in his determination to harness it.

Assuming the development of a black student union on all the local campuses, Harry explained to Sandra and me, and assuming a minimum of several hundred members per campus, within no time a vehicle such as the Alliance could call thousands of black students together to effectively carry out a single action. Thousands of black students—under Harry's tutelage and direction, evidently—could be mobilized into a mighty force on a moment's notice. Moreover, that number could increase exponentially, according to Harry's vision, as the field of the Alliance expanded. Imagine the magnitude of the thing, Harry excitedly suggested, if the Alliance incorporated black student unions in Southern California with those in Northern California, then the entire West Coast, then the East Coast, the whole country.

It was Harry's theory that the student was the natural ally of revolution. He explained his vision to Sandra and me night after night in his hillside house, as we sat around drinking lots of wine and watching Los Angeles sparkle beneath us.

"Proletarian, socialist revolution is waged by the masses of working people, irrespective of race," Harry taught us. "Although the student is not a worker, he is also not a member of the bourgeoisie, at least not as a student. He has no relation to the means of production and thus has no real class status. The student's youthful fervor, however, combined with his biological moment of rebellion against all authority, make him a prime candidate for a revolutionary.

"If the black college student can get past the bullshit and into the legitimate cause of black liberation, it will produce a campus concoction that will blow the lid off this state and even this country."

Harry went on to explain that it was our role, the role of the Alliance, to agitate such fervor among black students. Although there were "radical" white campus groups, like Students for a

Democratic Society (SDS) already in place, Harry emphasized that
they were not reliable allies of revolution. The war against the
Vietnamese, around which SDS and other white student groups
were primarily organized, would inevitably end, and whites could
resume their "natural place" in America. Black students, though
still sleeping, were a sleeping revolutionary giant, because black
students had no stake whatsoever in corporate America—which
they would learn sooner or later, especially on graduation into the
white world.

I could not resist Harry's heady language and logic. I agreed
to be part of the nucleus of his new Black Student Alliance, though
I was not a student anywhere.

I began spending a lot of time with the others who had become the mainstay of the new organization, Brothers with African
names like Dedan, Weusi, and Rashidi. They were not typical
students, not even as blacks. They were, however, an emerging
prototype of a new black student. They had come from the streets
with Black Power hearts, and had forced their way onto college
campuses through previously closed doors via the post-Watts
pacifying programs of the Johnson Administration's War on
Poverty.

SDS and its free-speech precursor, led by people like Mario
Savio in Berkeley, were addressing broad national and international issues, from a student perspective—a white student perspective. Dedan and Rashidi and the other campus leaders who
were now part of Harry's Alliance were building a student movement that had as its expressed goal the use of the college campus
as a staging area for revolution, black revolution.

Sometime during that period, Harry ordained me as the Alliance's first representative to the Black Congress, making me the
second woman on its executive committee. Now I was working
during the day, attending Black Congress meetings once a week,
contributing articles to the expanded staff of its newspaper, and
reading and studying, mostly with Sandra Scott, black literature
and revolutionary treatises—particularly works like Frantz Fanon's *Wretched of the Earth*—at night. I had also begun to wear my
hair in a huge Afro style, no longer setting it on rollers to keep it
straight, and arguing with my mother that my hair *was* really "like
that."

Karenga always chaired the weekly Black Congress meetings,
mostly because, I came to see, everyone was too terrified of him

to challenge him. They not only deferred to him, they called him Maulana, his self-conferred title, which was a Swahili term loosely translated as "great teacher." There were usually about a dozen organization representatives at the Congress meetings. We sat around a large oval table, with Karenga at the head, discussing issues we would collectively support. Mrs. Wright's welfare mothers, for example, might be attacking a cutback in services; or Crook's organization, the Community Alert Patrol, might be organizing a rally to denounce another police murder of a young black fellow; or Bremond would bring up the necessity of supporting a black running for public office. We would vote not only to support a particular issue but also to decide how we would support it, as a group and as individual organizations.

The force of our organizational unity could be secured with a single vote, but it had to be a unanimous one. Karenga had convinced everyone in the Congress that unanimity was an "African" method of deciding a question. It was in the spirit of African communalism, Karenga had expounded, that the collective act only when the collective will had spoken in this way.

There had not been any discussion at all in the Black Congress of a particularly significant recent event, although news of this event had been spreading like wildfire through the entire country. It was an event that had forced people to consider the real meaning of black pride and black power, setting aside the significance of Afro hairstyles and dashikis. It was a street-corner episode that had challenged the oppressor and the oppressed.

Earl Anthony came to discuss the event at an early November 1967 meeting of the Black Congress Executive Committee. He wore the Black Panther uniform: black leather jacket, black pants, powder-blue shirt. He told us he was on the Central Committee of the Black Panther Party for Self-defense. Like the rest of the black militant organizations, the Black Panthers had come into being only in the last year or so. Unlike the rest, they had drawn their guns. They walked the streets of Oakland openly armed, to challenge any police who were assaulting blacks.

"Brothers, this is an emergency," Anthony announced. "Last month, Brother Huey P. Newton, minister of defense of the Black Panther Party for Self-Defense, was taken hostage by the pig. He was seized off the streets of Oakland after an armed agent of the Man was shot and killed in a righteous act of self-defense. One of the pigs was killed when they tried to kill Huey. Yeah, Brothers, it was a 'red-light trial,' a trial by fire on the streets of Babylon. Brother Huey took care of business. Now he is the political prisoner of our enemy. I'm here to get you Brothers . . ."

Karenga interrupted. He spoke from his chair at the head of the table. "Brother, we would love to hear more, but we have an agenda to follow. Perhaps we could schedule you for next week."

"Uh, excuse me, Maulana," Walter Bremond said weakly, "but I took the liberty of telling Brother Earl here that he could address the Congress because he had come all the way from the Bay Area in this time of crisis to rally support for Huey Newton in Southern California."

"Walter Bremond," Karenga said in his singsong manner, "I appreciate your concern, but you do not vote in the Congress, you do not chair the Congress, and therefore you cannot set the agenda for the Congress."

My voice came through the air like a zephyr, ringing in the huge hall in which we were sitting, causing all heads to turn and mouths to open. "Well, I'd like to hear the rest of what this Brother has to say." I had begun to think of Karenga as an obnoxious prig. I snatched the opportunity to oppose him. Moreover, I was charmed by the Black Panther stuff; and Earl Anthony had style, I thought.

"Fine, Sister," Karenga muttered confidently. "Let us put it to a vote, to gain African consensus on the issue."

Everybody mumbled approval that a vote should be taken.

Crook and I were the only two to vote to hear Earl continue. It was enough to throw things into "African" confusion, however. No one knew what to do, because there was no absolute consensus. This had apparently never happened before. After much debate, Earl Anthony was permitted to continue his pitch for support for the Huey P. Newton Legal Defense Fund.

Karenga's main lieutenant, Tayari, brushed past me after the meeting, whispering to me in a threatening tone that black women did not wear miniskirts such as I was wearing. I stopped long enough to toss Tayari a street-corner comment to the effect that when black men paid for what black women wore, they could talk about it. I found my way over to Earl Anthony. He was taking the names of those whose organizations might form a support committee for Huey Newton.

Earl Anthony began attending the weekly Black Congress meetings, though he never petitioned the Congress to include the Oakland Panthers in its membership. Perhaps it had to do with the technicality that Earl represented only the Huey Newton Legal Defense Fund, which was organized around a limited agenda, unlike the NAACP and other organizations which had representatives in the Congress. Nevertheless, Earl was coming every week to report on the progress of the Huey Newton Legal Defense Fund and, afterward, inviting me to ride with him.

I became Earl's entourage of one. I would accompany him after the Congress meetings to gatherings of black professionals or college students or neighborhood groups, whom he would call upon to "join the struggle," to support Huey Newton. Earl also invited me to his bed.

I wondered, later, what made me accept Earl's nagging invitation. Perhaps I thought of it as having to do with the freedom of black people. Earl had suggested such a thing. He had actually told me that a true Sister would be happy to sleep with a revolutionary Brother. Obviously, revolutionariness was not close to cleanliness, I thought as I entered Earl's unkempt house. One night with him was enough. If I was guilty of having just discovered the Tommy Jacquettes, of having loved a white man named Jay Kennedy, of having done nothing to improve the sad condition of my people, I certainly would not be redeemed in the unclean house of Earl Anthony.

Avoiding Earl was why I missed the Black Congress meeting the week after the members' early-December retreat in the mountains to resolve a variety of internal conflicts—which retreat Karenga had refused to attend. At the retreat, Crook and I had forced a vote that Karenga no longer be referred to by the grandiose title of Maulana. "Call him Brother or nigger," Crook had said, which I had seconded. But I missed that next Black Congress meeting, in which it was revealed that the Brother who had come to the retreat known only as Ken, a telephone company employee who had begun working on *Harambee*, was really Ken Msimaji, a member of Karenga's hierarchy. I was shamefully grateful that I had missed that meeting, trying to avoid Earl, who had been pressuring me for another romp, the last time by pushing me up against a wall in the Black Congress building.

At least fifty US Organization members surrounded the Black Congress building at the beginning of the meeting, I was later told. Most of them were armed with shotguns. Karenga then paraded inside, but did not take his seat at the head of the table. Instead, accompanied by Tayari and Jomo and Ken Msimaji and several other bald clones, all armed (though Karenga was not), he stood at the head of the table. Some of his followers raised their shotguns at the Black Congress members sitting at the oval table. Franklin Alexander, the head of the Du Bois Clubs, a fledgling front organization of the Communist Party, USA, dove under the table for cover. John Floyd made a weak attempt to reach for his briefcase with his pistol in it. Everybody was terrified.

"I understand some people want to criticize US, Brothers," Karenga said, referring to his organization. "I understand somebody has something to say to Maulana."

When the response was only silence, he continued: "I have something to say to you, Brothers. If you cannot deal with me politically, perhaps you might want to deal with me militarily. Can you dig that, Brother Crook?"

Everyone talked about how Crook stood his ground that evening at the Black Congress. Everyone talked about how everybody but Crook started backing down about referring to Karenga as Maulana, leaving Crook with no backup for the collective position. The point was lost at the point of Karenga's goons' shotguns. Karenga had solidified his position as head of what would come to be considered the most militant black organization in Southern California—in Los Angeles, the city where only two years before young black men armed with indignation and Molotov cocktails had terrified all of America.

Even after that meeting, Sandra Scott and I continued our practice of laughing about Karenga and his US Organization. Whenever we met, we always got around to finding something demeaning to say about Karenga. We might laugh about his effeminate voice or his squatty body or his tiny hands. Sandra was a kind of feminist, though she would never have agreed to that label; and I had become as much her protégée as she was Harry's. Karenga was certainly not a promoter of equal opportunity for black women, inside or outside his ranks, Sandra and I agreed. We laughed about Karenga to keep from crying. Encouraged by Harry one night, Sandra and I decided we just had to fuel our sessions with new stories. We decided to attend an US Organization meeting held at the so-called Hakalu, the US Organization's headquarters.

It was a meeting open to the black community at large. People could come in off the street and listen to the teachings of Karenga, most of which were articulated in a pamphlet that might have been entitled *The Wisdom of Maulana Karenga*. Sandra and I were given the pamphlets as we entered the rear door of the small building. We secreted ourselves in the back row of folding chairs. On a small platform before the gathering, Tayari gave a pep talk, after which Karenga spoke. Each sentence he uttered rhymed, and was set off by his followers' choruses of "Speak, Maulana!" and "Tell the truth!"—the women chanting "A-la-la" over and over, in high, piercing tones. Sandra and I snickered one too many times and were spotted in the darkened room by Tayari. We were immediately asked to leave by two of the "Simbas," so-called young lions, duplicates of Karenga. We reported the details to Harry in between tears of laughter.

Harry had his own enjoyment in all of this. It allowed him to indulge his dream. Harry Truly wanted to replace Karenga. That is, I felt Harry wanted to hold the position of supreme black militant leader. Harry seemed to see that as a real possibility, through the Alliance, though he never articulated this aim. That would have suited me, however, having learned that Karenga had posted a notice in his building to the effect that Crook *and* I were "enemies" of the US Organization. As more and more black student unions were popping up like wildflowers in the Los Angeles area at the end of 1967, Harry began focusing everything on building the Alliance, which, he said, could become greater than the sum of its parts.

Harry insisted we wear long African *bubas* for the grand year-end Alliance fund-raising event—something Sandra refused to do. We Sisters had to look our part, Harry remarked in his leprechaun way. We also had to act our part, as hostesses, selling drink tickets and seating everybody at the benefit. The Brothers' part was handling the nebulous security. Miraculously, it all worked according to Harry's plan. A "sell-out crowd," as he referred to it, piled into the supper club to support the Black Student Alliance, Harry having convinced the club's owner to donate the place to us for the evening. Harry had also gotten the jazz/folk singer-songwriter Oscar Brown, Jr., and his wife to put on a show for our benefit.

For me, those few hours provided a bit of sanity and clarity in an evolving confusion, a tenderness squeezed between the hard edges of the Movement, to which I seemed to be committing body and soul. Listening to the words of Oscar Brown, sung by his strikingly beautiful wife, Jean Pace, I found time to remember why I had come that far by faith, it seemed. Brown sang his famous "Work Song," the music of which had been written by Nat Adderly. He also performed his well-known piece "Bid 'Em In," which depicted the auction of a young slave girl. Together, he and Jean sang the lilting bossa nova "Laia Ladaia," Brown closing with his sweet lullaby "Brown Baby."

> . . . When all of men's hate
> Is hurled away,
> You're gonna live
> In a better day,
> Oh, you little Brown Baby . . .

Afterward, about ten of us went to the apartment of two Alliance members, Razell and Nathalie, to assess our work. Nathalie, Angela Davis, and I, still bedecked in our African apparel, were the only women there. We all patted ourselves on the back for a job well done and began listening, as usual, to Harry pontificate about the future—the future of America, the future of black people in America. Soon Angela, a graduate student and a political theoretician like Harry, was debating the lack of merit of some point Harry had made, a point no one else even understood.

Their academic wrangling was interrupted by a grand entrance. He seemingly came out of nowhere. Perhaps Razell had invited him. He said he had heard about the Alliance and wanted to speak to some of us.

"My name is Bunchy," he said coolly. "Bunchy," he reiterated, "like a bunch of greens," answering a question someone a long time ago had found the courage to ask.

His face was black alabaster; his eyes, black diamonds, set off by carved eyebrows and distinct black eyelashes. His skin was as smooth as melted chocolate, unflawed, with a reddish gloss. He was the vision of Revelations, a head of soft black wool refined to an African crown. He stroked his rich mustache as he spoke, head back, feet apart, an olive-green leather coat tossed over his strong shoulders. Everybody had heard of Bunchy. He was a lion from the streets of L.A., the former head of the Slauson gang, five-thousand strong, originator of its feared hardcore, the Slauson Renegades. He was considered the most dangerous black man in Los Angeles, known as the "Mayor of the Ghetto." He was with another fellow, called Wilbur Terry, who was taller but less significant at first glance.

Harry did not bother to rise. He remained in his conversational posture, bent over like *The Thinker*, sitting on a low stool in Razell and Nathalie's living room, still fixed on Angela. The atmosphere in the room had changed, however. Harry felt it as strongly as we all did. He peered up at Bunchy through the thick lenses of his eyeglasses. He extended his hand without moving any other part of his body.

"Right on, Brother—ah, what? Bunchy?" Harry said as though he had a death wish.

"Bunchy," he confirmed for Harry, smiling.

Perhaps Harry did not understand, I felt. Perhaps he had been swathed in intellectualism too long. I knew this man Bunchy. He was the Crump brothers and all the other Brothers from the Avenue and Norris Street and Camac and Diamond, style transformed, rage directed, spirit defined by the ghetto streets and raised to a revolutionary level. He was a conscious and articulate member of the black proletariat, up from the industrial ghetto. He was different from the patient, agrarian Negro of the New South, different even from the new militants and Black Power brokers. He was an angry black man who had survived with a conscious understanding of the ruthless Northern urban centers that had forgotten what to do with "niggers" after the Civil War was over. I knew this man, and I wanted to know him.

He looked at Angela and Nathalie and me. "You Sisters sure look black and beautiful tonight," he said. "I'd love to take you Sisters down to the De La Soul with me, all dressed up like African queens. Yeah," he continued relentlessly, "I know you Sisters sure could organize some of those ignorant niggers down at the De La Soul."

I swore immediately that I would never, ever wear such a costume again. He had challenged us with his imagery. The De La Soul was obviously where "real" black people lived, raw and real, not dressed up—up, as in superior to the "ignorant masses" who "partied" at the De La Soul with wigs and sequined dresses and flashy suits bought the hard way. We had, he said with his picture-words, placed ourselves above the people, not as leaders or role models, but as intellects of a higher order, who did not deign to go down to the De La Soul but who sat around in living rooms in pseudo-African garb discussing the implications of a struggle from which we had safely distanced ourselves.

There was something else in the air that Bunchy had brought in with him. There were the rumors that Bunchy Carter was organizing the streets of which he was "mayor" into a chapter of the Black Panther Party in L.A., presumably a military wing of John Floyd's Black Panther Political Party. The combination of those thousands of gritty young Brothers from the Slausons, who still saw Bunchy as their leader, with the ideals of the Black Panther Party had sent chills through everybody at the Black Congress that had dared to speak about it.

Bunchy had just finished four years in Soledad prison, it was whispered, for armed robbery. He had become a Muslim minister in prison, a devotee of Malcolm X. Earl Anthony had verified to me the rumor that Bunchy had met Huey Newton right before the cop-killing incident and had, on the spot, pledged devotion to Newton's organization. It had been after the well-publicized event involving Betty Shabazz, the widow of Malcolm X. Huey Newton had led his Black Panthers, outfitted in their now-well-known Panther uniforms and openly armed with shotguns, into the San Francisco airport, right up to the airplane, to meet and escort Betty Shabazz. She was in the Bay Area on her first speaking tour since the assassination of her husband. Newton and his Panthers had dared anybody to attempt to assassinate the widow. The audaciousness of such an act, followed by their face-to-face meeting, had done it for Bunchy, Earl had said. I recalled that as I sat looking at Bunchy.

"I'd love to ask you to stay, Brother," Harry said fearlessly, "but we're having a meeting."

"I didn't come to interrupt, Brother," Bunchy replied. "As I said, I came to get involved. I've been out of the joint for only a little while now and I've been observing the black organizations here in L.A. to get a handle on things. It seems you are all doing a fine job of articulating the problems of our people." He placed one leg on the bottom rung of a wooden chair near Harry.

"I think the Alliance is doing more than that, Brother," Harry bristled. "We're struggling over a solution. Trying to initiate black revolution."

"Right on. That's right on. Even though I never heard of revolution without the gun . . ."

"The gun? The gun, Brother? Nobody's scared of the gun. We've got . . ."

"I'm just making an observation. I haven't seen anybody picking up the gun against the Man. Weapons of words won't deal with the Man. I think history has taught us that. The Man is a beast, and he's armed against us. The only thing that will deal with the Man is the gun, and men willing to use the gun."

"Spoken like a true Fidelista," Harry said, referring to those who adhered to the doctrines of Fidel Castro, and showing himself to be stronger than any of us had imagined.

We watched in silence.

"Spoken like a socialist, Professor," Bunchy shot back. "Lenin, Mao, Che, as well as Fidel understood the absolute necessity of *armed* struggle."

"We're not in a position to wage armed struggle right now, Brother. We have a ragtag army and a sorry arsenal. We can't deal with the Man with bullshit. We'd only lose. Is that what you'd have us do, fight to lose?"

" 'In revolution, one wins or dies,' " Bunchy answered, quoting Che Guevara.

Their conversation went on for an hour, it seemed. No other voices were heard. When it was over, when the wine was gone and nothing was resolved, Bunchy bid us farewell in rather swashbuckling style. Before leaving, he winked at us women with a remark about going down to the De La Soul. He had challenged us and left us dazzled, knowing we could never speak about black power or black nations or black struggle again without feeling the weightlessness of our words. It seemed he had offered us an opportunity to step into the real battle if we dared. Nothing much was said among us after he left.

No one I knew saw Bunchy again for weeks after that. The year ended only with the rumors. Maybe the rumors were untrue, everyone hoped, rumors of Bunchy heading an arm of the Black Panthers, of Bunchy bringing his transformed troops into the Southern California black militant scene.

Sandra Scott called me excitedly one evening during those last days of the year. She had purchased Black Panther Eldridge Cleaver's book *Soul on Ice*. I *had* to read it, she said. She could not read another word without calling me. We went through the entire book together the next night, each of us reading alternate chapters aloud, analyzing and praising each sentence and drinking about two bottles of wine. It was an incisive autobiographical excursion into the mind of a black man driven by racism to rape, for which Eldridge had spent nine years in prison. When we finished the book, we vowed we would meet him: the minister of information of the Black Panther Party, Eldridge Cleaver. When Sandra dropped me off at home early the next morning, I stayed up to write a poem for him. My mother, with whom I still lived, thought I was insane.

Spending less energy on my work with the Alliance than on discussing Eldridge Cleaver with Sandra, I brought in the new year with Rashidi. While making love was freer than ever at the end of 1967, I really liked Rashidi. He enjoyed ideas, and he liked to talk about them, and he enjoyed talking with women about them. It seemed appropriate to welcome in a new year with him. One of the core members of the Alliance, Rashidi was committed to the cause of black liberation and was excited by the prospect of the coming of Bunchy Carter and his L.A. Panthers. Our discussion was punctuated by a lot of wine and sex on the floor of my Westwood apartment.

A late-morning sun woke us from the deep sleep produced by the wine and the heat of the fireplace. When the closed bedroom door informed us that my mother had come home earlier than expected, and had had virtually to walk over our bodies to get to the bedroom, it shocked us from our lovely stupor. We dressed, cleaned up things hurriedly, and sneaked out into the cold new year. When I found the courage to return home late that night, my mother announced, as though it were a weather report, that we might consider getting separate apartments.

In his never-ending effort to organize the organizers and, ultimately, to control the black revolutionary struggle that was clearly building, Harry decided to create what he classified as a significant event, one that would bring together all the black organizations in Los Angeles under the sponsorship of the Alliance. A black culture was evolving, he explained, one that reflected the militant tone of the time. An art was coming into being that would not only define but inspire black revolution. The Alliance, as a student group, had a duty to encourage such revolutionary art.

Now we were inviting all black organizations in the area to participate in a community poetry reading. We distributed leaflets throughout black L.A., inviting the community to come together in the "spirit of struggle" one Sunday afternoon. Clyde Halisi of the US Organization would read some poems, our Alliance fliers promised. There would also be readings by the intense young poet Stanley Crouch, and by two of the original, well-known Watts Poets, Quincy Troupe and Ojenke. There would be plenty more. We drew an audience of about three hundred to the Black Congress's auditorium.

Representing the Alliance, I would recite a poem. I seated myself in the front row of chairs next to Stanley Crouch, along with the others who would read. Serious though he was, Stanley was the only humorist around. Whenever I saw him, I would end up a ball of laughter about this or that bit of pretentiousness of the latter-day militants. I had saved a chair next to him so I could share his funny fire, which would be the only relief, I felt, in what was going to be a long afternoon.

Harry played host and took charge of establishing the meaning of the day with lengthy introductions of each reader.

Stanley read his "Howlin' Wolf." Halisi read some words he had written about "our" African heritage. John Floyd and Aiuko Babu, of the Black Panther Political Party, read poems they had written. I read my "poem," which was really a metric denunciation of black men who were exploiting the struggle to cajole their Sisters into their beds with the slick rhetoric that to refuse a warrior was counterrevolutionary. Quincy Troupe read his elegiac tribute to John Coltrane:

Trane, Trane,
Runaway Trane,
Breaking all known dimensions . . .

Everyone was "black" and satisfied as the sun set after two hours of "blowing," as such readings were called—a very masculine reference: "Blow, Brother!" Everyone was black and satisfied until the double doors to the large Black Congress hall where we were seated were brusquely flung open. In he walked, "entering" as he had the last time, at Razell's. Down the aisle, past the many rows of folding chairs to the front, to face us. The waning winter sun burst around him. He was wearing a black leather jacket tossed over shoulders broadened by Soledad workouts. Wilbur Terry was with him again, along with about twenty others, the fiercest-looking Brothers I had ever seen.

He stood where the other poets had stood. His men swaggered into standing positions against the walls, surrounding the gathering. Some of them wore leather gloves, at least those with sawed-off shotguns pressed to the sides of their thighs. Some wore hats cocked over one eye and pistols in shoulder holsters. They postured in streetwise stances, holding up the walls that seemed to be closing in. Once they were in place, all eyes, all heads turned from them to the figure of Bunchy Carter.

"No one invited us, but we thought we'd come anyway," he said right off, without even a glance at Harry, quietly seated in the front row.

"Right on, Bunchy!" a deep voice exclaimed from the wall.

I could feel everyone straightening up, though no one spoke or made any overt moves.

"I've got a few poems, though."

It was said Bunchy wrote poems that he recited on the street corners of Los Angeles.

"Blow, Bunchy!" a voice cried out from the wall. "Blow 'Niggertown.' "

"Right on . . . 'Niggertown,' " he announced.

"Right on! Right on!" came the chorus from the wall.

Bunchy recited his confrontational "Niggertown" and a few other poems, finishing with the tender "Black Mother."

After that, he put an end to the rumors.

"Thank you for letting me blow," Bunchy said, after a beat, "but actually, I didn't come here for that. I came here to make an announcement: we have just officially formed the Southern California chapter of the Black Panther Party for Self Defense."

"Right on" came the chorus, covering the sound of gasps.

Stanley Crouch and I smiled at each other out of the corners of our eyes, for we knew. It was all changing irrevocably now. The Karengas and the John Floyds and even the Harry Trulys were being called to task, to back up rhetoric with action.

"I came here also to make it crystal clear that *we* are the Black Panther Party, that there is but *one* Black Panther Party and that is the party headed by Minister of Defense Huey P. Newton—ain't that right, John Floyd," Bunchy said in one sentence, walking down the center aisle of chairs toward John, who was a silent stone. "I said, ain't that right, John Floyd! There's only *one* Black Panther Party. And we don't want to hear about another soul trying to use our name again unless authorized by the Central Committee of the Black Panther Party. Is that *clear*, John Floyd!"

John Floyd, like everyone else, was immobile. People stole glances at John, however, grateful they had not exploited the name. Stanley Crouch and I nudged each other.

"I also came here to let you know that it is the position of the Black Panther Party for Self Defense that we are the vanguard of revolution in the United States. We are the vanguard party. And the vanguard party is declaring all-out-war on the pig. We are declaring war, and we are declaring that from this point forward, nobody will speak about Black Power or revolution unless he's willing to follow the example of the vanguard, willing to pick up the gun, ready to die for the people."

He snapped his fingers, eyes still fixed on all of us. One of the Brothers walked over and handed him a rolled-up banner. He unfurled it with a flourish, revealing a photo, blown up into a large poster: a poster of Huey Newton seated in a high-back rattan chair, wearing a black leather jacket and a black beret.

"This here is Huey P. Newton, Brothers and Sisters," he said in his streetwise timbre, modified by the tonality of Louisiana roots, one generation removed. "And this poster's got to hang on every wall in the black community, because Huey P. Newton is the leader of the black liberation movement in this country. He is the leader of the vanguard party. Why, Huey P. Newton has done what you niggers are talking about, thinking about, doing. He has dealt with the pig!"

"Right on!" came the chorus.

"He has set the example and showed us that we, too, must deal with the pig if we are to call ourselves men. We can no longer allow the pig's armed forces to come into our communities and kill our young men and disrespect our Sisters and rob us of our lives. The pig can no longer attack and suppress our people, or send his occupying army to maraud and maim our communities, without suffering grave consequences . . .

"From this point forward, Brothers and Sisters, if the pig moves on this community, the Black Panther Party will deal with him . . . What will we do, Brothers?" he said to his compatriots.

One stepped forward, sawed-off shotgun now raised across his chest, a gloved fist at his side. "We'll put his dick in the dirt, Bunchy."

"That's right. That's right. Right on." Bunchy nodded. "We're here to say that the vanguard party will deal with the pig. We'll kill the pig! Off the motherfucker! We will destroy him absolutely and completely or, in the process, destroy the gravitational pull between the earth and the moon!"

It was hard to believe Earl Anthony had found the nerve to call me again. I had made it clear to him months ago that he disgusted me, at best. He was still in Southern California, still working for the Huey Newton Legal Defense Fund and now also working with Bunchy Carter. He was writing press statements and pamphlets for the new Southern California chapter, he told me, as though I had an interest in him. He was also telling me something about attending a rally for Huey Newton's birthday. It was a political rally to raise funds and consciousness in connection with the pend-

ing trial of Huey Newton for the killing of the white Oakland cop
back in October.

There were about ten thousand people inside the Los Angeles
Sports Arena. There were hundreds more outside, involved in cir-
cuslike pandemonium. Posters of Huey Newton in the rattan chair
were being sold on the streets all around the arena. Young blacks
were also hawking Black Panther buttons and powder-blue sweat-
shirts, all carrying the same slogan, the same message: FREE HUEY!

Women and men in black leather coats were marching
military-style, back and forth outside the huge arena, backed up
by the beat of several parade drums, chanting the battle cry, a
clarion call that was thundering in the ghettoes of black America
and being carried in banner headlines in every news journal in
the country:

> Free Huey!
> Or else!
> The sky-y-y's the limit!

They marched and waved huge powder-blue flags on which
the stalking Black Panther symbol was emblazoned; now singing,
to the tune of the spiritual "Wade in the Water":

> Free Huey Newton,
> Free Huey Newton, fascist dogs,
> Free Huey Newton,
> We need our leader to guide us.

Inside, petitions and collection plates were being passed
around as the auditorium filled to overflowing, each person having
been searched for weapons on entry. Men in berets, holding shotguns, stood along the walls.

Seated in a row on the huge stage, waiting for the program
to get under way, was the entire leadership of the new black militant movement, a national movement neither supported by,
endorsed by, nor involving white people. They were a new generation of black men, divorced completely now from the old, the
civil-rights movement of the NAACP and the Urban League and
Martin Luther King's Southern Christian Leadership Conference.
They were young black men no longer concerned with the business
of segregation or integration. They were young black men who

were calling for an end, not only to discrimination, an end not only to the denial of civil rights, but to all forms of oppression of blacks—social, political, *and* economic—on all fronts. This new leadership was not begging the question but making a demand, a demand it declared it was backing up with armed force, as symbolized in the hero of that new movement: Huey P. Newton.

A new black leadership had gathered in Los Angeles that day in February 1968, as it had in Oakland the day before, to, as Eldridge Cleaver had defined it, declare war on "Babylon," the United States of America.

Now Eldridge was standing before the thousands in Los Angeles, spreading out his arms like a godly force. He wore dark glasses and spoke with his head to the side. He told us we were gathered there to celebrate the life of the leader of the vanguard party, Huey P. Newton. There were constant cheers as he spoke, and standing ovations, with fists raised in the air. A giant banner-poster of Huey formed the visual backdrop to Eldridge's words. When he finished, he introduced the other speakers, who stood up as he called their names.

"The vanguard party has drafted this Brother. He has been drafted into the army," Eldridge announced. "Brothers and Sisters, Brother Stokely Carmichael, the new prime minister of the Black Panther Party!"

"Power to the people!" the crowd cheered, up on their feet as Stokely stood, raising two fists high above his head. "Power to the people!" the people cried again, fists raised in return.

"Next to Brother Stokely," Eldridge continued, "is another draftee. He has put down his plow and picked up the gun," referring to the inductee's SNCC affiliation, as symbolized by SNCC members' wearing of overalls as they trudged through the Southern backwoods registering blacks to vote. "Brothers and Sisters, another new member of the Central Committee of the Black Panther Party, Brother H. Rap Brown!"

Rap Brown stood, wearing dark glasses and a black beret, acknowledging his transformation. He, like Stokely, was a leader of SNCC. The meaning of their donning the Panther black beret was not lost on the crowd, which roared its approval.

Eldridge continued the introductions of speakers: James Foreman, Ron Karenga, Bunchy Carter, and other local black community leaders. The crowd continued to cheer and stomp and shout.

When the introductions were finished, Stokely got up again to address the cheering crowd.

"Brothers and Sisters, we are calling for the freedom of Huey P. Newton. Huey Newton must be set free! Must be set free! Set free!"

It was a charismatic delivery that turned the crowd wild. There was a long, standing ovation.

"We're talking about freedom, the freedom of Huey, the freedom of all black people!"

Every sentence was punctuated by rousing cheers and raised fists from thousands.

"The honky has enslaved us and robbed us and killed us. But now, like Brother Huey, we're here to say, 'No more! No more! No more!' "

His words bounced off the walls, touching even those high in the balcony, where I was sitting, stunned.

"Malcolm told us. They killed him. Huey Newton told us. They're trying to put him in the gas chamber."

"Nooo!" came the cry from the throng.

"Huey Newton must be set free! Black people, black people must be set free! Free from poverty. Free from oppression. We have nothing to lose but our chains! Free Huey Newton! Power to the people!"

The speeches went on for hours. I sat in the balcony convinced, like everyone else, apparently, that the battle had begun. As Eldridge Cleaver said over and again during that evening, now we had to choose: we would be part of the solution or part of the problem. I was terrified.

Sandra Scott and I seemed on our own now. We were reading and holding our own political discussions without the benefit of Harry Truly's wisdom. After Bunchy's announcement and the Huey Newton birthday rally, Harry seemed to have withdrawn from everything. Besides, Sandra and I had grown up, in a manner of thinking.

The Alliance was muddling along, nevertheless, and I was muddling along, having just celebrated my twenty-fifth birthday, when Sandra called me several weeks after the Huey Newton rally to tell me Eldridge Cleaver was back in L.A. The local SNCC chapter was holding a fund-raiser for the family of one of their members who had died. A popular national figure with the success of his book, Eldridge had been invited to appear at the benefit to attract wider community support. Sandra's on-again, off-again lover, Crook—now working with SNCC—had called her and told her about it, assuring her Eldridge would be there, which guaranteed that Sandra and I would be there.

When Sandra came to pick me up in her Volkswagen, we joked and screamed about which one of us would go home with him. In fact, we actually made a friendly bet that one of us would go home with Eldridge Cleaver that very night.

When we pulled up and parked in front of SNCC's storefront office, where the benefit was being held, I saw that there were about 150 people inside, including Bunchy Carter and the ever-present Wilbur Terry. From the street, we could hear the Temptations singing from a blasting record player. Sandra and I sauntered in, smiling at each other.

My eyes scanned the dark room for the captivating Eldridge Cleaver. We both spotted him and did all the stuff girls do when they want to impress a fellow or catch his eye. We giggled loudly and whispered obviously and got drinks when he moved anywhere near the bar, and danced with everyone we could—me thrilled to be asked to do the African Twist by Bunchy, as dashing a dancer as he was a man.

When I could stand it no longer, I boldly walked over to where Eldridge was seated, holding conversation in the dark, and introduced myself to him.

"I really loved your book," I said cavalierly. "I just wanted to thank you for writing it."

He seemed genuinely grateful for my compliment. He stood up to kiss my hand. He was much bigger than he had appeared from a distance at the Sports Arena. He was about six feet five inches tall, and weighed about 250 pounds. Even in the dark, even with his dark glasses, his face was sensuously appealing, an appeal accentuated by a small earring he wore in one ear. His hands were massive, and his speech was poetic. I could see Sandra nearby, out of the corner of my eye, as I wondered, like the teenager I now was, where Crook was.

Eldridge told me he would ask me to dance but he did not dance. We talked a bit about Bunchy, whom he had known when both of them were in Soledad prison, and about the new Southern California chapter of the Black Panther Party. I avoided his silent exhortation that I become part of it. Finally, in desperation, when I saw there was little else to say, I told him I had written a poem for him, about him.

"How flattering," he said. "Where is it?"

"At my house."

"Can I see it?"

"Sure."

"How about now?" he said, rising simultaneously and indicating to the Brothers nearby that he was leaving.

"Fine," I stuttered, and threw a glance at Sandra.

Eldridge grabbed Bunchy as he walked toward the door, with me following. Bunchy shot a look at several of the Panthers in the room, who stumbled together quickly to escort the minister of information.

On his way outside, Eldridge held numerous short conversations with admirers. He got into the driver's seat of a black sedan that someone brought up to him, after wheeling it out of its parking space in front of Sandra's Volkswagen. I sat next to him. Bunchy and some other Brother got into the back seat.

When we dropped off Bunchy and the other fellow, Bunchy leaned forward and kissed me on the cheek. "Take good care of 'Papa,' Sister," he said with a smile.

We drove to my house to get the poem. I introduced Eldridge to my mother. When he realized that my mother lived with me, he asked if I would like to go somewhere else with him. He read the poem over almost ten times before we left, and praised it and me profusely.

After a bit of debate, we ended up at a motel. He smoked some marijuana and forcefully made love to me. Looking directly into his gray catlike eyes, I listened to him for hours, talking about revolution, about Huey Newton and his "redlight trial," about the struggle of black people. We lay awake next to each other till sunrise.

He drove me home in the early light. He had to get back to Oakland by that afternoon, he said. He would call me, he swore, not knowing that within a week that would be impossible.

On April 3, 1968, there was a massive earthquake in Los Angeles.

On April 4, Dr. Martin Luther King, Jr., was assassinated in Memphis, Tennessee, triggering the most massive uprising of black people in the history of America, in over one hundred cities throughout the country, wherever black people were concentrated, including in Los Angeles. Nonviolence was dead.

National Guardsmen all over the United States were still trying to put down the wrath of black people over King's assassination when seventeen-year-old Panther Bobby Hutton was killed in a ferocious shoot-out with Oakland police, on April 6.

In the same battle, the police shot and wounded Eldridge. A thousand charges were brought against him, any one of which could and did mean a parole violation. By the next day, Eldridge was back in a California state prison, at Vacaville. The following week, I received a letter he wrote me from there.

Sometime before the end of April 1968, I knocked on the office door in the Black Congress building that had been set aside for its newest member organization. A pretty woman named Ericka Huggins, whom I had noticed at the Huey Newton birthday rally, was inside. She spoke in a gentle manner as she wrote down my name and address and asked me a few questions about my life. Eventually, she told me what time to show up for the next membership meeting of the Southern California chapter of the Black Panther Party.

CHAPTER 7

LIVING FOR
THE PEOPLE

WHEN I FIRST ENCOUNTERED CAPTAIN JOHN HUGGINS, his clothes looked as if every piece had been stolen from a rummage sale. He had on a worn dark-green jacket, a pair of brown-and-tan-check pants, a nondescript "golf" shirt, and brown brogues with laces. This miscellany seemed to be holding up his slight body, not much taller than my five feet six inches. His hair was an African mane, reminiscent of Frederick Douglass. Under his disheveled exterior, however, was some kind of genteel breeding. There was no way I could have suspected he really was a Black Panther, much less a Black Panther "captain." He was surely no Panther, I thought when he approached me. Perhaps he was a black variation of a hippie, lost in the ghetto.

"Could I get the Sister's number," he said without introduction. We were in the main office of the Black Congress building.

I had been about to make my next call to Sandra Scott. I was supposed to call her every half hour, to get a report on the Brother's condition. I was to relay that report to Bunchy, who was trying to get medical help.

Somehow Sandra and I had been recruited on the spot earlier that evening to provide assistance. We were recruited because we were safe, I supposed. We were women who were not known as Panthers, who were not actually Panthers but who were certainly sympathetic. Moreover, Sandra had a car of her own, and she lived alone.

It was the night after the Oakland shoot-out in which Bobby Hutton had been killed and Eldridge wounded, three days after the King assassination. Black communities all over the United States were still burning in the wake of King's death.

It seemed that the entire black community of Los Angeles was in the Black Congress building that night. Black organizers were on telephones, in meetings, assessing news reports of street violence, holding spontaneous discussions. Everyone was making an effort either to maintain calm in the community or to direct the madness. It was hard to believe John Huggins was connected to any of it.

"What?" I finally responded to his question, with one eyebrow raised. I immediately hung up the telephone receiver. We were standing almost nose-to-nose.

"We've found a doctor for the Brother," he continued as though I ought to have been listening. "I need to arrange to move him."

"I don't know what you're talking about. Anyway, who are you?" I said, fixed guardedly in front of the telephone.

"Bunchy told me to find you and get the Sister's number."

"Sure," I said sarcastically.

I refused to communicate with him any longer, or to relinquish use of the telephone. I refused to dial Sandra's number in front of him. Finally, after a long moment of mutual glaring, he left.

"Killer" Wells had been severely wounded in the Oakland incident. I had seen him a few hours before, at Sandra's. He had miraculously escaped to Los Angeles. A doctor was being sought to treat Wells's police-inflicted gunshot wound, which had become gangrenous—a doctor who would not report it to the police.

Though his hip was horribly infected, Warren "Killer" Wells was toughing it out. He had driven himself to L.A., and shown even more bravado by passing the time waiting for medical care with dramatic vignettes about the engagement.

"Yeah, we spread out once the shooting started. We took our positions. They called for backup . . ."

I was certainly not going to violate my pledge to keep silent about Wells to some black hippie-looking fellow who claimed he was Captain John Huggins of the Black Panther Party. I waited a bit to make sure he was gone before starting to redial Sandra's number. He suddenly reappeared with Shermont Banks.

Banks was a known Panther. He strode into the room and immediately told me to give them Sandra's number so they could arrange to move Wells. Banks was a big fellow whose officious

manner forced one to dislike him instantly. I surely did. He had
the characteristics of a petty functionary, the type who moves up
a chain of command by luck and snitching. He was "Captain"
Banks, however, so I conceded the point. Out of the corner of my
eye, I watched John Huggins chuckle.

Now, two weeks later, John Huggins was standing before me
and the other Panther recruits, giving us our first orders. I smiled
at him from my chair in the front row. He smiled back without
missing a beat.

As members of the Black Panther Party, he was saying, we
would have to attend political education classes regularly and read
certain books. There was a long list of intraparty disciplinary rules
to be memorized and followed to the letter, including rules of
obedience and the prohibition of lying, theft, and drug use. Violations carried severe penalties or expulsion. We would eventually have to learn to use firearms, and also emergency medical
techniques. We had to learn, and know, verbatim, the Black
Panther Party ten-point platform and program.

The party's platform and program was a declaration and an
outline for black empowerment. It demanded restitution for slavery, food, education, decent housing and land for black people.
It demanded that the constitutional guarantees relating to "justice
for all" be enforced for blacks; the exemption of blacks from the
military service; the release of all black prisoners and the granting
of new trials by juries of their peers. Finally, the platform stated
that blacks in America had the right of self-determination and
called for a UN-supervised plebiscite to establish this claim.

The significance of the party platform lay in the fact that it
was underwritten by the gun, and by the goal of revolution as a
final step to power.

John explained that the party considered itself the vanguard
of that revolution, as emblematized by the beret worn by modern
revolutionists and the black leather jacket that typified the rebellious spirit in the urban ghettoes. The party was also a link in the
chain of the long and bloody history of black people struggling
for freedom.

The original name of the party, the Black Panther Party for
Self-Defense, was more than descriptive of our program. It was
an adaptation of the name of the organization that had preceded
us, the Louisiana-based Deacons for Defense. The Deacons for
Defense had been the only civil-rights group that was openly

armed and defended blacks in Klan country from being maimed or murdered for trying to exercise their constitutional rights. The black panther was the mark of the Lowndes County (Alabama) Freedom Organization. That organization had encouraged blacks to vote in their own interest by making a mark for freedom where the black panther leaped off the ballot.

Before he finished, John explained the structure of the organization to us. There was a Central Committee which governed the party. The Central Committee was guided by the Politburo, which made all policy decisions. Huey P. Newton was the leading member of the party as the minister of defense. Second in command was the chairman, Bobby Seale. Eldridge Cleaver was the minister of information. David Hilliard was the chief of staff, who administered the party on a day-to-day basis—especially now, when the minister of defense was imprisoned.

The party's chapters were organized by state, except in California, where there was a chapter for Northern California and the one we were members of, the Southern California chapter. Within a chapter were branches, organized by city, and within the branches were sections. These were divided into subsections, which were divided into squads. Ideas and information flowed up and down the chain of command. Orders went from the top to the bottom. It was a paramilitary structure.

After John spoke, we broke into small groups according to gender. Ericka Huggins, who was John's wife and captain of the women, talked first to the relatively few women who were new recruits.

Ericka told us we were now in the vanguard of revolution. Our job was to encourage the revolution that would bring true freedom to black people. The goal of the revolution was to overthrow the racist U.S. government and to institute socialism in the United States of America.

Our primary job was to organize the people to work for that goal—black people in particular, but also all the other oppressed people in the United States, including the *lumpen proletariat*. She was making that clear, she explained, because the party disagreed on that point with the analysis of Karl Marx. Marx, she said, deemed the *lumpen* the scum of the earth: they had no relationship to industrial production and could have no relevancy to socialist revolution. They could even be counterrevolutionary. Since the Black Panther Party fundamentally followed principles promulgated by Marx—whose writings were mandatory reading—that digression from a strict Marxist analysis was important to appreciate, she said.

These were new terms, new ideas to me. Though Jay had introduced me to the language, it had been an abstraction. Now the words were real. Revolution was becoming real. Like the other twenty or so women, I sat openmouthed, trying to comprehend the kind of commitment I had made.

A significant percentage of black people fell into the *lumpen proletariat* class, Ericka continued: the underemployed, the unemployed, and the unemployable. Moreover, a significant part of the membership of the party came from that class. Indeed, the party reached out to the black *lumpen proletariat* because the party held that it was the most motivated sector in America to lead the revolution.

The black *lumpen proletariat*, unlike Marx's working class, had absolutely no stake in industrial America. They existed at the bottom level of society in America, outside the capitalist system that was the basis for the oppression of black people. They were the millions of black domestics and porters, nurses' aides and maintenance men, laundresses and cooks, sharecroppers, unpropertied ghetto dwellers, welfare mothers, and street hustlers. At their lowest level, at the core, they were the gang members and the gangsters, the pimps and the prostitutes, the drug users and dealers, the common thieves and murderers.

The recent riots—and those in the early decades of the century—had demonstrated not only their rage but their readiness. Carried out by the hard core, those rebellions, from Harlem to Watts, had been endorsed by the entire black underclass, shouting "Hallelujah." The party intended to educate and politicize that mass of energy, creating vanguard soldiers from the hard core and a mass of black people ready for revolution.

Revolution was not beautiful, Ericka said. It was guns and bloodshed. It meant sacrificing everything, for, as the Russian revolutionary Mikhail Bakunin had written, "The revolutionist is a doomed man."

As women, our role was not very different from that of the men, except in certain particulars. Ericka told us point-blank that as women we might have to have a sexual encounter with "the enemy" at night and slit his throat in the morning—at which we all groaned. She reminded us of the Vietnamese guerrilla women, who were not only carrying guns but using their very bodies against the American forces. She reminded us of the courage of the other women fighting against oppression, those who had fought in Cuba, those still fighting in Angola and Mozambique. Our gender was but another weapon, another tool of the revolution. We also had the task of producing children, progeny of revolution who would carry the flame when we fell, knowing that generations after us would prevail.

No matter how impossible our objective, she went on in the softest manner, the revolution would be won. There was substance to the Panther slogan we would memorize: "The spirit of the People is greater than the Man's technology." The will to be free had proven itself stronger than the overwhelming machinery of oppressors. Proof of this was in the struggle for independence of the Vietnamese against the U.S. imperialists: knocking down B-52 bombers with ancient weapons, devastating American will and technological superiority in the recent Tet Offensive. They would win. And we would win. We had to have faith. Faith would give us the courage to live for the people and to die for the people, she said. We were all silent for a very long time.

During the ensuing weeks, I watched the ranks swell. At each Wednesday-night meeting, there would be fifty to a hundred new recruits. The party was popular, especially among gang members and young girls who lived on the streets. It was admirable and "tough," they felt, to be a Panther. There was the uniform: black leather jackets and berets. There were the guns. There was the manhood and the respect to be claimed. There was the heroic image of the leadership.

Most of those who came were men. Many did not return. They were driven away by the discipline and the reading. There were, however, those like me who signed on for the duration.

"Wherever death may surprise us, it will be welcome." These words of Che Guevara leaped off the page when I read them in the early Panther political education classes. We were given a *Red Book* to read, a collection of Mao Zedong's philosophical treatises and statements on revolution and revolutionaries. We were ordered to study his writings, to be prepared to recite portions of them on command, and to distribute his books to the masses. We were also to sell Black Panther newspapers every day, and to follow any other instructions given us by our squad leaders. We were on twenty-four-hour call. There were no part-time revolutionaries. We were full-time revolutionaries, full-time Panthers.

Early on, Ericka assigned me to ride from time to time with a young Brother named Tommy Lewis. On one occasion, he and two other Brothers had to transport a cache of weapons. The police were less likely to stop a car traveling in broad daylight, especially one with a woman in it, particularly a "bourgeois-looking Sister like yourself," Ericka said. I resented that label, as did Angela Davis, who had also begun working in the party. It was an unacceptable characterization of my life; it separated me from the other Panthers, the *lumpen*. I was not a member of the petit bourgeoisie, I wanted to say to Ericka. Despite appearances, I was from the same hard streets as most of the others, the hard streets of North Philadelphia. I was a genuine child of the black working class. It would not have mattered to Ericka. She knew all of that. She was not making a personal observation; she was carrying out a job.

The weapons Tommy and the others placed in the car were wrapped in baby blankets. There were shotguns and a few rifles. They were to be transported to Ericka and John's one-room apartment in a poor black section of town. Tommy Lewis, who was sixteen or seventeen, an abandoned boy who was becoming a man under their tutelage, lived with them.

The place smelled old and dusty. Greasy food odors from the hallways seeped under the door and defied the cleaning that had apparently been done. The apartment's main piece of furniture was a huge, high bed that overwhelmed the other odds and ends. There was joy there, though, the joy that comes with a sense of commitment to an ideal. In that, it seemed a beautiful place to me.

Ericka was taller than John and fashion-model-slim. She had ringlets of close-cropped hair and full lips. She was brown and quite pretty, without pretension. She and John had met at Lincoln University, the place for which, I remembered, Frank Constant had left me in my teen years, and where Kwame Nkrumah had gone to school with Aunt Frances's husband. Lincoln had been an all-male black college until the year Ericka and about eight other black women integrated it. John arrived the same year, having been discharged, not quite dishonorably, from the Navy after serving in the Vietnam War. That year they met, fell in love, and pledged their lives to the freedom of black people.

Once we arrived at Ericka and John's place with the weapons, Tommy took John aside. The others left. Tommy wanted John to test him on his political reading. That was really quite impossible, since Tommy could not read at all, Ericka whispered to me. Tommy pretended to read, though. He would have someone read the political education assignments to him and then memorize whole passages of text. Later, he would hold a book to his face and recite its words from memory. Quite a few people knew this, but nobody acknowledged it openly.

Tommy was explaining to John the meaning of something Mao had written. He was standing and speaking in the same style as his idol, Bunchy Carter. Bunchy was, in fact, the model for most of the Brothers on the ghetto streets of Los Angeles. They knew his swagger, his speaking style, his poems. Virtually illiterate Brothers could recite the poems of Bunchy Carter. I was thinking about that as I looked at little Tommy, astounded by his commitment to freedom and revolution when only a short time ago he had been a gun-toting member of the Baby Slausons. At about that moment, the second most dangerous man in L.A. opened the door.

"Captain Franco!" Ericka exclaimed happily.

She had told me about Franco. Everybody talked about him. Frank Diggs, Captain Franco, was reputedly leader of the Panther underground. He had spent twelve years in Sing Sing Prison in New York on robbery and murder charges. Now he was Bunchy's right hand.

He was older than most Panthers. I was, at twenty-five, the same age as Bunchy, and we were older than most of the rank and file. Franco, however, was thirty-five or so. His looks belied his age; he had flawless skin and the face of a boy. His clothing was impeccably neat and clean.

Franco was slightly insane, Ericka had told me. Prison had done it. He thought he had been fed peas in prison that contained small microphones, which, remaining in his body, allowed guards and police to monitor his life. That was why, even now, he lived so carefully, outright paranoid about everything, especially dirt. He showered at least twice a day and never wore any item of clothing more than once without it being cleaned or washed. He polished his shoes daily, tops *and* bottoms. The result was spectacular.

Franco spoke with a strange pitch to his voice, sounding oddly like the old actor Peter Lorre. "How're you doin', Sister Ericka," he said, carefully placing what appeared to be a piccolo or flute case he had brought with him on John and Ericka's bed.

John and Tommy stopped talking and looked curiously at Franco's black instrument case. Ericka introduced me to Franco. He lifted my hand to his mouth and kissed it. He spoke formally, telling me it was a pleasure to meet me. John gave me an impish grin.

"Captain John," Franco said, "take a look at this."

He opened the case. We gathered around the bed to look. Sitting neatly in the deep blue velvet lining of the case were lots and lots of bullets.

"This is what we need for the pig," Franco said. He lifted a cloth from a pocket of the case. We moved closer.

He picked up one of the highly glossed bullets with the cloth. "First of all, John, you should make sure your people always polish their bullets. It will help prevent jams."

Nobody responded.

"But these bullets are special," Franco continued. "I filled each cartridge myself with a mixture of gunpowder and garlic paste. You know why, John? Want to know why?" Franco said anxiously, like a child with a secret.

John nodded his head.

"Because garlic combined with the elements of gunpowder creates a deadly lead poison. If you hit a pig with one of these bullets, he's dead—even if you hit him in the toe. He'll die of lead poisoning. His blood will carry the poison throughout his body within a half hour. No doctor will be able to save his ass. They won't even realize what's happening. If they ever do, it'll be too late."

Everybody's breathing was audibly heavy.

Suddenly, Franco looked at me. "You know, Sister, you're so beautiful, I'd like you to ride with me tonight. Would you like to do that?"

"Franco, she's got other work to do," Ericka said before I could respond.

"All right, then, some other night," he said, tenderly brushing my cheek with his hand. "When you ride with me, I'll take out two pigs just for you. Would you like me to do that for you?"

"Stop scaring her, Franco," Ericka said with a careful smile.

"You don't have to be afraid, Sister Elaine. I would make it so beautiful for you. Other than making love to a Sister, downing a pig is the greatest feeling in the world. Have you ever seen a pig shot with a .45 automatic, Sister Elaine?"

"Ah n-no," I stammered, trying to imagine there was another answer to his very serious question.

"Well, it's a magnificent sight. Why, if a pig were standing right over there," he said, pointing across the room, "and I were to take my .45 and shoot him, his body would hit that wall hard, at about a thirty-degree angle, bounce off it, and fall forward, just about where you're standing."

"That's enough stories, Franco," Ericka said.

"It's not a story, Sister Ericka, it's revolution. This is what we're dealing with. You know that."

"Right on, Franco," John said in his deep baritone voice, which did not fit his slight physique.

In time, I began to see the dark reality of the revolution according to Franco, the revolution that was not some mystical battle of glory in some distant land of time. At the deepest level, there was blood, nothing but blood, unsanitized by political polemic. That was where Franco worked, in the vanguard of the vanguard, the underground.

Bunchy had created that workforce out of the bottom level of the lumpen, men he had recruited, as he put it, "from under the rock." They were a collage of his former Slauson partners, associates from prison, men from other L.A. gangs. Working side by side, they were armed with Bunchy's politics combined with a history of violence and a street code of silence and loyalty. All of them were loyal to Bunchy. Franco was their captain.

Bunchy had given most of them, like Franco, *noms de guerre*. In old street style, he had assigned new names to men who would be new men. There was "Pretty Pennywell." I had seen him a few times strolling through a Panther house, outfitted in a flashy suit that was a holdover from his pimping days. He would enter or leave with a smile and a rhyme:

The fellas say I'm hell,
The women think I'm swell,
But everybody knows
I'm the pretty, pretty Pennywell.

There was "Blue," whom I met when I was assigned to take a medical kit to an apartment on a little street on the edge of

Watts. It was for a girl, a teenager who was part of Blue's squad. She had shot herself accidentally. The underground had to repair its own wounds, I learned.

There was also "Bug" and "Wolf" and "Bird" from the Slausons. There was "Bright Eyes," who became "Masai." There were those with unembellished names, like Fred and Paul and Danny and Kenny. Few people knew their real names or their complete names, and none of us knew where they lived. Everybody aboveground had heard of them. Only Bunchy knew all of them. They were his Southern California Panther underground, whom he referred to as his "wolves."

Other than Franco, though, and Wilbur Terry, I did not recognize any of the faces that Wednesday night. About twenty-five of them burst into our general membership meeting.

Just before the meeting, most of us had been laughing about the words that had been scrawled across Ron Karenga's picture, which hung on the door of the US Organization office. The Black Congress had rented our chapter its first and only office, the one available being next door to that of the US Organization. That juxtaposition had stirred up basic conflicts between the two groups.

The most fundamental problem was that Karenga resented Bunchy's organizing a Black Panther chapter in Los Angeles, which had, if nothing else, damaged Karenga's reputation as the most militant black in the area. Moreover, Karenga's philosophy was in certain conflict with that of the party. Karenga promoted the idea that the development of an African-based culture among blacks would unite blacks and lead to black liberation. This represented what was generally referred to as a "cultural nationalist" philosophy. The main feature of Karenga's particular program was the denigration of all things white, or not black. The Black Panther Party held that the freedom of black people was tied to armed socialist revolution, which incorporated, by definition, the liberation of all oppressed people, including poor and working-class whites. As a result, the party had allied itself with white organizations such as the new Peace and Freedom Party.

These differences had fostered petty, day-to-day conflicts. Karenga's people taunted party members for not being "black," mostly in reference to our wearing European-style clothing, having members who did not sport "naturals," using our "slave names," and associating with Whitey. The party members laughed at Karenga's followers' bald heads and pseudo-African garb, mocked their empty militancy, and mimicked their mangled Swahili, castigating it even as a bastard African tongue—bearing on the language's Arabic roots and utilization by Portuguese and other slave traders as a lingua franca. The writing all over Karenga's photograph was the proverbial last straw.

No one knew who wrote MAMA LLAMA IS A PUNK across Karenga's face, but everybody assumed it was somebody in the party. It was a clever little play on words that questioned Karenga's manhood. We had loved it and laughed about it until Bunchy's "wolves" surprised us that Wednesday night.

We were sitting, listening to Shermont Banks, who had been elevated to the position of deputy chairman. He was telling us about the need to raise the amount of newspaper sales.

"Sit down, Banks. Now!" Bunchy's voice boomed from behind us as he and his wolves came through the door.

Bunchy walked down the gender-divided aisle looking from side to side at each row. There was fire in his eyes. Except for the fact that he was wearing house slippers, he was, as usual, sharply dressed.

Franco positioned the others, whose names and faces we did not know. Franco held a Thompson submachine gun, as did a couple of the others. Banks sat down immediately in one of the chairs in the front, next to John, and waited for Bunchy to speak.

"I want to know right now," Bunchy said, standing before all of us, "who is the backward lowlife, the ignorant, simpleminded reprobate who defaced Karenga's picture! If any of you niggers is the one who did it, or knows who did it, and does not step forward now, when we find you, you will be dealt with. Do you understand me, niggers?!"

"Right on," we said sullenly.

"I got *wolves*, niggers!" Bunchy shouted, making sure we knew who the Brothers were who had come with him.

Nobody said a word.

"I got wolves, niggers. Brothers foaming at the mouth begging me to kill something. I always have to hold them back. I have to tell them, 'No, *don't* kill that nigger.' I have to keep them locked up. *Do not*, niggers, do not let me unleash the wolves."

"Right on," we whispered.

"Now I want to know who caused Karenga's bald heads to come to my house armed to the teeth! To my house, where my woman lives! Who caused them to surround my house and call

me out! Had the gall to threaten to off me. Why?! Because some
silly motherfucker, probably in this room, wrote on that fool's
picture! Do you niggers understand?!"

"Right on, Bunchy," we said reverently.

"No. You do not understand. So I'm going to make you understand . . ."

He began to walk up and down the aisle, talking to us and
looking for clues in our faces, in our eyes. I was terrified he would
know—like teachers and parents always know—that I had been
one who had laughed about it. I was very thankful I had no clue
about who might have done it. He was preaching, like the former
Muslim minister that he was, telling us the mythical story of the
mad scientist Yacuub, who had "erroneously" saved white people.
He was explaining that we could not, by nature, be enemies of
black people.

"Whatever Karenga is about, he's *not* our enemy. The black
man is *not* our enemy. Do you niggers understand that?"

"Right on, Bunchy," we mumbled.

"What, niggers?! Tes-ti-fy, niggers! I said, we do *not* stand
against our own. Do we, niggers?!"

"No, Bunchy!"

"And white *people* are not our enemy, even though the color
of our enemy is white. Can you niggers comprehend that?! Testify,
niggers!"

"Right on, Bunchy," we said again.

"If you niggers are confused, try to remember that the black
man is *never* our enemy."

"Right on," we said again and again that evening as Bunchy
walked the floor, preached, and drove the point home. We pledged
never to publicly denounce or antagonize another black person
or organization.

"If we have a conflict with a black organization," he concluded, "we will settle our differences *nonantagonistically*. We will
settle differences antagonistically only with our enemy, who cannot
be black."

He then issued, as the head of the Southern California chapter, as the deputy minister of defense, Executive Order No. 1. It
was to be typed and distributed to all members and recruits of the
chapter: No member of the Southern California chapter of the
Black Panther Party would behave antagonistically toward another
black person or black organization. If a member violated the order,
he would face the severest discipline.

As soon as the meeting ended, I felt the terror creeping back. The old fears were climbing all over me. I began contemplating whether I was capable of being a Black Panther.

Bunchy sensed my feelings. I was plodding toward the front door when he came up behind me. He put his arm around my shoulder. "You know, we can't be sidetracked," he said. "We're dealing with volatile elements—pigs, niggers, and fools. We're trying to create a revolutionary force out of insanity, an insanity the Man created."

"I know, Bunchy," I said, scared.

"We need people who can articulate the struggle, who can come through the mud and represent us . . . Most of those niggers are soldiers, just soldiers, revolutionary infantry. They're beautiful Brothers, but they're rough. I have to do what I can to keep them in check. They don't know where it's headed, and they'll probably go down before we get to the starting line."

We were standing outside now, in front of the Black Congress building. The traffic on Broadway was loud. Over the din, he continued speaking.

"We need writers and thinkers for the struggle, as well as soldiers. Those who can wield the pen as well as the sword, like Papa," he said, referring to Eldridge by the name he had dubbed him. "And Angela, I'm hoping Angela will stay with us despite these fools, you know."

"I know, Bunchy; but I'm fine," I said, trying also to convince myself.

Suddenly, Bunchy turned away from me. He had spotted a familiar car driving along Broadway.

"Terry, Terry!" Bunchy shouted to Wilbur Terry, who had been walking with him. "There's that car! Get those motherfuckers, Terry!" Bunchy's hand rose and pointed out the car as he gave the command.

Had the car been following Bunchy, I wondered, setting aside my own confusion. I wondered if the police had an underground, too.

It was a movie. The light on the corner changed to red. The occupants of the car, seeing Bunchy point them out, swerved their car around the one in front and took off through the intersection like a bullet. Wilbur Terry's long legs propelled him through the heavy traffic. He actually caught up with the car, dove through the open passenger window, and began pounding away at the passenger's face. Others ran out of the building to watch. Bunchy sent some of his wolves after the still-rolling car. The driver was jerking the car from side to side to shake off Wilbur Terry. Terry was being flipped back and forth in the middle of traffic, but was still fighting, beating the passenger.

Finally, the car halted nearly two blocks away. Somebody drove Bunchy's yellow Mustang in a screech up to the front of the building. Bunchy kissed my cheek, jumped into the car, and was sped off toward the area where Wilbur Terry and the others had stopped the car.

The old fears consumed me over the next week. The dissociation, the separation from everything, the feeling of being disembodied began to be part of my nights. I sold Panther newspapers in the evenings with a Sister named Marsha, worked during the day, and read what I was supposed to read. Most of the time, I tried to ignore the old fears, as I tried to ignore my mother's implicit questions about what I was doing with my life.

My mother and I now occupied an apartment in a black area near Crenshaw Boulevard, in the foothills of Baldwin Hills, a little oasis for middle-class blacks. It was a decent and reasonable place—accent on reasonable. It was like our relationship, I reflected. If my mother had an opinion about my new life, she did not express it openly.

This might have been because she was afraid it would further tear the tattered dress our relationship wore, exposing its nakedness. I had no idea why, beyond the trumped-up image of motherhood, she held on to me. I had some idea why I passively nurtured the guilt I felt. I was not the kind of daughter-mate she desired, or planned. She was surely not pleased with this adventuristic turn of events, as she might have characterized it, if she had dared. Yet she did hold on.

Perhaps it was because she was afraid of something else. Acts of faith, feeling, passion were untrustworthy, not at all like money in the bank. Whatever ideals, values, or even passion she had ever held lay buried in her bitterness, between layers of defense and layers of fear. It had something to do with fear, I thought, consumed by it as I was.

Day by day, I was finding it more and more difficult to function. It was a task simply to take the bus to the crowded filth of downtown L.A. and survive the elevator ride up to the Office of

..mic Opportunity, where I worked as a clerk-typist, much less to go to the Panther offices later.

It was nearly lunchtime when the nighttime horror stole over me in the light of day. It was my monster, the thing I dreaded. I watched my fingers at the typewriter keyboard. I could not hear the sound, however, not any sound. My heart was beating, but I could not seem to draw a breath. My fingers, *those* fingers, continued to type. They were not my fingers or my hands. I tried to shake off the feeling that had made me call out for my mother in my childhood nights. It was full-blown now, though. I could not force myself back. My mother could not hold me until it went away. It would not go away.

I leaped from my seat in panic and rushed into the ladies' room. I looked around for a magazine or a newspaper or something to bring myself back from that monstrous place where I did not exist. I ran out of the ladies' room into the hallway to a pay telephone. I flipped furiously through the advertisements in the yellow pages, looking for a picture or a word that would connect me to something, to feeling. A person I recognized passed by and spoke to me. My mouth could not open.

I dialed the operator for the number of a mental-health clinic. I remembered hearing Walter Bremond mention its director's name. My brain spit forth the file of his name, the name of his clinic. I was able to dial the number. I heard a foreign voice emanating from my throat ask to see someone at the clinic immediately. The directions to the clinic were recorded.

I simply walked out of the Office of Economic Opportunity. I pushed through the crowds on the street like a maniac and found my way to the bus stop. Once I boarded the bus and sat down, the stillness added terror to my panic. I could not sense myself at all, could not feel my body anymore. I held myself tight, tighter, until I could feel only the sting of my own fingers on my arms. I was now only arms and fingers. I would remain that way forever, I felt. I would go deeper and deeper into that state. I would be frozen alive, locked into a nonexistent body, eyes only, eyes seeing but not recognizing.

I managed to get off the bus at the right place. I found the mental-health clinic. I unlocked my jaw to say my name, more terrified that I would not be able to speak than concerned with showing panic. I did not want to sit down, I thanked the receptionist, through tight lips. I preferred pacing in front of the front window.

"Miss Brown," a female voice called. "Please follow me."

She looked like a schoolteacher or an office worker. She introduced herself, but I did not hear her name. Her brown face was patient, adorned with very little makeup. Her clothes were "sensible," the way one is taught to dress for business.

"Your call was urgent, Miss Brown. How do you feel right now?" she asked once we entered her office. She showed me to a chair across from hers.

"Oh, actually, I feel fine now. I don't know why I called you because I really don't have a problem at least a problem that you can resolve because what can be resolved by talking about the past other than you can learn that I hate my father and really do love my mother that sort of thing but that has nothing to do with it and even if it did what good would it be for me to tell you that I tried or at least I'm trying to be a Panther you know a member of the Black Panther Party but that's impossible but if that's impossible I don't have anything else to do in life although I thought I could write songs but I really can't because what has that got to do with anything and what has anything got to do with anything if you understand what I mean."

"All right," she said calmly. "Now, what's really wrong?"

"Oh God! I don't know!" I sobbed, tears streaming, my hands catching my head as it fell.

She got up and came over to embrace me as I sobbed and tried to tell her about what seemed like a lifetime of desperation and fear and self-hatred. She held me as hives began to break out on my arms and hands, as though a time-lapse photographic process were occurring. I tried to explain the "feeling" and what my life had been like, carrying it with me everywhere. My skin began itching and my breath was short.

After a time, she told me it was best we start fresh the next day. She wanted to give me something to help me feel calm, she said, to get me through the night.

I was afraid to take drugs, I told her, recalling the horror of my acid trip with Bruce. She was not giving me a mind-altering drug, she assured me, and it was not addictive. Thorazine would simply calm me down so I could make it to our next appointment without incident. She gave me four pills, 25 milligrams each. She told me to take one every six hours.

By the time I arrived home, my fear of a recurring episode of my madness was greater than my fear of the Thorazine. I found the courage to choke down the first pill. Within a short time my skin was tingly. My heartbeat was slowing down. I became a bit drowsy, pleasantly so. I was actually experiencing something pleasant. I dozed off on the couch next to my mother, who was watching television.

The next afternoon I found out that the woman at the clinic was a psychiatric social worker. I thought she should have been some sort of doctor. Nevertheless, she was so kind, so caring, I felt confident she could help me survive.

She gave me more Thorazine. In about a week, she had a doctor write out a renewable prescription for me. Apparently I could refill it as often as I needed to. I continued taking 100 milligrams of Thorazine per day. In another week, I started missing my daily appointments and, ultimately, stopped going. I did not stop the Thorazine.

I did not need a psychotherapist or psychiatrist or psychiatric social worker. There was nothing to discuss. I was fine now. I lived in a lovely stupor. Thinking was no longer required. Pain was a memory.

I was now working in Watts, at an outpost field operation of the Office of Economic Opportunity. I had requested a change the day I started taking Thorazine. My superiors had suggested the Watts Happening Coffee House, one of their pet projects, a euphemism for one in which they could not find anybody willing to work.

Working there was no problem to me. Getting to the Coffee House on 103rd Street was, however. It was a complex bus ride from Baldwin Hills. Because of the Thorazine, I always fell asleep on the first bus. I would wake up at the end of the line, having fallen over into the seat next to me or onto the receptive shoulder of some faceless man. Retracing my steps, I would fall asleep on the second bus. Only after riding from the end of one bus line to another would I eventually wend my way to the Office of Economic Opportunity's field project in Watts.

The Watts Happening Coffee House had been Diamond Jim's Furniture Store before the Watts uprising in August 1965. Then it had been the object of Molotov cocktails and looting. Now it was a rivulet of the Johnson Administration's new-deal wash dubbed the War on Poverty. It was supposed to be a cultural center operated by and for the black residents of Watts.

There were six people working there, including me. There were over forty on the payroll, however. Otis, the executive director of the program, whose reputation for meanness was known throughout Watts, took most of the money for himself and his unemployed cronies. Nobody from the government had the nerve to monitor Otis's program, so Otis's word was law.

I was a perfect monitor, if that was what the Office of Economic Opportunity had had in mind. I kept Otis happy, and he kept me happy. Otis had not the slightest concern that I was always late or that I sat at my desk "composing" and typing up his payroll and employee-activity reports in between my Thorazine-induced nods. I was doing the only work I had to do. Otis and his other employees were free to do their work, which was to manage life out on 103rd Street. Otis did have a desk, which was the other piece of furniture in our small office. It contained the only tool he needed for his job: his pistol.

The other thing I poured equal energy into during the day was eating. The Thorazine made me very hungry. For lunch, usually every day, I ate a double-chili-cheeseburger with French fries and a soft taco, made by Mrs. Hamilton at her stand on 103rd Street. I usually washed it all down with a grape soda and topped it off with four or five Reese's peanut butter candies. After lunch, as happened after completing my other "activity," I fell asleep at my desk.

In between creating payroll data, nodding, and eating, I simply watched the post-Watts revolution from my desk. I spent hours talking to Otis's friends, who came through the Coffee House every day. I could identify with them, and they with me. They, too, were always high. Most of them were addicted to "reds," or Seconal, the drug of choice in Watts in 1968. I did not deal with the idea of the Black Panther Party. I did not deal with the Black Panther Party.

Otis was addicted to making money. I assumed that had something to do with his sudden decision to actually have some "programming." He decided to produce cultural shows every Sunday. Not ungratifyingly, the Coffee House came alive, became true to its name despite Otis and his nonexistent employees. It became a small Mecca for black musicians and artists in the area, creative ghetto dwellers who had no other place to take their product.

Singing groups began rehearsing in the huge, two-story main room that Diamond Jim had used to display his furniture. Bands warmed up. Poets tested the new microphones and lights on the newly installed stage that had increased Otis's budget. Whatever the backdrop, a little life rhythm was miraculously being restored to the heart of Watts.

Every Sunday now there was a performance. Horace Tapscott's jazz band might play the sounds of Coltrane or Miles or
Ornette Coleman or the hard bop of Eric Dolphy. Various poets
read their original works. Assuming I could keep my head from
falling forward, I even played piano some Sundays, and sang some
of my songs.

On days other than Sunday, Otis paraded along 103rd Street
and cashed his checks, rehearsal sounds filtered into the office, a
fight was started or finished by Otis and his gun, and I tried to
keep my drugged head from banging onto the typewriter as often
as I typed on it.

He was standing over me one of those days when I lifted my head
from the Coffee House desk. I could barely make out his face. I
could detect that cherubic contradiction I had seen that had fooled
me the first time we met. It had been a couple of months since I
had seen him.

"How've you been, Elaine?" I heard John Huggins say to me.

"Oh fine, John," I responded, blinking to bring his face
into focus. "Just fine," I whispered, feeling myself lapsing into
another nod.

"What's the matter?" he asked softly. "What're you taking?"
His voice echoed in my head.

"What do you mean?" I slurred.

"All right," he said. "Anyway, I'm down here looking for an
office for our new subsection in Watts."

I did not understand.

"For the party . . . You know, that was Tommy who was killed
in the incident at Adams and Montclair last week. Little Tommy
Lewis."

"No, John," I whispered, wiping the saliva from the corner
of my mouth, "I didn't . . . I mean . . ."

I closed my eyes and tried to understand the tears under their
lids. His voice took over.

It had happened at a gas station, in the Watts that was all of
black Los Angeles. Three men had been shot and killed by the
police. It was August. It was the third anniversary of the Watts
uprising. Everybody had heard about it, talked about it. Everybody
at the Coffee House had predicted it would trigger another riot.

"They blew Steve Bartholomew's head off his shoulders and
shot Robert Lawrence in the back. Tommy 'dealt,' though. He

dealt from the car, emptying his pistol. They kicked him to death in the ambulance on the way to the hospital."

"No, Johnny . . . I didn't know." I opened my eyes and forced my head to stay erect. "I didn't know . . . Little Tommy . . . He couldn't even read."

I remembered something. Executive Mandate No. 1, issued by Huey P. Newton: No Panther was to allow a pig to violate his home or his person. It was mandated that he defend himself. Now I understood. Little Tommy had memorized it. He had been slain clinging to the word.

"Come back, Elaine."

"Can't, Johnny. Scared. Panthers. Guns." Tears and shame and Thorazine produced a welcome toxin. I tried to respond to it—to die. He called me yet again.

"Come on back, Elaine. I'll help you. We need you."

He touched my head as I slumped into a grateful nod. He disappeared.

Horace Tapscott drove me home later. It had become his habit once he realized I was riding from one end of the bus line to another.

John came back the next day. He came the following day, and the one after that, and nearly every day after that. He told me, instructed me, implored me to stop taking the Thorazine. In a while, I was able to get by on only three pills a day. John kept coming, though, bringing me a hug and some little thing—a piece of candy, a poem he had copied. He might sing a song to me, his own renditions of currently popular ones:

Oh, I've got love for my [people],
Oh, I've got love for my [people] . . .
Well, who makes me happy
When I'm feeling sad
And who makes me forget
All the trouble I've had . . .

In time, he weaned me away from the Thorazine. He coaxed me into doing something with my life, guiding me back to consciousness, back to our people, back to the question of their freedom, back to his party, Bunchy's party, their revolution which was my revolution, which was my struggle, which was my freedom.

I ignored Shermont Banks's accusatory grimaces over my absence. I wrote and typed things furiously for the party; sold more Panther newspapers than nearly anybody, including Marsha, who was among the best; studied every revolutionary book and pamphlet I could lay my hands on. Soon I learned to shoot a pistol and an automatic rifle, out in the Mojave Desert. Soon I moved into "Camelot."

It was only a house. It was only in another poor black neighborhood, on Century Boulevard near the Hollywood racetrack, which was not in Hollywood. It was the new house of John and Ericka and their love.

Weeks before I moved in, John and Bunchy and Elmer Pratt (a recent veteran of Vietnam whom Bunchy had renamed Geronimo) and I had registered as students in a special program at UCLA. Ironically, that program had been put together by Beverlee Bruce, who, having gotten her master's degree, was moving up. She had designed it and convinced the university to fund it. Its purpose was to open the university's doors to otherwise unqualified ghetto youth who had a high potential for success. Thus, it was called the High Potential Program.

It had opened a door for us. Bunchy could finally satisfy his parole conditions. John could expand the party's reach by organizing students. Geronimo was to accompany Bunchy as his bodyguard; I was to work with John and take care of the superficialities of class assignments for everybody. Under the circumstances, I stopped working and moved into John and Ericka's house, leaving my mother.

The hippies might have called us a collective. We lived communally on Century Boulevard in a place shared principally by Ericka and John and Janice and Long John and me; but it was where the central nervous system of our chapter lived most of the time. It was where Bunchy was most of the time—typically keeping everybody up through the night—and therefore, it was where Blue and Geronimo and Franco, or Fred and Paul, were most of the time. It was for me a Camelot house, where ideals could be nourished into reality.

The house was actually an apartment, a two-story, wood-framed fixture that sat one story off the ground. The bottom floor was a garage, which was now becoming a library and office area. That was where I slept, on a mattress on the floor—a few nights with a hatchet John gave me, with a chuckle, to ward off the obnoxious advances of Long John, a definite blight in Camelot. Bunchy would ride through around midnight to offer his future plan, to discuss the black economy or culture, to talk about rev-

olution. He would tell funny stories and drink the "bitter motherfucker," Gallo port wine and lemon juice, and eat a "hot-link"
sausage sandwich garnished with hot sauce and hot peppers.

Every morning, John and I left early for UCLA. John would
have smoked his morning joint in the bathroom before joining
me to go outside to hitch a ride. While John hid behind a clump
of bushes, I would do my Claudette Colbert imitation to get a
driver to stop. As soon as a car pulled over and a door was opened,
John would pop out from his hiding place. A disgruntled man
would drive us the distance, or nearly, to UCLA, where Bunchy
and Geronimo usually joined us in the afternoon.

In the late afternoons, we sold newspapers. Evenings, we
attended political education classes at our building on Central
Avenue. The chapter had finally obtained its own building, a two-
story thing held up mostly by the other buildings on the block
that gave us the relief of independence from the structure of the
Black Congress and from trifling with US Organization members.
In the late evenings, we returned to Century Boulevard to eat,
clean guns, work on the library we were building, or listen to
Bunchy.

Some nights John and I did not go back to Camelot. I had
obtained a room in a UCLA dormitory, Weyburn Hall. A limited
number of rooms had been made available to High Potential students, with the presumption of maximizing the success ratio by
minimizing the distance between Westwood and the outlands
where the blacks lived. We used it as a way station.

Driving with all that gasoline the short distance from the UCLA
dormitory was scary. Making the Molotov cocktails had been easy.
It was my first "mission." John had gone over everything thoroughly: the political significance of our action, the details of our
plan. We were ready. We wore black clothing and gloves. When
we arrived at the designated empty building, we simply lit the
gasoline-filled bottles and tossed them through the windows. We
ran back to the car and watched the miniexplosions as we drove
away.

The other two people with us, a man and a woman I had
never met, were to take the car. John and I would stay at the
dormitory, where we had been seen earlier. We jumped out of
the car quickly and quietly climbed the fourteen flights of stairs
to the room. We would not need to make our way to the campus

in the morning, we laughed. We climbed into the small bed together and made love, willingly, not urgently, as though we had done it before, without guilt or explanation. It was all one, I thought, pieces joined by the whole. There was the beauty and the ugliness, the love and the violence, and the surrender of lives.

Some nights at Camelot, we sang songs together, John singing bass to my contralto and Bunchy's falsetto. We might have a spontaneous party and allow ourselves a dance or two. We talked a lot to Ericka's stomach, which was fat with a baby. Sometimes we ate the food I tried to cook. Every other minute we worked and talked. There was one theme: the revolution, our revolution. We accepted Mao Zedong's summation of our destiny.

Death comes to everyone, but it varies in its significance.
To die for the reactionaries is lighter than a feather.
To die for the people is heavier than Mount Tai.

The Christmas holiday period came and went. We paid no attention. It was contradictory to our work, another opiate of the reactionaries.

On New Year's Eve, we held our first formal coalition meeting with the Brown Berets. Mexicans, or Chicanos, had joined with other Latinos to form the group. Patterning their program after ours, they wore brown berets, à la the Panther black beret, to represent the unity of our common revolutionary commitment. Black Panthers and Brown Berets welcomed in the new year: 1969.

Later, in the early hours of that new year, Bunchy gathered together a number of us at Camelot. He made a simple announcement: Franco had been killed.

He had been shot in the head three times in an alley in Long Beach. It had happened earlier that evening.

CHAPTER 8

JANUARY 17th

OUR TEARS FOR FRANCO had to be deferred. FBI Director J. Edgar Hoover announced to America that 1969 would be the last year of the Panther.

In the latter days of 1968, Hoover had proclaimed: "The Black Panther Party is the single greatest threat to the internal security of the United States." Hoover's insidious lifelong crusade to crush the "Comm-uh-nis" threat to the "American way of life" had exploded into a declaration of war. Hoover would show Americans the ultimate price to be paid for dissidence by bringing down on the Black Panthers the full force of the FBI and its subservient institutions. The potency of the Panther "Comm-uh-nis" threat lay not so much in the puny Panther guns, Hoover had warned America, as in the "butter" the Panthers were spreading over the minds of the ignorant black masses, Panther propaganda promoted as social programs for the poor.

Hoover had, in a manner of speaking, hit the nail on the head. The more the party sharpened the contradictions between haves and the have-nots, between the powerful and the powerless, the oppressor and the oppressed, the more the people would seek to resolve them. That, and the desire to temporarily alleviate the pain of poverty, was precisely the purpose of the party's Free Breakfast for Children program.

The Free Breakfast for Children programs had begun thriving in the San Francisco Bay Area not long before Hoover made his declaration. Breakfasts had initially been served in Sacred Heart Church. An Irish Catholic priest, Father Eugene Boyle, had been the first to open his doors to the party's new breakfast program, providing a place big enough to feed the children of San Francisco's Fillmore district. Soon after, Father Earl Neil, a black Episcopalian, had opened the doors of his church in Oakland. Thereafter, breakfast programs began springing up everywhere in Northern California. There was no such program in L.A., however, at the start of the new year.

Although we had served free dinners from time to time in the L.A. black community, we had found it virtually impossible to feed hungry black people with any regularity, much less to institute a breakfast program. We had no access to a proper facility, and nearly all the money and energy we could have mustered for a breakfast program were being depleted by our daily efforts to simply keep our people on the street.

Ever-increasing police arrests of our members kept us running from jail to jail, getting medical treatment for Panthers beaten when arrested, paying excessive fees to retrieve our few cars from police impoundment, financing high bails. Indeed, police assaults on Panthers in L.A. were becoming more intense than in any other chapter of the party—from the national headquarters to all the others springing up in city after city. We expected the onslaught; we were not prepared for the intensity.

There was so much food at UCLA's Weyburn Hall that the steam tables were never depleted. John and I had decided there ought to be a way to obtain the excess food that was being dumped into UCLA's garbage bins every night. We had decided, during the holiday break, that when we returned to UCLA in January, we would approach the dormitory officials. It would be a small act of charity, we would say, for UCLA to dump the leftover food on the party, to feed some children who needed it.

January 17 was the first day I could arrange to meet with the head of Weyburn Hall's food services. We had been very busy since classes had resumed a few weeks before. Much had occurred in those weeks.

The campus had become radically different, at least in terms of the black students. They had grown up overnight, it seemed. They had been forced to come together as black people, after having languished in a middle-class myopia the semester before.

We too, it seemed, had grown up overnight. Franco had been buried. Ericka and John's baby girl had been born. Shermont Banks had been expelled, and John was now chairman of the chapter. The chapter had opened another new section office, on the west side of L.A., where middle-class, white-collar blacks had rooted themselves. We had also opened several new branches, in San Diego, Santa Ana, and Pasadena.

Marsha's golden Afro curls were bouncing in the early sunlight of January 17 as we started out for UCLA. She, too, was bouncing, in her continuing effort to define herself as "blacker than black." At one time many had even believed that Marsha was white. She defied the effect of her very fair complexion by always speaking in loud street parlance and carrying herself with a kind of "ghetto attitude."

We were standing on Century Boulevard trying to hitch a ride. First, we had to make recorded announcements about the opening of our west side office at a radio station in Hollywood. After that, we would meet with the Weyburn Hall people. Later, I was to see a lawyer about setting up a stable legal defense program for the chapter, in light of the frequency of our arrests. Before seeing the lawyer, Marsha and I were to attend an important black students' meeting at UCLA's Campbell Hall, an unusual building that had been set aside for the High Potential program. There we would meet John, Bunchy, and Geronimo.

Maybe Marsha was bouncing to make herself alert, I thought. We had all been up most of the night at Camelot. I had been in the basement working late at our new typewriter when Bunchy came down the stairs, followed by Cotton, one of his wolves.

"With these, with these, Elaine, we will *deal* with the pig," he announced.

I responded with a puzzled silence.

He flung open his jacket and lifted a sawed-off M-1 carbine from a shoulder holster.

"Hah! You didn't see a thing . . . This is beautiful work, Cotton. Beautiful," Bunchy said, patting the weapon.

Cotton had filed down a series of carbines for him. He was standing straight and looking at Bunchy with unadulterated pride.

"We can carry these under our coats, on the streets. On the outside we'll look very, shall we say, 'ordinary.' " He laughed. "But we'll be armed righteously."

John joined us. Geronimo soon came down with Blue. I could hear Ericka upstairs, walking with the baby. Marsha was upstairs, too, cleaning the kitchen.

Bunchy kissed the weapon, and everybody laughed. The men toasted with small bottles of Champale. Bunchy had banned the traditional Gallo wine concoction in support of the Cesar Chavez–led United Farm Workers' grape boycott.

I left the men and the guns to see Ericka and the baby. We joked about funny names for her baby, my favorite being "Huggie Girl." I teased her about taking control and giving the child a name immediately. Otherwise, I would spread the word that my first suspicions about John being a hippie had been confirmed, and that, like him, she was a closet hippie. She and John had refused to name the baby, insisting that she had the right to name herself when she was old enough.

Ericka parried with a threat to tell Bunchy about the poem I had written for him. He would love it, she assured me, giggling. I had written it almost a month before but had not found the courage to let him see it. If I did not give it to him that night, Ericka threatened, she would. She and I had reduced ourselves to giggling fools by the time we heard Bunchy's footsteps on the basement stairs. When Bunchy opened the door to the kitchen, Ericka forced me into it. I simply handed the poem to him, with a smirk to her.

He sipped his drink. " 'The Deputy,' " he said, reading the title.

"Please don't read it out loud, Bunchy."

He said nothing. Everything was very quiet. He read the poem. Then he read it again.

"Let's hear it, Bunchy," Geronimo said.

"Naw, niggers. This is too deep for you," he said, throwing his head back with a laugh.

He thanked me with a sweet kiss on my cheek. Folding the piece of paper with my poem on it into his pant pocket, he talked on for a long time.

He was still wearing those pants, I noticed, when Marsha and I finally arrived at the Black Student Union meeting at Campbell Hall. He had not taken time to change. He had had no sleep at all.

Marsha and I had made the public service announcements at the radio station. More important, we had also extracted a commitment from the director of Weyburn Hall to give us the dormitory's leftover food, along with all the dented canned goods we could handle. I was happy to be able to report to Bunchy that some kind of free-food program could now be instituted by our chapter.

"I'm sorry we're late," I whispered as Marsha and I approached the room where the Black Student Union was meeting.

"It's cool," Bunchy said matter-of-factly, leaning against a doorjamb at the entrance of the meeting room. Over two hundred black students were inside. The meeting had been under way for some time.

"John will fill you in," Bunchy said.

As usual, John was wearing a ridiculous costume. This time, a secondhand gray suit was draped over his 125-pound body, complemented by heavy black combat boots.

"What's happening?" I whispered to John as Marsha and I sat down.

"Nothing much," he whispered back, leaning toward me so that I could see his .44 magnum pistol, which was bigger than his hands. "They're trying to create a man on paper," he said somewhat cryptically.

"Is there anything you want me to do?" I asked.

"Not yet. Just listen."

Although there were only a few members of the US Organization at the meeting, Marsha and I had noted as we entered the building how Karenga's look-alike members were in force that day. Milling about Campbell Hall, they had seemed a thundercloud of clones, bald heads, dark glasses, pressed dashikis. Karenga was nowhere in sight. He rarely appeared anywhere personally, outside of the Black Congress and his own building.

The midday sun penetrated the cavernous room through its floor-to-ceiling windows. It brought warmth and character to the otherwise institutional dullness of the room. The meeting was, at best, boring and anticlimactic. I drifted into thinking about the meeting I had in the next hour with the lawyer George Slaff, from Beverly Hills. I was wondering how I was going to get to Slaff's office on time.

As I looked around the room, I also thought about how strange the meeting was, UCLA's Black Student Union having come into being only months before.

It was a time when every college student, black and white, across America seemed to be part of a campus organization. Everywhere, students were making demands on college administrations, expressing political concerns, addressing social issues, marching for causes. The black students at UCLA, however, had been reluctant to form any kind of association. If they had any desire for organized protest, it was less about the CIA recruiting office that sat conspicuously on UCLA's campus than about forcing the various dormitory cafeterias to serve "soul" food. They had not concerned themselves at all with the raging war in Vietnam, worrying more, it seemed, about whether Marvin Gaye's version of "I Heard It Through the Grapevine" would be piped into the dormitories.

John had faith, however, that the small population of black students on UCLA's sprawling campus could be educated to at least join with the SDS and other campus organizations in denouncing the war in Vietnam, and maybe in getting rid of the CIA recruiting office. He also believed they could be politicized to build a network between the campus and the community, a network to filter the intellectual resources of the students to the black community, a network that would bridge the disparities between "bourgeois" blacks and "street" blacks, a network that would forge a necessary link in the chain toward ultimately making the revolution.

The work John had proposed, which the chapter had tried to implement from the day the four of us enrolled in September, had moved very slowly. Even the poorer black students, the others in the High Potential Program, wanted to break their bonds with the ghetto. All of them wanted to avoid the issues and relax in the sunshine of Westwood. Nevertheless, John pushed us to push them. Every day, every evening, he would intone over and over: "Educate to liberate."

In those months since September, most of the black students had remained reluctant to become even peripherally involved with any of John's causes. A few students did initiate a Black Student Union, however, and somewhere in the process, a handful even joined the Black Panther Party, including Nathaniel Clark, Joe Brown, and Albert Armour.

That was the irony of that meeting, I was thinking. Only one month before, even the small Black Student Union that had been formed on UCLA's campus had become moribund. Indeed, the Black Studies Program we were now discussing had originally existed in a vacuum.

It was not the black students who had proposed the program, but rather the university in an attempt to forestall the kind of black student agitation that was on the rise on most college campuses. The program was suggested by the few blacks who peppered the ranks of UCLA's administration.

During the off-session holiday period, Ron Karenga, on information provided by one of the black architects of the proposed Black Studies Program, seized the opportunity to take advantage of the inactivity of the black students. Karenga recruited a Dr. Charles Thomas to serve as titular head of the proposed Black

Studies Program, which involved hundreds of thousands of university dollars—a High Potential Program with higher stakes. Then, just before Christmas Day, Karenga sent about fifty of his US members to the university administration offices to assert that they represented the Black Student Union, which represented the majority of black students at UCLA. They demanded that Charles Thomas be hired to direct the proposed Black Studies Program and that the program be instituted by the beginning of the next semester.

That show, coupled with the support of Karenga by Vice Chancellor Charles Young, turned the proverbial trick. As of the commencement of the Spring 1969 semester, UCLA had authorized funding for "Karenga's" Black Studies Program.

When classes resumed, though, and the black students learned about the program and Karenga's holiday machinations, they became fired up. Sure, they seemed to say in one voice, they had been passive about most issues. They were grumbling, however, that they would not stand for some self-proclaimed messiah to come to "their" campus and take over "their" program. Black student leaders suddenly evolved, reconstituting the Black Student Union. They demanded that the vice chancellor rescind his contractual pledge to the Karenga program. They demanded that Karenga come to the campus and explain himself.

But they became confused about their next step; as confused as most of the university administration became, responding with waves of rumblings that they did not want the campus to experience any disruption and would review the decision. Moreover, the students were terrified of dealing with Karenga.

That was when a few student leaders asked John and the rest of us if the Black Panther Party would support them—specifically by acting as "security" for their meeting with Karenga. Our answer was that we would not be their bodyguards, much less openly oppose another black organization—despite our attitude about Karenga. We would, however, we assured them, back up whatever decision the majority of black students made about the proposed program.

There had been a showdown of sorts on January 15—just two days before. Nearly a hundred US members had shown up, flashing their teeth and, as usual, their .45s. Unusually, Karenga himself had actually appeared, and addressed the students.

"*Maulana* means great teacher," he had begun. "I am the teacher. You are the students," he proclaimed, standing at a podium before the black students who had crammed into the Campbell Hall classroom. "The teacher must teach. The student must learn."

"Speak, Maulana!" one of the US members standing intimidatingly in the rear of the meeting room chanted on cue.

"Therefore, Brothers and Sisters," Karenga continued behind dark glasses, which emphasized his nearly white complexion, "you cannot advise me of what you want. I advise you of what you need!"

"A la la! A la la!" numerous followers chanted in simulated Swahili approval.

"US has taken the lead because you have shown yourselves too weak!"

The room froze. No one spoke for what seemed an interminable time. Finally, a freshman Brother, sitting in the back of the room, which was by then packed with about three hundred students, stood up.

"Brother Karenga," he said, pointedly not addressing Karenga as Maulana. "*We* are the students here, and we alone will determine our destinies!"

The Black Panthers in the room found each other's eyes. We smiled. His words had been lifted directly from our rhetoric, reflecting the main point of the party's platform and program.

There was sparse applause for his bold assertion. Then more students began to applaud, and more. They stomped their feet. They rose to their feet. Karenga could say no more as the students demanded that Karenga "get out!"

Having ushered Karenga and his troops out of the meeting, the students intensified their bravado. First, they voted to have a representative group immediately contact Vice Chancellor Young. They elected that small committee on the spot; it included Joan Kelley, a student sympathetic to the party, John, and me.

The ad hoc committee was to advise Young that the *real* Black Student Union had reformed and was electing a formal committee from the membership that would be the only group with which the university was to deal on the issue of a Black Studies Program. Their message warned the university that there would be massive problems on campus if anyone else tried to usurp the program or if the program was canceled. Only the black students of UCLA would determine how the already-allocated program dollars would be expended.

Their message to Young concluded with the specific command that neither Ron Karenga nor his lackey Charles Thomas, nor any other such lackey, was to be involved in any way with the Black Studies Program of UCLA.

Another meeting was scheduled for the seventeenth, so that the general body of the now-active Black Student Union could begin the process of developing a student-controlled Black Studies Program.

John was leaning over and whispering to me. His deep voice created a funny little tingle in my ear. "Move to adjourn. This is going nowhere. There're too many loose ends. I don't know how they think they can create a thing in the abstract."

I agreed it was time to adjourn, realizing that I was definitely late for my meeting with Slaff.

Then he added, whispering nearly inaudibly, "I hope they go for this, I'm starving."

"What?" I whispered back.

"I said," he enunciated each word carefully and very seriously, "I hope they go for this. I'm starv-ing."

I tossed him the kind of strained look I knew he loved to evoke with such silliness.

I moved that the meeting be adjourned and that the committee elected on the fifteenth meet and confer. It would simplify the task, I suggested, if that smaller group developed some guidelines and came back to the general body of the Black Student Union in a couple of weeks with specific recommendations. Everyone was so tired of discussing curricula and credentials, they readily agreed to my suggestion by an overwhelming vote.

"You need to watch what you say, Sister," one of Karenga's robots said to me afterward. He caught me as I was moving through the mass of students toward the hallway.

The only thing that differentiated that Karenga robot from the others, I noted, was the mustache outline he had drawn over his protruding lips with eyeliner. I could hardly feel frightened of anybody wearing a painted-on manhood. Indeed, I had an impulse to smear the thing. I was certainly not terrorized as I tried to move past him, when he grabbed me so hard the button snapped off my black leather coat.

I moved on, in a rush to get Joe Brown, who had gone to an upstairs office. John had arranged for Joe to drive me to the meeting with Slaff. Bunchy stopped me.

"What did that nigger say to you?" he asked.

"Nothing, really, Bunchy. The fool was babbling the usual US threats."

"Elaine!"

"Yes, Bunchy," I said, almost snapping to attention. When Bunchy spoke, one listened, because Bunchy was, at twenty-six, an uncanny composite of artist, "street nigger," poet, and revolutionary.

"Elaine," he repeated, head thrown back majestically, "as long as you live, don't let another nigger talk crazy to you or put his hand on you. You slap the nigger! The nigger is punk and a sissy. So you slap him. Do you understand?"

"Yes, Bunchy, I do. Right on."

I turned away then and quickly climbed the three flights of stairs of Campbell Hall, to find Joe Brown. I climbed the stairs and never heard the first shot that ripped into John's back—only ten feet away from the assassin.

I climbed the stairs and never heard the second shot that blasted into Bunchy's powerful chest.

"Joe! Come on. I'm late!" I said, hurrying Joe Brown.

Dashing down the stairs from the third floor with Joe, I heard gunshots for the first time.

What the fuck is going on? I thought.

The number-one marksman in UCLA's ROTC program, Joe started back up the stairs to retrieve his Browning 9mm, left locked in the third-floor office. He shouted to me to come with him. We quickly scurried back up the stairs.

Returning to the first-floor landing with Joe, I heard the sound of feet moving fast down the marble corridor. Fearful whisperings rose above the sound of running feet. Then gunfire again, and more gunfire. One, two shots at a time. Short bursts of fire, very loud, horrible echoes. I felt cold.

This is it.

I heard more feet running. The taste of salt came into my mouth. More shots rang out. I heard glass break, then the crash of more breakage. Students were leaping through the huge windows to escape. There were many screams now, following the report of each round of fire.

What should I do? Not the rough streets of North Philadelphia, nothing in my life, not even in the party, had prepared me to respond to so much gunfire. I felt ridiculous. Joe forced me back up to the second-floor landing, pushing me against the wall like a dress into an overstuffed suitcase, and ran off. Others were taking refuge on that landing. I could not see their faces. Joe ran back to me.

"Elaine, take this and get it out of here," he said in panic, shoving his Browning into my hand.

"John's dead!" he shouted, running down the stairs again.

"Not John!" I screamed.

Somebody tried to hold me. I knew what to do. I ran down the stairwell.

Get to John! Get an ambulance! John does not die! Get the gun out!

I saw Albert Armour and Nathaniel Clark moving quickly down the hallway on the first floor.

Where's John?

"Get out! Get out!" they were shouting.

I heard sirens. Then the old, long-ago feeling crept over my soul, that sense of lifelessness. I shook it off. I looked around and spotted Joan Kelley hovering in a corner. She had a purse. I grabbed her, put the Browning into her purse, and led her out a side door. We had to go to UCLA's Medical Center to get help for John, an ambulance. We had to get the gun out. *Find Geronimo. Call for backup—Bunchy's underground.*

"We don't have ambulance service," the hospital's emergency registration clerk said casually. I drew the Browning from Joan's purse. I aimed it at the clerk's face and cocked it. There was a round in the chamber.

"Well, *you're* going to need one, bitch!"

People in the emergency room panicked. Joan remained calm. Some of the hospital staff started getting a medical team together as I spilled out what had happened at Campbell Hall. I ran around the hospital until I found Geronimo, in the outpatient clinic. I remembered where he was: Bunchy had instructed him to stay with that hypochondriacal Janice. A lone soldier, Geronimo moved into action toward Campbell Hall. I dialed each underground number I knew. I talked to those I could reach. They were so far away from UCLA in distance and in life that I had to give them directions on how to get there. It was hopeless, absurd. Nothing would be done. But John was not dead, and somebody would pay.

Two hours passed. The police had arrived at Campbell Hall before Geronimo and had sealed off the building. He could not get in. No ambulance or medical team returned. No urgency filled the hospital rooms. A doctor finally emerged. I was so dazed I barely heard him.

"They're both dead," he said to me.

"Who's dead, motherfucker?" I demanded, consciousness shocked into comprehension, hoping he meant the stupid Karenga robot with the phony mustache was dead, hoping Joe had been wrong.

"Calm down, miss. Are you a member of either family?"

"How do I know. Who's dead?!"

He said their names formally. Bunchy and John were dead.

My mind reeled . . . What made me join this Black Panther Party? Why had Jay Kennedy let me leave the comfort and safety of his very rich and very white world? Had Joe used the Browning? Why had it been so urgent to take it out of Campbell Hall? What had happened?

The bodies of Bunchy and John were still lying in the meeting hall. They had fallen in such a way that their fingers touched. To escape, students had trampled them. When he was hit, John had emptied his gun at the assassin fruitlessly. After the first shot, Bunchy had whirled around, empty-handed, to face the assassin down, fruitlessly. The assassin, a high-ranking US member, who was positively identified as the killer by numerous black student witnesses, had escaped unscathed.

Those of us who had been able to find each other were gathered at the hospital: Geronimo, Nathaniel, Janice, Joan, and I.

"We've got to get the shit out of that house. We have to get back there to Ericka," Geronimo said, taking charge.

We returned to Camelot.

"What happened at UCLA today?" Ericka said, looking at me. Earlier, while feeding her three-week-old daughter, Ericka had seen the televised news bulletins about a shooting at UCLA.

I spat it out point-blank. "Two people were killed, Ericka."

"Was John one of them?"

I nodded. "And Bunchy," I finished.

We began organizing the guns, the ammunition, the grenades that were kept there, to haul them, along with Ericka and the baby, away. There would be war among the natives.

Ericka Huggins left the world then, it seemed. I watched her stand at the kitchen sink, her long, thin body surrendered, her eyes glazed, her artistic fingers pulling twenty-odd cups from the cupboard. Then she started to boil pots of water.

"I suppose everyone is upset. I'll make some coffee," she said insanely.

The six of us—with others now on the way—busied ourselves with cleaning out the house. We would all be underground soon.

"Cotton, take the first load away. Now!" Geronimo commanded when Cotton arrived. Cotton dragged several metal boxes and weapons wrapped in blankets down the outside stairs to the driveway. He loaded his station wagon and sped off.

"Mama, I want to bring Ericka's baby to you to take care of John and Bunchy are dead," I said into the telephone to my mother in a run-on sentence.

"Oh my God! You get out of there now!" my mother pleaded. "Oh God! All right. Maybe I can find somebody to take care of the baby, but you get out! Please, Elaine! Whatever you're after, it's not worth this. Nothing's worth this!"

She was saying nothing I wanted to hear. I slammed down the receiver.

"All you motherfuckers come out or we'll blow their heads off!"

"It's the pigs!" Janice screamed.

At least 150 uniformed and plainclothes pigs were moving around outside, getting into position. They were led by Detective Captain Lucey of the LAPD's 77th Division. I peeked out of the front window and saw the pigs crawling out of a fumigation tarpaulin that had been placed over the house across the street. It occurred to me that that tarpaulin had not been there when I left with Marsha in the morning.

The pigs had punched shotguns into Geronimo's and Nathaniel Clark's ears, and pressed their bodies flat onto the driveway cement outside. They had been caught loading up another car. Now there were footsteps in the garage-library area below. Now there was the sound of boots on the roof. The pigs repeated their demand.

"Come out now, or we'll blow their heads off!"

Ericka snatched the baby out of her crib; she had on only a diaper and an undershirt. I took off my coat to roll the baby into the warmth and safety of it. The four of us, Ericka, Joan, Janice, and I, swiftly and stealthily moved into the main bedroom, away from the front of the house. We rolled the coat with the baby in it under the bed and lay face down on the floor surrounding the bed. The four of us stayed there quietly, hoping our bodies would protect the baby, hoping the coat would muffle her little cries, hoping we would not die or, if we did, that we would be dignified.

We lay there listening. We heard Geronimo shouting: "There ain't nothing but women in there, man!" We lay there listening to 12-gauge shotgun rounds being "jacked" into police shotgun chambers. We lay there listening to our last breaths and wondering about the "other side." I heard an old hymn: "Yes, we'll gather at the river, the beautiful, beautiful river . . ." We held each other's hands and remembered our mothers. We listened to footsteps approaching the closed bedroom door. We looked at each other with sad, not fearful, eyes. We squeezed each other's hands to say goodbye.

"You motherfuckin' bitches, get up!" a pig with no face said, kicking in the door combat-style, joined by his faceless brothers and their shotguns.

We were four stones. We buried our faces in the floor so as not to hear the sound of our deaths. There was silence. Then four stones simply rose, gathering the coat from under the bed, gathering life from death. Lethargically, four stones rose and moved like one stone outside, into the chilly January setting sun.

Outside, we saw some of the underground, who had come too late. They were shouting at the pigs not to kill us.

"You're the oldest whore of the pink pussies," they said to me on the ride to the 77th Precinct, "so you must be the one with the biggest hole."

I sang: "How many roads must a man walk down . . ."

At the precinct, Joan and I were shackled together, even when they finally allowed us to use the toilet. Marsha was there, too, handcuffed and crying. Ericka had been placed in a corner alone and was breast-feeding the baby. The men were in some other part of the precinct.

The police eventually allowed one of the many Panther supporters that had gathered there to take the baby out of the precinct. Ericka had named her in the police car: Mai.

By four in the morning, after hours of so-called interrogation, we were all finally charged: conspiracy with the intent to commit murder. We were being held, we were told, to "prevent a bloody retaliation" against the US Organization for the assassinations of John and Bunchy.

More than seventy-five Panthers in the area were known to

have been rounded up and arrested. Not one US member had been arrested.

Ericka, Joan, Marsha, Janice, and the rest of us women were taken to the Sybil Brand Institute, the county's jail for women. We were booked and fingerprinted. We were put into bathtubs, sprayed for bugs, separated, and locked into seven-by-eight-foot maximum-security cells. The morning sun was almost rising.

CHAPTER 9

POSTMORTEM

THE CLANK OF THE IRON DOOR closing on me aroused the old fear. "The feeling" tried to creep inside my cell.

But John was with me. His brown skin, his softness, his love, his crown of hair, his voice, his humanity were with me. *John, my beloved John, I'm sorry it was you and not me.* I wrote him a thousand words in my head. I would not cry. I would live to fight. I would live to join him.

Then I lapsed into a dream. Bunchy was not dead. He had tricked them. He was on Century Boulevard hiding in the kitchen. In the dream I discovered him in the wall unit that encased the ironing board. He was laughing at us over his prankish pretense at being dead. He put his finger to his mouth to quiet my surprised reaction. He winked and motioned to me to close the wall unit. I promised to keep his secret.

Suddenly, a voice was speaking to me in the distance outside my dreamy reverie. Indistinct words were being said. Someone else was in the dark cell. I had heard no breathing and felt no movement. But the voice spoke again, above my head resting on the bottom bunk bed against the bars. An eerie voice was whispering above my head.

"What're you in for?" the voice lisped more distinctly.

"What?" I responded, annoyed.

She repeated her question. The daylight was beginning to filter through frosted windows high above the cell, beyond an outer set of bars. A heavy rain had begun.

"Conspiracy," I responded. "Conspiracy to commit murder. What about you?" I asked.

"For killing my two kids," she lisped sadly.

I nearly laughed. How very bizarre of the pigs, I thought.

The regimen was introduced to me by my white cellmate. When the alarm rang, we were to get up and dress in the blue, smocklike dresses that had been issued. There was no staying in bed. There was no shower, unless one had previously signed up to fill one of the ten shower slots. There was no soap, unless one had purchased it. There was no borrowing of soap or any other item.

Breakfast was at 7 A.M., announced by the clanking of cell doors automatically opening. There was to be no talking outside the cell block of approximately twenty-four women. On the way to the dining hall, there was only the soft scraping sound of rubber sandals on stone floors.

Dried out from my mandatory bath of a few hours ago, when we were processed into Sybil Brand, the skin on my wrist crackled when the guard roughly turned my plastic identification bracelet to record my number. That was how one entered the dining hall. No communication was allowed in the dining hall, verbal or otherwise. That included touching and eye contact. There were hundreds of other silent prisoners in there.

We stood in a cafeteria-style line for food, which was flipped onto a steel tray. Starchy carbohydrates were spread over the tray's three compartments. A spoon was issued. Salt shakers and steel cups were on the tables. Once seated, we were to raise the cups for coffee or water, served from stainless-steel pitchers by other inmates.

Uniformed guards were everywhere, along the walls and between the rows of long tables. They were black women and white women, in seemingly equal number. They stood with arms folded across their chests, looking down on us county jail inmates. If a woman erred, they hollered at her, pointed her out, and shouted that she show them her plastic bracelet. Before the end of breakfast, they had "written up" at least three women for communicating with other prisoners.

As we rose on cue to leave, a woman across from me took a chance and indicated to me she wanted my orange. I had eaten nothing, none of the potatoes or powdered eggs. My eyes told her it was hers. Looking up, my eyes fell upon Joan Kelley, several tables away.

Joan should not be there, I thought. She was not in the party. She was only a nineteen-year-old student from UCLA whose passion had been more for Nathaniel Clark than for Black Panthers or revolution. But she was standing strong.

You are very brave was my eye message to Joan. *Hold on, Sister.*

Joan shifted her eyes quickly to her left, indicating Ericka Huggins. Ericka and I spoke with blinking eyes.

I love you, my Sister, I felt, I sent.

We'll survive, she seemed to answer with her large eyes.

Rubber thongs shuffled back to the various cell blocks. Once we were inside our cells, we could talk, though no more than three women could gather in any cell at one time.

The black women greeted me warmly. They had heard about the Panther arrests. I talked to some of them. I ignored my cell-mate, the white woman who had killed her children and who spoke to herself in a lisp.

The black women wanted me to learn all the rules, but I had my own rules. I would ask the pigs for nothing. I had no money for or interest in the soap-and-shower routine. Nor was I interested in the candy-and-canteen routine. All I wanted was a pencil and paper to write out my words to John.

One woman handed them to me on the promise that I not tell anyone from whom I had gotten them. She seemed genuinely afraid. This was maximum-security, she warned. It was dangerous. Infraction of rules could send one to the "daddy tank." The daddy tank was solitary confinement, so called because it was reputedly run by tough lesbian guards who were like men, "daddys." They would have their way with a violator if she ever wanted to see the light of day. I told her not to worry. I had nothing to say to pigs.

Now that I had pencil and paper, I could write my letters to John. I could confess my guilt about the past and my fears about the future. I could tell him how much I loved him, again and again. I would not write to Bunchy. He was still hiding on Century Boulevard, which was not Camelot anymore.

On the next day, I was told I had a visitor. Since I did not recognize the name, I assumed it was a ploy. I refused the visit. The guard who had come to take me to the visiting area returned immediately. She said the visitor was a lawyer, referred by a name I seemed to recall, Don Freed—yes, a friend.

Jean Kidwell's manner was no-nonsense, straightforward, and kind, untypical for a white woman, I thought. She whispered reassuringly to me. She was there to help.

She had already seen Ericka and would be seeing the other women next. She told me some of the names of the many others arrested and news of related events of the last two days. The police had actually arrested two members of the US Organization in connection with the murders.

"Oh, the stupid Stiner brothers," I responded dryly. They were US underlings who were students in the High Potential Program. "What's that supposed to mean? Where's the assassin? Where's fucking Jomo? He was there.—A hundred of them were there."

"It means that everybody's supporting you. The people have the streets in such pandemonium, the police had to do something. We're all working to get you out," she continued. "We've gotten bail set. Your mother has raised six hundred dollars toward your bail."

Jean Kidwell was a member of something called the National Lawyers Guild, she told me. They were a collection of radical lawyers, some of whom had volunteered to handle the numerous Panther arrests of January 17.

Jean went on to explain the charges and how she was sure she could defeat them. I was fighting back tears. Her compassion had seeped through the barrier of my bravado.

I thought about my mother. What had she had to do, I wondered, to find six hundred dollars in so little time? I felt the constancy of her support, feeling sorry that I was who I was, feeling sorry that I had dragged her into all of this, feeling glad that I had not died and could thank her.

It was time for Jean to go. "Whatever bail money there is," I said, as she rose to leave, "get Ericka Huggins out first."

Geronimo had already made it clear to everyone, she told me, that Ericka was to be the first to get out.

She swore she would be back soon. I said nothing else to her, pushing back the touch of her genuineness.

Ericka was released on bail the next day. Within the next few days, Jean Kidwell returned. The charges against all of us had been suddenly, strangely dropped. Jean had come to take some of us women home.

Home would be a battleground. We had to regroup, find each other, pull together the pieces of our pathetic army.

"Jay, how've you been?" I said softly, for the second time in a month.

Jay Kennedy was in his Connecticut house.

"Jay, it's all horrible. Can you help? There's to be a funeral in the next few days. We need help with everything. We don't even have a place to live . . . It's all horrible."

I had confessed my love affair with Jay to Bunchy. We had been talking about poetry and things beyond our revolutionary dreams. He had made no judgmental comment, simply accepted what I had been.

How I had loved Bunchy that night of my confession. He had wished for other times for me, for all of us. He had kissed me strongly, on the lips, for the first and only time, which seemed a goodbye to our youth. He had even suggested dispelling the disparity I felt between the past and the present by involving Jay, who was clearly on our side. That was how I had come to make the first contact with Jay a month before. It had been nearly two years.

Jay had been warm and receptive when I reached him through Eileen. I had told him point-blank about my membership in the Black Panther Party. He knew, he told me. He would be happy to help. He knew someone who could alleviate our day-to-day police problems. He gave me the number of an ACLU lawyer friend of his, George Slaff, who was also, amazingly, the mayor of Beverly Hills. January 17 had been the day I was supposed to meet Slaff.

Now I urgently needed Jay again. We had to have money to rescue our chapter. Nearly everything had been lost, especially Century Boulevard. We were being erased, as J. Edgar Hoover had promised.

We would not be erased, Geronimo had insisted, assuming leadership over our chapter. We would start over, again and again, to instigate revolution in the United States of America. We would use Bunchy's very funeral to start over. We would demonstrate that Bunchy's death was "heavier than Mount Tai." We would show that even though the pigs could kill a revolutionary, they could not kill the revolution.

"Yes, dear," Jay responded after I strung together bits of the events of the past days for him. "I heard about the murders at UCLA . . . I can be in L.A. tomorrow. We can meet then, if you like," he said.

I took Janice with me to the Bel Air Hotel to see Jay. It was safer, better.

His eyes were so very blue and sad. He wanted, and I wanted him, to hold me. The tears were restrained. I should not have brought Janice, I thought, but I was glad I had brought her.

"I was there, Jay. The shots were so loud. We had all been together the night before, laughing . . . We've just gotten out of jail. We were all rounded up and arrested for conspiracy. The pigs claimed we were conspiring for revenge against the US members and their great leader, Karenga. So many of us. The US trigger man got away. Everybody knows who did it. Later, there was a token arrest of two US members. Even the black students are shocked—maybe into consciousness. We hear there was a plan to kill all Panthers on campus that day."

"Who is this Karenga?" he asked.

"Who knows? His real name is Ronald Everett. He's from Baltimore. He received a master's degree from UCLA in sociology, I think. I've been told that he had an affected British accent when he was a graduate student. Now he's very black," I told Jay. "Anyway, he started the US Organization several years ago." The organization attracted mostly middle-class blacks, students, and a sprinkling of former members of a limp west-side L.A. gang called the Gladiators." I explained to Jay that a street rivalry had existed between the Gladiators and Bunchy's former gang, the Slausons, many of whom had joined the chapter.

"But the rift between Karenga and the party stems from something else . . . Karenga postures himself as a fanatical Black Nationalist," I said. "He runs around denouncing 'Whitey' and assailing other black organizations for not being black or militant enough . . ."

Janice laughed out loud.

"This rhetoric bought him a place at the top of the Black Power pyramid," I continued, "until the chapter opened in L.A. After that, Karenga started putting all his energy into attacking the party. This new posture didn't mean much to us, even when we began noticing, recently, how the US Organization was getting seriously armed. They don't hesitate to flash their guns. And we barely thought about how, around the same time, they began acquiring fleets of new vans and cars, and spiffing up their head-quarters. In retrospect, it seems they became financially sound overnight. And remember, I'm not talking here about some long-standing Urban League or NAACP, with a substantial network. I'm talking about a group that makes dramatic declarations, that would bite any hand that feeds the others, a group that militantly opposes 'Whitey's' system.

"What we did notice was how they flash their new guns all over L.A. and San Diego without the slightest interference from the police. The police who stop party members if we make a move, assault us, arrest us every day, it seems, put wiretaps on our houses and offices, try to push their way into them with phony search warrants."

"Do you think it's a police setup: divide and conquer?"

"There's no doubt that's part of it. The police are in it. But the question is, how. The other question is, who's suffering . . .

"Look at the results of January 17. Two Panther leaders are killed by an US assassin, who skips past the police. A loose conspiracy charge is leveled, *later*, against two US foot soldiers. But on that day, nearly a hundred *Panthers* are rounded up and put in jail, 'to prevent' a so-called retaliatory bloodbath. And then there's a thing like that tarpaulin on the house across the street when they came for us. It's stretching the imagination to think it was a fluke that the police orchestrated and executed such a well-planned assault on a Panther facility on the very day, in the very same time period, that US people were murdering Panthers. There's some kind of concert going on here. That's all."

"So who's calling the tune?"

"The fucking FBI!" I shouted. "And Karenga's dancing. No matter how bizarre it sounds, I believe it.

"In addition to everything else, there's one very glaring reason to believe this. Karenga's thin line about black culture cloaks an otherwise empty program. I mean, he hasn't got one real project to *do* one single thing, black or militant. Just words. His US Organization is clearly only a shell of a thing that now seems bent on doing only one thing, the same thing as the police: killing Black Panthers."

"There's something I want to tell you that you may not know," Jay said with solemnity, after a minute. "Are you aware that Hoover issued a directive about black militants, instructing all FBI offices to eliminate or prevent the rise of another black 'messiah' figure, as Malcolm X and Martin Luther King were perceived to be?

"Well, the shocking thing is contained in the other part of that directive. It states that an alternative or related plan is for the FBI *itself* to *develop* such a black messiah."

The chills ran from Janice to me.

When it was time to go, Jay handed me an envelope full of cash. He told me he would get more to us on a monthly basis. I could pick it up at a black church in Los Angeles. The pastor, the Reverend H. H. Brookins, was his friend. We allowed ourselves an embrace, a soft kiss on the mouth, a look.

The taxicab carrying Janice and me back followed familiar curves along Sunset Boulevard out of Bel Air, through a pouring rain. We passed Delfern Drive. We passed the Beverly Hills Hotel. The past and the present became confused. There was then and there was now, and all of it seemed fused by love, by passion.

The rain had been phenomenal. It had rained every day of that week after Friday, January 17. The weather reports said it was the longest and hardest rain in the Los Angeles area in nearly a century. On the day of the funeral, one week later, the downpour was powerful. It did not restrain the thousands who came out to attend the funeral of Alprentice Bunchy Carter.

The rain pounded on the rooftops of South Central Los Angeles, the black ghetto. It beat on the cars of Black Panthers and black people driving in procession to the church. It beat on the flock of black umbrellas that barely protected those who could not get inside and had to listen to the service on the street. It pounded on the umbrellas and yellow raincoats of the hundreds of police who invaded the territory of the Mayor of the Ghetto.

Wreaths of flowers on stands surrounded the open casket. Wreaths and garlands were everywhere. Panthers in blue shirts and black berets and black leather jackets stood at attention along the walls. David Hilliard gave the eulogy, speaking on behalf of the Central Committee of the Black Panther Party. I sang the song Mrs. Carter had requested.

> Through the storm, through the night,
> lead me on to the light.
> Take my hand,
> Precious Lord,
> and lead me home . . .

I could not look into the casket. I pretended I did not know. I reembraced my dream and saw Bunchy on Century Boulevard, laughing.

Now the procession lined up outside to go to the cemetery. Masai, up from Bunchy's underground, had worked to organize everything while we were in jail. More than one hundred cars moved in an orderly fashion, slowly, through the slick streets of the ghetto. Panthers and former Slausons and mothers and sisters trailed the hearse. Blocks of headlights pierced the drenching rain. Plainclothes and uniformed pigs followed, slipping in and out of the procession headed toward the grave.

I was in a car with Masai and two other Brothers. We were near the head of the long, funereal column of cars. We were happy for the rain. It was Bunchy, we said, pissing on racist America. It was Bunchy raging on, for death could not destroy him. We talked in this way as we wound south toward Inglewood, toward the muddy grave that was to swallow the cadaver.

They swooped upon us, signaling our car with their sirens. We pulled out of the procession and stopped. Yellow raincoats and galoshes and black umbrellas were everywhere. Pigs were all over us. We laughed and waited as the train of black cars swished past ours.

One Brother in the car suddenly confessed he had three joints in his coat. Masai ordered him to eat them. He was swallowing the last bit when the four car doors were opened. We were told at gunpoint to get out.

The rain beat down on our heads and our black leather and the palms of our raised hands. The pigs meticulously searched the car. Fifteen minutes passed. Soon, half an hour had passed. After forty-five minutes, they let us get back into the car. We never found the procession. We did not see the casket lowered into the grave.

The airplane tempered the grief of Los Angeles. It was only days after Bunchy's funeral and after John's funeral in New Haven, Connecticut, where Janice and I were now headed.

John's family had tried to conduct a dignified service. But the FBI had invaded the small church and taken photographs of John's body in the casket and of every person who came there. They had even seized the guest sign-in book.

Once Ericka had arrived with her baby and John's body, a platoon of FBI agents had converged in New Haven, where the very refined Huggins family had always lived. They had followed Mr. and Mrs. Huggins every day after that, Ericka reported to us when we arrived. They had posted themselves across the street from the Huggins family home. They had photographed every visitor, every coming and going.

"This is Johnny's room," Mrs. Huggins said, showing Janice and me through the family's New England home. We were planning to say there for about a week.

"Here's Johnny's desk and all his papers from the Boston Latin School," she reminisced.

She had been angry with us at first, with the Black Panthers who had seemingly stolen his life. But the FBI's intrusion into the orderly lives of a librarian and a Yale Club steward had clarified matters. Her rage was redirected, though more frustrated. The *State* had snatched her Johnny's life.

She and John Sr. had always been good citizens of the State. Their marriage had been bonded by the State for all those years. They had educated their Carolyn and Joan and John under the laws of the State. They had paid their property taxes and gone to church and followed all the rules of the State for their whole lives. It seemed now that the State had ordered and orchestrated the assassination of their only son. There were so many of its agents everywhere, "investigating" them while the assassin ran free.

In the cold of our first night in New Haven, sleeping near Johnny's room, I was awakened by her. I reached for my watch and the bedside lamp. It was nearly 2 A.M. The shower water could not muffle the sound.

"Oh, Johnny! Johnny!" I heard Mrs. Huggins scream through the beating of shower water, through the shower door and the bathroom door and the cold night air.

"Why?! Oh God, why?!" I heard her pound into the shower wall.

"She does it nearly every night," Ericka said the next day. "We pretend not to hear her. But it's every night."

We cried and held on to each other for that week. Ericka told us she would not be returning to L.A. She would be staying in New Haven with the baby.

She could not leave Mrs. Huggins alone. She needed John's baby. Ericka would stay on and work to build the small chapter of the party in New Haven, as John would have wanted.

She kissed Janice and me goodbye, and reminded us of what we had to do.

◄ ►

The next few months were devoted to rebuilding. We found places to live. I moved in with Evon Carter, Bunchy's wife, six months pregnant with his baby. We sold the party newspapers. We distributed the UCLA food. We finally formalized a legal defense program, with what I felt was the courageous help of Jean Kidwell and the young white lawyers in the National Lawyers Guild, Ken Cloke and Joan Anderson and Dan Lund. Most of the few black lawyers that existed were afraid to associate with Panthers. And despite the early 1969 FBI directive to "eradicate [the Panthers'] serve the people programs," we finally started a breakfast program.

The only rent-free facility we had been able to find for our first Breakfast for Children program in L.A. was a Seventh-Day Adventist church. The black pastor welcomed us with one admonition: that we serve no meat. Joan Kelley, now a full-fledged Panther—despite her father and mother's fearful refusal to speak to her as long as she remained a Panther—found something called "vegeburgers." With the donations we were beginning to receive from some Hollywood whites, we purchased the burgers, passed them off as sausages, and started our program.

We organized rallies around police brutality against blacks. We organized rallies to denounce Karenga throughout black Los Angeles. We made speeches and circulated leaflets about every social and political issue affecting black and poor people locally, nationally, and internationally. We organized Panther support groups among whites. We opened a free clinic. We started a busing-to-prisons program, the first in the party, which provided transport and expenses to black families without the means to visit relatives in the vast California prison network—which could have included every black in L.A. We bought and stole more guns with new Hollywood and other money. We practiced shooting and guerrilla warfare tactics in the Mojave Desert. We developed and carried out retaliatory actions against the US Organization. We confronted and tried to deal with the daily assaults of the pigs.

The award-winning Los Angeles Police Department had primped itself up with no fanfare. There was now the LAPD Metro Squad. The Metro Squad had been its Vice Squad. Now it was its Panther unit, billed as an "urban counterinsurgency task force."

Nobody knew all of this initially, because the Metro Squad operated clandestinely, out of a small juvenile jail facility on Georgia Street, under a freeway in downtown Los Angeles. We eventually learned that the Metro Squad was deemed so important and elite that any one of its units could command an entire LAPD precinct at any given moment.

Joan and I were among the first in the chapter to learn of the Metro Squad. We were riding down Central Avenue, not far from our office. I was driving. Joan was weeks pregnant with Nathaniel Clark's baby. We had just come from a fund-raising brunch at the home of a white supporter.

I spotted the ordinary brown car following us. Suddenly, I saw, in the rearview mirror, an arm flip out of the passenger window of the car and place a flashing light on its roof. The loudspeaker from the brown car blared: "This is the police! Pull over now!"

Two pigs in uniform approached our car in standard fashion: one moved toward the driver's side and the other remained near the rear window. I rolled down my window—but only a few inches, as was my custom, since it always irritated them.

"What is it," I said dryly, without looking at him.

I was preparing to slip my driver's license through the little slot in the window when he spoke.

"Why don't you get your black ass out of the car, Elaine."

I turned to toss him a smart remark. I found myself facing the barrel of something that looked like a .44 magnum.

He cocked it. "Get your fuckin' ass out!"

I carefully, silently placed my hands, fingers spread, on the dashboard. Joan followed suit.

"If you open the door, I'll get out," I said carefully.

He laughed.

The two of them opened the car doors. We stepped out.

"Spread 'em," the pig named Panzica said, indicating that we should lean over the car hood with our legs spread apart.

That it was illegal for male police to perform a body search on women did not concern him or us. The barrel of that non-standard issue .44 concerned me. His attitude concerned me.

Panzica's partner, Pollock, searched us while Panzica gave us a little speech.

"You think you're doin' something for your people. That's a fuckin' joke. Niggers don't want nothin'. I know niggers. I kicked niggers' asses all over Hell's Kitchen. A Sicilian can kick the shit out of a nigger, *and* a spic. I hate niggers. How do you feel about that?"

Finding nothing else to do, they ripped out the back seat and kicked out a brake light—on the assumption we could not replace the light before another set of pigs would stop us for failing to have it. That was standard. My eye was still on the gun. It was not standard.

Only the L.A. Panthers appreciated the Metro Squad. Given the constancy of police assaults and the recent murders, the national headquarters had assigned key Panthers from the Bay Area to work with us. Among them was Captain Randy Williams and "Frisco" Eddie. We tried to tell them about the Metro Squad.

"A pig is a pig," they had laughed at us.

They were unmoved by Al Armour's report of his personal experience with the Metro Squad. While one of them commanded Al to stand against a wall near where he was stopped, his partner forced the Brother riding with Al onto his knees with a shotgun. The first one then fired five or six rounds over Al's head from an automatic pistol—also not standard—and asked Al what he thought about that. He *was* pretty good, this pig boasted, explaining that he practiced every day, with a thousand rounds, to make sure he could kill a nigger like Al.

The Bay Area Panthers were not moved by Masai's account of his introduction to the Metro Squad's team of Fisher and Hole. While it took Fisher one hour to rip up, one by one, every copy of a press statement Masai and I were about to present, Hole's gun kept us holding on to a utility pole in the middle of Grand Avenue, downtown, in broad daylight. Randy actually laughed when I told him about the time Fisher—who carried his pistol in the small of his back—told me how he would like to shoot me. Rousted from the car, I had refused to move to retrieve my driver's license from it, to give him an excuse to shoot me. "Hell, I wouldn't shoot you right here, princess. If I shot you in the face right here, why all your fuckin' blood would mess up my uniform. If you want to take a little hop down the street a bit, say fifty feet, it'd give me great pleasure to blow your brains out."

It was when two Metro Squad units caught the fearless Captain Randy Williams from national headquarters alone one night and, never charging or booking him, shuffled him from precinct to precinct for about two hours, beating him all over L.A., that the Bay Area Panthers became convinced. Los Angeles, they finally agreed, had a new breed of pig, one that was trying to reestablish the Wild West.

We all laughed about it later. We could appreciate clarity.

The escalating conflict with the US Organization was not so clear. There were frequent incidents, the most treacherous of which involved Panthers selling newspapers on the street. Seven or eight US members might spring out of a van and pounce upon a Brother or Sister and fire a few rounds. Ronald Freeman had been shot like that. We would retaliate by shooting up their facilities or homes.

Those confrontations were actually generating more terror than the conflicts with the pigs. The substance of it was so intangible. There was something unnatural about the look and style and feel of the US Organization, something sinister and dark. They made me think of Haitian dictator Papa Doc and his army of "tontons macoutes." Karenga was their priest, an agent of evil wearing the mask of a black man. J. Edgar Hoover was Papa Doc.

Sometime in the tempest of that period, Geronimo gave me a snub-nosed .38 pistol. However tricky it would be to have it with me without getting arrested, I intended to carry it in my purse every day.

CHAPTER 10

DYING FOR
THE PEOPLE

ON THE EVENING OF BUNCHY'S FUNERAL, after the rain stopped, I sang a few of my songs for David Hilliard. He had been impressed by my voice at the funeral, he said. I had been impressed by him, the chief of staff of the Black Panther Party.

Masai had told him I wrote revolutionary songs. David wanted to hear them before going back to Oakland. He ordered Geronimo to find a piano and to gather everyone in the area together to listen. There had been too much pain for me to be embarrassed about it. I sang him the song for Franco, "The Panther," and the one for Eldridge, "The Meeting." I sang the one written at Sybil Brand for Bunchy and John: "Assassination." David cried and ordained that the one for Eldridge become the Black Panther National Anthem. He had cassettes of it duplicated and distributed, and ordered all party members to learn it.

Having survived to April, everyone was now singing the new anthem with me. A capella, my voice echoed with several hundred others in the apple-crisp morning air of Oakland. We were assembled to honor the "first to fall."

" 'Li'l Bobby' was the first," we said. He was the first Panther to give his life to the struggle, we meant. It had been a year since the police had murdered seventeen-year-old Bobby Hutton.

They sang along with me quietly, huddling together in the early-morning chill of Defremery Park. Defremery was a tattered park. Its thinning grass patches reflected the poverty of West Oakland, where Bobby Hutton had lived and died. But it was our park now, the people's park. It had come to be called "Bobby

Hutton Memorial Park." Some held hands, some cried as we remembered and sang the anthem.

> Yes, he turned and he walked
> past the eyes of my life,
> and he nodded and sang without sound,
> and his face had the look of a man who knew strife,
> and a feeling familiarly came around.
> I said, "Man,
> where have you been for all these years?
> Man, where were you when I sought you?
> Man, do you know me as I know you?
> Man, am I coming through . . . ?

It was a strange song for an anthem, I thought, but not for the black man who had touched my life so powerfully I had surrendered to his party of men and ideas. It had been one year since I had seen him. Eldridge had by then eased out of Vacaville prison on a technicality and bail. After his release, he had defied the laws of our enemy by refusing to appear in court in connection with the April 6 charges. Consequently, his house in San Francisco, as well as other Panther facilities in the Bay Area, had been placed under close police surveillance. Finally, a host of police had surrounded Eldridge's house to force him to surrender, but Papa had slipped away. He was now in exile in Cuba.

After the memorial, those on the Central Committee and in the leadership of Northern California gathered in a "safe house" that belonged to a Sister named Shirley Neeley. Geronimo and Masai and Blue and I joined them, representing the other chapter in the state.

About twenty-five Panthers were present. There was the reputedly mad Captain Landon Williams, brother of the more vicious Randy—still temporarily assigned to the Wild West territory of L.A. There were Van Taylor and Charles Bursey and "Baby D" and June Hilliard and Dexter Woods and the artist Emory Douglas, minister of culture, and others whose names I did not know, all armed. Most significant among them were the chairman of the Black Panther Party, Bobby Seale, and David, chief of staff. They were sitting around the living room laughing about Eldridge's escape from the pigs.

We were in a characteristic West Oakland house, wood-framed and raised above the ground. Concrete steps led up from the street to the front door. Security people were in the back and on the roof. The smell of bacon and home-fried potatoes being cooked filled the house. The late-morning sun was strong. It shone through the house's many windows on the men with black leather and guns.

David was relaying the story of one year ago to a group gathered off the living room. It had been a horrible day in Oakland, David was saying. He reflected on how it had been one thing or another all day. "Niggers" were still trying to burn down Oakland over the King assassination. Panthers were still trying to stop the suicide. There had been only small incidents with the police. Now there was an all-out confrontation. Police and gunfire were all over West Oakland.

Panthers, including himself, had been patrolling the raging streets of West Oakland. The area around the house owned by a couple named Allen was suddenly overtaken by pigs opening fire. Panthers leaped to take cover; and one, David, pushed his way inside the Allen house.

It was like the end of the world, Mrs. Allen had said. All of America seemed to be on fire. Mr. and Mrs. Allen had hardly had time to grieve for the loss of King two days before. The house they had scrimped and saved for was now being threatened.

Having forced his way inside the Allens' house, David was crouching in fear, he said without shame, behind the bedroom door. All his twenty-four years of dedicated ducking and dodging on the streets of Oakland had not prepared him for this onslaught. There had been no automatic rifle fire in West Oakland when he was "gang-banging." Now, legions of pigs were outside firing automatic rifles. Actually, he corrected himself with a smile, there were only hundreds outside the Allen home. A Lieutenant Newton was among the police leadership, David noted, stressing the irony of the name. There were all kinds of pigs under Lieutenant Newton's command, including sharpshooters and grenadiers.

The police suddenly commanded from loudspeakers that they come out. They threatened to raid the house or raze it.

Mr. Allen begged his wife to give up the "boy," the chief of staff of the Black Panther Party.

David had beseeched them with wide eyes, he told us without hesitation. A shotgun shell pierced the living-room window and fell right before his eyes, even as he implored them to hold on.

"Burn that son-of-a-bitch down!" The order came over the loudspeakers outside Mrs. Allen's house.

A fire was started.

It was a shack the pigs were attacking and burning, the shack attached to the Allen house, the shack from which the three of them could now hear gunfire being returned.

As he talked, I lost concentration for a minute and focused on David. His dark velvet skin was glistening as he related how Mrs. Allen had held strong, boldly asserting that certain death was outside and nobody was walking into it.

Tears were filling David's eyes. He whispered that he did not know it had been Li'l Bobby in the shack. He whispered the rhythmical refrain: Li'l Bobby was the first, Li'l Bobby was the beginning. It was Li'l Bobby, the first member of the party, a boy who had been an ordinary little "finger popper," caught in the hail of police bullets and fire in a West Oakland shack. Li'l Bobby had not been driven by abstract political or intellectual issues, David recalled. For Bobby, commitment lay in the love of black people—including one of his role models, David himself, which he did not say but which everyone knew. David had been known on the streets of West Oakland as a streetwise hustler, a sharp dresser, and a smooth talker, whom the women loved and the men respected. When David joined the party of his friends Huey Newton and Bobby Seale, Li'l Bobby had latched on to him.

On April 6, David said, seventeen-year-old Bobby Hutton stood strong for himself and his people, and found his own freedom.

Eldridge was with Bobby, a man and a man-child firing back at hundreds of police.

When it had become hopeless and Eldridge determined it was time to surrender, he and Bobby put down their guns. Eldridge preceded Bobby out of the shack, emerging virtually naked to avoid any impression that he was still armed. He had ordered Bobby to follow suit.

Bobby Hutton came out after Eldridge. His hands were raised, his body covered by the clothing he was too shy to remove. The dark was suddenly pierced by spotlights and by bullets that tore into the face and chest and arms of Li'l Bobby. The pigs even stood over him in the end, pumping bullets rapid-fire into him.

After the surrender, Panthers in the area were quickly flushed out of their positions. David, Charles Bursey, and many others were arrested. Of course, there had been those like "Killer" Wells who got away, although he, too, was eventually indicted.

I was thinking now of Tommy Lewis, also seventeen when

he was cut down. Suddenly, Landon Williams broke through the quiet.

"Motherfuck that pig!" Captain Landon shouted from the other room. Angry about some comment made on a television news broadcast, Landon drew his pistol from his leather shoulder holster and shot out the television screen.

The sound of the shot stunned everyone. Within seconds, though, we were doubled over with laughter. The alteration of mood was welcome. As some of the men cleaned up the television glass, Bobby Seale spoke to me.

"Sister Elaine, your chairman," he said of himself, "thought you sang righteously today. I understand from David that you've written a bunch of other songs."

"Not so many, but some," I said.

He snapped his fingers and motioned to the only other Sister in the room to join us.

"This here is Sister Marsha," Bobby said. "I want you to meet her. Although she's a young Sister, she's got a full-grown dedication to this party. That's why she's the only Sister on a security squad. She's one of the toughest Sisters in the party . . .

"Marsha, tell the Sister here what a Brother has to do to get some from you," Bobby commanded.

Marsha was a child, maybe fifteen years old. She was nearly white—like the other Marsha in L.A. She had reputedly come from the San Francisco Tenderloin, the streets of the Fillmore district. Like the other Marsha, she spoke like a Brother.

She stood at attention. "First of all, a Brother's got to be righteous. He's got to be a Panther. He's got to be able to recite the ten-point platform and program, and be ready to off the pig and die for the People."

"Right on, Sister Marsha!" the Brothers shouted.

"Can't no motherfucker get no pussy from me unless he can get down with the party," she added without prompting.

"Right on!" they responded again.

"And what's a Sister got to do?" Bobby pushed.

"A Sister has to learn to shoot as well as to cook, and be ready to back up the Brothers. A Sister's got to know the ten-point platform and program by heart."

"And what else?" Bobby urged.

"A Sister has to give up the pussy when the Brother is on his job and hold it back when he's not. 'Cause Sisters got pussy power."

"Ooh-wee!" the Brothers laughed.

I tried to remember where I was. I thought of Bunchy and became enraged. There was no such verbiage being slung around in L.A.

If there had been any chauvinism in Bunchy, it had had to do with chivalry. He had even corrected his own, Black Muslim–inspired imposition of gender divisions in the ranks. I could not imagine Bunchy, and certainly not John, allowing, much less pushing, any Sister in L.A. to be so degraded as this pathetic child before me. If nothing else, there was too much work, too little time, too much danger. I was filled with fury. The word "Sister" was sounding like "bitch" to me.

"We need *all* the Sisters to help with the food, Sister," Shirley Neeley said to me while the men were still applauding Marsha.

Shirley had tapped me on the shoulder and was standing before me and the chairman, with her hand placed on her hip. She was annoyed with me, she shouted with her eyes and body, because I was just sitting in the living room with the Brothers.

Who do you think you are, her eyes said. There was also some kind of street jealousy there, some kind of you-must-think-you're-cute attitude.

I don't work in the kitchen, my eyes shot back. My mouth said, "Sure," with a slightly sarcastic smile, as I wondered if there were some pancakes to be flipped.

Walking behind Shirley toward the kitchen, I chuckled inside, thinking that the one thing Dorothy Clark had never taught her child to do was cook. I had to restrain a laugh thinking about the time a man gave my mother a new pressure cooker for a birthday present—the same man she eventually tried to cut the life out of, her ex-husband. She handed his gift right back to him and told him if he really wanted to help her have an easy time in the kitchen, he could get in there with her or take her out of it.

There were about ten women in the kitchen. I realized I had not seen them during the whole time. I had smelled the bacon and biscuits they had cooked but had given no thought to who was doing the cooking. I had been too busy listening to David to notice. Besides, it was not unusual to see very few women at a gathering. There was a low ratio of women to men in L.A. and, really, everywhere in our paramilitary organization.

I contemplated that as I angrily slopped eggs and bacon and biscuits and potatoes onto plates, poured orange juice into plastic cups, and served the Brothers in the living room.

Of course, the women were to clean up the kitchen in which

they had eaten, standing. When the meal was over, the men remained in the living room discussing guns and politics—and "pussy power," I presumed.

"Oh, please, let me wash," I said snidely to a Sister named Rosalee, who seemed to be in charge of the kitchen.

I banged dishes into soapy water in the sink while the other Sisters scraped plates and wiped tables and condiment containers. I also preached.

"At no time since I've been in this party have I seen such bullshit," I said loudly to the air, loudly enough for the men to hear.

Another plate was washed and handed to the Sister rinsing and drying. Nobody else said a word.

Masai came into the kitchen to talk to me, to calm me.

"What's the problem?" he asked, irritated. He was apparently embarrassed by his L.A. comrade.

"The problem? The problem? You want to join me in here so we can talk about the problem? Ignorant motherfuckers," I grumbled. "Bunchy didn't die for this stupid shit . . ."

Masai silenced me with an admonishing look, but turned away. He knew me well enough by then to know that agitating the situation any further would only encourage an uglier tirade. Finally, when the kitchen was in perfect order and I had successfully alienated most of the Brothers and Sisters there, I asked Geronimo if we could leave.

He and Blue had separated themselves from everyone else and were talking to David. Geronimo had his own problems with Northern California. He felt the orders he was receiving from the Central Committee limited him. I seized upon that in the car and spat out a laundry list of invectives as to our Bay Area comrades. On the ride to David's house, all four of us, including Masai, concluded that L.A. was where the real Panthers were.

When I returned to L.A., I told Joan and a few other Sisters about the way the women were treated up north. I even called Ericka Huggins about it. We all vowed to be watchful.

We knew Brothers dragged their old habits into the party. We all did. The party's role, however, was not limited to external revolution but incorporated the revolutionizing of its ranks. If, however, the very leadership of a male-dominated organization was bent on clinging to old habits about women, we had a problem. We would have to fight for the right to fight for freedom.

Like most black women of the time, we considered the notion

of women's liberation to be a "white girl's thing." Unlike the new feminists, we were not going to take a position against men. Our men did not have to "change or die," as the most radical of the feminists were saying. Black men were our Brothers in the struggle for black liberation. We had no intention, however, of allowing Panther men to assign us an inferior role in our revolution. Joan and Ericka and Evon Carter and Gwen Goodloe and I concluded that they better not try to fuck with us. We would not be rewarding *any* Brother with our bodies, in the bedroom or in the kitchen.

Our collective posture emerged, and we became known as "the clique." As the Brothers in Southern California began to feel the change in our consciousness, they whined that we had "bad attitudes." They initiated little verbal challenges to those of us designated members of the clique; even to Evon, the mother of Bunchy's baby, Osceola—after the Seminole Indian warrior—who had been born after Bunchy died. They even began to assail Ericka's name, venerated though she was, and absent though she was.

The reputation of the clique spread. Brothers throughout the many chapters that had emerged all over the country were mumbling about the clique in L.A., we learned. "Smart bitches" like us, they were saying, needed to be silenced. But we would silence them in the end by our hard work and dedication; and by the specter of the fierce Brothers who supported us, the leadership of Southern California, Geronimo and Masai.

The matter was hardly noteworthy over the next months, in any case, as Hoover's all-out campaign to destroy the Black Panther Party by the end of 1969 seemed to be moving on us like a bulldozer.

Bobby Seale was facing the conspiracy trial in Chicago that came to be known as the trial of the Chicago Seven. Bobby was the eighth defendant (though he was tried separately), but the press, and even most of the radical whites supporting the defendants, failed to acknowledge the only black defendant in their dubbing of the trial.

The Chicago Eight, Bobby Seale and Dave Dellinger, Abbie Hoffman, Tom Hayden, Rennie Davis, Jerry Rubin, Lee Weiner, and John Froines, were being tried for conspiracy to start a riot at the site of the 1968 Democratic National Convention. Thousands of mostly white radicals and leftists and antiwar activists had gathered there to denounce the Democrats and to demonstrate their opposition to the war in Vietnam, carried out under the Democratic President Lyndon Johnson.

Bobby had gone to Chicago to speak on behalf of the party. He had addressed the thousands assembled outside the convention, adding the voice of the party to the roaring denunciations of the war in Vietnam and the warmonger Johnson. It was the first time the party had positioned itself strongly with the massive antiwar movement, though in our newspaper and our rhetoric, we had not only condemned U.S. aggression but had openly urged black men to defy being drafted into the war. Bobby's representation of the party in Chicago was one of the strongest antiwar statements made by any black organization. Most moderate and even so-called militant blacks had defined the war as a "non-black issue"; many black organizations, including the NAACP, challenged even Martin Luther King, Jr.'s moral opposition to the war.

Chicago's mayor, Richard Daley, had ordered his police to get rid of the demonstrators by any means. More than being disruptive to the convention, the demonstrators were embarrassing to him, a Democrat and the political leader of the convention's host city. Daley had justified sweeping the Chicago streets clean of demonstrators on the flimsy assertion that proper permits had not been obtained to enjoy the constitutionally guaranteed right of freedom of assembly.

There had been several melees between demonstrators and police after that. The police had prevailed by brutally beating and arresting hundreds of demonstrators, including Bobby and the other men who were to be tried for conspiracy to incite riot.

In May, there was an additional charge. The ante had been raised. Bobby was charged with a murder conspiracy. Bobby had just visited New Haven to assist Ericka and the others in building up the chapter. Right after Bobby left, the body of a young black man was "discovered" in New Haven. A black government witness was produced who charged that Bobby and Ericka Huggins had conspired to have the man killed.

On the basis of that single piece of information, the government formally charged Bobby and Ericka with conspiracy. The prosecutor offered the theory that the dead man was a police informant who had tried to infiltrate the party, had been uncovered and murdered. Others were also swept into the conspiracy.

J. Edgar Hoover seemed to be working after hours. Four

months after burying John, Ericka Huggins was isolated in a cell in a rural Connecticut jail. Huey Newton was still in prison. Bobby Seale, arrested on the second charge in San Francisco, was now in jail awaiting two trials. Eldridge Cleaver was in exile. Bunchy and John and others were dead. Panthers were being arrested every day in L.A., in Chicago, in New York, Oakland, and San Francisco.

We clung to each other fiercely. We forgot cliques and chauvinism and any bit of internal strife.

That was why I continued to ignore Masai's advances. How could he even think of approaching me in that way, I had snarled at him during all those months since the time he rose from the underground. How could he imagine that I would relate to him, make love with him, in the middle of making war?

Masai had been Raymond Hewitt when he was growing up a few blocks from Bunchy. He had been a Slauson, and then, with Bunchy, a Slauson Renegade. He had been called "Bright Eyes" in those days. He was still called "Bright" by the Brothers who remained underground.

He had begun introducing them to me—just in case. They should know me, he felt, and I them: Wolf and Bug and Danny Brown and Kenny Favre and the others, including Masai's brother, Deacon. He would take me on midnight runs to their secret houses, noting over and over that nothing could be written down about them, their names or addresses or telephone numbers. Everything had to be remembered, like the connection between and among us, the roots of which sprang from Bunchy.

It was during those midnight runs through the black ghettoes of L.A. that Masai would turn his gruff manner to tenderness. He was not polished like Bunchy or David. He was a big man with a booming, deep voice and a strong body. He was well read, though not an abstract thinker, for he was cut from the cloth of the street and had a street fighter's mentality. He had a justifiable reputation as an accurate shot and a martial arts expert, and as being unyielding on ideological questions.

When Masai changed his name, he re-created himself as a black man, he told me. He showed me his real self in his soft moments on our night rides. He told me he had known me all along, even when I was singing my songs back in the Watts Happening Coffee House days. I told him about the Thorazine and my salvation by John.

What he offered was not love, he said eventually. We had, he said, faced marauding pigs and narrow nationalists together, written press statements together, treated the wounded and studied revolutionary philosophy together, all because we believed in and loved the people, black people. There was already love. It was part of each of us. "The true revolutionary is guided by great feelings of love," we acknowledged, quoting Che Guevara.

"What I'm looking for is the right woman to die with," he said one night. Then he laughed reminiscently over my behavior at Shirley Neeley's after the Bobby Hutton memorial. "You're a woman, all right. I could love you under any circumstances."

"It's been six months, twelve shootings, and six funerals since we met, since January seventeenth," he continued. "I've known you were the right woman since then."

I was leaning against the arm of the couch in Evon's living room on which we were sitting. I was resting my legs and feet on the couch pillows, my toes touching his thighs.

We were in a dream, mixed with vodka and tears. We needed each other. We would die soon. It was a foregone conclusion. He laughed. We made love, all night, into the morning. Our lovemaking was not desperate. It was a drink of water, a passionate moment of gratitude for a moment of living. He was the first man with whom I had made love since the assassinations.

It was Masai's face I was singing to on the other side of the glass recording booth. I was doing what David had ordered: recording an album of my songs. Masai smiled at me as I sang. I was several weeks pregnant with his child, though neither of us knew.

> And I'd cry with the man.
> And I'd die with the man.
> I'd lie with the man.
> 'Cause I know that I am
> the woman I am
> just with a Very Black Man . . .

The piano and horn arrangements of Horace Tapscott blended wonderfully with my messages, with "their" songs, which my hand wrote. Under Horace's direction, his jazz orchestra lifted my unembellished piano-playing. Horace had also orchestrated the arrangements with Vault Records to have the album made—

Seize the Time, after which Bobby Seale, still in jail, named his book that was soon to be published.

The joy I felt in making the music was undercut by the presence of the police, who followed us every day, who sat outside the Vault recording studio during the sessions, who stopped and delayed us going to and from the studio. They were omnipresent. The Metro Squad's brown and blue and pastel-pink and lime-green and canary-yellow cars seemed attached to our bodies. They became part of our lives, adding colorful twists, like the Negro team of Adams and Farwell. Adams and Farwell habitually rode by Central Avenue wearing dashikis and exaggerated Afros, shouting "Power to the people!" from their loudspeakers. In the Los Angeles County sheriff's department, where I was once taken to be charged, I saw a banner draped across a wall: PIGS 11—PANTHERS 0.

The regular black-and-white LAPD units also rode the expressways of our affairs. Among them was the notorious Sergeant William Davis—known throughout Watts as "Cigar"—who never let up. Panthers were being stopped and/or arrested, and/or beaten, en route to or from breakfast programs, rallies, offices, and homes. Panthers were arrested selling newspapers and had their papers confiscated. It was the same going to or from our free clinic; our medical supplies were crushed under police boots on the spot. It was the same leaving fund-raisers given by our white supporters, near the Westwood and Beverly Hills homes of Don Freed, or Shirley and Don Sutherland, or Bert Schneider. Donation checks were ripped up and strewn onto the street. It was the same for the branches beyond the borders of L.A., in Pasadena, Santa Ana, and especially San Diego, where party members tried to attend the funerals of two Panthers killed on the street by US Organization gunmen while selling newspapers.

We were so conditioned to police assaults by October, it was hard to recognize the urgency in Glenda's voice when she called me at the apartment that Evon, Gwen, Joan, and I now shared.

"The pigs shot Bruce!" Glenda screamed at me into the telephone. "Oh my God, he's bleeding everywhere! Toure is dead!"

She was alone, she cried. She was afraid.

"I'll be right there!" I threw down the telephone.

Gwen Goodloe and I hopped into our car, leaving Evon behind with Bunchy's baby. We stopped at a pay telephone to call Geronimo. He would meet us at the house on 55th Street.

Glenda was outside the house, bent over the railing on the darkened porch, sobbing.

Inside, Bruce Richard was lying on the couch in the living room. Nineteen years old and long and lanky, he was clutching his bleeding abdomen. Toure was dead, he reported in military style. The police had stopped them. There had been a gunfight. Toure's gun had jammed. Bruce had escaped. Shot twice, he had driven the Volkswagen in which they had been riding back to the house where Toure lived.

Geronimo arrived with Long John. He sent Gwen to find a doctor, gave Bruce a Seconal, and ordered me to stay with Bruce until the doctor arrived. After that, Geronimo left, charging Long John to stay with us as "security."

I went into the room with Bruce and closed the door, to dull the sound of Glenda's sobbing.

I peeled Bruce's bloody shirt from him, but I knew nothing about how to treat bullet wounds. We were alone, and I was afraid. I had not seen John or Bunchy die. This was the first time I had to face death in the present tense. I started talking to Bruce—this would ward off death, I imagined.

We talked about my baby, and laughed about "the pussy" Bruce had gotten and had lied about getting. We talked about the clique, Bruce laughing about how confused the Brothers were about Sisters, me laughing about how crazy that was, how much we really loved our Brothers. We talked about Toure—very briefly. We tried to keep laughing.

It was two hours before Geronimo returned and Gwen came back with Terry Kupers, a white doctor friend of ours.

Terry stood Bruce on his feet. Bruce wobbled from Seconal and pain. Terry stripped Bruce's pants down. As Bruce stood weakly, blood poured from his penis like water. Terry examined the wounds. One bullet had passed through his body. The other was lodged inside, probably in a kidney, Terry estimated. He could not operate on him there. Bruce had only a few more hours to live without treatment.

Geronimo decided: Bruce would have to be taken to a hospital, even though he would face certain imprisonment. The alternative was the certainty of death. Within less than forty-eight hours after being dropped off at a local hospital, he was shifted to the jail ward of the county hospital, charged with assault on police officers. He would spend the next seven years of his life in prison.

Only weeks before, Toure and I had been laughing over how wildly he had driven Joan to the hospital to have the baby she and Nathaniel Clark had made—me hanging out of the passenger window screaming to other cars to make way. We had cried at the hospital, waiting for news of Joan's baby, whom Nathaniel would never see—he had been shot and killed three weeks before that.

Now Toure's laugh was stilled, his face battered by the impression of police boots inflicted after they shot him dead.

On the plane to Chicago, the night of Toure's funeral, David Hilliard and I reflected on the devastation the party was suffering. David had decided, seemingly spontaneously, that I should accompany him to Chicago, where he planned to chastise the popular Illinois chapter chairman, Fred Hampton.

Fred had denounced the Weather Underground, or Weathermen group, for trashing some streets and stores in Chicago one night, allegedly in rage over the Chicago Eight trial. As a result of their trashing, the Chicago Police Department had brought down all hell on the black community, indiscriminately kicking in doors and making arbitrary arrests, under the guise of trying to find the perpetrators. Black people in Chicago blamed the party for instigating the police reign of terror. The party had some kind of alliance with the whites everyone knew had done the deed. When Fred, therefore, publicly denounced the action of the Weathermen as counterproductive to the goal of black liberation, Bernardine Dohrn and other Weather leadership demanded a meeting with him.

After an ugly argument, Fred had kicked Dohrn and the others out of the Chicago office. That conflict had so outraged Eldridge in exile that he had openly criticized Fred, in an essay he sent for publication in the party newspaper. He charged Fred with failing to appreciate that any attack on the pig power structure was correct, and for failing to respect the party's coalitions with white radical organizations. He demanded that Fred retract his statements. Fred refused.

I did not care about the Cleaver-Hampton dispute. It did not seem significant to me. I was numbed by day-to-day life in L.A.; and neutralized by the fact that while I could agree with the Illinois chapter chairman, I loved and respected the minister of information. In any event, since I was not on the Central Committee, I could not affect any of it.

David had not suddenly decided to take me with him to Chicago because he felt I should meet Fred Hampton, as he suggested. He was taking me because he felt a special trip with him would boost my morale and solidify what he perceived as my wavering commitment to the party. Maybe he felt that was important because the *Seize the Time* album might sell well, I was thinking cynically.

I had indeed contemplated leaving the party, and had told him so only days before Toure's murder.

How could I seriously allow the "subjective" to supersede the "objective," David had asked me angrily, when I told him my feelings over the telephone. That Masai had suddenly, without notice, married Shirley Neeley in Oakland when I was in my fourth month of pregnancy with his child should not turn me from the struggle. If I were a *true* revolutionary, David scolded me over the telephone, my commitment to the freedom of our people could not be swayed by "dick and pussy" problems.

He had tried to make my pain seem absurd—when I knew it was not. I also knew he was right. The question of Masai's marriage to another woman had no bearing on the times. Nevertheless, an airplane was carrying us to the cold of Chicago, where, among other things, David presumed my commitment would be rekindled.

The cold and the poverty through which we drove from the airport in Chicago seemed harder than anything on any street in North Philadelphia. In the car with Fred and Bobby Rush, deputy minister of defense, two Panther security cars following us, we drove by the Cabrini Green Housing Project. It was the worst place I had ever seen: a collection of government-built ghetto mausoleums, buildings twenty stories or so high, that sealed up thousands of poor blacks. It was more oppressive than Jordan Downs or the James Weldon Johnson Project. The caravan slid through other bitter streets, trying to avoid the infamous Chicago PD.

Deborah, Fred's wife, was pregnant, too, I saw when we arrived at their place. She and I talked about babies, while Fred and David and the rest of the Brothers argued. She told me their baby was due in January. My baby was due in March, I said. If she had a boy, she would name him after Fred. I would name a boy after John Huggins—which was amusing to both of us, as his name would be John Brown.

About 4 A.M., Deborah and I decided we needed to sleep.

She showed me their new bed, which took up most of a small room in the cracker box of a house. It was the first she and Fred had had, she confided. Like most Panthers, they had been sleeping on a mattress on the floor or in a sleeping bag—makeshift fashion, temporary arrangements for temporary living. Deborah and I rolled our pregnant bodies into the new bed, while the Brothers talked on.

"I'm high on the People!" they shouted in the awful gray of seven in the morning.

Hundreds of Panthers were lined up in a West Side Chicago schoolyard, ready to start the day's work. "Chairman Fred" was making sure his chief of staff would see the good work the Illinois chapter was doing. Chicago Panthers, Fred explained, lined up that way every morning. It was a demonstration of discipline and commitment. Fred felt it was an inspirational way to get the day started. It was.

"I ain't gon' die slippin' on no ice!" Fred shouted into a bull-horn, walking up and down the aisles of Panthers like a Baptist preacher.

"I ain't gon' die slippin' on no ice!" Panthers shouted back.

"I ain't gon' die in no airplane crash!"

"I ain't gon' die in no airplane crash!" they responded in unison.

"I'm gon' die for the People!" the chairman continued, his fist high, the steam of his breath bursting into the bitter early-morning cold.

"I'm gon' die for the People!" came the echo.

" 'Cause I live for the People!"

". . . live for the People!"

" 'Cause I'm high on the People!"

". . . high on the People!"

" 'Cause I *love* the People!"

". . . *love* the People!"

"Power to the People! Power to the People! Power to the People!"

Tears were streaming down my face, stinging my frozen cheeks. This young, twenty-one-year-old Fred Hampton had aroused in me a surge of love for my people stronger than I had ever felt. David had had the right idea. He had heard Fred before.

◀ ▶

Fred came to L.A. the next month, after the Eldridge rift was over; nobody had apologized to the Weather people. He made several speeches in the area. Once again, he brought the tears. He was saying things I had heard before. He was, however, so masterful, so forceful in his delivery, he stood me on my feet, along with everyone else to whom he spoke.

During his stay, he and Masai—who had brought his new wife to L.A., I "objectively" noted—jokingly argued over whether the Chicago police were more brutal than the LAPD. There was no comparison, I said. If nothing else, Masai and I asserted, the proof was in the fact that Panthers in other chapters were now being "threatened" with being sent to L.A. if they violated a party rule. As Masai and I outnumbered Fred in the discussion, it was decided that the LAPD was the most vicious police department in the country.

A week or so after Fred left, the LAPD bore out our assessment. Hundreds of them surrounded our main headquarters on Central Avenue.

Joan, Gwen, and I were about to leave the chapter. The two of them had been reassigned to Northern California. Having been recognized as an effective party propagandist and thereby now designated deputy minister of information for our chapter, I was being sent to New Haven to organize a publicity campaign around the impending trial of Bobby and Ericka. Of course, we felt that the changes had more to do with answering the now more vociferous whinings of the Brothers about the problem of the clique. Its leadership was being dismantled and dispersed.

About a hundred of us were on the second floor of the building, winding up the weekly dinner meeting. One Brother, on watch, suddenly shouted that the pigs were outside. We all dropped to the floor. Geronimo ordered the lights extinguished. He returned to Vietnam.

He ordered shotguns and rifles stripped from their racks and distributed quietly, quickly. He positioned men near all the windows, behind the sandbags we had sweated to place there over the last months. He sent others to cover the doors and windows downstairs.

Joan and I took refuge under the main desk. We grabbed the telephone and our news media list from the desktop. We would at least record what was about to happen.

Geronimo gave the command: "Do not fire until you hear the order. Do not waste bullets."

Everything became silent. Police sharpshooters were reported to be in position on rooftops outside. Police tow trucks were hauling away parked cars on Central Avenue. Huge dark police vans nobody had ever seen before were reportedly parked at each end of Central Avenue.

As Joan and I began calling the news media, we laughed bizarrely about how it hardly required all of that to break up our clique—we were already being separated. I called every television and radio station in the area. Joan whispered the numbers to me in the dark, by the light on the telephone buttons.

An hour later, it was still silent outside. Suddenly, the telephone rang. It was the captain of the LAPD Newton Street Division. He wanted to know why he was being called by so many press people.

I explained, quite casually as Joan crawled to Geronimo to tell him about the call, that we were concerned about the hundreds of police surrounding our building. Just as casually, he acknowledged that they were under his command.

Geronimo crawled over to me and squatted under the desk, holding his M-16. He signaled me to continue talking.

I explained to the captain that there were women and children in the building who wanted to leave but were afraid. He told me that he had had a report of a man in our window with a shotgun, which had triggered his order to surround our office. With my word he would order his men to leave. There was no one like that, I said politely. The hundreds of police, with their sharpshooters and vans, simply withdrew.

Ericka Huggins could hardly believe what had happened when I recounted that night to her. We tried to analyze what it meant. Was it actually a kind of "dry run," a pig experiment, we wondered.

She was being very brave in her isolation. She had been separated from the other women in the jail population, and ate and bathed and lived in her cell completely alone. I had gone to see her the day I arrived in New Haven, only two days after the "raid." I was not permitted to see Bobby Seale.

Ericka cried about not being with her Mai, though Mrs. Huggins did bring her to visit. Nobody else visited her; party members were restricted, and her mother had no money to get there from

Washington, D.C. Ericka was happy I was pregnant. She was sad about the business with Masai, who, I reported, had just been moved permanently back to Oakland as a new member of the Central Committee, the minister of education. I had gotten over Masai's marriage, I lied with a laugh. However, since I considered it her fault that I had stopped taking birth-control pills, after she encouraged all of us to have at least one baby for the revolution, if my baby were a girl, I was naming her Ericka.

We talked about her grim charges. We talked about her life with the Huggins family and about her own family; she painfully talked about how she felt seeing her mother beaten up by her father for years. I told her about my feelings on York Street, and about my overnight visit with my grandmother there, on my way to New Haven. It had been the first night I had spent on York Street since my mother and I left. I was not sure why I went there, I told Ericka—not until I left.

Carrie Brown had always been my grandmother, not a woman unto herself, as grandmothers never are. I saw that she was the same, as Aunt Mary was the same, as the roaches and rats and darkness were the same. The only thing that was new was my sense that my grandmother and aunt seemed so little and alone there on York Street. Aunt Mary went to bed not much after I arrived. She had to get up early to go to work. My grandmother hobbled into the dining room, beckoning me to follow. She poured us a glass of her homemade elderberry wine, which was in a pretty decanter on the buffet brought from Richmond, Virginia, when she was young, waiting for such a moment. She began to talk.

She told me about my grandfather, not her long-gone husband but the father of my father. Dignified man, she said, as she easily found a book among a collection of papers and junk stuffed inside the buffet, a history book, to show me his picture. She showed me other pictures, the most noteworthy of which was her wedding photograph, more than half a century old. I was thinking that I understood why she had been charmed by my grandfather, seeing his youthful face—fine, and very black, "to get some color back into the family," she always said. That was what made me think about her, what she had been, what she was, as a woman, a woman other than my hobbling, hymn-singing grandmother.

We talked through the night, until dawn. During those hours I began to see the woman. She told me stories about Randolph, the dressed-up twenty-two-year-old in the wedding picture; stories about Virginia and how she had been one of the only colored women in her time to learn to read and write; she even had her certificate. Listening, I wondered if I should tell her what I was doing.

She did not blink an eye. I wondered if she understood me.

"You know something, girl," she said after a bit of sighing when I told her, "back in the old days, white men used to have their way with black gals."

It was "black," she said, I noted to Ericka. Her voice was strong.

"Yes, and, Lord, some of them men would *make* those black gals have a baby for 'em."

She did not say rape. She just sat there, rocking a bit, with her light, almost-white skin flushed, her thin lips tight.

"And sometimes—Lord, forgive me," she said finally, "forgive me, Lord! Sometimes I've wanted to burn 'em all up. *All* of 'em!"

Ericka howled one of her deep-down laughs, teeth and all, which was the first real gut laugh I had known her to have since January 17.

I had been in New Haven less than a week when the news bulletins raged out of Chicago on December 4: Fred Hampton had been murdered.

An early-morning police raid had been made on Fred's house. He and another Brother in the house, Mark Clark, had been killed. Fred's body had been riddled with bullets while he slept in his bed.

Another news bulletin about Panthers came over the radio as I was preparing to leave for Chicago on the morning of December 8. Another police assault, on other Panthers. This time, it was in Los Angeles.

Once again in the predawn hours, a massive police force had assaulted three of our facilities there. The battle at the headquarters on Central Avenue was still going on. Police had sealed off blocks around Central Avenue. Gunfire had been exchanged for the past three hours, and was continuing even as I listened. Police were still being pushed back by Panther bullets from rapid-fire rifles, the radio was saying. Police helicopters had been unable to land or fire on or take the building.

An hour passed. There were continuing reports. Those of us in New Haven gathered around radios and television sets. There was no one to call. Another hour passed. It was a standoff, the reports said. We cheered. We cried. I was sure everyone I knew would soon be dead.

The television bulletins soon flashed pictures of my comrades, walking out of Central Avenue, hands above their heads, alive. The battle was over. There were only eleven of them. There they were, Cotton and Robert Bryan and Wayne Pharr and Mims, along with Peaches and Tommye Williams, the only women. The press immediately dubbed the assault a "mini-Vietnam." Still photographs were shown of those who had been arrested after assaults on the other facilities: Evon Carter, Craig Williams, and Al Armour, even Geronimo. There were eighteen of them in all.

Masai was just hours away, at a speaking engagement at a college in Boston. He called me. I met him in Boston, and together we headed for Chicago, to attend Fred Hampton's funeral.

I found Deborah. Our bellies touched as we fell into a weeping embrace.

She had been in bed in the back of the house, next to Fred, whom she could not wake, not even after they kicked in the front door. As she had struggled to wake him, her nineteen-year-old body had been rocked with the forty-two rounds that were pounded into the bed. Her body had been stained by his blood. Not one bullet hit her. It was a premeditated assassination.

Masai and I went to the house. Thousands of people were lined up to look inside, at the place where "Chairman Fred," as he was known all over Black Chicago, had been assassinated. The chapter wanted black people to see, to know the extent to which the police would go to repress resistance to their oppression.

I touched the bed, the bed where Deborah and I had laughed only a month or so before. It was still soaking wet with Fred's blood, five days after the assassination.

All of the West Side and South Side of Chicago was preparing for the funeral of Fred Hampton that night. Bobby Rush had Panthers all over Black Chicago, manning sound trucks playing Fred's recorded speeches. They were organizing to arouse the wrath of the people.

Ralph Abernathy, the post–Martin Luther King, Jr., head of the SCLC, spoke at the funeral. Civil-rights activist Jesse Jackson spoke, despite his negative attitude about Fred and the Chicago Panthers. Other local black community leaders came and spoke.

At least a thousand Brothers came from the P-Stone Nation, formerly the Black Stone Rangers, the nation's largest organized black street gang. Fred had finally developed a coalition with the Nation, despite the FBI's campaign to "promote disharmony" between Fred and Nation leader Jeff Fort, between the Black Panther Party and the P-Stone Nation.

Panthers from Boston and Philadelphia and Washington, D.C., and everywhere else came. Thousands of people were lined up outside the church listening to the eulogies for the twenty-one-year-old hero. Hundreds more were inside. Yes, everyone repeated, the police had assassinated Chairman Fred. They had kicked in the door and slain him in his sleep.

Dozens of bullets from Thompson submachine guns had been pumped into his bed, two bullets fired point-blank into his head. It had been an FBI assassination under the direction of special agent Marlin Johnson, carried out by Illinois state police wielding twenty-seven guns and led by their nigger, James "Gloves" Davis. Davis and his cohorts had blasted the entire cracker box of a house in the dark before dawn, wounding Brenda Harris, Satchell, and Verlina Brewer and killing young Mark Clark in their determination to reach their real target. Though the *Chicago Tribune* headlines produced by longtime FBI friend and *Tribune* editor Clayton Kirkpatrick supported the lie that the raiding police had been assaulted, everyone knew it was an assassination. It was according to plan: to eliminate the rise of a messianic black man, in the person of Fred Hampton.

As the eulogies concluded, I could hear Panther sound trucks outside, winding through the icy streets, blasting Fred's favorite contemporary song, the one he had been making everybody sing along with him in those last days in Chicago. It was a Motown song, a Motown sound, the sound that seemed to be the sound of black rebellion. Diana Ross and the Supremes were singing.

> . . . Someday
> we'll be together—
> Say it, say it, say it, say it again . . .

Now the procession passed before Fred's casket. I watched thousands file by with raised fists to Fred, hundreds of members of the P-Stone Nation, uniformed in red berets, pounding fists against their chests in homage—"to the Nation!" It occurred to me that it was the end of 1969. I wiped away my tears, the voice of Fred Hampton now filling me as it rang out in the church and beyond.

I ain't gon' die slippin' on no ice. I ain't gon' die in no airplane crash. I'm gon' die for the People. 'Cause I live for the People. 'Cause I love the People. Power to the People! Power to the People!

CHAPTER 11

WHERE IS
THE LOVE?

HER SKIN WAS VERY WHITE. She was a porcelain doll, and just as delicate. I never resented what Masai felt for her. It was understandable. Jean Seberg was truly beautiful.

We had met Jean in the early part of that terrible year of 1969. David had "assigned" Masai and me to see her. She was another white movie star who wanted to help.

A small group of Hollywood helpers had already begun to astound us with their support for our chapter by the time we met Jean. If we had thought about it, it was a natural alliance.

Historically, artists were the traditional allies of movements for social change. In the twentieth century, the art of filmmaking had produced men like Charlie Chaplin, so progressive he became a personal target of J. Edgar Hoover's anti-Communist campaign. There had been the Hollywood Ten, and tens more, who were blacklisted from the film industry for refusing to cower before U.S. Senator Joseph McCarthy's anti-Communist raid on America.

Recent history gave further testimony to that affiliation. The civil-rights movement, the most potent surge for social change in the history of America, had been vigorously supported by artists, black and white. When the latter-day Black Power people seized leadership of the black struggle, they shunned all white involvement, raising fists in white faces. White artists found their support of that movement rejected. Whatever the hazards of association, the Black Panther Party seemed to make a place in the sun for sympathetic whites. White artists were the first to come in out of the cold.

As Los Angeles and New York were the main homes of the artistic communities America fostered, the party chapters there began developing relationships with liberal and progressive white artists. In New York, there were such notable supporters as Leonard Bernstein. Our chapter in Southern California, however, was becoming the beneficiary of the support of the most powerful collection of artists in America: the Hollywood film industry's actors, actresses, producers, writers, and directors.

People like Don and Shirley Sutherland, and the writer Don Freed, and actors like Jon Voigt and Susan St. James and Jane Fonda, and, most consistent of all, producer Bert Schneider had begun lending us their homes for fund-raising soirees that produced thousands of dollars in hard cash. They subscribed to and helped obtain other subscriptions for our newspaper. They sent monthly checks for our breakfast program, and paid our incessant bails. As most black artists, along with other black professionals, steered around and away from us, we clutched Hollywood, and did not analyze it. We thanked our stars.

That was what made me so resentful of author Tom Wolfe's wholesale appraisal of such white supporters with the epithet "radical chic." The influential and popular Wolfe coined that phrase to characterize the rich and famous suddenly latching on to the Panther cause—with the added counterimage of the black Mau Mau, who operated a flimflam to privately exploit the radical chic.

The bevy of white "star" supporters were, the cosmopolitan Wolfe suggested, only casting themselves in a more interesting role, to enliven the boring comfort of life between their real roles. I thought his well-touted term was, at best, a superficial stereotype. At worst, that label, as it seeped into the lingo of the times, ridiculed our supporters with a judgment that could make them recoil.

It was true that some of those cinematic souls were motivated by something less than concern over the plight of poor and oppressed black people. It was equally true that there were ordinary black opportunists in our revolution, as in our ranks. Among those at the various parties and brunches our steady supporters sponsored, there were surely those who wanted to satisfy their curiosity about mythical black men. There were surely those titillated by the danger and daring seemingly involved in being near real black "militants." There were surely those who imagined themselves vicariously linked to some dramatic revolutionary act. There were surely those who simply found it the thing to do in 1969.

None of that was the point. We were dying, and all of them, the strongest and the most frivolous, were helping us survive another day.

There was nothing at all radically chic about Jean Seberg. From the moment Masai and I entered her rented house in Beverly Hills, I felt her genuineness and decency. She was expressive, like a little girl, excitedly interested in our programs. Transplanted from an all-white, all-American youth in Iowa, she really wanted to know about black people, about the nature of our oppression and the price of our freedom.

She had supported other efforts of blacks in the past: the NAACP—surprisingly, when she was a teenager in Iowa; and, more recently, the school and other social programs of a flashy, independent Muslim named Hakim Jamal (whom Masai knew). She had come to the realization, she told us, that black people could never be treated fairly or justly unless entire systems in America were revolutionized. She wanted to support such an effort.

Her friend, fellow actress Vanessa Redgrave, through whom she had made initial contact with us, considered Jean foolish to become involved with the Black Panther Party. While it was never clear to me precisely why Redgrave felt that way, Jean had her own ideals. She simply believed what she had been taught back in Marshalltown, embodied in the words about freedom and equality found in the Declaration of Independence. To me, Jean seemed a free spirit and a true believer.

After several hours of listening to Masai and I discuss the ideals and goals of the party, and the specifics of our programs, she offered her financial support—and something more, I sensed, as she and Masai lapsed into a long, personal conversation about Hakim Jamal.

Masai and I visited her about once a week after that. Soon I saw no point in going with him.

That was months before the raid on our office and Fred's assassination. Jean had given us quite a bit of money by then. She gave it in incremental amounts, several thousand dollars at a time. Our arrangement was that she would telephone Masai or me when she had a contribution to make. She would simply leave a message that she had called. An envelope of cash would then be delivered to my mother's house for one of us to pick up. She used a pseudonym when she called, "Aretha," after the Queen of Soul. The three of us had laughed in deciding on that name. Jean felt if she was known as a major contributor to the party, she would not get work in Hollywood, and would not, in turn, have the resources to continue. It was logical.

That first meeting with Jean was also some time before I became pregnant with Masai's child, before he began spending most of his time in Oakland, before his sudden marriage. It was also before Masai's wife, too, became pregnant—which gave rise to Jean's dubbing him "Johnny Appleseed."

When I returned to Los Angeles after Fred's funeral in Chicago, I called Jean. She was out of the country, but she made arrangements to get some money to our chapter as soon as possible.

The main office on Central Avenue could not be occupied. Thousands of rounds of Los Angeles Police Department ammunition had punctured and destroyed the walls of our two-story building. There were so many bulletholes that light from the front of the building shone through to the back. So many tear-gas canisters had been tossed into the building's windows and doors that people passing by the building on the street still became nauseous and teary-eyed.

The damage had been done by an army: the LAPD's new, and previously unknown, Special Weapons and Tactics team, known as SWAT. SWAT, a funny acronym, its sound descriptive of its intentions for us, was billed as an "urban guerrilla counterinsurgency team"—superior to and superseding the Metro Squad.

Before the raid on our office, no one had heard of SWAT. People had seemed incredulous when we told them about those dark blue trucks containing heavy artillery and military materials and specially trained men that had sat outside the Central Avenue office in November, a month before. Now it was clear that the LAPD had spent several hundred thousand dollars to actually create a military force to do one thing: eliminate the Black Panther Party in their domain.

In one fell swoop, they had tried to destroy our Southern California office and our Southern California chapter. They had come at three in the morning with a search warrant and a battering ram and a helicopter and a tank and those dark blue trucks. They had assaulted the headquarters building, as well as two other facilities.

SWAT team members assaulting our headquarters had sustained substantial wounds, while Panthers had not—at least not any serious bullet wounds. Albert Armour, at another facility, had even survived, after fighting SWAT team units alone for half an hour, firing from the rooftop when the building was overtaken and the few others there were forced to surrender. Tommye Williams had been the most serious casualty of the assault, taking a ricocheted bullet in her leg.

Later, however, they had all been beaten mercilessly. Kidneys had been collapsed by gun butts. Teeth had been kicked out by combat boots. Eyes had been stomped closed.

Later, after the five-hour battle on Central Avenue, our typewriters and mimeograph machines and telephones had been smashed. Our posters had been ripped from the walls. Our pots and pans and food and books had been strewn wildly, angrily, over the second-story floors. Our files had been demolished. Our furniture had been broken; our roof caved in.

As I walked through the headquarters building with a gas mask, I was overcome by the wreckage committed by rage. I stared at the hundreds of cigarette filters sprinkled on the floors. My comrades had stuffed them into their nostrils when gas masks had failed them, to keep from being forced outside. They had hunkered down behind the sandbags and reinforced walls and fought like madmen and survived. Now they were all in jail under exorbitant bails for extravagant charges.

Reviewing the devastation, I wondered how long our spirit could last. After visiting my eighteen comrades in jail and the hospital wards of the jail, I knew the police had damaged us severely. Still, they had destroyed neither our chapter nor our will. We would start again.

It was hard to be pregnant under the circumstances. As March 1970 drew near, however, and I began to feel the regular movements of a living being inside me, the anger and rage of 1969 were assuaged. In the hours of quiet in my bed in the chapter's house in Compton, where I now lived, I would touch the outline of my swelled belly. There would come what seemed a response. I could see it! It was delightful, the sight and feeling of a little being turning, reaching, moving inside my body. I took to talking to the baby and telling it what was happening.

Now we were being stopped in our car by a pig named Zeigler. He was forcing us out of the car at gunpoint and delightedly announcing that if he shot me in the stomach, he could "kill two birds with one stone."

Second birthday celebration. My mother tried to make me "the most beautiful girl in the world."

At a neighbor's Halloween party on York Street where I grew up. It would not be long before I hated life there. Here with the women of my house, left to right: *my grandmother, Aunt Mary, and mother (and me in costume).*

First ballet recital, after which I came to
consider the ballet part of the repertoire of
"white things" I could do.

Some of my best friends forever, particularly during summertime, when
the boundaries of my world shrunk to those of my ghetto neighborhood.
Clockwise from top left: *Barbara Taylor, Kathy Neal, me, and Darlese*
Reid.

Having left behind the black ghetto and a white lover, I stumbled upon Sandra Scott. She became a beacon of black womanhood as I entered the maelstrom called the sixties.

When the force of the Free Huey movement erupted in 1968, I was driven to decide whether to be "part of the problem or part of the solution." I joined the Black Panther Party.

John Huggins, Black Panther captain, then Southern California chapter chairman. Only twenty-three when he lost his life, he had already retrieved mine.

Bunchy Carter, founder of the party's Southern California chapter, formerly head of the 5,000-strong Slauson gang, was so formidable a man it was hard to come to terms with his assassination in 1969.

Ericka Huggins remained strong through the assassination of her husband, John, in Los Angeles and her own arrest in New Haven. She spent two years isolated in jail awaiting trial.

An early moment of unity among black power advocates (1967). Seated left to right: *Dick Gregory, Ron Karenga, H. Rap Brown, and Ralph Featherstone.* Standing: *US members Tayari,* second left, *and Msimaji,* second right.

The FBI (agent at right) *directed the innumerable violent police raids on Panther facilities. This raid in Chicago occurred six months before the murder of Fred Hampton.*

It would take ten years to prove that the assassination by state police of Fred Hampton, Illinois chapter chairman of the Black Panther Party, was orchestrated by the FBI under J. Edgar Hoover's directive to "stop the rise of a black messiah."

Only eleven Panthers were inside the Los Angeles headquarters when hundreds of the L.A.P.D.'s new SWAT team assaulted it in December of 1969. Because the battle lasted an incredible five hours, it was characterized by the press as a "mini-Vietnam."

David Hilliard, insightful and faithful Black Panther chief of staff (1967-1974), survived being viciously assailed by Eldridge Cleaver only to be later casually expelled from the party—a casualty of Huey Newton's rage.

The provocative rhetoric of Black Panther minister of information Eldridge Cleaver not only shocked America but also drove a dangerous wedge into the heart of the party.

Masai Hewitt, Panther minister of education, father of my only child, was the center of an FBI scheme to destroy film actress Jean Seberg.

By the time I reached Beijing, traveling as part of a group headed by Eldridge Cleaver, I was living in terror from Cleaver's threat to bury me at our final destination.

Huey Newton, founder and leader of the Black Panther Party. Not long after he was freed from prison in July 1970, I met him and came to think of him as my lover and leader.

*George Jackson, writer
and field marshal of the
Black Panther Party,
was assassinated by San
Quentin prison guards
one year after other
California prison guards
cut down his seventeen-
year-old brother,
Jonathan.*

*Ten thousand came to Oakland to celebrate the life of George Jackson after
his assassination in August 1971.*

The success of the Panther free-breakfast program inspired numerous other party service programs for the poor, including distribution of free food and the establishment of free health clinics. These programs as much as Panther guns triggered J. Edgar Hoover's targeting of the party for the most massive and violent FBI assault ever committed.

When Black Panther Party chairman Bobby Seale and I launched our campaign for Oakland political office in 1972, it was not because the party had set aside the "bullet for the ballot." This was a change in tactics, not in strategy.

Returning with Huey from my second trip to China. I was named the party's new minister of information, replacing Eldridge Cleaver.

Early formal school for Panther children soon developed into the well-regarded Oakland Community School. Among the students pictured here are: Ericka Brown, bottom row, far right; *Geronimo Clark,* left of Ericka Brown, *the son of Joan Kelley and Nathaniel Clark; John and Ericka Huggins' daughter Mai,* same row, far left; *Al and Norma Armour's son, Al Jr.,* second row, far right; *Gwen Fountaine's daughter, Jessica,* second row, second from right, *and son, Ronnie,* third row, second from left.

I found it difficult to be a real mother to Ericka Brown, whose love for me remained constant nevertheless.

Stealing time together just before Huey would go into exile in Cuba. Here with Gwen Fountaine, second from right, and Darron Perkins, far left, an unsung hero whose sharp witticisms always reduced me to a helpless state of laughter.

After Bobby Seale's expulsion from the party and Huey's designation of me as chairman in 1974, I ran for Oakland political office alone.

After I became chairman of the party, other women were finally placed on the Central Committee. Among them were: Ericka Huggins, seated; Norma Armour, standing, right; and Phyllis Jackson, whom I came to admire more than nearly anyone else in the party.

I was able to secure the endorsement of California governor Jerry Brown, left, for Lionel Wilson, the Panther-sponsored candidate for Oakland mayor.

Huey and I spent the days alone together during my one visit with him in Cuba in 1975, though he lived in exile with Gwen Fountaine. It was there I learned to appreciate that Gwen was not so much "his" woman as she was my sister.

Only months after Huey returned from three years of exile in Cuba, I suffered a nervous breakdown and was forced to reexamine my commitment to him and his party.

Now we were speaking at a huge mass rally for the eighteen L.A. Panthers in jail from the December raids; and cheering with the thousands over the testimonial of "Bebe," the lady who lived around the corner from the Central Avenue headquarters. She was addressing the crowd, her wig cocked "ace-deuce": "Yeah, the police come *early* in the mornin', rootin' us up out of our houses, tellin' us not to say a thing. And I say to my friend, 'Why they doin' this to the Panters? When I'm sick, I can't call no doctor. I calls the Panters, and they come see 'bout me.' And she say, 'That's right, honey.' And then I say, 'And when I ain't got no food for my chil'ren, I calls the Panters, and they come see 'bout me . . .' "

Now we were making a speech at an Emma Lazarus Jewish Women's Club meeting, where old Polish ladies who had fought the Nazis with guns and refused to go to the gas chambers were telling me to stop smoking while I was pregnant.

Now we were singing to a hundred thousand people gathered in San Francisco's Golden Gate Park for an antiwar rally, where David's speech, which suggested the war be ended by killing Nixon, triggered his arrest for "*conspiracy* to kill the President."

Now we were meeting "Aunt Jean" at the airport, where she announced that she, too, was pregnant.

"Can you believe it?" Jean Seberg declared excitedly above the din as I greeted her at the L.A. airport.

She touched my stomach and spoke to the baby: "Aunt Jean is having a baby, too!"

This, I thought, was the "wonderful secret" she had told me about over the telephone, girlishly enticing me to meet her at the airport if I wanted to hear more.

"No, Jean, I can't believe it," I said, feeling afraid for her.

I felt no one would understand about the boy in Mexico she was telling me had fathered the child. For all intents and purposes, she was still married to French author Romain Gary. She still lived with him officially in France. It was a marriage headed for divorce, but a divorce that would be complicated given the Catholic-grounded French divorce laws.

I told her all that.

"Romain is my friend more than my husband. He'll understand when he sees how happy I am," she said, beaming.

She had met the father in Mexico, where she had just completed a film about Mexican revolutionaries. The boy had a part in the film. He was more than an actor, she swore. He was a revolutionary himself, she said, as I recalled another love affair she had had during a different film. Maybe she had confused everything. Maybe Tom Wolfe was right. But I had come to love Jean. She was happy, and she needed to be loved.

"So you had a love affair," I finally declared, "but this is really foolish, Jean." I tried suggesting she return to Mexico to have an abortion.

"You should be happy for me," she exclaimed brightly, side-stepping everything I had said. "You, of all people, should be really happy for me. I want this baby, don't you see?"

She was going back to France, anyway, to wind up her life with Gary.

"I *am* happy for you," I said, resigned to the notion that she did not live by the rules.

Her blond hair was still close-cropped, a remnant of her debut film *Saint Joan*. She looked the part even then. She *was* the part, an absurd girl who could never accept brutality or oppression or injustice, and who really believed in love.

She handed me a present she had bought for her "niece or nephew" and kissed me goodbye.

I was sure Jean would have held my hand. I longed for someone to do so, though I tried to be stalwart. I realized I had done nothing to prepare for the moment of the birth of my baby. The Vietnamese women had their babies one day and got back into battle the next, I had told myself. I was, after all, a revolutionary. There were bullets or prisons waiting to take me. There was the grave, ultimately. Surely I could have a baby.

The pain was more than I could bear. I felt alone, and sad for being so. I felt powerless. I did not want to go through with it. I could not believe I would have to give birth to that baby who had been with me for those past months, whose face I did not know. A living being would actually have to emerge from my body. I was frightened.

Masai, who in the last month had decided to behave like the father of my child, arrived at the hospital. He brought my mother with him. Dorothy Phillips, a Sister in the party who lived with me and the others in the Compton house, was there. She had driven me to the hospital at four in the morning, Masai being elsewhere with his pregnant wife. Neither my mother nor Dorothy, nor even Masai, however, was allowed to see me. Because he was not married to me, Masai's paternity was irrelevant to the Catholics who operated Queen of Angels Hospital—none of whom, I thought, had to have this baby.

Giving birth was endurable until the moment there was no break between the labor pains. I had thought it would be a 5-4-3-2-1-0 operation. There was one sustaining pain now, hard and unbearable. I begged the nurse coming to check on me for something to ease the pain. She responded by telling me to breathe properly. I had forgotten to go to those stupid classes for breathing, I now remembered. I was changing my mind about natural childbirth, I told her arrogantly. She went off in a huff.

On each of her more-frequent returns to my room, I implored her to give me something to help ease the pain, simultaneously trying to retain some pittance of dignity—lost in my physical appearance; reduced to absurdity by the enema I had been forced by some unknown person to take; stripped away by the shaving of my pubic hair. She remained firm.

After about five hours of such exchanges, beside myself with pain and frustration, I changed tactics. "Fuck you, then," I finally shouted at her back, banging my elbows on the bed's sidebars, which she had furiously raised.

Marie Branch, the only black medical professional who helped us at our free clinics in L.A. arrived and took command. She forced them to accept her as my private nurse.

She made them unstrap me. Before she arrived, I had been given a shot of something known commonly as "twilight sleep," to temper my hostile attitude. I had tried to get out of bed, where, according to medical text, I was to remain prone. The drug had only made me hysterical. To keep me in place, leather straps had been harnessed across my feet and chest. Marie ordered the staff to free me and let me have my baby sitting up, which, by then, was all I wanted.

The hysteria and pain subsided. My mind grew silent, contemplating the magnitude of the process. A being was coming out of my body; a being who had been breathing inside my dark womb would soon open its eyes to me, a separate person, its mother. Would he be happy? I wondered. Would she be whole, not damaged by my life and the way I was living it? Would he grow up in a welcome world or a still-hostile one? I suddenly loved that little being whose face I did not know. She was more than revolutions or oppression or freedom or time or death. To give that being

life, I would die. I did die, for my ego vanished at the moment of
her birth. Ericka.

It was June of 1970, three months after Ericka was born, right
after the fantastic and dirty little story had been printed in the *Los
Angeles Times* about Jean Seberg. We were still reeling from the
repercussions of columnist Joyce Haber's FBI-sponsored story.

> *Let us call her Miss A . . . She is beautiful and she's blond . . .*
> *. . . According to those really "in" international sources, Topic A is*
> *the baby Miss A is expecting, and its father. Papa's said to be a rather*
> *prominent Black Panther.*

Jean had called me and cried over the story. It had been
published around the world, landing on the front covers of French
journals. She had pledged she would never return to the United
States.

Romain Gary had slapped her around because of it. He had
accepted the pregnancy at first, but the publicity hurt him, and
he hurt her.

Panthers were outraged by the possibility of its truth, grumbling about which Central Committee member had "fucked that
white bitch." Hollywood supporters were worried about their own
association with the party.

No one was interested in the truth. The FBI had done well.
Its telephone wiretaps had picked up information about "Aretha"
in conversations between her and me, or her and Masai. They had
placed FBI "interpretation" on the funny little appellation
"Johnny Appleseed," which Jean had given Masai after she learned
he was fathering two children, his wife's and mine. They had
followed him on his visits to her. They had made their move.

The secret, internal memorandum the FBI's Los Angeles office forwarded to Hoover in April 1970 read:

> Bureau permission is requested to publicize pregnancy of Jean
> Seberg, well-known movie actress, by Raymond Hewitt ("Masai")
> of the Black Panther Party by advising Hollywood gossip columnists
> in the Los Angeles area of the situation.
> It is felt that the possible publication of Seberg's pregnancy
> could cause her embarrassment and serve to cheapen her image
> with the general public.

Hoover's immediate response had been:

Jean Seberg has been a financial supporter of the Black Panther Party and should be neutralized. Her current pregnancy by Raymond Hewitt while still married affords an opportunity for such effort.

I talked to Jean a few times afterward. I would never see her again. She would return to Marshalltown to have a bizarre funeral for her stillborn baby, madly displaying the little corpus in a glass casket to refute the FBI. Years later, she would commit suicide in France.

Now, in June, Eldridge was calling me away from the never-ending madness. That was how I felt as I listened to David Hilliard. Eldridge was forming a delegation of radical American journalists to join him in North Korea. He had left Cuba and was now in exile in Algeria, where he had met the North Koreans.

I was to join this delegation to North Korea, David was saying, as a representative of the Black Panther newspaper. David was slightly perturbed about that. Eldridge had specifically ordered that I be sent, as deputy minister of information for Southern California. While David said he was comfortable with the idea of my going, he seemed distraught that Eldridge had not requested that a member of the Central Committee be part of the delegation. After all, Emory Douglas, minister of culture, and Masai, minister of education, had accompanied David to see Eldridge in Algiers in 1969.

In any event, David himself could not leave the country. He was facing trial. The federal "kill Nixon" charge had been dismissed. David was, however, preparing for the trial on charges stemming from the April 6 events that had sent Eldridge into exile.

We would be in North Korea three weeks, David was explaining. Eldridge would outline everything about the nature of the trip when we met him in Moscow. My heart sang.

I returned to Oakland weeks later, in early July. David wanted to see me before I left the country. I was planning to leave that evening and had with me my packed bags and passport. It was rather ludicrous to have a passport, I thought with a smile, since travel to North Korea was specifically forbidden to U.S. citizens. But we were not U.S. citizens. We were outsiders, runaway slaves. At any rate, I was ready. I had made arrangements for my little

Ericka to be cared for by my comrades; Gwen Goodloe would personally supervise it all. I was ready to see Papa again.

"Find out when Eldridge plans on opening the International Section office," David said in our secret meeting.

I made mental notes.

"Find out if Kathleen is returning," he said, referring to Eldridge's wife, who had joined him when he moved to Algiers. "Ask him what really happened to Byron Booth. Did D.C. make it to Algiers?" he continued, speaking about San Francisco captain Don Cox, who had disappeared after a shoot-out in the Hunters Point section of San Francisco. "Tell Papa my case looks bad. I'll probably do some time . . ."

David went on for almost an hour, thrusting me into a whole new world. I had not known that D.C. had been sent to Algiers. I had never heard of Byron Booth. Apparently he had disappeared after arriving in Algiers. I did not know there was to be an International Section of the Black Panther Party. In listening to David, I realized that the party seemed to be growing into a legitimate member of the international family of Communists.

Before taking me to the airport, David had to make a stop at the party's national headquarters. The aroma of spicy barbecue was wafting through the rooms of the building. The Bay Area branches were about to hold an anti-Fourth-of-July picnic and rally in West Oakland. Tons of ribs and chicken were being roasted over charcoal in the facility's back yard. The kitchen was filled with Sisters *and* Brothers making potato salad and lemonade.

David ushered me into a small office to wait for him. There were several Panthers inside awaiting work assignments. I sat down next to the only one I knew, Jonathan Jackson. He was reading a book by Che Guevara.

"Have you spoken to your brother, lately?" I asked, interrupting.

He had, he said, without looking up. It was typical behavior for Jonathan. I thought he was too serious most of the time, though he was only seventeen years old.

The year before, he had seriously asked Angela Davis to permit him to be her bodyguard. Angela had become caught in a morass of media and police attention over her battle with UCLA, based on the university's refusal to reinstate her faculty position because she was—by then—a member of the Communist Party, U.S.A. Jonathan had also learned most of the songs on my album, *Seize the Time*, after I brought it to his family's home in Pasadena on one of my visits there; in particular, the song written for Franco, "The Panther," dubbed "Get Guns and Be Men." He was most serious about his beloved brother, George Jackson, his imprisoned hero, whose book, *Soledad Brother*, was about to be published.

Jonathan and his mother, Georgia, had recently moved their things from Pasadena to Berkeley, into one of the party's houses there, so that they could visit George regularly at nearby San Quentin prison. He had been transferred from Soledad prison after he was charged with the murder of a prison guard.

Even when Georgia joined us in the little office, Jonathan did not look up from his reading.

"Jonathan! At least stop long enough to give Georgia a chair," I said, giving him an admonishing smile.

Georgia greeted me with a hug and a wink.

"Oh yeah. Right on," he said, getting up without putting down his book. He leaned against a wall near his mother and continued reading.

I chatted with Georgia a few minutes, until I saw David waiting in the doorway for me.

I kissed Jonathan goodbye on the cheek. It was the sweetest face, one had to kiss it. His fair complexion took on the blush of a boy. He finally looked up with his big, questioning, sad eyes.

"Okay. See you later, Sister Elaine," he eked out with unbelievable shyness.

I boarded an Oakland-to-Los Angeles shuttle flight and waited in the L.A. airport to meet Robert Scheer. By arrangement, he was to be my traveling companion. Scheer and I took a nonstop flight from Los Angeles to Paris a few hours later.

Scheer was a writer, and one of the editors of *Ramparts* magazine. He was also some sort of radical hippie, it seemed, from Berkeley. With a group of his white radical friends in the area, he had formed something called the Red Brigade, whose purpose was unclear to me, even as he talked about it. Scheer also, according to David, had been instrumental in getting Eldridge into Cuba.

He and I would be joining some of the others in Paris. We would meet Eldridge and the rest in Moscow. The United States had diplomatic relations with the French; the French had diplomatic relations with the Russians; the Russians had diplomatic relations with the North Koreans, the Democratic People's Republic of Korea.

Those who met Scheer and me in Paris were also white, Jan

Austin and Andy Truskier and Anne Froines and other radical journalists. There would be eleven of us in all, including Eldridge.

When the Aeroflot jet landed in Moscow, it was dark. Eldridge loomed forward out of the crush of heavyweight Russians. He was elegant and not in the least worn. He had on an all-white suit and was still wearing the earring in his pierced ear. He greeted me first, expansively taking me into his arms. It had been a long way back to him.

Surely the Russian tsars and nobility were frustrated even in their death. Ordinary peasants had not only seized power from them, their peasant hands had laid claim to the vestiges of their royal reign. The beautiful Baroque hotel we entered had once belonged to them. Its wide marble stairwells had been theirs. Its crystal chandeliers and Byzantine rugs and tapestried walls had been theirs. The elegant balcony doors of the room where Eldridge and I slept had been theirs. The turrets of the basilican edifices rising in the distance sparkled in the morning light. The Russian summer sun filled the room when we flung open our balcony doors.

I was musing about the history it all represented as I listened to the voice of Eldridge. He was addressing the entire delegation, now gathered in our room. Of the eleven members, only he and I were black. Besides the whites, there were two Asians: a young, diminutive Japanese woman and a fellow from San Francisco's Chinatown, whose face was overwhelmed by acne.

"Babylon must be burned," Eldridge was saying. "But the Black Panther Party is abandoning its duty to take Babylon down . . ."

I grew attentive.

"The fact is, there's a split in the party. The right wing has seized the reins of leadership and put a muzzle on the Panther. The vanguard party has become a breakfast-for-children club."

Was he serious? Was he constructing another of his well-known grand metaphors, a bizarre one? Like me, the others were stilled by incredulity, their pens frozen over the notepads they held.

"But I represent the left wing of the party," he proclaimed, "the International Section, headquartered in Algiers. We're saying it's time to clip the right wing operating out of national head-quarters, dominated by the reformist David Hilliard and his nep-otistic hierarchy, which includes his reactionary brother, June, and his silly wife, Pat."

I could hardly think, much less respond. It was impossible to believe what I was hearing.

"Babylon is quiet. Pigs are comfortable. Why? Because the vanguard is cooking fucking breakfasts instead of drawing guns!" he boomed.

Had exile driven him so mad he did not see? Had he been given some new mind-altering drug that had erased the police raids and assassinations from his brain? He had obviously forgotten the detail of the party mandate, based on the teachings of Malcolm X, that no member speak against another outside the ranks.

"The entire movement will follow suit," Eldridge went on to open mouths. "I'm not going to stand for it. *You* can't stand for it . . ."

"The left wing of the vanguard party is calling upon you, our white, radical Mother Country brothers and sisters—and you others—to stand with us. Support the International Section, the hijackers and the ex-cons and revolutionary warriors in exile, who mean to set fire to Babylon. With your assistance, the real party can rise again, and we can return to finish what we started," he finished in a dramatic whisper.

"I'm sorry," Jan Austin boldly interrupted, putting down her pen and notepad. "What exactly do you want *us* to do? *We're* not in the party. We're journalists and writers. Why are you telling us this?"

"So that," Eldridge said with a sigh, "with the might of your pens you will spread the word throughout Babylon. Recognize the left wing. Tell everybody who the true revolutionaries are. Take the correct line. Call for the bombing of pig strongholds. Urge the kidnapping of the children of the bourgeoisie. Demand that the bastions of Wall Street be burned to the ground. Stir some shit in Babylon. Show some fucking spirit!"

"Is that why you asked us to travel all the way here?" Andy Truskier asked, unmoved.

"Basically. I had to talk to all of you in person. I had to personally let you know what was happening to the party. With the help of Scheer, I handpicked each of you for this mission."

I noted Bob Scheer's silence.

"I'm trying to get this train rolling again. But I can no longer communicate with any of the members of the Central Committee in Oakland. They're all Hilliard lackeys. I brought Sister Elaine here to be my personal emissary. She's loyal to me. She and I go a long way back. She's going to take the message back to the true believers in the party, so they'll know it came from my lips. I've had word a lot of them are sick and tired of the bullshit. So you don't have to worry about the party's business. Do your thing, and we'll deal with the party . . ."

Looking out of a window, all I could wonder was when and how he had come to the conclusion that I would be his emissary to advance a rift inside the party. Was he so arrogant as to imagine that my expressions of love for him had meant I would help him destroy the Black Panther Party?

"Of course, we'll go to Korea and talk to them about promoting the thoughts and writings of good ole Comrade Kim Il Sung," he continued. I promised them we'd get Kim's entire works published in the U.S. I'm sure we can do that, can't we, Scheer? That's why they arranged this whole thing. But yes, I needed to see all of you on this more serious matter. I need your understanding. Can you dig it?"

"Right on," those who opened their mouths mumbled, new acolytes of the massive man who sat before us, one whom I did not know and, it occurred to me, never really had known.

It lasted another hour—Eldridge's attacks on the party, on David, on everything sacred. Later, when we were away from the others, I challenged the minister of information of the Black Panther Party.

I told him flat out that the saddest thing about how absolutely wrong he was about David was that David respected him. I asked him why he could not see that it was David who had held the party together through all of the hell we had faced since he left. Furthermore, David had always been in constant communication with the minister of defense, the leader of the party, Huey P. Newton, in prison at San Luis Obispo, whom Eldridge had not attacked.

He told me I did not understand. He knew David. David was ignoring the directives of Huey, whose hands were tied, because David was "pussy." That was why the party was stuck in reform. He knew what was happening. I did not, for which he might forgive me. David was destroying the vanguard, buying more eggs than guns.

The rank and file wanted to move. Loyalty to the party was the only thing holding them back. He had solid information about that from Brothers out of New York who had joined him in Algiers. Who *were* these "Brothers," I asked him. All I needed to know was that they were *the* bad motherfuckers. Anyway, anybody with eyes could see how weak the party had become. This had been echoed, Eldridge said, by a Trinidadian Sister named Connie Matthews. She worked with a Panther support group in Europe and had come to Algiers to talk to him about how the party's reputation in the international community was stained, how nobody was taking the party seriously anymore.

"And after sitting in Algiers," I said, "listening to these so-called Brothers and this Connie Matthews, you want to . . ."

"Listen! Shut up and listen!" he commanded. "They just confirmed what I already know. There's unrest in the rank and file, and even on the streets—remember the Weathermen thing?—over the fact that the Hilliard dynasty has damn near forced everybody to put down their guns. I hear this shit everywhere. Even in Algiers! I'm not going to stand for it!"

We argued for hours. Rather, I more and more patiently tried to explain that David was seriously committed to the revolution and that the party was on the correct road.

"The party can't do battle with the pigs alone," I said earnestly. "Take a look at our losses, if nothing else, Eldridge. Our own people are becoming afraid of us. Every time the pigs attack us, the whole community suffers. The people just aren't ready for that. The only thing holding the party and the people together is the programs . . ."

"Bullshit!" he shot back. "Revolution has to be won, not coddled like eggs. The Hilliards are so punked-out and gun-shy, they're making the vanguard look like a reformist bitch."

"Nobody's put down the gun, Eldridge, but if we don't have the programs, we won't organize the people to pick up the gun. And it's the people," I reminded him as forcefully as I dared, "who will, after all, ultimately make the revolution . . . Face it, Eldridge," I pleaded, "the only thing we've done so far to advance the struggle, besides losing a lot of Brothers, *is* the programs."

"I don't give a fuck about some serve-the-people programs. Anybody who doesn't want to deal with the struggle has to have his ass dragged down the revolutionary road, kicking and screaming if necessary. I'm talking about the same thing I've always talked about, 'revolution in our lifetime' and I mean it . . ."

"You mean the revolution that will die with its secret because all the revolutionaries will have died trying . . ."

"You're too emotional. Can't you see I'm drafting Whitey to take the first heat—Weathermen and all that, and these motherfuckers. Look. I just want to get rid of those weak-assed Hilliards

right now. That's all. There's only one way to get that done and
hold the party together . . . Now, I brought you here to help me
accomplish that.

"All you have to do is sound the alarm. Do it because you
love me. What the fuck. Take a .45 or something, walk into national headquarters," he went on seriously, "and put it to David's
head. Tell the motherfucker you've come with a message from
me: I'm taking back the Black Panther Party in the name of the
true revolutionaries. And don't worry, I've got backup for you,
Brothers waiting for the word from me."

"You must be kidding, Eldridge."

By dinnertime, after we had drunk a second round of vodka
and the beef Stroganoff had been served to the "delegation" at
long tables in the opulent, mirrored dining hall, Eldridge and I
had stopped speaking. The last thing he said to me before I left
his room and tried to find another for myself was that he would
bury me in Algiers.

"I picked you!" he had shouted furiously. "I picked you to
take care of this. You're the perfect candidate. A woman that
everybody in the party knows and that everybody knows loves me.
Just like I know it. The fucking anthem is my song . . . Stop acting
up, and 'let your love come down,' " he said with a chuckle.

"Eldridge, you're crazy . . . I can't deny I loved you. I have
truly loved the idea of you. But you can't be serious about any of
this . . . Please . . . Look, I'll go back and I'll leave the party, and
I won't tell anyone anything. I know you can find yourself another
emissary. 'Cause it's over for me. It's all over, Eldridge."

"You won't get back, bitch, unless you do what I say! Do you
actually think I'd let you walk away from here and mess up the
cha-cha?!" he shouted, standing over me now, seated in the room
with blue taffeta drapes and bedspread. "Besides, there ain't nobody else. I couldn't exactly tell David to send one of the rank and
file. I certainly couldn't call on any of those studs on the Central
Committee. All their sorry asses belong to the Hilliards. You're it,
bitch!"

I tried not to cry or shake.

"If you don't want to work with me, it's simple. I'll bury your
ass. In Algiers. I've got a burial ground there, you know." He
laughed, throwing his head back. "I've put two niggers in the
ground already. Boumédienne doesn't give a fuck," he said referring to the Algerian president. "I do as I please. It ain't Cuba.

I got AK-47's and twenty niggers, and I will put your ass in the fucking ground!"

"I'm not going anywhere but back to the States," I cried out, getting up from the bed. "I'm leaving now. I'll take a plane from here, alone—tonight, if necessary."

"And I'll beat your ass right here and now if you move . . . Anyway, it'll be a hard way back." He laughed again. "I've got your passport. Remember? Got all the passports. If you want it, deal with the Russians or the Koreans. But I don't think you have the heart to put yourself in the middle of an international scandal over it. Do you?"

"You're right, Eldridge. It's more than I can handle," I said in a resigned whisper.

I stepped away from him, trembling.

In that second, I suddenly saw him, knew him. Eldridge was a man so afraid of facing prison again, he had left David behind to take the weight of the charges of April 6. Eldridge was a man who had stood naked before the police, walking away with a sur- face wound to his heel, while Bobby Hutton, half his size and age, had been mowed down before his very eyes. Eldridge was a man who was a rapist, a man who lashed out at women—in fear.

He was undoubtedly capable of inspiring others to act. There was no question that if I were pushed to Algiers, he could inflame his nebulous "niggers" to do what he willed with me. But his own claims to manhood hovered beneath the skin of a man who was, more than anything, a rapist.

"You're right," I repeated. "Right about the passport. Wrong about me. I'm not Kathleen. I do not take ass-kicking. You can kill me here and now, but that's what it's going to take. 'Cause if you touch me, I guarantee you, one of us will die tonight! And I don't think *you've* got the heart to risk an international scandal. You wouldn't have any more countries to run to."

His eyes smiled as he walked past me. He quietly opened the door of the room to leave.

"Later, baby. Later."

Our arrival in Pyongyang, Democratic People's Republic of Korea, postponed the terror. The Koreans seemed genuinely happy to see us, hoping we would enjoy what they announced was our one- month stay in North Korea.

We had already spent one week in Paris and one week in Moscow. The three-week trip Eldridge had originally proposed was now going to be six weeks. It was a reality that I had to accept, while trying to invent a plan of escape, while trying to appreciate the people and places in Pyongyang under the circumstances. The circumstances were only exacerbated by the fact that not only were Eldridge and I not speaking, he had influenced most of the others to isolate themselves from me.

Our hotel was actually a charming place, I thought, as I put away my things. I had a room to myself. The other ten were grouped two to a bedroom, Eldridge sharing one with Scheer, now ordained the cochief of the delegation.

Despite the chill, I smiled along with everyone else as we toured museums, war memorials, factories, clinics, schools, farms. I even found the mental strength to appreciate what I saw was the genuine development of socialism in action. There were no homeless beggars on the streets of Pyongyang, no prostitutes, no hustlers. There were no gambling houses or cheap bars, no run-down houses or apartment buildings. Connected to every work-place were a free clinic and a free child-care facility or school.

Most dominant in Pyongyang and the surrounding country-side were tributes to Kim Il Sung. On every corner on every street there were large colorful paintings or framed photographs of Comrade Kim Il Sung, often adorned with flowers or lighted sun-bursts emanating from his head. Kim Il Sung was more than their hero or leader who had led the Koreans to victory in the fifteen-year guerrilla war against the Japanese imperialists in the 1940s. He was their virtual god, their "Illustrious Leader," around whom they had created a cult of the individual.

We saw a passionate, dramatic, four-hour film, *Sea of Blood*, which depicted the bloody later years of the Koreans' long struggle for liberation from Japanese colonialism. It made most of us cry and walk away with an appreciation for the Koreans' unabashed elevation of the man who led them, finally, to liberation. We also saw the film the Koreans had made of the famous capture of the U.S.S. *Pueblo*. There was actual film footage of the nighttime cap-ture of the *Pueblo*, caught in North Korean waters years after the end of the so-called Korean War—referred to by the Koreans as the "U.S. Imperialist War of Aggression."

During that month, we learned a great deal about the Korean War. We heard personal testimonies about the famous battles known to Americans as Porkchop Hill and Heartbreak Ridge. We saw film footage of the Chinese volunteer soldiers as they greeted their Korean comrades; the Chinese "hordes" that had walked to Korea to fight and had turned the tide of war back to the bargaining tables—despite General MacArthur's bold promise of American victory. We eventually went to the demilitarized zone at Panmunjom and, from the North Korean side, looked into the faces of U.N. and U.S. soldiers "guarding" the border for the U.S.– backed government in the South.

Early one morning, our Korean guides excitedly knocked on our respective hotel room doors. They had important news from the United States: Huey Newton had been released from prison.

Eldridge was genuinely elated. Huey would understand his position, he told me, entering my room without a knock. It was the first time we had spoken since Moscow.

"You don't know Huey, Sister. But you will. He'll be with me. If you want to be part of the vanguard, go back and tell him what I'm talking about. Explain everything to him. Tell him how the Hilliards are making the party lose face in the international revolutionary community with their bullshit breakfasts for children . . .

"Yeah, Huey'll understand. Huey had a red-light trial! He *wanted* a red-light trial! Huey knows revolution is guns and bloodshed, not bullshit . . ."

He rambled on like that for a while as I listened with a serious façade, hoping that, given his sudden burst of enthusiasm for the unknown hero, Huey Newton, he would see I was no longer a problem to be dealt with in Algeria.

That hope was quickly diminished when Eldridge, in his moment of reconciliation with me and the party, dragged me to see Kathleen. I had not wondered about her at all, I realized. She was in a North Korean hospital preparing to have their second child.

Seeing Kathleen was not what bothered me. A part of me admired her. There was something sadly heroic about Kathleen. There was the audacity with which she played her role as one of the first and most significant women in the party. There was her defiant acceptance of Eldridge's well-known brutality toward her. There was her willingness to stick with everything under a variety of adverse conditions, including being uprooted from San Francisco, and now from Algiers to Pyongyang to have her baby.

What threw me back into a shell of fear was Eldridge's behavior on the visit to Kathleen. She was weak and less than one month from delivering. Nevertheless, Eldridge immediately launched into an attack on her about nothing in particular, something personal to them. Her listless response only increased his hostility to her. He did not feel shit about her condition, he told her, since the baby she was carrying was probably not his.

When she tried to defend herself, he shouted her down. "Shut up! Shut up, bitch!" True to form, Kathleen hung on, chiding him with spitfire responses, pushing further with her high-bred intelligence. Incapable of shutting her up, he finally slapped her hard, right there in the pristine orderliness of a North Korean hospital reserved for Communist Party leaders. He slapped her again, as I stood stoically, stupidly helpless. She just sat there in bed, holding her pregnant belly with one hand and wiping away tears with the other. She bravely screamed at him to leave. As he left her room, me trailing, he tossed her a laugh and a last ugly comment that he would have nothing to do with the bastard she was carrying.

My hope of finding a way to survive the trip was finally extinguished on one of our last days in North Korea. We visited the embassy of the Democratic Republic of Vietnam. It was one of the few diplomatic outposts of North Vietnam, as the war with the United States was still raging in the South. The Marxist government of the North, established by the Vietminh (*Viet Nam Doc Lap Dong Minh*) under the leadership of Ho Chi Minh, who had recently died, was the administration the United States was waging war to topple. We had tea there late one afternoon.

We exchanged pleasantries with the Vietnamese through interpreters, drank our tea, and listened to them invite the delegation of radical American journalists to Hanoi for two weeks. With no hesitation at all, Eldridge, on behalf of our delegation, accepted their invitation.

The Vietnamese people seemed small and serious compared to their robust and cheerful Asian comrades in Korea. Of course, there was the debilitation that came from constant war. There had been hardly a breath of peace since Dien Bien Phu, where, in 1954, they had, using the guerrilla warfare tactics of General Giap, finally ousted the French colonialists. From that point forward, a country divided by the 1954 postwar Geneva Conference had suffered internal struggle, due to the refusal of the United States–backed provisional government in the South to hold free elections and its declaration that the South was a separate state.

It was easy to feel at home in Vietnam, although the poverty and underdevelopment were pervasive. Perhaps the influence of years of French domination had so Westernized the people they seemed familiar, the Koreans having seemed more "Asian." Moreover, the Vietnamese offered us their best, when they had so little. They were passionate, unabashedly weeping as they spoke of the horrors of the war, and able to laugh with equal vigor—even about the war. Every time the United States dropped bombs on them, they told us, a big crater was created. The most efficient thing to do with the deep holes the bombs made was fill them with water. Then they became "lakes." "We have many lakes in Vietnam," they laughed.

In contrast to the warmth of the Vietnamese, I was still feeling the chill of Algiers, still coldly isolated from the group. Although we had been eating and touring museums and war memorials, hospitals and farms together, by the time we reached Hanoi, most of the delegation was barely speaking to me at all—thanks, of course, to Eldridge.

I was surprised, then, when Jan Austin burst into my room one afternoon. She was, on the other hand, the only one with whom I did talk beyond the diplomatic doors, and whom I rather liked. She was waving a Vietnamese news bulletin in front of me and speaking about it excitedly, incoherently.

News about the United States was a rare item. We had been isolated from the affairs outside our cloistered world. Other than the brief information we had been given in Korea about Huey Newton's release, we knew nothing of life back in the United States.

Jan was animatedly pointing to several bizarre sentences in the Vietnamese wire service page she held. They said that Huey Newton had spoken at the funeral of Jonathan Jackson.

Jonathan Jackson?! It could not be the same one. What had happened?!

Jan and I raced down the stone stairs of the hotel. We tried to find an English-language magazine or newspaper. Some of the other members of the group were already in the lobby, trying to do the same thing. Eldridge was nowhere in sight. We were told there was a Swiss chargé d'affaires in Hanoi who had an office in the hotel. He might have a journal. We rushed, en masse, into his offices. Inside was a French-language version of *Newsweek* magazine. The secretary let us borrow it.

There was Jonathan Jackson on the cover. There was the sweet face of a boy taking charge of life like a man. His blondish Afro was lit by the photographers' flashes. His beautiful eyes were

covered by smoke-colored glasses. His back was to the camera, but
he had turned his face and upper body around as the picture had
been taken. He held an M-1 carbine at the ready, at waist level.

We sat down on the stairs near the hotel lobby. Jan read the
French and did her best to translate. On August 7, Jonathan Jackson had gone to a courtroom in Marin County, California, where
certain prison inmates were having a hearing. He was alone. He
had taken the parts of a folding-stock M-1 carbine, secreted in a
bag he had brought into the courtroom, put them together, and
stood up in the back.

"All right, gentlemen, I'm taking over now," he was quoted
as having said.

He had passed out automatic pistols to the inmates at the
hearing who had joined him: Arthur Christmas, Ruchell Magee,
and James McClain. A shotgun had been tied to the neck of the
judge. The prosecutor, selected members of the jury, and the
judge had been marched outside at gunpoint, one inmate shouting, "Free the Soledad Brothers by twelve-thirty!" I could smell
the lush beauty of the San Rafael countryside that surrounded the
courthouse that Frank Lloyd Wright designed. I could see the sun
bouncing off the subtle mosaic colors of Wright's building. They
had marched outside to a van, all hostages, and entered the van.
Then the bullets had rained down. Hundreds and hundreds of
rounds from the weapons of San Quentin guards and sharpshooters had been rapidly sprayed into and around the van. The judge's
head had been blown off. The prosecutor had been critically
wounded by San Quentin guard bullets. McClain and Christmas
were killed, and Jonathan Jackson, sitting in the driver's seat, had
been riddled with bullets, slain in his seventeenth year.

I had no more breath in my body. I wondered why I was
there and Jonathan was dead. I wondered why I was still involved
in any of it, if it meant the loss of so much tenderness. Eldridge
Cleaver was a stupid detail. Another man-child was gone. Yes, the
Vietnamese were suffering, and far more; as were the Angolans
and the blacks in South Africa and all the other oppressed peoples
struggling to live. It was still too much. Jonathan was only a boy,
a boy who had had a crush on Angela Davis, a boy who was a
science genius, a boy who loved songs, my songs, and, above all,
a boy who loved his only brother more than life.

Lying on my bed in the waning light and crying, I wrote
another song, a ballad, a lamentation for the man-child who should
not have died so alone . . .

> You weren't there, you didn't see
> Jonathan
> Or do you care, what do you mean
> Jonathan
> What he would do none of us knew
> Jonathan
> for a man was he . . .

Dismissing Eldridge from my mind and focusing on the strength of the Vietnamese for the duration of our two-week stay brought the alleviation of understanding. So many of them had died and would die for their independence.

There were the young guerrilla girls we met on the beach at the Gulf of Tonkin, thirteen- and fourteen-year-olds, up from Saigon for a rest, girls who should have been giggling about boys or lipstick or hairstyles. There were the children we met whose bodies had been maimed by napalm, and those who had only one arm or one leg, the missing limbs destroyed by U.S. bombs. There were the stalwart old women who had lost everyone in their families in U.S. troop destructions of their villages.

So, there would be many Jonathans. There would be more bloodshed and suffering. Perhaps Eldridge was right, I thought. Perhaps we should force the thing fast to its inevitable, ultimate confrontation. No, I decided, Eldridge was wrong. Ours was truly a vanguard organization, a small unit in a big endeavor, whose purpose was to trigger a step-by-step revolutionary process, to clarify the issues, develop the mass mind, solidify a base of struggle, prepare our people to achieve freedom as nonantagonistically as possible—or to prevail in a conflict decided by bloodshed.

We were still not returning to the United States. We were now, according to Eldridge's private arrangements, going to Beijing. We would stay only one week, Eldridge promised, a few of his cherished delegates having found the fortitude to suggest they had to return to their lives. I had been gone from my baby for over two months.

I put on my happy, diplomatic face and found that Beijing in early autumn was not too burdensome. Even as I dragged myself around to the factories and hospitals and new housing developments, I was challenged by the enthusiasm of the Chinese people. Old and young would spontaneously give emotional testimonies,

like Baptist converts, to the glories of socialism. There was a refrain, it seemed:

*If it hadn't been for Chairman Mao and the Chinese Communist
Party, I never would have lived in a house of brick . . .*

*If it hadn't been for Chairman Mao and the Chinese Communist
Party, I never would have eaten meat and vegetables, or educated myself
and my children, or had running water, or medical care . . .*

They affirmed that, but for the revolution, they would not
have had the possibility of a decent life. Most of them would have
lived and died eating the garbage of the feudal landlords for whom
they had toiled, simply surviving the brutalities of the landlords
and the warlords and the opium wars and the invading armies of
eight different colonizing nations, never imagining happiness.

In comparison to the clean crispness of Beijing, Algiers, a crum-
bling, dirty city, was a disaster. It was also a study in contradictions,
eight years after liberation from French colonialism. As we rode
along the highway abutting the Mediterranean, all the signs were
in French. Along the streets, however, women were babbling in
Arabic, still hidden behind the veil. There were open, native marketplaces selling indigenous fruits and grains alongside French
bistros advertising ice-cold Coca-Cola.

The building that Eldridge referred to as the embassy of the
International Section of the Black Panther Party had previously
been the residence of the North Vietnamese ambassador and his
staff. Eldridge had secured it with the help of the Koreans,
probably with another revolutionary lie. It was a white stucco-and-
marble building, with open, airy, arched doorways, very Mediterranean in its feeling. There were three levels, the ground floor
and one above and below, connected by whitewashed stairwells.
A maid and cook lived on the lower level.

A small black woman was the first person I saw, standing in
front of the house. Eldridge introduced her: Connie Mathews. I
did not bother to speak to her. There were several Panthers inside
from New York, men who had actually hijacked airplanes to get
there. There was also the dashing D.C., Don Cox from San
Francisco.

They all greeted Eldridge as though he were a nobleman
returning from a Crusade, taking his bags, showing him telephone
messages and stacks of mail and newspapers. All their hustle and
bustle was overshadowed, I felt, by the racks of AK-47 rifles I saw

lining an entire wall of one of the rooms. I heard somebody tell
Eldridge that Huey Newton had just called.

As Eldridge placed a return call to the United States, some
of his Panthers took Scheer and the rest of the journalists to hotels.
I would be staying at the embassy.

"Yeah, Brother, I know you'll dig where I'm coming from.
The Sister will run it down to you," Eldridge said into the receiver.

I read a Black Panther newspaper as I listened. It was the
July issue, which headlined the release of Huey Newton. Ten
thousand or more had greeted him when he exited the Alameda
County courthouse. The front-page photograph showed him
standing on top of a car, shirtless, surrounded by a mob that filled
the camera lens. Impressive, I thought, ears cocked to Eldridge's
conversation.

"Naw, Huey, you don't need to talk with her now. She'll tell
you everything in person," Eldridge was saying.

I was not sure whether that meant I would really be able to
escape finally, or whether he was covering up a plan to keep me
there indefinitely or, as he had threatened, to "off" me.

I sat up for the next three nights, avoiding sleep as much as
possible, and took quick baths whenever Eldridge went out. I ate
nearly nothing though I had already been reduced to just over
100 pounds. During the day, as "ordered" by Eldridge, I wrote
and typed various press statements that were to be delivered in a
few days. Eldridge was preparing to formally announce the opening of the International Section.

Every news organization in the world arrived at the embassy
for Eldridge's press conference, along with various ambassadors
and leaders of numerous revolutionary organizations based in Algiers. Eldridge was, as usual, effusively dramatic in his delivery,
announcing that the Black Panther Party was establishing an International Section, "to join with our Third World comrades in the
assault on U.S. imperialism." The Brothers stood around in strategic places looking stern and revolutionary. Finally, it was over.
The lights were out, the press was gone. It seemed time to leave.

The next morning, Eldridge gathered together his delegation. Once everyone was obediently seated in a sitting room in the
embassy, Eldridge handed out our passports with a smirk. His
cook served us a meal of couscous. Finally, he told us that he had
made reservations for us on a flight to Paris that would be leaving
in a few hours.

It took me only minutes to pack, despite having to do so while acknowledging Eldridge's various admonitions and reiterations about exactly what I was to tell Huey Newton. Tears of relief clouded my vision, which Eldridge actually presumed to have something to do with my leaving him. My façade had been effective, I smiled weakly inside, alive.

I forgot my fear of flying. I had eleven hours between Paris and New York to contemplate what lay before me. I had eleven hours to decide whether to run from everything or to face it. I had eleven hours to determine what any of it meant to me, or whether everything I had become meant anything or nothing at all. There were eleven hours to develop the courage to tell everything to David and the unknown Huey Newton.

Huey was free. His imprisonment had been a symbolic victory for the reactionary forces in America, which had been gathering momentum since World War II. Achieving his freedom seemed a concrete victory for all of us fighting for real change.

The atomic bombing of Hiroshima and Nagasaki had purchased for the United States the position of dominant world power. The sun had set on the British Empire, and on the other European colonialists. There was only one postwar issue for the United States: holding on to the number-one position. There was only one external threat to that: the Soviet Union, its wartime ally.

The most critical issue facing America at home was the maintenance of internal security. Strife or disruption inside the stronghold would waylay the global march, rust the new imperial sword, give free rein to the voracious appetite of former friend Stalin. Ranks had to be closed.

A postwar anti-Communist paranoia was constructed by J. Edgar Hoover, a friend and manipulator of every president since the 1920s. It flared in the machinations of the House Un-American Activities Committee (HUAC), formerly the Dies Committee. It spread like the proverbial prairie fire, fanned by the shameful Senate hearings conducted by Hoover's close friend Joseph McCarthy. In 1956, the FBI's Counter Intelligence Program (COINTELPRO) was created, the aim of which was not merely to investigate dissidents but to "disrupt, disorganize, and neutralize" them. Now there was wholesale suppression of all dissident citizens of the United States. The new public enemies were anybody and everybody designated as Communists.

The majority of people in the United States were unaffected by all of this. The war had introduced them to a new credit system which could confer great comfort on the lives of Depression survivors. Production and consumption boomed. There were new cars and radios and washing machines and toasters and refrigerators for everyone. There was a wonderful new thing called television. Everybody liked Ike and J. Edgar Hoover. Happy days had come again.

It was okay to round up and jail or even kill Communists and Communist sympathizers. Whoever they might be, they were enemies of freedom.

"Freedom" was the watchword. "Free enterprise," they meant, the men whose monopolies controlled the United States of America, the only interested parties in the business of being number one. It was in the name of freedom that surviving Nazis were employed by the U.S. government, and Ethel and Julius Rosenberg were burned at the stake of the state.

By the end of the fifties, Hoover and his FBI had expanded their investigations and disruptions to civil-rights activities. The civil-rights movement had begun marching with a momentum that was unsettling.

There was the emerging leadership of Martin Luther King, Jr., who could not be labeled a Communist. He could not be assailed as an enemy of freedom, with his nonviolence. But he was charging that there was something wrong with America. Freed slaves had no real freedom, he was saying, had no ability to exercise their life-liberty-pursuit-of-happiness rights. People were listening to him. Blacks sitting in their ghettos and sharecropper shanties were getting ideas and even speaking out.

A lot of white Americans were being shaken from a comfortable sleep. The color of things was being radically changed, blighting the all-white mashed-potatoes American culture of comfort, bringing disharmony to the internal peace.

Ordinary Americans were titillated by the sounds of new music, that had originated in darkest Africa. The new music was spreading into a psychedelic culture, accompanied by long hair and missing brassieres. Young whites were flowering into rebels, and young blacks were rising up in the streets.

In 1968, Hoover forced a massive augmentation of his COIN-TELPRO budget and forces. The timing seemed strange since the two men who had embodied for Hoover the only real danger to the internal security of the United States, Martin Luther King, Jr., and Malcolm X, were by then dead.

It had been the embrace of reputed opponents Martin Luther King, Jr., and Malcolm X in 1964 that had most alarmed Hoover. It was not a strong embrace, but it had certainly signaled a red alert.

Before 1964, Malcolm X had been dismissible as a racist and hate monger, with his visions of black independence from "the Devil." His appeal had been limited to a relatively small segment of the black population, even though his freedom-by-any-means-necessary exhortation had quickened the rebellious pulse of black urban youth. Besides, Malcolm's Muslims had been talking mostly about a separate program, and that did not interfere with the free-enterprise designs of the rich. Then Malcolm had abruptly left the Nation of Islam, disavowed narrow nationalism, and begun espousing an internationalist ideology. Through his new Organization of Afro-American Unity, he began linking blacks "impatient" for "freedom" to the international community. At the same time, the program of Martin Luther King was receiving international acclaim. In 1964 he was named *Time* magazine's Man of the Year and awarded the Nobel Peace Prize.

Hoover saw that the union of Malcolm and Martin was the worst possible threat to the internal security of America. The synthesis of their philosophies and, even worse, their forces, directed toward an aggressive campaign to gain "freedom" for black people, was a real danger. Both men were assassinated not long after that embrace: Malcolm X in 1965 and King in 1968.

Nevertheless, in 1968 Hoover intensified his COINTELPRO activities. The domestic situation had become a brewing tempest that Hoover knew could not even be stemmed by the millions of dollars assigned to waging the War on Poverty of his close friend Lyndon Johnson.

Young whites, the generation born after the war, the children of the days of civil-defense drills and Hiroshima and James Dean, the kids of good American families who had been bred on *Father Knows Best* philosophies, were doing more than dancing in the streets like their black counterparts. Grown up, they were sitting in front of their television sets watching the brutal realities of the war their freedom-loving government was waging in Vietnam, outraged.

Young urban blacks, who had idealized Malcolm X, who had always thought nonviolence an absurdity, who had tossed Molotov cocktails at America, were militantly claiming they were "black and proud."

The domestic threat that caused Hoover to bolster his COIN-TELPRO forces arose the moment these two groups, black and white, came together—not under a psychedelic umbrella of "flower power" or to sing "We Shall Overcome," but to shout "Free Huey! Free Huey!"

Before then, Hoover had not even noticed Huey Newton. Huey Newton had been characterized by Oakland police reports as a small-time gangster. Hoover did not even pretend to deal with gangsters, any more than he dealt with American Nazis, the Ku Klux Klan, or organized crime syndicates.

Hoover had been busy with his post–Malcolm X campaign against Martin Luther King. He had also been watching the angry new generation of war babies dancing to the music of the legatees of Malcolm X. Even after the King assassination, Hoover had been trying to keep a handle on the residue of dissatisfied, alienated, and disenfranchised Americans, who were complaining about their government.

On the day in October 1967 when Huey Newton was arrested for killing a white cop, a hush had fallen over that cacophony of disgruntled voices. Huey Newton had specifically stated that "for every act of aggression, the oppressor must suffer a 'political consequence.' " Huey Newton was not grumbling about problems, he was addressing problems. It was a Jeffersonian address.

The cop-killing charge against Huey was soon defined as a "revolutionary act," and Huey became a "political prisoner." By the time Huey was put on trial in 1968, he was gasoline on a nationwide spark. The question of change in America had become a matter of revolution.

It was the year "Free Huey" erupted as a kind of universal battle cry that J. Edgar Hoover openly pronounced: "The Black Panther Party is the single greatest threat to the internal security of the United States." By early 1970, Hoover and his new best friend in the White House, Richard Nixon, declared that the destruction of the Black Panther Party was a national security "priority." Huey Newton had become more than just another leader of a black organization. He was the symbol of change for Americans questioning everything sacred to the American way of life.

Now Huey was free. But what did this mean? During the eleven hours on my way to New York I smoked a lot and drank a lot of Bordeaux, and thought about that. And I thought about

John and Bunchy and Fred Hampton—and Jonathan Jackson.

Whatever I would do, I felt I had come to the end of a road, a glorious revolutionary road on which I had been traveling for the past two years. Whether I ran or resisted the temptation, I was convinced the Black Panther Party was facing its final days.

It was more horrible to think of, because after all we had endured, the party's destruction would come from inside, from Eldridge. Malcolm X had predicted such a thing, and had been the victim of it. "We had a beautiful thing and 'niggers' messed it up," Malcolm had said. History, I felt, would substantiate that the destruction of the Black Panther Party marked a tragic episode in the struggle of black people in America for freedom. No one would record that it marked the end of my life.

Our feet had barely touched the terminal floor when we were snatched up, as such, by unknown officials, men in suits, perhaps customs agents. Their guns were their identification. They cordoned us off into a single corner of the customs entry area. Dragging our bags into the same area with us, they began shouting to us to open everything. Scheer tried to protest; to no avail, of course. I was too stunned to care. What difference did it make to me if they questioned us forever about the "Commie" countries to which they very well knew we had traveled, though our passports bore no indication of the fact. Everything was doomed as far as I was concerned.

In the midst of all the shuffling around that was going on as to our passport stamps and the identification of our luggage, I noticed, out of the corner of my eye, a number of familiar-looking faces. They were smiling at me. I saw David among them. There appeared to be quite a few, maybe a hundred, other party members. They were crushed against a glass wall, a sound barrier. They were on the side that was United States soil. I was on the other side, in a kind of limbo land that seemed to belong to the unknown agents. They were smiling and waving fisted hands in muted animation. What was there to be excited about, I wondered. I stared at them sadly, especially David. They did not know.

"Exactly where have you been, Miss Brown?" a voice suddenly asked me.

"Paris," I said matter-of-factly, still staring at my doomed comrades. France was the only country whose stamp was on my passport.

Of course, the volumes of Mao's writings and the works of Kim Il Sung in my suitcases, which were being opened before me now, provided conflicting testimony. Agents were strewing the contents of my bags everywhere, apparently waiting for an explanation. They wanted me to account for the bottles of ginseng liquor from Korea and the cigarettes from Vietnam. They wanted Scheer and Jan and the rest of us to explain how we acquired the complete works of the North Korean leader Kim Il Sung, as well as the film canisters from North Korea—one of which contained the documentary of the capture of the *Pueblo*. It seemed perfectly reasonable to me at the moment to insist such things had been purchased in Paris.

"Paris, motherfucker!" I snapped to no one in particular, hand on my bony hip. I glanced back at my supportive audience of comrades, who were furiously raising fists, shouting silently.

When the search was over, I was asked to accompany a few of the unknown agents to an investigation room. The rest were free to go, their bags sufficiently stripped of all "Communist" paraphernalia.

It was while two of the agents and I were walking past the glass wall that I saw a sight so stunning it halted me. David was pressing kisses against the glass and pointing to that imposing sight—which was a man.

The agents touched my elbow to move along. I could not move. What could they do? I thought. There were too many witnesses for them to get too rough. I threw kisses back to David, my eyes fixed on the man. I did not hear David's introduction of him. Then I recognized him. It was Huey Newton.

He was certainly not the poster. He was certainly not the picture Eldridge had painted. His face gleamed with beauty and sensitivity, and his smile was familiar, in a haunting way.

His body was built up, apparently from prison exercise. Behind the rimless glasses he was wearing, I could see eyes that were large dark almonds. His face was angular, chiseled. He wore a fastidiously groomed Afro hairstyle, and had beautiful teeth and flawless skin, the color of honey.

He sort of bowed to me, and I felt a loss of energy, like finishing a foot race or reaching a climax. It was an exquisite exhaustion that buckled my knees.

Somehow, Huey and Charles Garry, the party's chief legal counsel—who, I realized, had been standing next to Huey against the glass—moved along laterally with me and the armed agents to an open area. It seemed to be a bridge between the territory beyond the glass wall and our limbo land. As we passed that area, Garry called out to me not to worry if I was arrested. He would get me out immediately.

Before I could speak, or my agent escorts could move, Huey Newton stepped across the forbidden bridge into limbo land, stopping time. He reached out his powerful arms and embraced me.

"I have lived to touch you," he said softly.

My escorts were still immobilized.

"I've listened to your voice and your songs over and over in my prison cell and dreamed of you," he whispered into my ear, still holding me against his body. His breath was a kiss.

"Welcome home, Comrade."

CHAPTER 12

BECOMING HUEY'S QUEEN

"DO YOU KNOW who that was?!" I shouted at my interrogators, locked with them in a small room somewhere in the New York airport.

"That was Huey P. Newton! The minister of defense of the Black Panther Party!"

They were unimpressed. They took off their ill-fitting jackets to show their holstered guns. I was unimpressed.

They wanted to know if I realized that U.S. passports prohibited travel to Russia and North Korea. Cuba too, I added, noting that I could read. They wanted to know if I realized that the United States was at war with North Vietnam, and thus if I had gone there, I could be charged with treason. I wanted to know if that applied to the several hundred thousand U.S. troops on the border. They wanted to know if I had been to Algiers with the escaped criminal Eldridge Cleaver. I laughed in response, thinking that having been there was not the question; having survived was.

During the rest of the two hours, I laughed a lot, mostly thinking about Huey Newton and a funny thing my old girl friend Desiree Fountaine used to say whenever she met a fellow she thought was exceptionally "fine." "Girl," Desiree would say, "take me away now, 'cause I've seen all I came for."

When I left the airport interrogation room, a few party members were waiting for me. I walked with them in a daze. A car appeared and took me to a hotel suite where Huey was waiting.

Lots of people were inside, clinking cocktail glasses and chattering. Jane Fonda was the most prominent face I saw when I entered. She had paid for all of it, I recalled having been told in the car. They were there to celebrate Huey's signing of a publishing contract for his first book.

As I stood in the doorway, I concentrated on the people in the room, blacks and whites, Panthers and progressives, lawyers and writers. They looked gaudy and somewhat decadent to me. I was suffering from culture shock, having become accustomed to the ways of people in the socialist Asian countries I had just visited, people who wore plain clothes and lived simple lives.

Huey emerged from the crowd and rushed over to me.

"Would you stay here with me tonight?" he whispered in a strong embrace.

I nodded.

In a short time, Huey dismissed everyone from the suite. Only the Panther bodyguards remained, on guard in the sitting room.

At first I felt ashamed to be naked in front of him. It was something deeper than the skin disease I had contracted in Korea, which had left my body marred with discolored splotches. I felt unworthy somehow—not an unfamiliar feeling, I realized, as I showered behind a closed door. I walked out of the bathroom like a virgin, wrapped in a towel.

He did not remove the towel. Grabbing another one, he dried my back and neck and face. He was nude, thin legs and narrow waist, muscular torso and tight buttocks.

He took my hand as though he thought I might break, and led me to the bed. He whisked back the covers and bowed chivalrously, assisting me into the crispness of hotel sheets. We lay in the dark next to each other, neither speaking nor touching.

"I know you're exhausted," he whispered eventually. "I just wanted to be near you, after dreaming about you for so long. May I hold you?"

As I snuggled into the strength of his arms, I asked him how he had heard my songs. David's cassettes, I laughed, when he told me. He began to rock me back and forth, so gently that tears fell from my eyes. He brushed them away with the tenderest of kisses. When he spoke again, his Louisiana accent sweet and soft, it was very studied. He talked to me about loneliness.

"When I was more alone than I thought a human being ever could be, my insides screamed out begging to know why. Why was

I alive? Why couldn't I die . . . It was back in sixty-four, before the party. I was in the Alameda County jail, in the part they called the 'Soul Breaker'—which you've probably heard about."

It was an understatement. The Soul Breaker was as known in and around Oakland as his having been there was. It consisted of a series of special jail cells constructed to do exactly what its name implied. No inmate had lasted in there more than forty-eight hours. The most angry and rebellious, the most sturdy resisters, for whom the cells had been designed, were usually released in a day, having been reduced to screaming morons.

"I'd been in isolation in jail before, but this was harder than anything," he said. "Not a ray of light filtered into the cell. There wasn't a window. No knob on the door. No bed or toilet. Just four black walls, a rubber floor, and me, nearly naked.

"The minute I stepped inside, I wanted to beg them to let me out. I was ready to do anything they wanted me to do. I didn't care about appearing tough. I just wanted out.

"I was shaking with fear when it occurred to me that it was important to hold on. Not for them. But for me. If I could withstand the total deprivation of my senses, I might see something I needed to see. You know, learn something that could set me free forever. Free from all my fears, free enough to look at myself, into the dark corners, come to terms with myself and the universe I occupy."

I was sobbing and he was holding me hard in the dark.

"You don't have to shed any tears for me, 'cause I survived fifteen days of the pigs' so-called Soul Breaker, and came out more powerful than any of them . . . all of them," he said with a cocky laugh.

"It's not your pain," I told him. "It's—it's that I know that pain. I know who you are. I've known you in my soul. But I never thought you existed."

Here was a man who had stepped out boldly and begun an attack on the forces that dominated us. Yet here was a man who was opening all the wounds, boring through the rhetoric of rage to the point of pain. It was a place I knew. He was no hero. He was a man. It was ridiculous to feel sorry for him. I loved him.

At one point he said, "I'm not a man, I'm not a woman, I'm just a plain-born child."

He went on to tell me that after a while they slipped food through a slot in the bottom of the door of the Soul Breaker. He soon vomited up that food. Later, he became sick from the smells

of his vomit and his defecation and urine. He tried to calm himself
by imagining beautiful things and keeping close to a wall to place
himself. All his imaginary images began to rush together, turning
into gargoyles and monsters.

He fell on his back and tried to find a position that would
ward off madness. He began to hear the sound of his own breathing. He clung to it. He heard his heartbeat start to regulate. That
was when he "let go," reached out with his mind to the expanse
of infinity. He began to feel at peace, he said. He stopped throwing
up, and he stopped trying to mark time.

After what seemed hours of talking, he asked me to sing for
him. Lying there in the dark of the hotel room, I hoarsely sang a
few songs until I fell asleep.

Huey would heal everything, my heart said as I opened my
eyes to him the next morning. He seemed a giant hand that would
slap the grinning faces that shamed and shunned and severed lives
like mine.

He bought me yellow roses and a new pantsuit later that
morning. We were off to meet David Hilliard at a lawyer's office.

Seeing David, I remembered Moscow and Algiers. I tried to
focus instead on love, or at least on the business at hand.

"What do you think of the name Stronghold, Elaine?" Huey
was asking me.

He was very animated, his cologne filtering lightly through
the air as he walked, like a tiger, back and forth in front of the
lawyer's desk.

"That's a fine name, man," David offered, to fill the beat of
time in which I had not responded.

"Oh yes, it's wonderful," I said.

Stronghold was Huey's name for an entity under which the
party would legally receive revenues from various artistic and business enterprises, beginning with his first book to be published, a
collection of essays, *To Die for the People*. He was laughing about
the pun in it: a one-word idea that captured what the party intended to erect inside the walls of the citadel of capitalism.

Once the three of us returned to the hotel, Huey launched
right into the issue I had been dreading.

"Now, what the fuck is wrong with Eldridge? Is he crazy?"
he asked, easing the tension in my jaws and neck and back. "I told
you about all that bullshit he told me on the phone, didn't I,
David?"

"Yeah, man, but I think we need to hear Elaine run it down."

I told David everything Eldridge had said about him, how Eldridge had openly denounced him, how Eldridge had even proposed that I be part of a move to push him out of the leadership. Then, looking into Huey's almond eyes, I explained to him how Eldridge had insisted he would agree with him about the party, since he had had a "red-light trial."

"Is this what you're upset about?—Eldridge told me enough of that bullshit already. But worrying about what Eldridge *says* is like worrying about the paper he wipes his ass with . . . This is actually some funny shit, man, when you think about it," Huey said to David. "I mean the idea of Eldridge wanting to 'get down.' I guess that's how Bobby Hutton ended up dead," he added.

"I'll tell you what's happening with Eldridge, David," Huey continued, bolstering David's spirit. "This doesn't have a thing to do with you, man . . . Eldridge got his ass over there with all those African guerrillas and wants to have some dramatic shit to add to the conversation when he has cocktails with them. Just like he stuck us with his anti-Zionist rhetoric when he first moved to Algiers and found himself surrounded by all those Palestinians. Matter of fact, just like he did in the joint. Snapped his fingers and turned himself into a so-called Muslim minister when he saw all the Brothers around him picking up on Malcolm."

David was as speechless as I was.

"I only asked the motherfucker to help put together the newspaper. He's got words down pat. So I gave him a title and a pencil . . ."

David smiled.

"I didn't ask Eldridge to do shit but *write* about revolution, man. This is *my* party, and we'll have breakfast, lunch, *and* dinner programs if I say so. And I do . . . Eldridge can be happy he didn't lay his hand on you," he said, looking at me with a grin, "much as I wanted your pussy."

David's gratitude for Huey's support bowled him off his chair with laughter. He slapped Huey's palm. I nearly collapsed with relief.

"I need to see Eldridge in person, so I can smack him." Huey laughed finally. "When we get back, man, have somebody get me a passport. I'm going to Algiers."

We stayed about a week in New York, days that seemed to me a love montage in a movie. Huey bought me flowers almost every day and made love to me every night. He talked to me about everything and anything. He took me everywhere with him and made it known that I was his.

When author Mark Lane came to interview Huey for *Playboy* magazine, we were propped up in bed next to each other, both of us buck-naked. Huey said he felt clothing was too confining. I went with him to meetings with his publisher and lunches with well-to-do whites who wanted to support the party—and had to meet Huey Newton. When he made several visits to New York Panthers, we saw them together. He dismissed their irritation about that, and I dismissed the jealousy I saw. I was in a small, private world in the arms of Huey Newton; and also in a bigger world in the arms of Huey Newton.

"Man, this Eldridge shit could get serious," Huey was saying to David between swallows of orange juice.

David was having breakfast with us in the hotel room on one of our last mornings in New York.

"Did you check out the bad attitude of these New York comrades? Telling me the direction they felt the party ought to be moving in."

"Some disrespectful motherfuckers, Huey."

"David, man, we have to make these comrades understand what's really happening." He gulped down a raw egg. "Nothing in the universe remains the same. It's a law of nature. The party doesn't stand outside of that . . .

"The only constant we have is the goal of freedom for black people. And that's actually a *subjective* goal. It's certainly not in the interest of these capitalists. It's in *our* interest to be free. And we've come to see that our freedom can only be realized through revolution, the complete overthrow of the system of capitalism . . .

"But in order to attain our subjective goal, we have to become as objective as possible. We can't be free using strategies based on emotion or rhetoric. If a man has the subjective desire to drive a car, for instance, and jumps into one without knowing how to drive, he's bound to destroy himself, and whatever else. To get what we want, we have to look at the objective conditions and develop strategies and tactics related to them. And those conditions are in a constant state of flux—like everything else in nature. So our tactics must be adapted accordingly—you could say we have to know when to hold and when to fold.

"Now, when we jumped out on the streets with our guns, we had favorable conditions—the element of surprise. The pigs weren't ready for some niggers parading around town with guns pointed at them . . . Of course, they're ready now . . ."

"Ready like a motherfucker," David echoed.

"But that shouldn't come as a surprise. Superiority of guns is theirs—to put it mildly."

He got out of bed and started pacing.

"But originally, when we carried our guns openly, it was a tactic to introduce our people to an idea . . . The only government most black people had ever seen *was* the police—an armed force which we called an 'occupying army.' For black people, the police were all three prongs of the U.S. government, right out on the streets—legislative, judicial, and mostly executive. Black people understand a red-light trial—which I certainly did not want, whatever Eldridge has concocted in his mind about that.

"Before the party, you had Brothers operating the community-alert patrols. The joke was, after the patrols took their pictures and made notes about rampant police brutality on the streets, they reported that shit *to* the police. The party came along to heighten the contradiction, take it to a manageable level. Since the people viewed their primary relationship to the system's oppression on the street, we had to introduce dealing with the 'system' on the street. And that's one idea our people have gotten, I think. To an extent, so have the pigs, at least in Oakland.

"Sacramento was the same thing. It had less to do with guns than with organizing; even though a lot of people, even the so-called militants, had the mistaken idea we went there over a gun law."

"Manifest reform," David injected. "I remember that, man. As though we gave a fuck about pig laws."

"We have to go back over that, David, and explain that the fundamental reason we went to the legislature in Sacramento was to organize. To put forth a call. Not to arms in the narrow sense, but to people ready to take a vanguard step toward revolution . . . You know, Elaine, we just showed up with guns and used the gun legislation issue to startle the pig press into putting our message out."

"Matter of fact," David said, laughing, "there were only about seven *real* party members at the time. After Sacramento, thousands of Brothers signed up to be Panthers."

"Yes, well, that was about organizing the party. Now we've

got to move to organize millions of black *people* to sign up for revolution. So I think the first thing we have to make these comrades understand about all of this, David, is that, intrinsically, the gun is not necessarily revolutionary. The fascists have guns. It's the motivation behind the gun that determines the validity of its use. Vietnamese guns against imperialist guns. And it's the strategy that determines the value of the gun. Of course, Mao said, 'In order to get rid of the gun it is necessary to take up the gun.' And we believe that. But we have to emphasize that the idea is to get *rid* of the gun.

"As for the party, we need guns to keep ourselves from being obliterated, so we can push the momentum of revolution. And we need guns in the picture to politicize black people with the *concept* of the ultimate necessity of armed revolutionary struggle—which seems inevitable, unless the pigs change and throw down the guns that support the system. But the ultimate armed struggle is not the business of the vanguard. Our business is to develop and organize our *people* to carry out the revolution to achieve the subjective goal of freedom.

"As I see it, the next step in that process is to deemphasize the gun and emphasize the social programs, to widen the people's horizon. If we stayed on the pigs and the gun, per se, not only would the party go down, the people's spirit would be crushed as they watched, and they might remain blind to the forest for the trees. Not only that, they'd come dead on arrival at the door of revolution. It's the *people* who have to survive to the point of revolution.

"Elaine, would you make some notes on this. From now on, we're going to call the breakfast program and the clinics and so forth Survival Programs . . .

"We have to educate the comrades, David, that these programs are neither revolutionary *nor* reformist—no different than the gun. They have to understand that what the programs—Survival Programs—do is expose the contradictions *beyond* pigs with guns. The Survival Programs are a vehicle to move the people to a higher level.

"Now, Martin Luther King was dealing with—or had started to deal with—this primary contradiction, going beyond civil rights to the economic question. But his poor people's campaign had some major flaws. Not to mention that Martin had no chance to correct them, which I think he might have if he'd lived. And the pigs must've thought so, too, because it was at the start of that campaign that they cut him down. But first, the poor people's thing lacked dignity, had the tone of begging from the white man, maintaining the slave-master relationship. Second, it was doomed from the jump, as a moral appeal to an immoral bunch of thieves. Mostly, the idea went no further than getting jobs and housing and so forth. It was reformist, something like asking the slave master to make better slave shacks, avoiding the fundamental question of slavery.

"If that was our strategy with the Survival Programs, it *would* be reformist. And Eldridge would be right—in that sense. Not about you, David . . . But I hope he tells me that shit about you to my face, so I can put my revolutionary foot in his ass.

"Black people already know they're poor and powerless. They just don't understand the nature of their oppression. They haven't drawn the line from their condition to the *system* of capitalism. The Survival Programs begin to do that. The people will undoubtedly start asking themselves why the party can do so much with so little, and the capitalists so little with so much. That'll motivate them to start making some demands—not begging—for shit. And the Man will be forced to make little concessions. The more concessions, the more demands . . . In other words, the programs are another tactic for revolution."

It was more than love I was feeling for Huey. I was beginning to see a man who seemed the other part of my soul. Connected to him, I was a new force. Disconnected, I felt I might never exist again.

Huey, David, and I returned to Oakland, to sort out the pieces, or what might be the pieces, of the party, given Eldridge's machinations. In the meantime, Huey prepared to deal with Eldridge in person.

Everybody I saw on my arrival in L.A. was complaining about the heat, with the exception of one little being, who was concentrating all her energy on a lime Popsicle.

There was no interest in my hello-my-darling-baby, how-you-have-grown sentiments. Ericka Brown did not even look up from her crib. She never noticed the grand entrance of her mother. She did not concern herself with my tears, as I looked at her; or Gwen, her mother for half her life, standing over her, smiling.

It is very hard to eat a Popsicle with no teeth, especially when it is so hard to sit up. Thus, Gwen had propped a wardrobe of support pillows behind my baby's back and, wrapping a piece of wood with layers of cool white sheet, had invented a mouth-high plank across the small crib. It was a no-hands-necessary arrangement for licking a lime Popsicle at about forty miles an hour. The largest fan in the house was sending a breeze onto Ericka's topless torso, causing her eyelashes to flutter and the cloth napkin tied under her chin to billow. It did not interrupt her concentration.

After a few minutes of holding back, I jumped in front of her with a tap step.

It was that smile that shook me. She really remembered her mother, who had left her three months ago, off to save the world. A chubby beauty, she cracked the world with her smile and sent me to my knees with arms outstretched.

How could I explain myself? There were no words. I picked up that baby that was mine, and squeezed and squeezed her, staining the sticky remnants of lime Popsicle on her face with stupid tears. How forgiving her little body was to hug me back, to tell me she had been well. How forgiving to accept my embrace without question, to accept me back as her mother, a woman who claimed to care about millions of black children, yet had shown so little caring for the one that was hers. In kiss after kiss, I tried to ask her to hold on through the rest of my comings and goings.

I wanted some group of mothers to show up with a ribbon and tell her I really was one of them. I wanted somebody to tell her it was all right if I never baked a cake, all right if I knew nothing about teething, or what she was supposed to be eating at this stage. I wanted somebody to make amends for what I would not do for her, because I was doing this intangible thing, with this grand idea about my role in it. I wanted to explain myself.

If anything, I had the instincts of a father—to provide for and protect. I wondered if that was enough when you had a cold and needed your nose wiped; when you could not sleep and needed a hug; when you needed a ribbon in your hair, or your shoe tied.

My mother did not hesitate to inform me that no committee would be coming to give me the motherhood stamp of approval. She told me that if I were too busy to take care of my own child, the least I could have done was to leave her in a decent home: hers. I had, in point of fact, abandoned my child. That was something, for good or ill, she had never done.

She was right, right about everything I was not. I just listened. I did not want to be her. She did not want to be her.

Huey was ablaze. I had to come to Oakland right away. He had a proposal for rescuing the comrades from their ideological stagnation, from the undertow that Eldridge might create. Instead of directing the party leadership to study the guerrilla warfare treatises of Castro or Che, he wanted them to study the great ideas of the world, he told me when I arrived. He wanted to know what I thought about the creation of an Ideological Institute.

Such a forum, he was saying excitedly, would bring together the party's leading members to study ideas, expand their minds, come to conclusions, or find there were no conclusions. We could go beyond his own early treatise, *The Correct Handling of a Revolution*. We could set it aside with the rest. There was no correct way, no blueprint for socialist revolution in America. Through the leadership's collective investigation of the history of ideas and philosophies, however, we might develop some kind of road map.

If he wanted my endorsement, he had it, I said. I knew how Eldridge's jingoistic "revolution-now," "part-of-the-solution-part-of-the-problem" rhetoric had influenced the style of the party. I knew that if his latest rhetoric reached the ears of the rank and file, it would cut at the heart of the party. Such a college, I told Huey, certainly could be an antidote. To my mind, this was also a way for Huey to begin to re-establish his place in the Black Panther Party.

Huey had gone to prison within the first year of the party's formation. During his three years in prison, his small essays on revolution, printed and distributed in pamphlet form, had been required reading for party members, as his rattan-chair poster had been our introduction to revolutionary art. Thousands had joined the Black Panther Party while Huey was behind bars. To them he was a mythical figure, a godly photograph of a man, or a man's image of God.

When he emerged from prison, thousands were waiting for deliverance. He was David with a stone in hand, Perseus with sword raised. Even for those beyond the ranks, black and white, Huey's being set free raised the prospect of revolution in their lifetimes. For the party membership, he was the returning general who would reveal his plan for the decisive battle of victory over the abstractions of racism and oppression, and lead the charge that would propel us into paradise. For those who had known him on the streets of Oakland, not excluding David or his brother June or even Bobby Seale, Huey's mythical persona had supplanted the street image of "crazy Huey," the man they had known in pre-Panther days. He had become a kind of homegrown messiah.

Of course, I had my own Huey Newton fantasies, which did not exclude Prince Charming visions. As we grew closer in those weeks after Eldridge, though, I saw that he was bigger than the visions and fantasies of him. And I saw that that made him a misfit in his own place and time as much as in his own organization.

"A lot of what I am has to do with fear," he said to me out of nowhere one of those first nights I came to see him in Oakland. "And what I understand about fear. I wasn't afraid only in the Soul Breaker. Like you, I've been afraid much of my life."

I moved closer to him. We were curled up in a small bed in the apartment of Alex Hoffmann, a white attorney who provided regular refuge to Huey, who had had no residence of his own since his three-year residence in prison.

"You know, niggers on the street don't like 'pretty niggers,' " he continued, making me wonder whether he was speaking about him or me. "They called me 'pretty' and 'high-yellow nigger' and other motherfuckers. The problem with niggers on the street, of course, is that they don't know what to hate for their oppression."

"Or, as Frantz Fanon wrote, they're afraid to confront the real issue: 'draw the *oppressor's* blood,' as he said. My problem in North Philly was 'good' hair."

"Naturally . . . Anyway, it didn't take long to figure out that I was in trouble on the street. I reached a point where I was scared to go out of my house. Then Walter, my brother, tutored me on the game.

"Walter schooled me on how to confront my fear, how to see a motherfucker for what he was—in most cases, another scared individual. He taught me how to walk on the street, how to talk, how to carry myself, and how to use my hands . . . But I was still scared every day. Every blood on the street was a potential threat, unless I knew he was a friend. After my first fights, though, I recognized that they bled like me . . . By the time I became a teenager, I was challenging the first fool who looked at me wrong, and walking around with an ice pick in a paper bag."

"No, really?" I laughed.

"Really. And you can believe it kept most of them out of my

face." He laughed with me. "The rest I knew how to beat with my fists, unless they wanted to deal with my ice pick. I earned a reputation as 'crazy.' "

He went on to say that black people would never rise out of life at the bottom of the quagmire of America unless they took the same approach.

"The first question for black people is to get past fear, to see past the monolith to the man. That's why we started using the word 'pig,' a detestable image that takes away the image of omnipotence. A pig, whether running loose in the ghetto with a gun or sitting on Wall Street or in the White House, is a man who can bleed like a man and fall like a man.

"So, in many ways, the party represents a response to our collective fear of the Man—getting past the first barrier to walking free on the streets of life . . . Revolution will be our ultimate response. But that's a hell of a thing for black people to begin to comprehend, because their fear of the Man has been driven down so deep, down where they live. It comes out in the form of hatred, or self-hatred. That was another reason I felt we had to start there, where they lived and the armed pig wallowed. Putting guns out there was carrying ice picks in a collective paper bag."

"And so it's 'Free Huey' all around," I said with a smile.

"Something like that. But I'm still talking about fear. If we can now expose the whole face of the Man, tear off his mask, the people will see the capitalist system. They'll see that what keeps them down is a collection of men that can be dealt with by the collective effort of other men—and women.

"The hardest part for me right now, though, is trying to convince this party I invented that *we* can't do much more than that. The *party* can't take down the Man. And *I* can't do it. I can't save one soul. And I don't want to be Jesus or any other god. I want to *realize* 'God,' which is not some dominating power sitting above us. God is all humanity in concert with nature. *We* are God, though we've yet to *become* God. But mostly, I want to be free to live on my terms and die on my terms. But in order for Huey to be free, the party has to develop the collective will in the people to free us all. We say, 'Power to the people.' "

He talked on—then and each time I returned to him. Every word became a building block to the new world, the one where I knew I belonged—with him, who had become my other self, my lover, my confessor, and the only man I could imagine I would ever call my leader. And in that world, I saw that Huey was as much an outsider in life as he was in the party.

On his release from prison, Huey had made a formal public offer to the North Vietnamese of the entire Black Panther Party membership as comrades-in-arms to support them in defending their country in the vicious war against the "U.S. imperialists." For Huey, marching for peace or calling for an end to the war was futile. In war, he said, the only position was on the battlefield. Though his offer was not accepted, the North Vietnamese sent the party a formal expression of gratitude.

Just as the party membership and thousands of other leftists in America were applauding that act, Huey sent everything into a state of confusion. He renounced the party's Eldridge Cleaver–inspired position against the State of Israel. He sent a message to all Arab embassies and to that of Israel stating that the Black Panther Party now recognized both the State of Israel and the right of the Palestinian people to have a homeland.

The party's position, as his message outlined, was that the Arab-Israeli dispute could be settled quickly if Saudi Arabia or Egypt, or some other territory controlled by the Palestinians' rich brothers—who had been claiming since 1948 to be pressing to help them reclaim Palestine—simply gave a piece of territory inside their vast borders to the Palestinians and made them a new homeland. The wrong that had been done by the Stern Gang in collusion with the British gang and the U.S. gang in uprooting the Palestinians was a *fait accompli*. The resultant State of Israel had to be reckoned with, therefore. Life, like revolution, he said, looked forward, not backward.

His message contained the most daring conclusion. Ultimately, he exhorted, there was a revolutionary way to settle the conflict. He called upon Arabs and Israelis alike to recognize that the problems between them had to do with something larger than the territory of Israel or Palestine, larger than Judaism or Islam. It had to do with the theft and hoarding of the resources of the region—specifically the oil—by what he lambasted as a conspiracy of certain governments of the region with the United States. He urged them to lay down their arms against each other, rise up united, and overthrow the reactionary Zionist government in Israel and the reactionary Arab sheikdoms and kingdoms and create peace in the land of plenty.

Huey found a certain private delight in taking that position, no matter how befuddled his troops became over it or that it tainted our nominal alliance with the PLO—and notwithstanding the damage it did to Eldridge. Several nights before he proclaimed the party's new Middle East position, he told me about his father.

Huey's father, Walter, was half white, or half Jewish actually: the product of a black woman and a Southern Jew named Simon. The question of whether or not Walter Newton's mother was forcibly raped, working in the house of Simon, was a technicality lost to history as far as Huey was concerned. What disturbed him was the damage that had been done to his father, whose self-hatred and hatred of whites was that of the son of a presumed rapist— despite his mother's subsequent marriage to a black man named Newton, who gave him his name.

Somewhere in the outer regions of Huey's thinking, he saw a connection between the bitterness of Walter Newton and the bitterness of Arabs and of Jews, and that of black people in general. It was, to him, a useless response to the sting of the past. They had all looked back so long, he declared, the present was obliterated and the future eclipsed. The relief of change was only for those who could create the future. There was, therefore, something poetically proper, healing, even, he thought, for the black son of the bastard son of a Jew to take that position.

The confusion of Arab-Israeli positions for Black Panthers far from the Sahara was only temporary. It did, however, begin to disturb the poster image of the homecoming hero who was to "off the pig." As Huey was defining his leadership, his troops were trying to decipher the man they had created, with whom they were now face to face.

Now they were wondering about his Ideological Institute. I saw the questions as the local leadership cadres came trooping to Oakland from as far away as Boston, Philadelphia, and Chicago for bimonthly, two-day learning sessions led by Huey. Where was the stuff about the pigs? they seemed to ask, as we studied not only Mao and Marx but Aristotle and Plato. Where was the stuff about urban guerrilla warfare? their expressions conveyed, as Huey led us in discussions of the philosophies of Rousseau and Kant, Kirkegaard and Nietzsche, about existentialism and determinism and free will. I saw their faces when we examined and questioned the theories of capitalism and socialism and Communism, Huey asking whether our systematic use of the tests of dialectical materialism meant anything. If, under a dialectical materialist analysis, nothing "stood outside" of the process, did that negate the process itself? he asked.

In that time of reawakening, as I came to think of it, it never dawned on Huey that he ought to have a place to live. Other than Alex Hoffmann's, or the house of one of his six brothers and sisters, Huey slept at arbitrarily chosen locales nearly every night. On one hand, that arbitrariness had its benefits. A potential assassin could make no plan. It necessitated, however, that David undertake the difficult task of providing security for Huey, which was worsened by Huey's frequent, unannounced jaunts into the streets by himself, unarmed. Ignoring all admonitions, Huey would simply declare that "the People" would protect him. It was actually quite an amazing thing to behold Huey walking down an Oakland street. He drew large crowds of eager children and teary-eyed women with flowers and men reaching out to shake his hand.

It was definitely time for Huey to have a secure place to live, David kept insisting. I agreed. By the end of 1970, the police had increased the number and sophistication of their watchful eyes on Huey Newton. There was a lot of COINTELPRO money.

Police were, of course, watching all party members. That Huey Newton himself, however, was the target of an FBI-sponsored assassination plan was becoming more and more evident. The "heroic" cop killer who had defanged the Oakland Police Department, who had inspired others to do the same elsewhere, who was preaching revolution, had to be eliminated—though gunning him down openly did not appear, at the moment, politically practical.

I was staying in Oakland more than not and saw the increasing level of police surveillance. Wherever Huey was, it was certain the police would be—an apparent assortment of FBI and local police. When we woke up at Alex Hoffmann's, a plainclothes policeman would be outside our second-floor bedroom window on a telephone pole. Outside his parents', there might be police in phony mail trucks. Police drove taxicabs behind the car he was riding in; police walked down whatever street he walked on. They were so invasive, it became necessary—David insisted over Huey's protests—to post a bodyguard overnight with Huey wherever he stayed. In time, Huey himself began feeling the strain of looking over his shoulder, sleeping very lightly and eventually trying to keep alert with Ritalin pills.

"Huey, man, this arrangement of yours about housing has got to go," David commanded with finality one afternoon at his house. "I'm going to trial soon, man. And I'm sure to get a conviction. Then what happens? Even if Bobby gets out of his New Haven case, he's facing the Chicago trial. Anyway, you think Bobby can take care of things . . . I want you to get a place to live. Now."

"I have one—wherever I want." Huey laughed.

"This is not funny, Brother. Even I know that," Gene McKinney said. McKinney was one of Huey's myriad "street partners," who faithfully stayed close to their homegrown hero. McKinney, though, was a special one. He had been with Huey the night Oakland police officer Frey had been shot and killed—the incident that put a bullet into Huey's abdomen and sent him to prison, triggering the "Free Huey" campaign. It was Gene's dramatic testimony about that night—or his Fifth Amendment refusal to testify about that night—that had tossed judge and jury into a maelstrom at the end of the trial.

"But, Gene," Huey said, still laughing, "I've got *you*, Brother . . ."

"Man, this is *not* about you, Huey," David interrupted forcefully. "It's about this party. It's about taking care of the party by taking care of the leadership. We're on thin ice as it is . . . We need you, Brother."

"Because I'm the supreme commander?" Huey said, not laughing anymore. His title had been changed by the Central Committee from minister of defense when he was released from prison.

"Because you're . . ."

"Who came up with that title, anyway, David . . . See, that's the real problem. I don't want to be the supreme commander anymore. Let Gene be the supreme commander . . ."

"People love you, Huey," I said.

"Because they don't love themselves . . ."

"You can philosophize about this shit if you want to, Huey," David said, as if to an obstreperous child, "but I'm going to prison, and . . ."

"You want to put me in one."

"Call it what you want, Huey, but we've found a place for you to live, and you're going to live there."

"Why do you need all this convincing, Huey?" I added. "You can't even sleep anymore. Pigs everywhere."

"And will they go away if I get an address?"

"No, Huey," David said patiently, "but they'll have to go through some deep shit to get to you . . . Now be quiet a minute, man. Let me tell you about the place. It's an apartment on the twenty-fifth floor of the building. The penthouse. The pigs would have to use helicopters to get to you. Or burn down the building along with all those well-to-do white people in it. There's an internal security system in the building, television cameras and that shit. The point is, it'll give you some space, Brother, away from the bullshit."

"Sounds nice. But not for me," Huey said.

"Why not?" I asked.

We discussed the advantages and disadvantages, the latter being virtually nonexistent.

"It'll cost too much," Huey argued weakly in the end.

"Six hundred dollars a month?" I said. "You're not serious."

"I know one thing you'll appreciate about this place, Huey," David added. "A piece of poetry for you . . . The building faces the Alameda County courthouse. You can look down on it out of the windows—you know, reflect on the thousands of black people who stood out there all those months chanting 'Free Huey.' "

Huey was strangely quiet.

"You mean I can see the Soul Breaker, where I nearly died," he said solemnly.

Nobody said a word.

"Where nobody else will, really because of you, Huey," I said after a bit. After Charles Garry became Huey's trial attorney, and then legal counsel to the party, he had lobbied for a judicial ruling that such confinement was "cruel and unusual punishment," based on the atrocious treatment of Huey, effectively outlawing soul breakers in the state of California.

Still nothing.

"Get me a telescope!" Huey laughed at us, patting my rear end.

There was something more about that apartment I did not mention, and certainly could not. It had to do with one of the reasons for my enthusiasm for it, beyond my love for Huey and the obvious security question. It was a shameful, secret, personal reason. It was a woman thing, and not at all a revolutionary woman thing. I really wanted to be Huey's "woman," in the old sense, the nonrevolutionary, get-married, down-and-dirty street sense, even including the barefoot-and-pregnant sense.

The party's position about such relationships was being revolutionized. Indeed, it was Huey who was promoting a line that the primary relationship between men and women in the party was as comrades. That included love and sex. To define another party member as one's own—"my" man, "my" woman—was not merely taking a step backward, clinging to a bourgeois socialization. It was taking a step in the wrong direction, to support the most fundamental principle of capitalism, the private possession of property; and worse, it was to liken people to property, chattel. That socialization had to be rooted out of us, as did all the other old ways, if we were to follow a revolutionary road.

Thus, I traipsed back and forth between Los Angeles and Oakland like the comrade and lover that I was. Under my revolutionary façade, however, clinging like a cancer, was a woman with fairy-tale, teenage dreams. Moreover, I was doing nothing to improve myself—doing nothing that would distinguish me from all the other women I sadly discovered Huey had in his life.

How naïve I had been to imagine Huey had been looking for me, as I had been for him. I knew at that point that he truly loved me. I knew our relationship was special, outside the others—men and women, party and family. I knew also that the idea of his being "mine" could exist only in a very small place.

When Huey Newton walked into a room, he stunned both women and men with the combination of his image and physical appearance. I had seen even calculating journalists, looking for some Pulitzer Prize-winning angle in an interview with him, be halted in their tracks and thrown completely by his presence. I was not concerned about the part of him that belonged to the party or the struggle, or that was consumed by his numerous admiring friends, or his adoring family, or the public. It was Huey's absolute irresistibility to a host of women, particularly beautiful brown-skinned women, that was a problem, as I saw how many of them were also irresistible to him.

His arbitrary forays into the night, the many nights I was not in Oakland, were not, I had come to learn, limited to the home of Hoffmann or his mother or his street partners. There were the women, quite a few, exquisite brown-skinned ones. I saw them when we went out to dinner in Oakland, handing him telephone numbers, suggesting they wanted to be in the party, and I saw him saying he would personally call them to talk about it. And he *was* calling them, I knew.

It had only stung me at first, dismissible as part of the temperament of the times; dismissible at some higher plane of thought that Huey Newton ought to have love, all the love he could get; dismissible because most of the women were not in the party. They would come and they would go, with their beautiful bodies and painted nails and tantalizing perfumes. They would have their night with a "star," and he would let them go—while I would remain.

But there was Gwen Fountaine—one of them, I assumed, when Huey introduced us—who had actually been recruited into the party after a romp with him. And she was nothing like the other women in the party.

In general, Black Panther women were stripped of the pretty things, the "bourgeois" sweetnesses that could have made them glamorous women, the kind that I saw Huey adored, despite his revolutionized ways. Panther women were hard, in a way—soldiers, comrades, not pretty little things. Gwen was a pretty little thing with beautiful brown skin inherited from her absent black father and beautiful big eyes like her Greek mother's. She had actually shown up to do graphics work on the newspaper—more or less joining the ranks.

The problem with Gwen was not simply her nominal membership in the party. It was that Huey was leaving clothes at her private apartment in Berkeley, the one that was away from the collective. The problem was that I felt threatened, in that old "what-you-doin'-with-my-man," that old "bitch" sense.

As Huey was the leader of the party whose life was definitely at risk, as Huey was the man I loved in my ether world, I wanted him to have a secure place to live. I also wanted him to hang his clothes in a place that was not the place of Gwen or any other Gwen who might happen along. I would be queen in his world, I thought, as the bourgeois cancer began to infect my conscious thought.

The only issue remaining regarding the apartment, as far as David and I were concerned, was finding the $12,000 we determined was needed to pay for it. We thought one year's rent should be paid in advance, lest there be an early eviction notice once it was discovered who occupied the apartment. We also wanted to buy some furniture. Every dime the party had was locked up in publishing our newspaper, maintaining our Survival Programs, paying rent and operational expenses, and securing ammunition and guns.

◄ ►

By the beginning of the next year, we had become urgent about the apartment. David's trial was about to commence, and a problem more compelling than the police had begun to erupt.

Though Huey had talked to Eldridge every week over those months since my return, Eldridge remained adamant about ousting the Hilliards and instituting his "terrorist" agenda. Huey kept insisting he wanted to talk about it in person. Since Huey had not been able to obtain a passport, and Eldridge would not be coming to the United States, Huey suggested at one point that Eldridge send Kathleen to Oakland as his "emissary," to try to settle the differences sans police telephone monitors. Eldridge offered Connie Matthews instead.

She lied from the moment she stepped into Oakland. She said she had only agreed with Eldridge because she thought he was crazy. She said she was ready to take orders from Huey. In response, Huey had ordered her to stay in Oakland, perform secretarial duties for him only, and never do anything, not even receive or place a telephone call, without his express permission.

During this time, Huey continued to try to get his passport to go to Algiers. Legally, he was not free. The technicality that Fay Stender, Garry's associate on Huey's trial, had brilliantly unearthed had only stayed the serving of a prison term. Huey's potential fifteen-year prison sentence, for a manslaughter conviction—an irritation, at best, to the state which had charged him with murder—was simply overturned, pending a new trial. A passport for Huey Newton, under these circumstances, which included Eldridge's notorious escape from prosecution, was out of the question, the court finally ruled. By that time, however, Huey was finished with Eldridge Cleaver.

In the early part of 1971, Connie Matthews disappeared with a member of the party from New York and later surfaced in Algiers. At the same time, the Panthers who formed the highly publicized "New York 21" sent Huey a letter stating they were resigning from the party because it was no longer the vanguard of the revolution. And while the Weather Underground issued a statement that the party was "reformist," Eldridge openly declared that there was a "split" in the Black Panther Party.

In a nationally televised broadcast from Algiers, Eldridge claimed he and his International Section represented the "true vanguard," the "left wing" of the party, while the "right wing," headed by David Hilliard in Oakland, was a reformist faction that had taken over the party. He was issuing a call for other true revolutionaries to join his vanguard soldiers.

Huey responded through the party newspaper, castigating Eldridge as an ordinary renegade. He had me write many articles for the paper supporting the party and lambasting Eldridge. Message after message shot out from Oakland. There was no split in the party. As a result of Eldridge Cleaver's defection, he and all who supported him were now "expelled" from the Black Panther Party.

People inside and outside the party began to take sides, however. Most Panthers wandered around in confusion. Papa was an unknown dynamo whose rhetoric had fueled their passions. Huey was also unknown, but was the hero and near-deity who had created the Black Panther Party. A domestic battle line was drawn.

That Huey should have a secure place to live was no longer debatable. The only question was money. The emergency quickened my brain. I had not been the party's chief liaison to the stars in the land of movies and money for nothing. If no one else, there was certainly Bert Schneider.

I had met Bert in early 1969 as a result of one of my various calls to Jay in those desperate months. Jay knew Bert's father, who was president of Columbia Pictures. Bert had become a film producer in his own right, however, with the success of one of his company's early films *Easy Rider*.

The first time I met Bert was at his production company's offices on the sprawling Columbia film lot. His friend Abbie Hoffman was just leaving. I had become irritated with Bert at the very outset of that meeting. He and Hoffman were exchanging lighthearted word games about what I deemed the heaviness of our struggle. As I considered that either of them could dismiss that struggle whenever the spirit moved them, they seemed to me the prototypes of Bert's "easy riders."

Bert was very smooth, though. After showing Hoffman out, he displayed not the slightest sign of being flustered by my hostility. It was not at all what I felt was the typical white liberal attitude: that annoyingly patronizing attitude of ingratiation that was usually presented to surly blacks. He was a unique "white boy," I thought, trying not to notice how pretty I also thought he was. He was lean, as tall as a basketball player, with chiseled features, longish blond curls, and light blue eyes. Despite his lackadaisical "Hollywood" style, he was evidently very intelligent and well read. By the time I left, he had charmed me.

After that, Bert began to make significant monetary contributions to our Southern California chapter. He also introduced us to many of our other Hollywood supporters, the most noteworthy of whom was Jane Fonda.

"The boy's got that kind of money to throw around?" David said to me after I reminded him about Bert.

"He's got it, all right."

I immediately arranged to have lunch with Bert in L.A. Over those nearly two years since I had met him, we had had our share of lunches. We had had our share of private time. We had had our share of bantering foreplay, for which I had always felt mildly ashamed.

I could, of course, justify those times alone with Bert to my comrades. Along with Jean Seberg, he was the most serious of the Hollywood, or any of the other, supporters of our chapter. It was more than the sumptuous sums of cash he laid out without question, I could explain. He was with us for the ride, and it was not easy. It was one thing to fight against oppression from under the boot of the oppressor. It was another to do so when born with all the comforts of capitalism; when one is among the most popular producers in a million-dollar milieu; when one is the most sought-after prince of every beauty in a world of beauty.

I did not ask myself why I did not ignore Bert's signals, the sensuous ones that usually attended our lunches. I was pretty certain it had nothing to do with Huey and Gwen. I did not ask myself why I said nothing at lunch about why I had wanted to meet with him right away, about an apartment for the leader of the Black Panther Party. I just laughed with him a lot, and drank a lot of wine, and let the conversation drift to man and woman things, human things, not revolutions.

After lunch, we strolled out of the garden restaurant still laughing, hugging. I had to return to his office to get my car. When we got into his small blue BMW, the natural thing happened. He leaned across the center panel and kissed me, deliciously, deftly.

We drove in silence in the midafternoon to a small motel nearby. We barely breathed once inside, and did not speak.

I did not care about justifications, personal or political. I lost myself in the frenzy of stripping off clothing, tossing back bedcovers, making love, hard and passionate.

"Bert," I said finally, as we dressed, "we need some cash. Cash that can't be drawn from the party's main accounts, which, as you know, the FBI regularly reviews. Besides, as you can guess, what money we have can't be freed for another project . . . Well, this isn't really a project, it's an apartment. It's a place for Huey. His life is in real danger right now, more than ever, but he practically lives on the streets and . . ."

"How much, babe?" Bert interrupted.

"Well," I hesitated, "we want to pay an entire year's rent."

"How much?" He smiled.

"Twelve thousand," I mumbled.

"Can you pick it up from my office tomorrow? I'll have a cashier's check made out to you personally." It was the largest single contribution he had ever made to us.

I felt relief rush over me, along with shame. It was not about comrades, certainly not about morality, not even about Huey. I worried that Bert would think I had used him. And perhaps I had. Perhaps not.

He looked at me with a knowing smile. "Don't worry, Queenie," he said, using his shameless nickname for me, which I had insisted he never speak publicly. "Don't look so worried. If anybody sees us, you can say I'm a trick." He laughed.

"Or maybe I am," I responded, looking away from his blue eyes. ". . . Or maybe," I added, brightening, "I'll tell them it ain't true what they say 'bout white boys."

"And what's that?" He smiled, helping me into his car.

I brashly brushed my hand along the front of his pants. "Let's just say that you defy the cherished myths about black men."

The day before Huey moved into the apartment, the FBI leaked the information about it to one of their favored reporters in the Bay Area, Ed Montgomery. The front-page headlines blasted that the "declared revolutionary" Huey P. Newton would be moving into a "luxurious penthouse" apartment in a building on the "exclusive and fashionable" shores of Oakland's Lake Merritt.

The FBI had been ready. We had not. The "masses" turned on Huey. It was a sin, they whispered on the streets of Oakland and other places. By the time Huey actually settled in, letters to editors and barroom gossip carried their message. God was to live in man's image of him, a sacrificial lamb, a martyr, not a man living in a penthouse.

Party members were grumbling everywhere that it was

enough that they were faithfully adhering to Huey's party in light of the Eldridge conflict. Now they were being insulted, expected to swallow the hard, self-sacrificing lives they led in the Black Panther Party, housed in bare-bones collectives, working every waking hour, while the supreme commander lived in a glamorous bourgeois penthouse.

One Sister even confronted me over the matter. Like many Panthers, she believed that I influenced the supreme commander, though I was not a member of the Central Committee. Like most Panthers, she understood that the reality of our paramilitary structure was that the Politburo and the Central Committee and the other hierarchy in the party had come to function very much like the rank and file, under the supreme command of Huey Newton. I was the best person to approach about him, and the safest, not the intimidating figure of the men in leadership. She told me forthrightly that she was, at best, very disappointed in Huey Newton.

"Wait a minute, Sister," I said to her defensively. "Don't be ridiculous. Think . . . You know, when I was in China, everywhere I went, the people testified. They didn't talk about how thrilled they were that the motherland was finally free. They didn't declare how overjoyed they were over the blood they had shed for the revolution. No. Everywhere I went, this is what I heard: 'If it hadn't been for Chairman Mao, I never would have lived in a house of brick or had medical care . . .' and so forth. You see the point? In the end, that's what our fight is about. It's about people living, not dying . . .

"Notwithstanding the question of security against pigs and 'jackanapes,' " I continued, referring to the name we had begun using for the Cleaverites, "it's really a little thing to have the leader of our party live in a decent place. If nothing else, we show the world that we will *never* sacrifice our leader to our enemies' guns, much less allow him to live without the dignity and quality of life he's earned and deserves. Huey didn't want this. It was necessary."

She was, however, like the others, unmoved. Like the others, she wanted a leader who would be a suffering savior.

It was not the apartment per se that spawned the general anger. It was that confusion was replacing what had seemed the clarity of that glorious moment when everyone had cried "Free Huey!" Huey was no longer amorphous. He had stepped out of his poster and was breathing and eating and exhibiting ordinary attributes. People were angry with him because he was only a man, a man who might not bring about the instant upheaval of the world that would assuage their rage and pain.

"I can't save them," Huey actually sighed in frustration over the grumblings regarding his new apartment. "They want to love me as they created me, because they don't know how to love themselves."

Finally, he gave up. He locked himself defiantly inside his penthouse, alone. He decided the party members' anger with their god was transient. As for the "masses," they would have to discover their own power. Perhaps this would help put things into perspective. In any event, he was not going to die for the pigs, and certainly not on their terms. He would live for the people and the party, and they would forget their temporary insanity.

David and I, and Huey's other close associates and comrades, including the members of the Central Committee, had absolutely no regret about the decision regarding Huey's apartment. Eldridge was actually building an opposition army. That message was delivered with the brutal murder of Sam Napier.

Sam had been the backbone of the party's newspaper circulation. In spite of the fact that the pigs had forced airlines to "lose" bundles of our papers, or intimidated our printers into overinking the pages, or hired people to regularly turn water hoses or fire on bundles of our papers, Sam had miraculously gotten the newspaper distributed throughout the entire United States and beyond, on time, every week. Now Sam was dead, killed by "jackanapes" from the Eldridge faction in New York. He had been tied to a chair in our main newspaper distribution office in New York, beaten, shot in the head, and left in the building, which was then set on fire. His body was found charred nearly beyond recognition.

It had been a horrible warning. It was the beginning of a frightening, internecine battle as our troops, Huey's party, responded.

Bobby Seale, the party's well-known chairman, now acquitted of the murder-conspiracy charges in New Haven, came out of his Connecticut cell publicly praising Huey and denouncing Eldridge. Ericka Huggins, also acquitted in New Haven, returned to Oakland a heroine and condemned Eldridge. The powerfully influential prisoner-author George Jackson, now openly acknowledged as the field marshal of the Black Panther Party, attacked Eldridge scathingly, summarized in an open letter he wrote to author John Gerassi:

> My personal message to [Eldridge] was mild, considering that he was in fact leaving his old comrades open to [police] attack again. I sent a letter reminding him that his behavior while in prison was far from exemplary . . . I finally asked him simply to show proof now that he was not a compulsive disrupter or *agent provocateur*. A very mild request, I feel. He returned with a very scurrilous and profane set of invectives—in short, a piece of vendetta . . . Tell him that seven thousand miles, the walls of prison, steel and barbed wire do not make him safe from my special brand of discipline, tell him the dragon is coming . . .

The party foundation cracked. Nearly the entire New York chapter defected. Panthers in San Francisco, Eldridge's old base, were drifting away daily. Suspicions among all of us, about each of us, became rampant. Soon no one could be trusted. "Comrades" began carrying arms against one another.

Los Angeles was not spared its share of shooting incidents between former comrades after Sam's death. Adding insult to injury, Karenga's people began taking advantage of the war with Cleaver, accosting us openly. The ever-vigilant police certainly stepped up their attacks on our weakened corpus. The combination of police and Karenga's people and now Eldridge's forces made it a dangerous proposition to even identify oneself as a Panther in L.A., much less to brave the streets to sell a Panther newspaper.

It was then that Huey decided it was unsound for me to remain in L.A. It was inevitable, he said, that I would be specifically targeted by Eldridge's people—whoever they were. I was to move permanently to Oakland, immediately.

Everything I had come to be, everything I had come to feel, had been created in L.A. My reeducation as a human being had begun in L.A., with John and Bunchy. My close comrades had died in L.A., been jailed in L.A. Now I was to leave everything in L.A., I thought, packing up my child and our life.

CHAPTER 13

KISS OF THE PANTHER

GEORGE JACKSON SENT ME A LETTER in the early part of 1971. He was now in San Quentin prison's notorious Adjustment Center, but his words of fire were becoming internationally acclaimed through his book *Soledad Brother*. He called me by name and by position: "Comrade." Jonathan had spoken highly of me, his first letter said, and my songs. Later, his mother, Georgia, had told him about the song for Jonathan. We had to meet, his letter insisted. He was proud of Comrade Jon; Jon, the man-child. He was also on fire.

George had been "down" since he was eighteen years old, convicted of a seventy-dollar robbery. That had been over ten years earlier, when California liberals had traded with the Establishment. They had exchanged long-term, finite prison sentences for the possibility of shorter ones, the length to be determined by each prison administration: the wardens and the guards. That was how George had come to be sentenced to one-year-to-life for a comparatively minor infraction. That was why he had spent nearly half his life in prison—seven of those years in solitary confinement. The indeterminate sentence and the determined man were a volatile combination.

The years of prison, including isolation, had not driven him to his knees; and he had driven himself to comprehend the nature of his condition, not as a prisoner, but as a black man in America. He had concluded that his imprisonment had little to do with a seventy-dollar robbery. It had to do with trying to *live* in America, a social arrangement in which one's humanity had to be discarded in order to survive. He saw that if one was white, acts of survival in the American milieu might propel one to a corporate board-room. If one was black, these acts would most likely hurl one into an early grave or a prison cell. What George understood, he preached.

He taught his fellow inmates to really see how many rich white corporate raiders occupied cells in America's prisons; how many rich rapists, well-to-do wife beaters, high-class thieves, or murderers were inside. America's prisons, he showed them, were overpopulated with the poor, especially the black poor. In 1971, more than 50 percent of the inmates in America's prisons were black—more than five times the population ratio of blacks. Prisoners in America, George taught, were part of a larger class that was locked in a larger prison. He exhorted others to join him in changing their condition. He organized them around demands for reform, but challenged them to see that, in the end, prisons could not be reformed. Change had to be more fundamental. Change was revolution.

Not since Malcolm X had one man appealed so strongly to the hundreds of thousands of black prisoners in America. Not even Malcolm had done so from behind the walls. Not even Malcolm had issued a call for revolution. George Jackson would serve the maximum of his indeterminate sentence, it was determined. And redetermined in 1969 after a handful of black prisoners from Soledad prison's notorious segregated unit, O Wing, had been thrown into an exercise yard with a handful of white prisoners. The predictable racial fight was settled by four bullets from a guard tower. Three killed three of the blacks; the fourth wounded a white. Three days later, after a legal ruling of justifiable homicide, a white guard at Soledad was beaten to death. George was charged with that murder, along with two other "black militant" prisoners, Fleeta Drumgo and John Clutchette: the case of the Soledad Brothers.

George's was not a prisoner letter. I knew prisoner letters; I had received thousands, for the Black Panther Party was revered by black inmates in America. Our ten-point platform and program, written in 1966, specifically called for new trials for all black men held in prisons and jails. We believed blacks were, on the whole, the victims of crime, not the perpetrators of it. How could a man be said to steal to live the life that had been stolen from him, we reasoned. Blacks had been denied jobs and housing, education and health care, even a place to be buried, by de jure racism. That was grounded in the Supreme Court's dictum in the case of ex-slave Dred Scott: "A black man has no rights a white man is bound to respect."

Through the Black Panther Party and the writings of George Jackson, blacks in prison had come to see themselves not as criminals but as men, men whose potential was to form the backbone of an army to free our people. Black prisoners had begun building prison chapters of the party. They had begun pledging themselves to our struggle. The hero of all of them, the standard-bearer of that prisoner movement, was George Jackson. Breathing political fire into the hearts of thousands of angry black inmates across America, he was the Dragon of Ho Chi Minh. He was the field marshal of an army still in formation.

That was the title Huey had conferred on George when they were both inside the prison system. They never met, but they saw each other's photographs and communicated through mutual friends inside. Their vision of each other created a powerful bond. As I talked with Huey about George's first letter, I realized that George was, perhaps, the only man Huey really loved. There was a connection between them stronger than I could comprehend. When he spoke of George, Huey spoke of his brother, of his better self, of his ideal of a man. George Jackson was Huey's hero.

Huey was not really jealous of George's letters to me, in spite of the intimacies coloring his words of fire and the secondary subtleties inside his continuing demand that I arrange to visit him. It became a funny game, though, between us, among us. Huey would have given me to George, if such a thing could be said or done. It was only a funny game, mostly between them.

Gwen Fountaine had moved into the penthouse. Her lipsticks, perfumes, and leather purses filled the rooms. Huey had made the transition smoothly.

On my arrival in Oakland, Huey had showed me a large bedroom in David's house where there was a new bed with new sheets purchased for me. He had taken me to the penthouse, where new furnishings and a large telescope had put his mark on the rooms—pre-perfumes—including the bedroom where we stayed that first night in Oakland. He spent hours that night talking to me about how really useful the penthouse could be, as both office and home. He laughed about the Bert Schneider business, about my "twelve-thousand-dollar pussy." He talked on through most of the rest of the night, about love and revolution, and about how "fucking" had little to do with either. And he told me about Gwen, how he had reassigned her to work as his personal secretary in his office-home.

It was not a job for me, he explained, as I sobbed. I was more than a secretary-mistress who arranged his calendar and cooked his food and took care of his clothes and cleaned his house and "fucked" him any way he wanted, any time he wanted, and who got out of his bed on demand when he brought in all the others. We were not merely man and woman, he said, we were partners, revolutionary soulmates.

I came to a grudging acceptance of Gwen's presence, mostly because I came to feel a kind of admiration for her. Perhaps it was pity I felt, or maybe empathy. She did indeed do everything for Huey. She stayed up long hours with him, filling requests for exotic food or sex. She hosted the men, the rough underground men and street partners who were coming, more and more often, for one- and two-day nightmares, bringing Huey cocaine and cognac like myrrh. She served lunches to the legions of white intellectuals and journalists who wanted to take notes on the revolution of the dashing Huey P. Newton. She kept track of all the names, addresses, and faces of the rich and nearly rich who donated checks to the party in exchange for a few hours with Huey—including Bert Schneider, who was becoming Huey's new best friend. She served tea or champagne to the other women, the ones brought in for a night. She maintained his daily life with grace, and usually with a smile. Yes, she was stronger in a way that I never intended to be, I came to feel. It was not a job for me.

My job now was editor of the Black Panther newspaper. That was how Huey actually gave me to George, to find the proper format for, and publish the poetic power of, the words of his hero. Huey had installed me in that position by simply ousting the current editor, "Big Man." Besides my greater skill in the English language, my editorship gave Huey control over the party news organ. The absoluteness of my loyalty to Huey alone was clear, whereas Huey did not *really* know Big Man.

Huey did not intend to know Big Man, any more than he intended to know the majority of our comrades. He rarely saw them, leaving his penthouse less and less, never going to the party's national headquarters or other facilities. Besides, from Huey's point of view, most of them could not be trusted, the possible silent partners of the Cleaver faction that was still struggling to disrupt the party—though the voice of Eldridge himself was barely heard on United States shores; it was quieted by the personal dilemma his loss of party affiliation created for him with the Algerian government.

Huey did not want to know the comrades. They asked too much of him. He was claiming a space for himself where he could do what was required, no matter the fear of loneliness, for loneliness and fear were the raw points of human existence . . .

Nobody appreciated that more deeply than Armelia Newton's seventh son, her last child, her special child, who had been her own Second Coming. She had demanded that the world rejoice in the birth of her beautiful seventh son, whose hair she had brushed with sweet oils when he was a boy, whose face she had fanned in the intense humidity of Louisiana evenings, whose name she had made sacred to her entire world, especially her family. Of course, the streets of Oakland had not shared Armelia Newton's vision of Huey P. Newton, named for the infamous governor of Louisiana. On the streets of Oakland, her godsend had become the very embodiment of everything held in disdain by angry urban toughs, and "crazy"—until now.

Now he had risen again, sentenced to save those who had condemned him to know the raw loneliness and fear that pervaded the streets of West Oakland and that crystallized there on Seventh Street one night.

There were four men that night, Huey had confided in me —two white and two black, the oppressor and the oppressed. There had been Huey and Gene McKinney. There had been two pigs.

He and Gene had been driving down the liveliness of Seventh Street's bars and barbecue joints and gambling dens and dance halls, seeking the best barbecue in Oakland. Like the rest of the pigs, the two who stopped the car that night had come to see Huey, with his "high yellow" arrogance that taunted them, as the personification of what they hated about black men. They had decided to confront the object of their hatred that night.

The sequence of events was unclear. The results were not. The white cop had been killed by bullets from his white partner's weapon. The "high-yellow" black had been shot by a white cop before the very eyes of his black street partner. Only the four knew, but everybody else had a theory.

The black men, the others from the streets, acclaimed Huey.

He was now their Saint George, the dragon slayer. Now they were at his door calling him out, not to taunt him, but to exalt him. . . .

Now he played the game with them, as he always had, even inviting them to his penthouse door. There was Gene from Seventh Street, and others from other streets. There was the Bishop, from San Francisco. There had been the Jackal Dog—now mysteriously dead. There was Big Booker, from the prison years. There was June Hilliard, the party's new and more violent chief of staff—David had indeed been convicted and gone to prison. There were John Seale and Big Bob from Boston, and the others who had stood in opposition to Eldridge, including Steve, the vicious new leader of the Southern California chapter's underground. As he gathered them to him more and more, he ventured out less and less. There were usually no women at Huey's penthouse "stronghold"—unless one counted Gwen or me.

Bobby Seale, conspicuously absent from the penthouse, was, I saw up close in Oakland, duplicitous. With David gone, Bobby had taken over administration of the party's newspaper. He hated my presence at the newspaper the minute Huey placed me there, though he never dared challenge Huey about it. Despite being chairman of the party, he no more dared question Huey about my editorship than he dared question why he was never asked to the penthouse.

Big Man was Bobby's man. Big Man published all of Bobby's poorly worded diatribes, his pieces of puff, which Emory Douglas, minister of culture, then had to dress up with his graphics. Once I replaced Big Man as editor, I virtually eliminated all of Bobby's submissions.

I had insisted that Joan Kelley, working in the Bay Area, be reassigned to work with me on the newspaper staff. I needed a literate friend there. In the beginning, Joan and I had had to spend nearly two solid days each week trying to rework Bobby's hopeless prose. Finally, tiring of trying to make something out of nothing, I stopped printing most of what Bobby sent for publication.

Bobby was boiling—somewhat understandably—though he never confronted me directly about any article. He decided to confront the issue from the rear, under cover of his title. I appealed to Huey.

"He's an idiot," I insisted to Huey on a visit to the penthouse. "He's driving me crazy with his stupid orders. Every week he changes the deadline, and then, of course, he and Big Man fuck with me to make sure the paper's late."

"He's the chairman." Huey smiled sardonically, walking back and forth along the walls of windows that led to the balconies twenty-five stories high. He was sipping cognac, shirtless. "We have to let the chairman be the chairman," he chortled with a sarcasm that I did not think was funny. "Look, you're smart, you can get around Bobby. But definitely don't give him any pussy." He laughed.

I grimaced.

"All right. Just remind Bobby I put you there to do the job, and to let you do it . . .

"But the problem with you is," he continued, still chuckling, "that you don't appreciate history. I mean, Bobby started with me. You should've seen him in Sacramento. You know I didn't go. I sent Bobby. I wrote a little statement for the press and sent Bobby and the other Brothers, half of whom were just our partners from the street. And Bobby was fantastic. He did the thing right. Showed up at the legislature with his black leather and beret, a Kool cigarette hanging out of his mouth and his .45 strapped on, and read our statement beautifully."

It was true that Bobby Seale had been working hard for the party a long time, and long before the time I even knew I was black. He had been in the leadership of the party through the hard years and had never wavered, not in a courtroom in Chicago nor in a cell in Connecticut.

"You're right, Huey. And I'm sorry . . . But what *can* I do about . . ."

"And Bobby's stayed true to me and the party. Just look at Eldridge if you want a reference point."

I looked down.

"Okay. Now that you see my point, go on back and try to work with Bobby," he said seriously.

Then he laughed at me. "But we really can't have Bobby actually running the paper. I put you there to do it."

I rolled my eyes at him, and he laughed again.

Then he spoke softly. "Anyway, I promised George you would make sure no one would tamper with his articles."

I suffered Bobby a few weeks more. Joan and I stayed up longer, taking 20, then 40 milligrams of Ritalin a day to work against time, to edit and rewrite, to step around Bobby and Big

Man. What sleep we stole was in the wooden chairs in our second-floor office at national headquarters. I saw very little of my child, who was living in one of the houses in which we collectively cared for the party's children. I was tired all the time, even with the Ritalin. It was in that low moment that Bobby finally found a way to justify an outright attack on me.

The newspaper had to be ready for the press precisely at twelve noon on Wednesdays, Bobby suddenly ordered. After that, Bobby, accompanied by a few security people, began showing up on Wednesday mornings with last-minute articles. Bobby would waste time looking at Emory's layouts and criticizing everything. He would demand that an article be pulled, leaving a big hole. Then he would add insult to injury by standing over us at the layout tables until we finished, threatening "discipline" for failure to get the paper out on time.

One morning, we were an hour late. Bobby began screaming at me. It would cost the party money, he complained to everyone he had brought with him. Too much time had been spent editing, he shouted, looking at me. I was the editor, and I was responsible, and I was subject to discipline for that.

I took the punishment, the way most comrades did. Bobby's order was sufficient. There was no real appeal. It was our judicial system, made up mostly as we went along. If we had been in Bolivia with Che, we told ourselves, we would be shot for violations of rules or orders. Discipline was essential in the vanguard, we told ourselves. So I silently faced the punishment, which was always an act of violence.

John Seale was strangely gentle with the ten lashes I received from the whip he held. We were in a small basement room at national headquarters. My bare back hardly felt the sting. Joan was standing in a corner quietly crying for me, for the outright, absurd unfairness of it. My rage was so intense, each lash stung me only with the face of Bobby, who was not there. My skin developed welts but was unbroken by the tenth lash. I refused the attempts of John and the other men there to put salve on my back.

"I've done more than I need to do, Huey. I won't take it again," I stated firmly.

"Okay, okay," he said, knowing he would have to stop avoiding the issue of Bobby Seale. "I'll make it up to you."

Then he laughed, and kissed me, over and over, until I

shamelessly abandoned the business of Bobby Seale and allowed myself to forget Gwen.

Huey was accelerating the progress of our Survival Programs. He was dictating numerous articles for me to print regarding their importance in a revolutionary context. To push the momentum, he ordered Bobby to take charge of all the Survival Programs. In one stroke, he changed the course of the party and removed Bobby's hand from the newspaper, which kept Bobby and his cronies out of my face for some time to come.

In his new role, Bobby blossomed, turning his true talent for rallying massive numbers of people into a tangible boon for the party and our people. He created the most magnificent food giveaways. The big ones became major community events, reported often in the media. Previously, there had been only the breakfast and other free-meal programs but Bobby organized a campaign to give away bags of groceries to whole families, with a stalking panther printed on each bag. The community and the press went wild.

Bobby's giant food giveaways begat tremendous support for all our other Survival Programs. Even middle-class blacks, theretofore reluctant to support or be identified with the party, began endorsing it and making contributions. As Bobby's spirit and leadership reached the other chapters, support for the party's free-food programs grew by leaps and bounds everywhere. We expanded our free clinics and preventive medicine projects—through which we placed the deadly blood disease peculiar to blacks, sickle-cell anemia, on the agenda of America's medical profession. We implemented new ideas, such as a shoe program—renting a factory and manufacturing shoes to give away to our people. These successful efforts spawned a true survival program for the party, as confused police and FBI had to regroup, bury their old assault plans, and invent new tactics to attack us.

From his penthouse, Huey now ordered that the party begin to close ranks. The strengthening of the Survival Programs boosted our support and morale, but the party apparatus was spread too thin. With everything in our forty-two chapters being duplicated, our money and energy were being so drained, the impact of our Survival Programs would inevitably be diminished. We were not, after all, trying to establish the Survival Programs as much as an idea. That was taking hold, as evidenced in the emergence of free-breakfast programs in a variety of schools in California and elsewhere that had come as a result of black community demands. It was time to move forward.

We could solidify our gains by concentrating everything we had in one operation, Huey analyzed. We would develop a real stronghold, Huey directed, a base of operation to move to higher ground.

Oakland, Huey declared, would be the base. It was not only historically relevant as the birthplace of our party, it was objectively significant. It was a territory in which we could, in fact, establish such a base. Oakland's relatively small population was nearly half black. Moreover, Oakland had solid economic strength and potential, primarily from its significant port. Oakland was a ripe environment, Huey decided, to establish a base.

This was more than a tactic to strengthen the party's apparatus. Huey considered our concentration on Oakland a first step in a long-range plan. There was the "mass line," and there was the "party line," and there was the bottom line, which was the vision of Huey P. Newton.

Sometime before I left L.A., he had ordered me to Oakland to talk about that vision.

"Take a look at this and tell me what you see," he said within seconds of my arrival.

He handed me a copy of an international magazine. It was opened to an advertisement.

"It's an ad for Ford cars" was all I could say.

"Yes, but what does it *say*? Look!"

He was pacing with excitement as I read the copy aloud: " 'We at Ford International fly the American flag . . .' "

" 'But we say,' " he repeated with me, fired with enthusiasm, " 'we say, what flag do *you* fly?' . . . It's incredible, isn't it?"

"In what way?" I responded, opening the door through which he was anxious to pass.

"Before I tell you, do you recall the Coca-Cola jingle: 'I'd love to buy the world a Coke . . .'? That. Remember?"

"Yes, with all those wonderful, perfect-looking, Americanized Africans and Asians and . . ."

"Exactly . . . But the bottom line is: they'd love to *sell* the world a Coke . . . 'We at Ford say what flag do *you* fly.'

"What does it mean? . . . It means that the U.S. capitalists have taken a turn, a right turn. And I think it's affecting the economic structure of the entire world. We're in a brand-new game.

"If I'm right, we can't define the world anymore as a collection of sovereign states with independent economies. What this bit of advertising bullshit triggered in my mind is that a new economic arrangement has taken hold, one that exists irrespective of language, custom, ideology, flags, and, most of all, *territory* . . .

"First you have to accept that a human being's life in society is determined by his relationship to its economy. Before industrialization, that relationship everywhere was to a land-based, agricultural economy. Generally speaking, if one had land, one was rich; if not, one was poor. A brutal but long-standing social arrangement.

"Industrialization disrupted that. It introduced mass production, new transportation methods, powerful infrastructures. It transformed the structure of society because it spurred the rise of capitalism, which killed the feudal landlord by opening the doors of wealth to a new class: the bourgeoisie. Wealth came to be determined not by landholding but by industrial-based profit.

"Most of the people in the countries that became industrialized, however, only left oppression in the field for oppression in the factory. Of course, none of that meant anything to people in the nonindustrialized countries.

"This shift was completed by the end of the last century. But I think the change was only quantitative. Because the social structures under both feudalism and capitalism were rooted in national economies. Now I think a shift has occurred that is more profound than the transformation from feudalism to capitalism—a *qualitative* shift. Modern technology has introduced a *global* economic structure that has wiped out capitalism . . .

"We've always accepted the Marxist analysis that our oppression was grounded in the rise of capitalism. For blacks here, of course, going from the post–Civil War fields to the industrial centers didn't put many of us into the industrial proletariat. Racism precluded that. But that's our class relationship in the U.S., and defines our present, postagrarian enslavement. So we concluded that socialist revolution was the road to our freedom. I don't believe that means anything anymore, if a *global* economic arrangement has succeeded in overwhelming capitalism.

"After the Russians sent up Sputnik, the U.S. poured every

dollar it had into technological exploration in space and other military adventures—notably by diverting billions of dollars from resolving the internal social ills U.S. capitalism had created. The government and the capitalists built what Eisenhower called the 'military-industrial complex.' As U.S. technology mushroomed. And the U.S. became, in fact, the most militarily powerful country in the world.

"The U.S. capitalists found their production capacity becoming manifold and unlimited. Up until then, they had followed the line of the other imperialist nations. To increase profits, they had to rip off raw materials and free or cheap labor from the darker continents. But the technological advances reduced the need for both labor and raw materials. The problem is, you can't sell shit if you don't have people with salaries to buy it. If they can produce more than the U.S. market can bear, they've reached the limits of profitability. They need to develop new *marketplaces* . . .

"The American way of life—capitalism—is no longer threatened by Communism. Soviet inroads into the undeveloped Third World are irrelevant. The U.S. capitalists are threatened by a limitation of marketplaces. They not only *need* to sell the whole world a Coke, they're moving to do it.

"Consider Vietnam. I think the war has very little to do with Vietnam's tungsten and bauxite. Technology will soon be able to accommodate the need for those raw materials without Vietnam —like the industrial diamonds that can be synthesized; or the way coal was replaced by oil production, due to technological development. And they don't need the unskilled labor. They need the marketplace! I think Vietnam is about developing a marketplace of forty million potential consumers. It's a play-or-pay proposition: they *will* buy a Coke.

"The rest of the world is just trying to keep up or survive. Take the communities in Africa and South America, with their vast copper and diamond deposits—discounting what hasn't already been stolen. The people can't eat these precious materials. And the territorial governments, neocolonialists, and local bourgeoisie don't have the technology to transform them into food and other basic necessities. But even if they could refine the raw materials and get around the massive distribution problems, they would be hard put to compete with U.S.-established price formulas and rates of exchange. And if they found their way around that, they'd find themselves facing the hard line of U.S. market

competition: the U.S. military machine. And they won't get around
that. The point is, technology has produced domination of the
entire world by one nation: the United States of America.

"Assuming this analysis is basically correct, there's a new so-
cioeconomic arrangement that is not bound by national territory
. . . We cannot, then, continue to use the term 'capitalism' or
'imperialism' to define the structure that governs and oppresses
us. A new language is required for this new arrangement. I'm
calling it 'reactionary intercommunalism.'

"I use this term because the new arrangement has not only
overwhelmed capitalism, it has obliterated nationhood. If we use
Stalin's definition, a nation is, primarily, a sovereign territory with
economic and social independence. I believe U.S. global power
has transformed things so that the world's nations have been reduced to a collection of integrated *communities*. What you have now
dominating all the communities of the new world economic order
is a global bourgeoisie: the owners of the U.S. corporate conglom-
erates, the reactionary intercommunalists . . .

"What is the functional difference in the relationship to the
U.S. economy of Africans living in Africa and Africans living in
Harlem? Or take Vietnam again. The U.S. refers to its war on the
Vietnamese as a 'police action'—and it basically is: no different in
kind from putting down a riot in Watts . . .

"The reactionary intercommunalists have obliterated national
independence and sovereignty. Of course, there are some liber-
ated territories, like Russia and China. At best, they are what I
would call 'provisional revolutionary administrations,' but not
independent, sovereign nations—not in the global shadow of
the U.S.

"And there're the Europeans. Can the French or the British,
two of the leading European economies, legitimately lay claim to
economic independence and national sovereignty when even the
old international gold standard has become the U.S. dollar
standard?

"That's why Ford can ask what flag do you fly. It's not important. When they control your market, they'll have the rest. If
you want to be 'black and proud,' they put Negroes in advertising
campaigns and have all the Negroes fighting for the right to drink
Coke over Pepsi. For the Chinese they throw up Bank of America
buildings that look like pagodas. And if you fly a flag with a ham-
mer and sickle, they'll slap it on the dashboard of a Ford and

control the Communist communities—that the Communists themselves can't accommodate.

"The important thing for us is to *see* this new reality. We have to abandon the idea of developing socialist states. That idea depends on the existence of nations, national economies. We have to embrace the idea of *global* revolution.

"But there's good news in this. As this new dominant force of reactionary intercommunalists necessarily has to continue to expand—sell more Fords and Cokes, open more marketplaces— they, like the old capitalists, build up the potential for their own negation. A *global* negation. This situation cuts out the microstep of installing socialism in one place only to have it threatened by capitalism in another—where we would end up running around like the Russians, trying to maintain and never being able to build.

"There's only *one* machinery to seize, the toppling of which makes way for an egalitarian redistribution of the wealth of the whole world—true communism. And there are only two classes: the billions of us and the few of them. Whatever the differences in the levels of oppression, from the industrial and technological workers to the impoverished Third World millions, the majority of the world's people have become *one* class of dominated people. In other words, we have a setup for global revolution: revolutionary intercommunalism.

"Blacks in the U.S. have a special duty to give up any claim to nationhood now more than ever. The U.S. has never been our country; and realistically there's no territory for us to claim. Of all the oppressed people in the world, we are in the best position to inspire global revolution."

I was stunned. Huey had spat out an idea that the most learned economists and sociologists had failed to articulate, an idea that encompassed an ultimate solution for us—the us that had been present and discounted for centuries.

Huey was now pushing the party to act on his theory of intercommunalism, despite the fact that some Central Committee members, particularly Masai, had challenged its validity. He commanded all chapters to begin sending their people to Oakland. Whatever anyone thought in the final analysis, our dispersed troops began their exodus to Oakland to build "the base"—for global revolution.

Huey remained isolated from all of them, however. More and more, he separated himself from the rest of the world. He had stopped making speeches, despite the demand. He hated speaking in public, he said, because he could not be honest. It was a show and he was not a good performer. He could function better one-on-one, or alone, where the complex parts of who he was could thrive. He had indeed been at his very best not long before in a set of recorded conversations, before a small, elite Yale University audience, with the world-renowned psychoanalyst Erik Erikson; the conversations were being transcribed and edited for a book: *In Search of Common Ground.* Even the last of those conversations between Erikson and Huey, however, had taken place at the penthouse. His most recent public speaking engagements had been miserable.

At what had been slated to be the last annual Huey Newton birthday rally, which became a March rather than a February event, touted as the "Intercommunal Day of Solidarity," he had stuttered through an arcane statement. The adoring audience of thousands had barely been able to applaud it, much less appreciate it.

Before that, at the party's assembly calling for a constitutional convention in Washington, D.C., he had recoiled from the thousands of people who had come to hear him, consuming an extra dose of Ritalin to face their cheers, and afterward, their bodies blocking the streets, enveloping our car like an octopus.

Huey had been reluctant to speak in Washington not only because he disliked the idea of speaking, but also because he was convinced that the idea of a black rewriting of the cherished document that was the basic law of the land had little merit. The convention had been an Eldridge Cleaver–engendered idea that had been foisted on the party—pre-defection. Huey had agreed to allow the party to continue to organize the convention primarily to buy time. He had still been pushing Eldridge to send Kathleen to the United States, suggesting she should address the convention along with him.

The drama of Kathleen's absence had only intensified Huey's dread. Every chapter was organizing black people to come to the nation's capital, to Howard University, the only distinguished black holding in what blacks referred to as "Chocolate City"—Washington having a nearly 90 percent black population.

What finally forced Huey to make that speech, however, was that Howard University reneged on its commitment to host the convention once it was announced that Huey Newton would be the keynote speaker. Despite the fact that Howard's traditionally middle-class black student population had recently become "blackenized"—as expressed in demonstrations over black studies and the selection of a campus "queen" who was not Howard's traditional "light-bright-and-almost-white" black woman—Howard's administration did not intend to be *that* "black." Having Huey Newton bring his Black Panther message to its distinguished grounds was out of the question. Before Huey reached the point of going to Washington and tearing down Howard's administration buildings and administration members, I advanced an appeasement. It had come to me, as ideas do, out of the necessity of the moment; and also out of an echo of the past. It appealed to Huey's fondness for linking past harm with action for the future.

It had to do, first, with the fact that my father's father, Emmett Scott, had been a major financial contributor to Howard University. Secondly, as my mother had reported to me a year or so before, my father, Horace Scott, had died. I had long stopped contemplating my contempt for him and my teenage promise to spit on his grave when he died. When I learned of his death, I only felt sad.

When Howard's administration closed its doors to Huey, it occurred to me to pull my father's dead hand from the grave to do something positive, something that would allow me to seize a piece of my lost heritage. Huey loved that.

I called the office of Howard's president. After suffering some bureaucratic "shucking and jiving," I was finally allowed to speak with the president of America's largest black institution of higher learning. My opening question as to whether he knew the name Dr. Emmett J. Scott was met with a warm Negro "Yes, ma'am" response. Indeed, Dr. Scott's contribution to Howard was memorialized in some statuary on campus, he said. In that case, as his granddaughter, I was requesting, on behalf of "our family," that the university change its "hard-ass" position on hosting the convention. His intellectualized circumvention of my personal "family" request was cut short by my hanging up the telephone.

I was now on the case, though, the case of doing something for Huey, for the party, and for making my father do right in death. My mother advised me that there was one living sibling of my father, his sister Evelyn, who was married to a well-known Chicago attorney, Aaron Payne. I called my father's sister then, with the intention of squeezing my blood from this last Scott relative to shove it down the throat of Howard, to remedy things past, and to relish the private joy that the only biological offspring of the grand Scott line was now the worst imaginable kind of embarrassment to it—a Black Panther.

Mrs. Payne spoke like a Georgia peach. "Yes, darling, I'm so thrilled to hear from you. We've always wondered what happened to you." She went on to say that she thought of me often, for I was—according to the photograph of me she had been given by my father, a "wonderful man"—the living replica of their dear sister Clarissa, now gone. She confirmed how "the family" had always wished that my mother would have simply allowed them to absorb me into the Scott family. She was so teary-eyed happy to hear from me, I could not break the spell with the facts about what I was actually doing, or why I had actually called.

So I wrote her a long letter, laying out my life as it existed in relation to my "wonderful" father. I finished with a few paragraphs about why I was now a dedicated member of the Black Panther Party, and why I would be pleased to have the family's support in bringing Howard to its senses—in light of the "family's" magnanimous contributions to the university.

As Howard remained unyielding, I called Mrs. Aaron Payne a week or so later. Her husband answered the telephone and immediately advised me never to call or make contact with his wife or their house again. His wife had nearly fainted upon reading my ugly words about her brother and the unmentionable "work" I was presently doing. How could I dare seek to involve her in such ugly business? My weak attempt to insist on speaking directly to "my aunt" was thwarted with an absolute refusal, and a final warning that, as she was his wife, and it was her family, and therefore his, I was "messing" with, he would see me in hell before he would allow me to connect myself to them again. The telephone connection was abruptly severed.

Huey had had to put his arms around me again, as I cried to him about it, hurt raw by what seemed the final rejection of my father, even from the grave; stunned by the frustration of being unable to accomplish what I had set out to do; disgraced by how weak and needing I was. Then Huey made me laugh, telling me how another location for the convention had been found after he personally advised the Washington, D.C., chapter leadership that they had better take care of the matter immediately. Then he told me one of his "insights," one of the poems he wrote in the moment of "realization," not a poem but an "insight"—which would introduce his second book, *Revolutionary Suicide*.

By having no family,
I inherited the family of humanity.
By having no possessions,
I have possessed all.
By rejecting the love of one,
I received the love of all.
By surrendering my life to the revolution,
I found eternal life . . .

That was the full expression of Huey Newton, which, while it bound me to him, was not a rousing idea for a public speech—in Washington, D.C., or anywhere else. Most people did not want to experience ideas at Huey's level of truth. And he had neither the patience nor the ability to dress up those ideas for public consumption. If he continued trying to place them in a big arena, people would, he predicted, ultimately come to hate him—and worse, the ideas. Most people preferred fantasy truths and fantasy heroes; and he hated the former and refused to be the latter. That was why Washington became one of his last major speeches, and why he now, less than a year after his release from prison, virtually locked himself inside his prison-penthouse.

Now he held the party reins alone from the twenty-fifth floor, and sent out his orders and directives. He virtually stopped convening Central Committee meetings, where ego haggling over minor issues generally resulted in indecisiveness. "Words are beautiful, but action is supreme," he would say, quoting Che Guevara. If he had an idea, he would spend days, weeks, struggling with it, usually alone, and then make a decision to act.

A visit to the penthouse had become an awesome experience. It was where truth was both explored and extracted, the house of redemption or damnation.

When the men with cocaine came, Huey laughed with them and snorted with them, for as long as they could stand it. When the intellectuals came, he wound them up with hours of debate. When the women came, he addressed their loneliness and his. When the rich came, he gave them absolution in return for their contributions to the party. When the few party members came, he offered enlightenment, sometimes with the back of his hand, or worse.

I became generally indifferent to the penthouse comings and goings. Huey had finally built the world in which he needed to function, and I was happy for that. I worked hard to produce the newspaper, had my own visits with Huey, stayed clear of Bobby Seale—still busy with his Survival Programs—and stayed on the spot of higher ground that Huey had reserved for me.

There were more people at the penthouse the night of Huey's meeting with Farrakhan than I had ever seen, however. There were quite a few Panthers, about ten men, all armed, and, of course, Gwen. It was 2 A.M., and the twenty-fifth floor's open windows were making all of us, except Huey, shiver. Perhaps it was the nature of the meeting Huey was about to have, I thought as we waited for the arrival of the bastard heir to Malcolm X, the Nation of Islam's Louis Farrakhan.

Farrakhan had been Elijah Muhammad's anointed replacement for Malcolm after Malcolm's defection had rocked the world of the Black Muslims, after Malcolm's assassination had been reputedly carried out by members of the Nation. Farrakhan had also been, strangely, I thought in retrospect, one of Malcolm's bodyguards. Louis Farrakhan—who had grown up in Boston as Gene Walcott—was a handsome man by any standard, glib of tongue, fearless in rhetoric, arrogant in style. He had built his reputation within and without the Nation on his denunciation of Malcolm X. Farrakhan would have a posthumous reputation for maligning the Black Panther Party, Huey had said, organizing this middle-of-the-night meeting at the penthouse.

Farrakhan had been running around the Northern California Bay Area, where *our* base was being built, incorporating foul little formulations subtly denigrating the party into his speeches. He was a speaker who generally drew relatively large audiences, not entirely Muslim. To denounce the party, even subtly, was a travesty worthy of harsh punishment. To do so in our base territory was a gauntlet thrown down.

My Brothers and Sisters, Farrakhan had been saying, *we in the Nation say that a man is what he eats . . . Now, some people, on one hand, denounce others as pigs, while, on the other hand, they themselves eat the pig . . . We say that if a man eats the pig, he must be the pig!*

Farrakhan arrived with about twenty members of the FOI, the Black Muslims' infamous security force: the Fruit of Islam.

Only five would be allowed entrance to the penthouse, they were informed by Panthers who were waiting in the lobby. They were all searched for weapons.

"Oh, we don't carry 'carnal' weapons, Brothers," Farrakhan had casually said on the elevator ride up to the twenty-fifth floor. The search had yielded none.

The double doors were flung open movie-style. The scene had been set perfectly by Huey. Panthers in full blue and black uniforms, including berets, were standing strategically at attention in the spacious living room. They were all holding shotguns, noticeable even in the dim light cast by the lamp over Huey's large oil painting of Che Guevara. Gwen and I were dressed in "costume," according to Huey's instruction, long skirts and long-sleeved blouses, befitting some ideal look of a Muslim woman. She was to serve tea; I was to take notes—appropriate roles for us as women, Huey had joked.

Reviewing the scene, I recalled another experience with a Black Muslim. During Huey's speechmaking stint, in a college auditorium a Black Muslim in the audience kept interrupting Huey's already-difficult exercise with taunts. He said something to the effect that the party was not providing a proper image for the black man and needed to embrace Allah. Huey had ignored the man for his entire speech; but two seconds after he had finished, he had jumped off the stage and walked through the audience to confront the man directly.

"Is Allah your god?" he asked the Muslim, inches away from his face. The audience was stunned into immobility.

"That right, Brother!"

"Well, Man is my god—and I hope your god will save your ass from the wrath of my god." Within a breath, Huey was all over the Muslim, pummeling him up and down the auditorium aisle.

Huey showed Farrakhan to a chair at one end of his massive, highly polished, ebony dining table. He sat at the opposite end. Interestingly, Huey and Farrakhan looked to me like mirror images of each other. The striking handsomeness of their faces seemed to say as much about each man as his reputation.

Gwen poured tea from an elegant pot, taking great care to serve each of Farrakhan's five lieutenants seated along one side of the table. She then poured for each of the party members seated on the opposite side, including John Seale and June Hilliard. The movie began as I took pen and notebook in hand to approximate my role, sitting slightly behind and to the right of Huey.

"My Brother," Huey began, with diplomatic formality, "I appreciate the time you've taken to meet with us." The "imperial" us, I noted, eyes appropriately downcast.

"We welcome the opportunity to speak with our good Brother in struggle," Farrakhan responded.

"We in the Black Panther Party have always appreciated the teachings of the Honorable Elijah Muhammad," Huey went on without batting an eyelash.

I swallowed very hard, wondering how Huey could open his mouth to make such a claim. It was true that the party's ten-point platform and program had been shaped by the Nation's doctrine, as printed on the back of every issue of *Muhammad Speaks!* However, notwithstanding Huey's own atheistic opinions about all religions, the party had always aligned itself specifically with Malcolm X—a proclaimed "enemy" of the Nation, before and since his assassination six years before.

"At the same time, my Brother," Huey added, before Farrakhan could turn a smiling response into a verbal pat on the head, "we identify completely with the principles taught by Minister Malcolm X."

That was when I thought the FOI seated at the table would jump up and initiate the inevitable battle.

"Indeed," he continued, adding insult to injury, "that was why I personally took charge of Sister Betty Shabazz's security when she came to speak here in the Bay Area some time ago—after Malcolm's murder." Nobody alive and black did not know about that time, when Huey and other Panthers carrying shotguns had marched up to the airplane in the San Francisco airport to escort Malcolm's widow.

Out of the corner of my eye, I saw a shotgun jump when he said that. The dangerous FOI at the table sat up—dangerous men, it was said, not merely because they were purportedly martial arts experts, but because they were "true believers," men pledged to be ready at any time to meet Allah in paradise for their beliefs. And I knew Huey was prepared to send them there that night.

"Yes, Brother Malcolm was an interesting man, though misguided," Farrakhan responded, his eyes motioning away the potential of his men's angry response. "He lost faith, though, and . . ."

"Yes, well anyway—excuse me, my Brother," Huey interrupted, "but I actually did not ask you here to speak about the dead past . . . I wanted to talk with you about a little thing you've been saying recently which has given me great concern, my Brother." There was a barely detectable bit of sarcasm.

"Speak on it, Brother," Farrakhan said, leaning forward with clasped hands under his chin, an emperor listening to the plea of his subject.

"First, I want to be sure I have understood you correctly . . . I believe you say that a man is what he eats, is that correct—uh, my Brother?"

"That is what we say, Brother."

"You have also said that if a man eats the pig, he must *be* the pig. Is that also correct, *Brother?*" His tone was very confrontational.

"Ah!" Farrakhan said, understanding. "Yes, that is so. You see, we in the Nation believe the pig is a dirty animal, and to eat any part of it is a sin against Allah."

"I understand, my Brother. I accept what you say, and I appreciate your saying it. I have, however, another question."

"Speak, Brother."

"Are you a man?" Huey threw back his head in anticipation of triumph.

Everyone looked puzzled, including Farrakhan.

"Why, of course," Farrakhan said, leaning back in the expensive ebony chair at the head of Huey's table. "Is that your question, Brother?" he added, given Huey's silent contemplation of his answer.

"Yes . . . Well, not quite. Here is my question: if a man is what he eats and you are a man, what part of the man do *you* eat?!"

With that, Huey dramatically slid to the edge of his chair, leaning forward to look directly into Farrakhan's eyes, waiting for an answer.

The shotguns no longer looked sufficient to me. The FOI left behind were surely climbing the sides of the building by now, secreting themselves in the dark corners of the balconies, having heard everything on small electronic devices, I wildly imagined, that had not been detected when their brothers were searched. I could see the morning newspaper reports of the carnage created by men who did not carry "carnal weapons."

The pause between Huey's last word and Farrakhan's resumption of breathing ended.

Farrakhan fell back in his chair, threw back his head, and laughed heartily, genuinely—thankfully.

"That's a good one, Brother," Farrakhan said, still laughing. "You got me there. I understand you completely, my Brother. And I assure you, we'll be more careful in our references . . ."

It was not an outright apology, but it sufficed. Huey talked pleasantly with Farrakhan for the next hour or so, the open penthouse windows cooling the heat that lingered.

The Brothers were prouder of their hero than ever, as the story circulated later, somewhat exaggerated, as stories become, passed among men like a joint or a new pistol or a new woman.

George Jackson seemed bigger than he had appeared in the courtroom months before, even though I had been only a slight distance from him then. He was about six feet four, with a broad chest and strong arms developed in his martial arts exercises. It had taken me six months to obtain San Quentin prison's permission to visit him. Even in the way he moved, George Jackson defied the state's repression with his dignity, his shackled hands pulling up his pants with a certain style. His smile was broad, fearless, terrifying, embracing.

"Greetings, Comrade!" he said with dramatic effervescence, adjusting the single chair on his side of the visiting chamber with his shackled feet. The chair's sharp scraping on the stone floor made one of the escorting guards twitch. "You look like my aunt in Chicago," he said, sliding like a lion into place, sitting tall, his large eyes looking me over thoroughly, flirtatiously, delectably.

After that, he spoke differently. He had perfected a speech pattern suitable for the life of a hated prisoner, tight lips that spoke softly. His eyes searched constantly.

"Why has Huey denied my request?" he said, looking directly at me, ignoring the presence of the guard behind the door at his back.

We were locked inside the cell, separated by a divider that rose to eye level, the top half of which was heavy glass and the bottom a concrete slab. A small counter protruded at desk height on either side.

"Your request?"

"To have you for my woman."

I simply blushed.

"You can give me your answer later. Then we'll convince the Servant," he continued, referring to Huey by his new title.

Huey had demanded that the "supreme commander" title be dropped, calling it an arrogant and ridiculous label. He had offered an appellation in its stead, "Servant of the People"—a rather biblical reference, I thought—asserting it represented what each party member was. Some had later tried to foist "Supreme Servant" onto that—also dismissed. He was now generally referred to as "the Servant."

George laughed at the concern on my face over how to respond to his "request" face-to-face. I had played the game in letters all along, and in lavish fantasies. Now I had to adjust words and fantasy to the reality of this incredibly big man who was looking at me, whom Huey, the man I loved more than any man, loved more than any man. There was one hour to make some kind of adjustment.

"Do you know Angela?" he asked, in a tone the meaning of which I could not interpret.

"Yes and no. When Bunchy was alive, she was in the party, in L.A. She was driven away by the stupidity of niggers. They attacked her because she was too light-skinned and too well educated, which they translated as too bourgeois.

"Deacon Alexander, Franklin's brother—head of the Communist Party's little Du Bois Clubs operating out of L.A.—stole her away with a few acts of kindness. Then the CP used her for everything she was worth, exploiting every line she was getting in the press in connection with her fight with UCLA. I haven't seen Angela since then."

"Jon thought she was wonderful," he said.

He and Angela communicated, he went on. They wrote letters from prison to prison. Angela had been in jail for months by then, charged with conspiring with Jonathan, by allegedly supplying the guns he used that August 7. She could not get bail. She was as wonderful as Jon had said.

"I'm just trying to convince her to leave the CP. She needs ten thousand dollars to do that. It's a ransom. Ask the Servant if we'll pay."

I did not have the courage to ask more about this exotic business.

My second visit, a week later, on August 19, seemed shorter than one hour.

I would see him before the next week's visit, I reminded him before leaving. He had a pretrial hearing set for the following Monday, August 23. As I rose to leave, he looked at me conspiratorially with his broad smile.

"Wear something next time so I can see your breasts. I want to remember them in my cell."

I responded with a smile and left the visiting cell. But I cried

as I walked past each of the two San Quentin metal detectors, and
all along the winding roads to the parking lot, and driving away
from the Romanesque prison, which looked like a castle as it disappeared in the rearview mirror of my car. It was such a painfully
pathetic request from such an extraordinarily strong man. I rushed
to the closet in the national headquarters where my clothes were
now kept to see what was there.

It was pointless, of course. Two days later George was assassinated. It was on August 21, 1971, nearly one year to the day
from the date of Jonathan's death.

Joan and I had been laughingly trying to create a newspaper
article out of a submission from one of our comrades. It was a
typically banal piece purporting to expose police brutality, perfect
fare for the stockpile of cynicisms we had developed about the
"black misery" stories we received. The early-afternoon sun filled
our workroom, crowded with two desks, stacks of papers, and a
useless file cabinet. Dust particles were flickering in the sunlight
as we tried to locate sense in the rhetoric, when we were halted
by the voice on the small radio as it spat out the first news bulletin.

There was a riot in progress at San Quentin, it said. It was
centered in the Adjustment Center wing of the prison.

George was surely in the heart of it. He was the center of
everything they did. I was imagining George knocking down the
enforcers of the petty bureaucrats with his self-trained hands and
feet, as he had in a courtroom in San Francisco, and at Soledad,
and before. They always came for him, to control him, eight and
ten at a time, routing him out of his cell under some pretext. It
happened all the time. It was simply another attack on George,
who would demonstrate that the spirit of a man is greater than
the suppression of his body, even by ten men.

The radio did not report how a marksman's bullets pierced
the brain of George Jackson. It reported that shots had been fired.
Shots had been fired at Soledad, and had killed three black inmates; but not George. He had survived that. The first shot from
San Quentin's rifles hit George in his foot, causing him to stumble
and fall. The second bullet, the deadly one, came minutes later,
after he was felled. It pierced the top of his head, ripping through
skull bone and brain tissue and brilliance.

Huey and I sat in his bed in the penthouse. We sat there for
nearly two days, teenagers at a pajama party talking about our
friend George. Huey had been at a bar with some of the men
when I reached him. He had dropped the telephone the minute

he heard the horrible words and immediately picked a fight with some fellow chosen randomly. He had broken his arm smashing the man's head into a table in the bar. His arm was in a cast now; the other lifted a glass of cognac.

We laughingly played the game for the final time, arguing over whether I would have given George "some." We tried to imagine why George thought ten thousand dollars would somehow free Angela of the CP, and why he wanted to do it. We tried to figure out what had really happened that afternoon. We planned the funeral for George. Mostly, however, we cried.

It was painful to select a black leather jacket for his body; it had to be purchased from a store for large-sized men. George had never really known such a thing as buying clothes for himself. He had worn state-issued prison garb for the last eleven of his twenty-nine years. His pants had been secured by chains and held up by string. Now I was selecting expensive black slacks, a fine leather belt, a powder-blue silk shirt, and a black leather jacket to cover his body, which was filled out by formaldehyde.

Nothing was more painful than accompanying Mrs. Jackson to the mortuary to see the body of her first son, the second to die in one year. Where had the bullets entered his body, she wanted to know, and wanted to see, her hands wringing, her sleepless eyes wild. Were there more than two bullets? she asked over and over. She wanted to touch the body of her boy, which they had refused to release to her for two days, driving rage forever into her blood. She wanted to take pictures of her child's body, to prove something, to right something. I had asked Steve Shames, a photographer who did a great deal of work for the party, to meet us at the mortuary, had taken two Librium, and driven her there. Fortunately, even the mortician was against her seeing the body of her only remaining son. He told her the scalp had been pulled back already. The body was in no state to view. She finally agreed to let Steve work alone, demanding he take pictures of "everything." I let the Librium take charge of me.

Father Neil allowed us to bring shotguns into his West Oakland church. They were for the honor guard. All the hundreds and hundreds of Panthers, including Huey, for the first time since I had known him, wore the full Panther uniform. Ten thousand came to the funeral of George Jackson.

I sang for George as I had for all the others, and Huey delivered the strongest speech I had ever heard him make. His lips were tight as he stood like a stone statue and eulogized George.

He pledged his life to George's memory and swore that the pigs would never defeat us: ". . . the oppressor is very strong and . . . he might beat us to our very knees, he might crush us to the ground, but it will be physically impossible for the oppressor to go on. At some point his legs will get tired, and when his legs get tired, then George Jackson and the people will tear his kneecaps off . . ."

One month later, several hundred Brothers at Attica state prison in New York tried to resurrect George—as I considered it, as I wrote about it in numerous articles for our newspaper. Like thousands of others, the prisoners at Attica had read George's book, or read about his book, or been touched by his words of fire. Black prisoners throughout California and the country had made protests of varying kinds over George's assassination. The prisoners at Attica, blacks and Puerto Ricans and a few whites, did that, and then took over Attica. They seized control of the prison to extract a variety of demands, the kinds of demands for better prison conditions around which George had organized California prisoners.

Huey sent Bobby to Attica on the first available flight, to be part of the prisoners' negotiating team, as their leadership had requested. The prisoners had organized themselves into a ragtag army and demanded that the state deal with them as men. We held our breath.

Nelson Rockefeller, governor of New York, ended the four-day protest by ordering death and destruction. Nearly forty men, including ten guards held as hostages, all unarmed, were murdered by the army of New York State Police under Rockefeller's command. Nearly ninety others were wounded by the hundreds of bullets Rockefeller had rained on unarmed men. Not much later, George's second and last book was published: *Blood in My Eye*.

CHAPTER 14

SANCTUARY

THERE WAS something pleasantly civil in the conservative order of Ottawa. Had the Chinese government not recently opened its first embassy in the Western world there, I would not have been in Ottawa. Huey had suddenly ordered me to arrange a trip to China for him and me. At the last minute he told me that his bodyguard, Robert Bay, would be accompanying us, which I considered an intrusion.

For Huey, the trip to China was a road out of the penthouse. It was an attempt to grasp life, a last chance for fulfillment, for heroes, it seemed, were headed too quickly toward death. There had been death at San Quentin less than two months before; death at Attica weeks before. It was autumn. Winter would come soon enough.

The Chinese ambassador offered me a cigarette, as we sat down after exchanging formal greetings. He had been in China's diplomatic corps for some time; and had been the chief negotiator on behalf of the Koreans at Panmunjom. He poured two large cups of black tea for us.

"You have been to China before," he affirmed, rather than asked, through his interpreter. A secretary was poised to take notes.

"Yes, Comrade Ambassador. It was little more than a year ago."

He poured more tea as the secretary wrote me a small note, which said that their embassy was under U.S. electronic surveillance. Therefore, we would not specify dates or routes regarding Huey's trip to China.

We would like Comrade Newton to be our guest, said the next note. We were verbally discussing the ballet.

Did you bring your passports? said the following note. I presented the *three* passports as I praised China's leadership in elevating the role of women in political and military affairs.

They could not hide their confusion. Our communication with them had indicated we were seeking permission for only Huey, leader of the Black Panther Party—the title given to them was minister of defense—and me, editor of the party's news organ, to visit China. Now that they were offering to make us their guests, we were adding a third person. I wondered if my face indicated my halfhearted attitude about that addition.

When the ambassador rose from his chair in the richly decorated sitting room to indicate our discussion had ended, he advised me I would be contacted very soon. That was all. I indicated, gently, that I was hoping to spend only two or three more days in Ottawa, as we were planning to leave immediately.

"Nixon has announced he's going to China! He's issued some kind of fucked-up statement about opening up avenues of diplomacy —meaning trade, of course. I have to get there before Nixon!" Huey was excitedly exclaiming into the telephone. "When're we leaving?!" He was a child.

"We have to wait a few more days," I said, with the hope that it was true.

Huey called me three or four times a day over the next several days.

When the call finally came, I went to the embassy again. An envelope was handed to me. Inside were our passports and visa papers along with three tickets to Hong Kong. There were also instructions on where in Hong Kong we were to obtain the tickets for Beijing. We were to leave in the next forty-eight hours. I scrambled to call Huey. Gwen informed me that he and Robert were already on their way to Ottawa.

The airline reservations clerk was swearing she could not find a third first-class seat for our flight to Hong Kong. Huey had decided to upgrade the tickets the Chinese had given us. I felt Robert should sit in the coach section anyway, but I said nothing. The rage was building up in Huey. I knew that rage well, as well as I knew the love and the brilliance.

Huey was now pacing the area in front of the counter. I implored the clerk to review her records one more time. Perhaps she understood my eyes or his. She finally found another cancellation for first class. She obligingly moved three single seats around so that we could sit together.

Huey's satisfaction lasted seconds. A well-dressed white man anxiously rushed to the check-in counter right after we received our upgraded boarding passes. The same clerk sold the man a first-class seat on the same flight. He did not seem to have a reservation.

"You know why he's getting a seat in first class with no problem?" Huey virtually shouted. "They had to change plans when we did. He's a pig! He's the FBI!"

"Yeah, Servant, he looks like FBI," Robert uttered, in what I felt was his simpleton voice.

"He better not get on this flight," Huey shouted at the desk, turning to walk very fast toward the first-class boarding lounge. Robert and I hurried after him.

"Even if he is the FBI, Huey," I whispered to him as we were escorted on board, "what can he do?"

"You do not understand anything," he chided, dismissing me.

The clerk and Fate were unkind. Huey sat down in his window seat. My oversized first-class seat was next to his, on the aisle. Across the aisle from me was Robert Bay. Seated next to Robert, at the window, was the "FBI agent."

"Now, perhaps, you understand," Huey said to me, looking out the window as we took off. "They follow me everywhere. Not you. Me."

He was, of course, right about his being followed, about the FBI surveillance to which he, more than any of us, was always subjected. It even occurred to me for a fleeting second that he was probably right about the passenger in question. But the man in the window seat was rendered harmless by the situation. The only harm that we could experience in the next eighteen hours would come if Huey acted on his rage. I was really becoming annoyed with him, for perhaps the first time.

"I know they follow you, Huey," I said softly, "but there's nothing we can do now but try to relax on this trip."

"Relax?! With a pig in my face?! Go to the pilot and tell him to have that pig seated somewhere else! Out of my sight!"

He was actually waiting for me to move.

"Huey, please. Let's just have a drink and try to ignore him. He can't hurt you here."

I was thinking I could work verbal magic, thinking I could strike a bargain with Fate.

"You don't think he's a pig, that's the problem. You're not with me."

"You know, of course, that that's not true, Huey. Please."

The conversation continued for a while, as the airplane reached cruising altitude and bottles of fine wine were opened.

"You know, if you think he's so harmless, why don't you sit with him" Huey finally said to me. "That's probably what you want anyway . . . In fact, I want you to sit with him. I don't want you near me."

He leaned over me to look at Robert. "Bay! Get up! Sit here! Let her sit with her pig friend!"

"Get up!" he ordered me.

I could not distinguish between fear and sorrow. Huey had never been angry with me before. We had all those hours ahead and two weeks in China.

I was not afraid of Huey in the conventional sense, not like the others in the real sense. Secure in my other world, where Huey's fists were arms and his rage was love, I had looked away from the others. *I was* afraid of Huey. I was afraid of falling from grace. I was afraid of being dismissed by him into a void. Life beyond Huey and his party would not be life. Life beyond Huey *was* a nothing little nigger girl. I would have ridden into hell with him to avoid the abyss.

His misplaced hostility would subside, I told myself, and I would be welcomed home. I had become, after all, the most important woman in the party. I was indeed the second most important person in the party, given David's imprisonment. Eldridge was a bad memory; Bobby was irrelevant. There was no one else.

That alone had allowed me to accept Gwen and Bobby Seale and cocaine. That alone had closed my eyes to the rod Huey had brought down on the others since his emergence from prison. I saw only the man who had greeted me at the airport, the man who created Survival Programs and intercommunalism. I refused to see the man who extracted heavy prices for minor frailties and infractions. I did not acknowledge his more and more frequent orders to violently discipline comrades and others, or the discipline he personally inflicted. I had not even looked at the way he had brutally put down the Eldridge faction. I was happy that he had driven the hard men to their knees, for his intuitive ability to develop ideas for change, change for the better, would have been otherwise crushed for all time.

It was by its own desire that the Central Committee had become a euphemism, a body of men with titles but no power. If there were no more Central Committee decisions, it was because they had begged Huey to lead them, guide them, take charge of their party and their lives, the way men always do with their gods. Their surrender of will had, paradoxically, generated his own surrender to the isolation of absolute leader.

It was in the absoluteness of that isolation that he always came to me. I supposed it was because I loved him while everyone else venerated him. With me he could be lover and friend, and abandon the roles of street hustler and brute, revolutionary and god.

The fact was that as much as I needed Huey, he needed me. I was his confessor as much as he was mine. I was the woman in him as much as he was the man in me. I carried his banner and kept his secrets, and did not judge him.

I had come to appreciate that Huey had always been seeking an end to the torture of his obsession with death. *To Die for the People* was the title of his first book. The one he was writing now was called *Revolutionary Suicide*. It was not dying that tormented him. It was living with the lingering knowledge of death's finality. That reduced the business of life to mere folly.

Thus, he agonized over and sought ultimate answers to ultimate questions. Before the Soul Breaker and after, before the party and now, he pushed life to see if it would reveal a hope of eternity. He tested life's edge every day, daring, challenging, hiding, and seeking at once. It was his best and worst attribute. It was what elevated him and diminished him. If there was no party, he would probably have lived and died not so much ingloriously as hopelessly. With the party, he could test his theories with action. He could turn his fantasies into realities. He could write and rewrite the rules, re-create the present, and shape the future.

His dabbling with cocaine was an aspect of the testing, a ritualistic requirement in a brutal man-game through which he could hold on to the power that allowed him to hold on to his life. And beneath that, it was another private test of his will. Would death devour him through cocaine, he seemed to ask, or could he defeat death once more, as he had on Seventh Street, as he had in the Soul Breaker, as he had in West Oakland?

Death, he had said, whispering, as I shivered in the cold of the twenty-fifth floor one night, is X, the unknown factor, like God. As we gain knowledge, X is diminished. There would surely come a time, he insisted, when man's knowledge would deliver up the ultimate answers, expose the face of God, and destroy the power of death. Until then, Huey believed, man could not truly be happy. Huey, I knew, could certainly not be happy.

Huey wanted to correct the losses of history, to resurrect the nobility of the African. He wanted to be involved in eliminating the alienation between human life on the planet and the rest of nature. He wanted to join the searches for life beyond this planet. He was consumed with frustration over being locked in a time in which it was impossible for him, or any other black in America, to reach for his best. He longed for freedom, the freedom to choose and to know all the choices.

The depth of his profound sorrow over life embraced my own, and I had been able to find a happiness with him in his party. I felt I was participating in a glorious experiment, the outcome of which might elevate the world. There was the headiness of defying the odds and seizing history by the throat, to throw off our accursed lot. There was expanding the vision of life with new designs for the way we might live. And there was, also, my place in the scheme of things. Huey offered me a life that was more than I had the potential to realize beyond his domain. So I ignored the day-to-day brutalities and relished my role as echo and scribe, who gave ordinary expression to the complexity of his extraordinary mind, and I accepted all of him, as he was, even now.

I waited for a signal from Huey that my banishment was over. It came when we landed in Tokyo for a one-hour layover. He simply asked if I wanted a drink. When I nodded, he went to the bar in the lounge where we were waiting for our next flight and brought one back to me. He said nothing more. It was enough. I knew he was laughing at himself as we boarded again for the four-hour flight to Hong Kong.

We landed in Kowloon, the peninsula that is the busy port of entry to the mainland of Hong Kong. The doorman at the Hong Kong Hilton was a big Chinese fellow. The hotel had attired him in a costume that approached some sort of Hollywood Ali Baba look, replete with gold brocade shoes that turned up at the toe. He bowed and opened the door.

As we walked through the corridors of the luxury hotel, I

tried not to glare at the fat, red-necked Australian and British men who were drunkenly sauntering to their rooms with twelve- and thirteen-year-old Chinese whores. I tried not to see that our bellman was dressed in a Hilton "coolie" outfit, including the obligatory white stockings and long black braid.

We entered an imposing living room filled with white rattan chairs and pastel-colored couches, complemented by a variety of tropical plants, all seeming to evoke a chorus of "Bali Ha'i." Huey told Robert to put his things in the smaller of the two bedrooms and to order food for us. He conducted me into our bedroom, his arm around my waist, his hand playfully patting my derriere.

He walked into the giant-sized bathroom and started a bath in the huge, sunken, guava-colored tub. He returned and began taking off my clothes, gently, as he had the first time.

"Come on," he said, grabbing my hand and leading me into the bathroom. "The food should be here by the time you take a bath. I know you can't hold out much longer. I saw you drooling over that prime rib on the plane." He laughed.

I pouted as he helped me into the deep tub. He washed me, splashing me, kissing me.

"You better get it now," he said, taking off his clothes to join me. "Remember you can't have it in China. No fucking in Peking," he said in the singsong style of a schoolyard rhyme.

"Yeah, each to his own room, so don't try to come into my room if you get desperate. And you better not try to touch those Chinese comrades. They're armed, you know." I laughed as he got into the tub with a big splash.

There was no sexual encounter, though. It would have diminished what we felt, what we had become. Somewhere in the transformation of our love, we had decided orgasm was only a biological response and that a sexual experience ought to be more. Love ought to be even more. We pretended we cared about the sex, though, to ourselves, to keep from being too lofty.

The sun was rising on the harbor. Nude under hotel terrycloth robes, Huey and I sat huddled together looking out our suite's living-room window at the new day. It was such a faraway sunrise, over a place that at once bound and divided East and West, Communists and capitalists. It was a never-never land that winked and winced at its preteen whores and hustling cabdrivers and coolie bellhops and signs in English first, with Chinese as a second language. But I saw that Hong Kong in that sunrise seemed to offer something more.

Huey had begun to weep in the first light. Hong Kong was a stepping-stone to a new world, he whispered, one created by men with vision and fortitude. China, Huey thought, was the triumph of the human spirit. He felt he could find peace in China—even if he never found happiness.

I had to step over the women and their children later that morning. They were squatting and cooking their breakfasts over flames from canned heat. Some were still huddled under the lean-tos in which they lived. It was more painful to see because of the incongruity. The women were languishing in tents staked out on the concrete that formed Queen's Road, Hong Kong's main financial thoroughfare, a hub of international finance. If there was something other than a lifetime of destitution for those women, I thought, it might lay in the hope of 1997. That was the year of transition, when the mainland of China would, by agreement with the British, completely subsume the business of Hong Kong, control, and, perhaps, correct the business of Queen's Road.

It occurred to me, as I wound my way on foot to the China Travel Agency, why there was a Hong Kong. It was a convenience for the People's Republic of China. Its significant port provided a road to the Western world, to necessary Western goods and services that were otherwise forbidden by governing mainland principle. It also furnished a corridor through which China could move its own trade, and could listen to the rest of the world and influence its machinations without apparent involvement. It was what Oakland could be to the Black Panther Party. I wondered, though, how meaningful that was to the lives of the women on Queen's Road. I thought about the many daily sacrifices my mother had made to put together a decent meal or pay our meager rent. The impact of social movements never seemed to reach down to Queen's Road or York Street, at least not in some lifetimes.

The freshness of autumn in Beijing the next day heightened Huey's sense of freedom. The tests and the sorrow were set aside. He was exuberant. He wanted to dress like the Chinese, eat Chinese food, be absorbed by Chinese life.

Every morning, Huey rose early, waiting for the old men and women, the children and the families, to appear on the streets, to begin the day with the national exercise, tai chi ch'uan. He wanted to understand everything. He read Mao's poems at night, recognizing the Buddhist philosophy interwoven in revolutionary verses. When we met Chou En-lai, he bowed.

The blacks we encountered in the hotel dining room one morning were from Mozambique. Huey sent me to their table to arrange a meeting. They told me they had such a busy schedule it was not clear when we could get together. When I relayed their response to Huey, he leaped up and went directly to their table, beckoning me to follow. He introduced himself and said that he would really appreciate it if they would accept copies of our newspapers and other materials we had brought. As they could not have tea with us, he was happy for the opportunity to just meet them, he told the apparent leader. They responded to his enthusiasm and offered to adjust their schedule to meet with us that afternoon.

They were surprised by what Huey told them when they came to his room. First, they had not realized he had officially expelled Eldridge Cleaver from the party. They were also not familiar with the party's Survival Programs and the political line that Huey espoused. They had thought we lived by the Cleaver rhetoric they had heard in Algiers.

After a while, their leader, Samora Machal, began to open up to Huey. He told us how he had been a military leader of their struggle and was now the head of FRELIMO, the revolutionary organization that was guiding the Mozambican struggle to throw off Portuguese colonialism. Before we parted, we agreed that when the inevitable day came for the Mozambicans, we wanted to be there to share the joy of victory.

Huey was more convinced than ever that the success of our struggle was tied to an internationalist philosophy. With the support of our comrades in China and Mozambique, and elsewhere, we might really be able to lay the groundwork for the overthrow of the U.S. government. We might really make way for the institution of a new order.

The party's character had to change, Huey concluded. We had to elevate our Survival Programs to models for alternative institutions, as the Mozambicans had. Machal had emphasized that the mass of their people had been inspired and educated and, ultimately, incorporated in their armed liberation struggle primarily because of FRELIMO's establishment of schools and hospitals. We had to develop mass organizing mechanisms, as the Chinese had. We had to do everything possible to embrace more and more of our people, if we were to become a serious revolutionary force in the world.

On the airplane that returned us to the United States, I wrote Huey's press statement. We had contacted June on our stopover in Hong Kong to organize a press conference for our arrival in San Francisco.

First, Huey wanted to denounce Nixon and his devious intentions with respect to his upcoming trip to China. He also wanted to promote the idea that Nixon had been allowed into China only *after* our visit. In addition, Huey wanted to praise the Chinese Revolution and its ongoing success. We would then reiterate our internationalist position. We would emphasize our bond with the struggles of all oppressed peoples throughout the world and the importance of unity in the worldwide struggle against U.S. imperialism.

A large body of press greeted us in San Francisco, along with hundreds of our comrades. At the last minute, Huey had decided that I should read his statement, in conformance with what he identified as a Maoist manner of making public statements. Before that, I was to make Huey's other announcement. Only June Hilliard would not be surprised.

"My name is Elaine Brown. I will read the statement of Huey P. Newton, minister of defense of the Black Panther Party, with respect to our visit to the People's Republic of China.

"First, however, I would like to make an announcement. The Black Panther Party acknowledges the progressive leadership of our Chinese comrades in all areas of revolution. Specifically, we embrace China's correct recognition of the proper status of women as equal to that of men.

"In that context, I hereby confirm, on behalf of the entire Black Panther Party, that I have been elected to the Central Committee of the party. As such, I am the first woman member of the Central Committee, filling the vacancy of the renegade Eldridge Cleaver as minister of information."

Steve's first blow struck all the glory out of that moment. It was only weeks after the press conference, and I was still basking in the comfort of Huey's validation.

Months before, I had begun some kind of relationship with Steve, albeit in the loosest definition of the word. He had come to Oakland from L.A. to discuss "security" matters. L.A. had become so dangerous for Panthers after the Cleaver rift erupted, Huey had finally reduced the entire Southern California chapter to an underground operation, which Steve headed. On Steve's last day in Oakland, a number of us from L.A. had gotten together. Though we were splintered, we L.A. Panthers still thought of ourselves as a rather select group; and the gathering that day was a kind of reunion. Steve and I had slept together that night. The next time was in L.A., where I had gone at Huey's demand.

Huey had commanded me to make another album of songs. Simply deciding that a black-owned company like Motown Records had a duty to record my songs, he had ordered me to make another album there. After a few telephone calls, and with the help of a white supporter of the party I had known in L.A., Ed Michel, I had, rather amazingly, been able to secure an appointment to meet with an executive at Motown at the company's new headquarters in Los Angeles.

Two members of Steve's underground had escorted me to the meeting. When the Motown executive saw my two "bodyguards," he became so terrified he told me right off that he realized Ed Michel had made a mistake. He was not the man I needed to see. I had to see the head of Motown's Creative Department, as all decisions to make an album at Motown, he stuttered, were made only by the head of that department.

"Where is he?" I had demanded, standing. Steve's underground escorts followed suit.

"It's *she*," he said quickly. "Her name's Suzanne de Passe, and her office is right down that hall."

I had had to stay two more days with Steve in Los Angeles bickering with the male secretary of the head of Motown's Creative Department to arrange to see her.

Suzanne de Passe had not been terrified of the bodyguards. Indeed, she had seemed quite oblivious to the reputation of the Black Panther Party. She sat down comfortably in a booth with me in the restaurant where we met for lunch; the men with me kept their distance, standard procedure, sitting a table or so away from us.

She was very "white" in a bourgeois way, I thought, seeing myself of not so long before. Her skin was that caramel color that seems to permeate the ranks of the black bourgeoisie. Her hair was soft, its last curls, vestiges of African ancestry, had been blow-dried away, as mine would have been but for the Black Panther Party. I knew the armed men with me detested women like her, like us, and I felt a sudden need to protect her.

We sat together in the restaurant for five hours. She started out by telling me she had heard my first album and liked what she heard. T-Boy Ross, Diana's brother, had loved it and had given it to her.

The conversation soon drifted away from the business at hand, and moved to the conversation of girl friends, a "yeah-girl" kind of conversation. It was funny, we thought, that we were both only children, the only daughters of our mothers, who had both tried to make princesses of us in the middle of black America—in Harlem and North Philly—and despite the absence of our fathers. She had missed my ballet lessons, and I her equestrian lessons, we laughed. There were Jewish schoolmates and friends in both our lives; and we had to laugh about how much we really, secretly loved Jewish things, from bagels and lox to canopied weddings.

We eventually laughed at each other, at our defensiveness over the absurd rumors, about Panthers being no more than a new kind of Mafia and Motown being a front for the real Mafia. Those rumors were signs of the changing times of power to the people, black people. The changes reflected a reality that other people, white people, had to redefine to find comfort in the times.

After we parted, I began to think of Suzanne as a little secret, a soft, womanly secret self, who was untainted by the hardness of the world in which I lived. She was the girl on the other side of the mirror with whom one plays, outside the very uninteresting world.

I met with her once again in L.A. after that. Now I had returned to see her a final time regarding the proposed album. As I had no lead sheets or demonstration tapes to give her, I had to present the songs to her in person, which now included a song for George.

Seeing Suzanne again, I was thinking when I arrived in L.A., was exciting; more like having a rendezvous with a new lover than a discussion with an executive about a business transaction.

The movie of my first meeting with Suzanne replayed in the single instant Steve struck me. Just after meticulously draping his expensive clothes over the bedroom chair, he had suddenly hollered at me, "Did you fuck him, bitch?!"

I was sitting up in his bed, looking at television, something innocuously distracting like Johnny Carson.

Steve had just returned to the apartment, having left me alone there for hours since my arrival earlier that evening. He and his fellows had been out somewhere. Only one of them had returned with him. I could hear him in the other bedroom. Perhaps they had just been drinking at a bar. Perhaps not.

Steve's underground, which included a very small number of women, had come to function at a rather sophisticated level. They wore the fashionable clothes of middle-class blacks to avoid any appearance of affiliation with the party. They lived in suburban, racially mixed neighborhoods. They held ordinary jobs to support themselves, or obtained money any way they could, for they received no real financial support from the party. Like the others elsewhere, if they were arrested, they accepted it in silence, keeping the party's name out of it. If they carried off a dramatic operation, they took no credit, making no connection with the party.

Perhaps it was the spirit of such commitment that had attracted me to Steve. He was certainly not a man to be loved. One could be titillated by the toughness, the strength of a commander, the fortitude of a man who took on the hard and dirty tasks. There was also the animalness of him, the danger in a man who terrified even the vicious men under him. But Steve and I were not matched for anything beyond fleeting fascination. Fear usually kept me from getting too close to this kind of man.

I would simply leave him in the morning, I thought after the first blow. I would pick up Horace Tapscott and we would meet with Suzanne. I would play her my new songs, discuss the arrangement for Horace to orchestrate the prospective album, leave L.A., and never see Steve again. He would not be hard to avoid. Or he would be replaced for violating the newest member of the Central Committee. Huey would decide.

"I said, did you fuck him, bitch!" he shouted again, smacking me again, hard. He grinned, and suddenly thrust himself on top of me, his knees across my breasts, pinning down my arms.

"I don't know what you mean," I said, trembling, too terrified to cry.

Johnny Carson's image had been erased from the television he had flipped off. He reached over and clicked off the bedside lamp. His muscular black body, the size of a solid middleweight, disappeared. There was only the outline of his white undershirt and undershorts, and the pressure of his weight.

A fist was struck to my temple. "Naw, bitch, I *know* you fucked him."

"He" was a Brother who had recently gotten out of prison. To celebrate his release we had held a small party in Oakland, and I had danced with him a few times. Some former L.A. girl friend of Steve's, now relocated in Oakland, had built up Steve's macho ego and jealousy with a lie meant to return herself to his favor. I learned all that in between the next blows.

"Who the fuck do you think you are, bitch! Answer me!" he bellowed, striking my head so hard my skull seemed to crash against my brain. "Did you come good, 'ho'?! Tell me 'bout it!"

Each ugly inquiry he shouted was punctuated with another hard blow.

"Don't no bitch disrespect me! Naw, motherfucker!"

Now came streams of blows, along with constant vituperation, his sweat dripping onto my face. His large fists alternately pummeled my temples and ears and the back of my head, and then my kidneys, as he turned my listless body to accommodate him. It was a serious, careful beating, the kind in which he was obviously expert, the kind designed to do serious damage without leaving a visible mark.

The pain left me. The restrained tears dried up into a glaucomatous haze. I lay there realizing I was being beaten senseless, grateful to be still conscious. As my body rocked under the force of each blow, my brain tried to find a way to survive, to summon the memory of survival.

He got up to go to the toilet, fooling me into thinking it was over. My body could not move as I listened to his urine splatter into the toilet water. I was stricken anew with terror when he returned, reinvigorated. He turned on a small radio on his way back to his business. It had been over an hour since the beating began, the radio time announcement confirmed between the next blows.

I suddenly became desperate not to urinate, or even defecate, on myself. I tried to faint, thinking that might end it. No, my brain commanded. I had to be conscious to survive. I had to hold on.

I separated myself from my face and ears and temples and kidneys and pain. Some part of my consciousness became curious about the amount of violence a body could sustain without expiring. It was fascinated by the image of what my beaten face might now look like, remembering the faces of boxers on television, seeing my own face at sixteen, when feet had trampled it. I began to focus on distinguishing between and among the different sounds of the blows, especially the ones to my ears, which rang like the pounding of tons of rushing water. In the corner of my mind that was holding on, I began to wonder exactly how many blows I would have to suffer before he stopped. I began to count them.

He would continue to fool me, though, pausing only to rest, and then resuming the beating with increased rage. There were no more insane inquiries or invective. Now he was just beating me, with so much force and vigor he was actually tiring, requiring rest more and more. I noted that, holding on.

Suddenly, I stopped calculating. I had to pull all my energy together to resist him. I stiffened my back and pressed my head against the pillow. He was trying to reach under the pillow. His .44 magnum pistol was there.

"Why do you want to kill me?" cried the voice that came from the body that was no longer mine. The image of a round hole being drilled into the center of my forehead flashed before me. I saw myself being swept back and out—something akin to the feeling I had had under a dentist's sodium pentothal.

"Why do you want to kill me?!" the scream came again, my head pressing firmly, urgently against the pillow under which his hand was reaching.

I could see his eyes in the October moonlight that was seeping through the opaque curtains of his bedroom. My cry seemed to startle him from his stupor.

"Shut the fuck up, bitch!" he shouted, and unexpectedly unstraddled me, rolling over to lie down next to me.

As he rolled over onto his stomach, one of his arms fell across my body, his strong biceps heavy on my breast and heart.

In a few minutes, he seemed to have fallen asleep. I lay still, though, waiting for the resumption of terror. It was almost three in the morning, the voice on the radio announced. He had been meting out his punishment to me for nearly three hours.

The soft baritone of an all-night disc jockey announced that the radio broadcast's jazz hours were ending. Now there would be early-morning gospel programming. I lay there for the next hours motionless, listening to the choirs and hearty voices singing about "Glory," listening for any twitch or new sound to emanate from the monster beside me, listening for the birds to announce the break of dawn.

Dawn comes late in October. My entire body became numb as I waited. I devised and dismissed numerous plans of escape during those hours. If I jumped up and leaped from the window of his second-story apartment, I might break a leg or an ankle. I would not be able to run, and he could shoot me from the balcony. If I tried to crawl away quietly, I would wake him as I stumbled through the apartment's unknown terrain, and he would shoot me. I finally found the courage to ease his arm off me, and did not move again. My hope was in the dawn, when I might be able to walk out of the apartment on my own two feet.

I was left to concentrate on the meeting I would have with Suzanne de Passe, and on the songs I would present to her. As I thought about those songs, all my songs, it occurred to me that most of them had been written to men and for men. That realization made me wonder what exactly there was in my life that had made me come to rely so on the power of men. I began to wonder if that was why I was really in the Black Panther Party, with its men and its guns.

People were oppressed, and I was one of them. The party held some solution to that, and I was part of it. Huey was the best of men, and I was part of him. It was a perfect formulation for my life—except that in those three hours of pain I had endured, I had felt more than physical pain. I had felt the weight of my aloneness. And I had seen the core of my fear, which was loneliness. This was the deepest truth of why I was in the Black Panther Party, of why I smothered my life with Huey Newton.

Life was as lonely as death. Huey and his party had built a bridge over that chasm. Huey offered God-deliverance, omnipotence that could allay loneliness like unconditional father-love, like unbroken wedding vows, like Jesus in the shadow of death. I had been in the shadow of death for three hours. But I had always been there. Life was the shadow of death. And I was still alone in that. There was no father, no God, no man to stand between me and death, or me and life, not if I wrote psalms to them forever. I held on to that until dawn, and thought about the girl on the other side of the mirror.

A NEW WAVE
TO RIDE

I ROSE from Steve's bed just after dawn broke. His regular snoring was my signal of safety. I made a quick assessment about clothing—what I would wear and what I would forfeit. I made sure all my songs were enclosed in my small valise. When I was ready, I gently woke him. One of his cars had to take me to the meeting. The other Brother in the apartment, who was to be my driver, was still asleep. I would have to get rid of him later.

I was casual with Steve. I was a demure, "good" woman, one willing to forget the ringing in my ears, the mandibular pain. I smiled inside at my performance, the image of the woman in an old Billie Holiday tune: "If I get beat by my poppa, I sure won't call no coppa . . ." I was thinking of vindication.

After Steve woke the other Brother, he began chatting. Waiting for the driver to dress, he offered his opinion about the possibility of my making an album with Motown. He asked if I liked his new .44 magnum pistol, grabbing it from under his pillow to show me. I smiled all the while, even at the door when he asked me where I would like to have dinner that night. He wondered if I liked frogs' legs. I kissed his cheek and told him that would be fine.

I convinced the driver that it was unnecessary to pick up the other bodyguard. The two of us arrived at Horace Tapscott's house at nine in the morning, though the appointment Horace and I had with Suzanne was not until one o'clock. I responded to the anxious grimace on Horace's face with an eye signal. The moment we arrived at his door, he saw, though there were no visible signs, no black-and-blue marks on my face. He recognized the danger

—that there had been danger, might be danger. He never hinted that I was several hours early. He dressed himself quickly and took up the hours before our meeting with Suzanne by having me go over the songs with him. He discussed every detail of his ideas for each arrangement. Steve's bodyguard seemed unsuspecting of my intention to escape him and his boss before the day was over, unsuspecting of my wrathful thoughts.

Suzanne was so easy, so open. Tears of gratitude stung the lids of my eyes. I had to hold them back throughout my presentation. I had offhandedly commanded the bodyguard to wait in an outer office. There were just Horace, Suzanne, and I in the room. I sang for Suzanne for all I was worth, for the renewal of life feelings.

Ignoring the pain at the back of my eyes, I sang the song for Jonathan and the new one for George. Despite the reverberations in my head, I sang the one nobody would know had been written for Jay Kennedy. Disregarding the swollen tissue in my ears, which seemed to be closing off sound, I sang the song written for my friends on the streets of North Philadelphia. It was the one that would become the title song of the new album: *Until We're Free.*

Though I could barely move my jaws without pain, I thanked Suzanne profusely for affirming then and there that Motown would produce an album of my songs—and for more. I would be recorded on Motown's "Black Forum" label, she said, proudly telling me that the only other product on that new label was the recorded speeches of Martin Luther King, Jr. Horace would be paid to arrange all the material, and the party would be advanced $10,000 against royalties on my signing a formal contract.

As she hugged me goodbye, Suzanne told me in her touch that she knew. In her touch, she offered me comfort, the comfort of her friendship. With her touch, I was shocked into the recognition that mine was a life without a real friend. There were comrades. There was Huey. There was no one like her, no girl-friend person with whom to share sins and other secrets, sort out the laughter and the tears that accompanied the men who came and mostly went, argue the point with an amen or a hug, right or wrong. I hugged her back hard. In my embrace, I asked her to be my friend, my first woman friend since I had become a woman, since youth and North Philly carried Nita and Barbara away. Girl friends were better than mothers or lovers, we agreed, without saying anything at all.

After escaping L.A., I ran to Huey's arms. He already knew.

I had told June by telephone after I left Suzanne. June had ordered Steve's man to leave me alone.

Huey's arms were strong. But he lowered them, surrendering to the men, most of whom thought "it was about time." I was an arrogant "bitch." I had been the backbone of that L.A. clique, had defied the chairman, hid behind Huey, been forced into their leadership, among other violations. Getting my ass kicked was just what I needed, the men had responded. What did I expect him to do in the face of such a tide of opinion? Huey shrugged. It was, arguably, a violation of party rules, but categorically not really party business, he finished. Anyway, I should never have been in the bed of such an "ugly black motherfucker," he concluded. He went on to say how proud he was of the album business.

That was all right. Not forgivable, but all right. Wobbling, I was still standing. I saw that. And Huey saw that. I was finding my sight. Months before, I would have considered that what Huey now proposed for the party contained an atonement for what had happened to me. I would have sparkled like a little girl. I was not a little girl. Huey was not a god.

We had to acknowledge, Huey was now telling me, that the blood we had shed was more than our party could continue to endure. The loss of George had brought the lessons home. China had been instructive.

China's recent entrance into the U.N. was neither contradictory to China's goal of toppling U.S. imperialism nor an abnegation of revolutionary principles. It was a tactic of socialist revolution. It was a tactic, Huey concluded, that offered us a great example. Those were the roots of Huey's new idea: to have Panthers run for political office.

The subtle criticisms made by the ultraleftists in the post-Eldridge period would pale in comparison with their response to this new item on Huey's agenda. But the doctrinal differences that had long beleaguered the so-called political left in the United States could not be indulged by the party. We would act, whether or not what we did conformed to the notions of the various leftist groups. If the left denounced our involvement in the system and the party members questioned the wisdom of the leadership, the benefits that could result from a Panther electoral campaign outweighed all of that.

The Survival Programs had accomplished a great deal by involving masses of black people in revolution at the primary level of raising consciousness. Casting a vote for a Black Panther candidate would be the first concrete expression of that consciousness.

Years before, Eldridge Cleaver had nominally placed his and Kathleen's names on an election ballot, under the Peace and Freedom Party banner. To imagine the effectiveness of that effort would be to consider the percentage of people in the United States registered as members of the Peace and Freedom Party—less than zero. The new effort, Huey said, would be a serious assault, not an elite educational game.

Bobby Seale's name was highly recognizable in and beyond Oakland. That was a prerequisite for an electoral campaign in the United States. We would, Huey declared, run Bobby for mayor of Oakland.

I waited, without comment, for my instruction, the one I knew would be forthcoming.

"And just to make the thing sweeter, if you don't mind my saying so," he added, as though on cue, "I want you to run with Bobby, for a City Council seat. You'll not only soften the blow, you can keep Bobby in check."

"No, Huey. No! I'll orchestrate the thing if you want. I'll manage the campaign, even. But don't put me face-to-face with Bobby every day."

"If you believe in me, you'll do it." He laughed. "And if you think about it, you'll see the wisdom in it. I can't let Bobby go out there alone. And can you see me running for office?"

Huey had a point. Besides his distaste for public speaking, he inevitably made statements that were either too academic or too antagonistic. Nevertheless, to forestall the inevitability of days and nights with Bobby Seale, I reminded Huey of how he had shone on a television broadcast not that long ago.

It was on a program hosted by rightist William F. Buckley. Buckley's first question to Huey was whether he intended to overthrow the United States government. It was a question to which either answer would have been damning. He told Buckley he would answer his question honestly if Buckley would first answer a question of his with honesty. Buckley agreed. Huey asked, if Buckley had been alive at the time of the American Revolution, circa 1776, on which side would he have fought? Buckley stuttered, then laughed, then called it a draw. Only Huey could have made such a clever response, extemporaneously.

"I *was* good, wasn't I?" Huey responded. "But you know I'm not running for office with Bobby. You are."

I said not another word.

"So I see you agree," he filled in with a laugh.

A few days later, the rest of the members of the Central Committee, including Bobby, were informed of Huey's new plan.

The end of the past was not so easily marked. There were those who were still committed to the Eldridge Cleaver view of what the Black Panther Party should be: a terrorist organization. While the most outspoken and dangerous of them were trapped behind the bars of California's prisons, trapped with them was Johnny Spain.

Johnny had been an unknown lieutenant in George Jackson's army. He had become known to me through a letter I received just after we buried George. I had ripped into his introductory letter because his handwriting so resembled George's, I imagined for a moment that it was a letter from the grave. In this letter, Johnny told me he had been at George's side at the end.

Now Johnny was facing trial on charges of conspiring with George to murder two San Quentin guards on the day of George's assassination. Six had died that day: George, three guards, and two white trusties. Other guards had survived the slitting of their throats with crudely fashioned implements. Afterward, Johnny and five other inmates, now collectively known as the "San Quentin Six," were charged with an assortment of crimes relating to the bloody events of that day. No one was charged with the crime of murdering George.

Johnny had rushed into the yard outside San Quentin's Adjustment Center with George, dodging the same bullets. When everything was over, he had been beaten and dragged nude across the prison yard, the skin ripped from his face and chest. He had healed in isolation. He was now allowed to exit his cell only in relation to the trial, and only while supporting twenty-five pounds of chains, from his neck to his wrists, waist, ankles. He was holding up to these ordeals bravely, and he was proudly wearing the badge of the Panther passed to him by George.

The party had put forth the most radical and forceful demands on behalf of all black prisoners in America. We had given body to our rhetoric with "free busing to prisons" and free legal-aid programs. We published articles about prisoner injustices, set up a correspondence network between inside and outside, sent reading materials, money, and other things necessary to at least survive years of life in prison. The Black Panther Party provided a voice and hope for thousands of black inmates.

Many of them, however, had used our political line to justify their personal crimes on the street—rape and mindless killings— and to excuse the capriciousness of their prison violence. When Huey denounced Eldridge's long-distance proposals for terrorism and expelled him from the party, a vociferous number of black prisoners were shocked. The party's political clarification of revolutionary violence had, at best, confused men who basically lived by the sword. That suited the government's aims.

With George's murder, the government did more than eliminate the one man who could have molded the prison contingent of black liberation forces. Through its COINTELPRO operation, using prison snitches and other propagandists, the government parlayed its very assassination of George into the breakdown of those forces. Government-promoted rumors and Cleaverism struck a chord, particularly in the California prisons, an atmosphere rife with gang mentalities on both sides of the bars. They converged on the same point: that George Jackson had rejected the party and the party had rejected him.

In death, of course, a man can become what his friends and enemies make of him. In life, George had foreseen this, having written to Huey only months before his death: "Be very careful of messages or any word that was supposed to have come from me . . . People lie for many reasons." In life, George had summarily denounced Eldridge Cleaver and his rhetoric. He had pledged his life to Huey and the party, of which George was field marshal until the day he died. Nevertheless, after his death, a crop of self-professed black "guerrilla" gangs erupted in the California prison system, denounced the party as reformist, and "claimed" George.

Although these guerrilla gangs acted in much the same way as the white, Mexican, and other black prison gangs, they asserted that they were "political," nay, "revolutionary" organizations, purportedly functioning under the revolutionary principles by which George Jackson had lived and died. They now deemed the multiple stabbings and beatings of white, Mexican, and other black inmates, suspected of "opposition," as revolutionary acts, just as they clothed themselves with the term "political prisoner." *They* were the revolutionaries, vanguards of revolution, as the party no longer was.

Huey had become frustrated by their posture, annoyed by

their counterproductive revisionism, furious over their misuse of George's name. This situation, I was convinced, would only become more volatile. Huey had come out of prison calling for the release of all of them. Now he was ready to quit them all, making no allowances for Johnny Spain, the only prisoner who had been with George Jackson at the end, and who still adhered to the party line of his chief. Johnny was isolated in a dangerous cross fire at San Quentin's Adjustment Center. Although I did what I could for Johnny during those months of preparing for the campaign, headlining his case in our newspaper and convincing Huey to employ Charles Garry as Johnny's attorney, it was not enough. He needed more.

This was why I felt justified in trying to slap the life out of her. Elaine Wender was a newly licensed white lawyer who had latched on to the case of Johnny Spain, as an assistant to Charles Garry. Like many young white women of that era, she seemed to be devoting her youth to "revolutionary" black men. When she had confronted me in front of a number of Marin County marshals and guards at a hearing on one of Johnny's pretrial motions, I had tried to ignore her. She had called after me, though, her nasty comments echoing in the hallway. She had shouted that she hoped the party was not going to exploit Johnny as it had George. I had walked over to her and advised her that I would gladly accept whatever charge all those pigs might impose on me for assaulting her on the spot if she uttered another word to me about George or anything else. Now she had opened her mouth again.

I was sure Huey would tell me it was the exact kind of petty dispute we could no longer indulge in. I decided not to speak with him about it. The problem had to do with publication of Johnny's poems.

I was preparing for the great electoral leap forward. I was overseeing the newspaper with Ericka Huggins, who was slated to replace me as editor during the campaign. I was trying to fill the motherhood gaps I was leaving in my own Ericka's young life. I was finishing an album of songs in between. I was exhausted. And the fact was, I really detested the Elaine Wenders of the world. I viewed them as comfortable white women who infringed on our struggle and our men. I resented what I felt were their fantasy interests in black people, particularly in black men. Moreover, I detested black men's often unabashed responses to them, to the lifeline they seemed to toss from more comfortable shores.

Substantively, Johnny's poems were significant in their purity, in their sad beauty. More significantly, their publication might help save Johnny's life through the awakening of public interest in his plight. The poems had been smuggled out of the prison and were in Elaine's possession for safekeeping, since the San Quentin guards habitually destroyed even the smallest possession of one of their most hated prisoners. Despite Johnny's request, Elaine was refusing to release the poems to me to have them typed for a prospective publisher. This, I believed, was enough.

I enlisted Joan Kelley and a Sister named Ukali to accompany me. We arrived at Elaine's law office without warning. It was the kind of office I had expected, consciously "political" in its decor. There were books of leftist writings filling the shelves of the converted old house near Berkeley. There was an abundance of house plants, to promote ecological balance in the interiors, I supposed, and a collective kitchen. The walls were covered with framed photographs and lithographs, capturing revolutionary faces and ideals.

We found Elaine upstairs, in her private office. She was with Ann Scheer, Bob Scheer's former wife, and a woman of the same cloth, I felt. When we burst in, they were drinking herbal tea.

Elaine glared at me as though I were a child interrupting adult affairs. Earlier, she had dismissed my final demand for the poems by hanging up the telephone on me. She was committed to holding on to the poems. Whatever her motivation, I wasted little time with her once we entered her office. Ann Scheer was terrified, imploring me to allow Elaine time to "find" the poems, suggesting it was possible they had been mislaid. Then Elaine was insisting, with a sigh, that she really had looked for them. That was when I slapped her face. She began crying. I felt inspired.

I ordered Joan and Ukali to begin searching for the poems with me. We cleared her desk and tabletops with sweeps of our hands. We tore open her oak file cabinets and strewed their contents onto her handmade rugs. Intermittently over that next half hour, I slapped Elaine several times more, to no avail. Finally, I gave her twenty-four hours to deliver the poems to me, lest her office be blown off the map, as I put it.

I was unequivocally denounced. A deluge of calls from protesting white leftists reached Huey over the next week. He rejected them, told them I had been mild in my punishment. He assured them my promise would have been kept had Elaine not personally delivered Johnny's poems to national headquarters the day after my visit.

It might have been a shameful admission to acknowledge that my behavior toward Elaine Wender had been unreasonable. I never made such an acknowledgment. I felt no regret and was even able to enjoy verbally sparring with Huey over his laughing depiction of me as a terrorist.

What I acknowledged about the Elaine Wender affair was that she was incidental to it, as were, even, Johnny's poems. That piece of the present was a very old business. It was not simply that the hatred in my genes for the "Miss Anne" syndrome had not been erased by the loveliness of Jean Seberg and Jean Kidwell. It was not so black and white. It is impossible to summarize the biological response to an act of will in a life of submission. It would be to capture the deliciousness of chocolate, the arousing aroma of a man or a perfume, the feel of water to the dry throat. What I had begun to experience was the sensation of personal freedom, like the tremor before orgasm. The Black Panther Party had awakened that thirst in me. And it had given me the power to satisfy it.

It is a sensuous thing to know that at one's will an enemy can be struck down, a friend saved. The corruption in that affirmation coexists comfortably with the senuousness and the seriousness in it. For a black woman in America to know that power is to experience being raised from the dead.

Sadly, during that time it was this very contradiction in the exercise of power that drove Masai out of the party.

It made me sad mostly because Masai was the father of my only child. No one more than I appreciated the affliction of a fatherless life. While Masai could lay far less claim to being Ericka's father in any meaningful way than I could to being her mother, I had come to believe that the presence of the two of us was critical to her growth. Leaving the party was a final rupture.

It was not surprising that this issue would propel Masai to break with the party. He had become the kind of man who favored argument over action, who forgot the battle in haggling over the plan. Taking his role as minister of education too literally, I concluded, Masai had reached the point where theory superseded practice; and he was unable to merge the two.

Masai's strict adherence to the party's theory and principle did provide a check on the violent elements of the party. On the other hand, his obsession with democratic detail resulted in the kind of indecision that could stifle the revolution itself. Also, troubling was the way he could twist a square reality into a round principle. While Masai could invoke every revolutionary sentence against the abuse of women comrades, for example, he had looked me in the face and repeated to me that the beating I had suffered in L.A., though awful, was too personal a matter for a party decision. Generally, though, I appreciated Masai because, in the main, he tried to live by his word, because he usually made cogent arguments, because his voice tended to soften the hard men and, very subjectively, because he was Ericka's father.

Even Masai accepted the fact that the party was not a democratic organization, either in principle or in fact. Specifically, we operated under "democratic centralism," whereby a central body dictated the work of the whole in its interest. That centralism had been essentially reduced to one man, Huey Newton, though the Central Committee still influenced the governance of the party, since its members held individual fields of sway.

There was no doubt that some Panthers conformed to the discipline as a result of blind faith in the leadership. There were some who accepted our internal scheme because their personal agendas coincided with the party's. There were those afraid to act alone. There were those with gang mentalities. The bases of individual adherence to the party's centralized structure were as varied as the members.

In a Central Committee meeting I did not attend, Masai brazenly stated, like the boy who announced the emperor was nude, that the party operated on the basis of Huey's will. The Central Committee had become no more than a rubber stamp for it. The party had to address that weakness, to allow for a true consensus of will, at least the will of the Central Committee under the principles of democratic centralism. Huey had reduced the governing body of the party to little more than glorified members of the rank and file, Masai added. He concluded by claiming that he was not in truth, therefore, a member of the Central Committee, as were none of the rest. He looked to the rest for agreement.

Their silence muffled his appeal and amplified Huey's response. Huey asked Masai if he was not truly a member of the Central Committee, of what committee did he believe he was a member. The rhetorical question was immediately answered by Huey. He declared that Masai should be what he deemed himself: a member of the rank and file. Everybody laughed and agreed. Huey then assigned Masai to sell Panther newspapers on the street from that point forward. It was only a matter of weeks before Masai packed his things and left the party.

I tried to keep him from leaving. Although I would not have laughed at him, I told him, I begged him to see that while Huey had indeed assumed absolute leadership and was capable of brutal abuses, he was the same man who had invented the Black Panther Party, who had developed the Survival Programs, had written the theory of intercommunalism, and had challenged our common oppressor—with his own life. The end did not justify the means, Masai responded. In a better world, I told him finally, he might be a better man than Huey. But we were not in a better world.

The party was, I believed, the true vanguard of a new revolution in America. The reactionary forces against change were so strong, we had to use a closed fist to break through. The individual rights that were forfeited were inconsequential to the task before us.

By the spring of 1972, we were prepared to undertake the electoral campaign. Before the announcement was made, Bobby Seale had organized the largest of our free-food projects. We gave away ten thousand bags of groceries, with a "chicken in every bag," in a single event at the Oakland Auditorium. Then we shed the last of our combat boots and berets, ignored the sound of ultraleft teeth-gnashing, and launched our new campaign.

We started appropriately in the middle of West Oakland. The party had been born there, Bobby Hutton had been slain there, and Huey had been raised there.

West Oakland's shabby wood-frame housing had been hurriedly thrown together to accommodate Henry Kaiser's World War II project. When Oakland's massive port had demonstrated its capacity to produce instant war profits for Kaiser, particularly if he had the support of cheap labor, he sent out his call. The blacks came. They came from sharecropper shanties in the South in response to Kaiser's promise of good wages on the wharfs and docks of Oakland. The blacks came as blacks had come to other industrial centers since the onset of the "great migration" in 1915. Like the others, the blacks in Oakland found that the end of war brought a return to joblessness, a return to the realities of racism, a return to abject poverty in most cases.

Our campaign was designed to inspire our people to take control of their own destinies, without reliance on the Henry Kaisers. Our campaign was to engender the idea of revolutionary change.

This was an idea my mother had once briefly embraced, I reflected. It was during those few years when she was really young, between high school and the burdensome birth of me.

She and her brother Grant had espoused Communist doctrines then. They had tried to organize unions of factory workers, in the spirit of A. Philip Randolph, who had successfully built the first black workers' union, the Brotherhood of Sleeping Car Porters. They and their friends would come together in political discussion groups, like thousands of other blacks in America at the time, seeing hope in Moscow's embrace, idealistically seeking any means to right centuries of wrongs.

It was an exciting time, my mother had told me. Despite the despair of being black in America, there was a general feeling of hope.

My mother actually had dreams for herself then. After joining the New Negro Theater, she dreamed of one day becoming a dramatic actress. For the moment, she was content to participate in the dynamic productions of the New Negro Theater, sometimes assisted by great artists like Paul Robeson. They were dramatic warriors urging an end to a long train of barbarities, the most urgent of which at the time was the rampant lynching of Negroes.

The liberal Roosevelt White House kept a chilling silence on the Southern tradition of lynching. Moreover, FDR, a supporter of J. Edgar Hoover, expanded the FBI's reach to include spying on American citizens. One result of this was that Congress began actively seeking out and attacking members of the New Negro Theater. One by one, my mother and her friends were subjected to the tentacles of the Dies Committee's frightening investigations of "un-American" activities. Large numbers of blacks began losing the meager jobs they had struggled so hard to obtain. When even the Communists abandoned the cause of blacks—the Communist Party withdrawing its powerful support from all race issues—there was a loss of hope. Along with the others, my mother resigned herself to what Huey termed the "spiritual death" of our people.

Our campaign would, of course, have no impact on the dashed hopes of the past. It might not help realize the dreams of the next generation. Yet when Bobby Seale and I launched our campaign on the streets of West Oakland I could see on the faces of our constituents something I had never seen on my mother's face. I saw a resurgence of hope. Whatever the outcome of the campaign, that alone gave it worth.

Along with the hundreds and hundreds of black people

cheering our announcement, there was a host of local, national, and even international press. Entrance into the U.S. Establishment's game by its most vehement opposition was news. Dressed in a handsome business suit, Bobby Seale, chairman of the Black Panther Party, declared that he was going to run for mayor of Oakland in the next city election. Similarly dressed, I announced that I would run with Bobby for a City Council seat.

Questions shot out at us about the Panthers' "new image." The press wanted to know whether our running for office was a sign we had become part of the system. They asked if we still believed in armed revolution. They took photograph after photograph, flashing Bobby Seale's image all over the country. National and international media carried major stories about the new image of the Panthers. Editorial analyses abounded as to what it all meant.

In Oakland, great public debate arose about the new Panthers, about whether we had decided that power grew out of a ballot box rather than the barrel of a gun. That the voting process had never changed the disposition of real power in America never seemed to occur to the powerless majority.

For blacks in America, voting had always been an exercise in futility, notwithstanding the Fifteenth Amendment to the Constitution. The year slavery was finally abolished was the year America created the Black Codes, which denied constitutional rights to blacks, including the right to vote.

Blacks, in the South particularly, were murdered attempting to vote. They were legally kept from voting by grandfather clauses and literacy tests. Blacks who actually made it to the ballot box found their votes decimated by the might of white political machines. Thus, blacks had come to the realization that black votes, like black lives, were always extinguished by the majority rule of whites. Voting for Black Panthers was another matter.

Our agenda was to overthrow the United States government. It was to defend the humanity of our people with armed force. It was to institute socialist revolution. That was not the program of the Republican Party. It was not the program of the Democratic Party. It was not the program of the traditional white-endorsed, black-faced candidates. It was not the program of the NAACP or the Urban League. It was not even the program of the black nationalists or SNCC or the radical Peace and Freedom Party. It was still the program of the Black Panther Party.

With a minor shift in style, however, we had begun a campaign that would turn the vote into a step in the revolutionary process. With a minor change in form, we might transform the content of the hope of black people. They understood what it meant. When Bobby and I began walking the streets of West Oakland and East Oakland with our new image in our new campaign, black people winked.

Soon they were applauding. They were proud of the Panthers, they were saying. Working black people were joining our constituent *lumpen*, as the so-called black middle class became more than a smattering of Survival Program supporters. Our electoral campaign was one all of them could openly support. It was that support we sought.

It was hard not to forgive Bobby's buffoonery during that time. The campaign was realizing its full potential because of his work. At dawn every day, Bobby pushed us onto the streets. We might ride a bus on a gray morning to talk to people going to work an early shift. We might parade through a school or a hospital or a shopping mall with balloons and trinkets to give away, along with Panthers to register people to vote. We might show up to greet factory workers when they came off shift. Every evening, we would walk the streets of Oakland, block by block, knocking on doors. At day's end, Bobby would gather together all those party members working on the campaign to review his voter maps, to plan the next day, the next week, the next month.

Black people began inviting us to speak in small gatherings in their homes or to massive church congregations on Sunday mornings—Bobby preaching and me singing—or to college campuses, social clubs, or professional organizations. Volunteers were joining the campaign in droves. Large pockets of Oakland's blacks who had not voted in years were registering. Black folks were talking proud, declaring they would no longer allow a rich white minority to retain domination over the politics of a city that was half black and over 75 percent Democratic. They were becoming citizens, ready to change the nature of things, to install Panthers where there had been only Republicans for the last three decades. This was certainly due in the main to Bobby Seale, whose dynamism, had returned full-blown. He was turning his elevated national image and his genuine commitment into a powerful boon to the campaign. I was truly gratified by his work, despite the difficulty of being with him day in and day out.

A major irritation was Bobby's refusal to use standard English, even though his speeches were always strong and spirited, delivered with passion. Generally, I felt it was important for us to promote the use of standard English, as this language had been a tool of our oppression. Through denial of access to the skills of reading and writing English over so many years, we had been kept ignorant of the machinations of those who dominated us. I believed we had to know the oppressor in order to overcome him.

Bobby liked playing the fool, however. His verbal clowning had always elicited foot-stomping responses from black people. That had, presumably, eliminated any desire on his part to learn to speak the language well. Now, because of the critical eye of the national media, because political campaigns in America were in truth media events, Bobby's nonsense phrases threatened to make our campaign a sideshow.

Bobby would announce each day that we had "shooken" the hands of so many potential voters and "tooken" so many press photographs. He liked the rhyme of "shooken" with "tooken." It made my back arch, especially when Huey only laughed at my frustration over being unable to get Bobby to change. "I know you right, Elaine," Bobby would say, only to go through the next day telling the troops and the people and the press how many hands and photos he had "shooken" and "tooken." There was also Bobby's insistence that the large "cooperations" in Oakland would, if we were elected, have to pay a capital-gains tax, his version of a campaign proposal developed by our legal advisor, Fred Hiestand. Huey finally admonished Bobby to stop the clowning and deal seriously with the national image of the campaign. For one whole year, however, I would have to stand by Bobby's side listening to him say over and over that when he became mayor, the big "cooperations" were in for "boo-coo" trouble.

By the last months of the campaign, we had begun tearing down the existing government foundation in order to install a building block of our own. We had attacked every institution in the city of Oakland.

There were the relatively small issues of poor city services, such as garbage collection and public transportation. There were the more sweeping problems, such as the poverty of the labor market in a city built on the solid economics of its port—a small city that was, interestingly, home to several Fortune 500 companies. We exposed not only the glaring failures of the present government but also the hidden ones, the means by which a clique of rich white men held on to control of the city. We showed our people that the port's vast resources were technically the property of the city and therefore of the people. Through a variety of legal machinations, all the port's funds had been diverted to the authority of an appointed board of men who had vested interests in the port. If we were elected, we promised that the port's economic benefits would be returned to the citizenry, in whose name it had been established.

Our most dynamic effort was our two-pronged assault on Oakland's educational system. First we attacked the system itself. At the outset, we began attending each and every school-board meeting. As the meetings were always held at a time and place that made them virtually inaccessible to most people, especially blacks, we publicly denounced the board for hiding from the people. After that, we provided busing and free meals to people who would join us at the board meetings. Eventually, we forced the board to change its schedule to accommodate mass participation. Then we attacked the board's misuse of its discretionary funds and lambasted it for failing to provide decent curricula, facilities, and materials. Soon, because of media attention to our campaign, we succeeded in arousing black people to denounce the board. They even called for the resignation of Marcus Foster, the black man who was superintendent of Oakland's schools.

Building on the momentum, we introduced the second part of our effort. We held a press conference to announce that the Black Panther Party was opening a school: the Intercommunal Youth Institute. Our school would demonstrate how black children ought to be educated.

The institute was Huey's creation, his private dream. Huey's had always been an untutored intellect. I had been shocked to learn how difficult cursive writing was for him. When he decided to present copies of his book to the Chinese, he had wanted to inscribe them first. In the privacy of our hotel room in Ottawa, I had helped him painstakingly write his dedications. His genius was so great, it had completely masked his lack of formal education. He had used tape recorders and transcribers to write his books. He had taught himself to read, and read only slowly, he confessed, always with the help of a dictionary. It was another of our secrets.

It had been more than a year of shaking hands, of speaking and singing in churches, of meetings with social clubs, of talks to high-school and college students, of campaign dinners and lunches, and, of course, of walking the streets of Oakland block by block. Now all this would end, one way or another, on Election Day. A part of us hoped for the miracle of victory.

As I watched the television reports of the election, it was clear that Bobby and I were losing. When the final results were tallied, we did not take seats in the house of the Establishment.

But we did win. We won the votes of approximately 40 percent of the electorate. We won the solid support of black people in Oakland. The Panther constituency had indeed expanded. We had planted our ideas a little deeper. We had established a foundation.

CHAPTER 16

CHAIRMAN

I DID NOT ASK Huey about the fire which had virtually destroyed the movie theater. I read about it. The theater owner was probably upset. I was not.

Black lives had been consumed by other fires. That was what I thought. There had always been sirens and flames swirling about York Street. There was the fire that left third-degree burns on most of eleven-year-old Herbie, I remembered, the result of a profit-motivated contractor's faulty wiring. There was the cheap, combustible wall paint of absentee slumlords, which frequently set off fires in the tenements along 21st Street. I recalled my mother's frenzy about my schooling after the antiquated heating system at Claghorn Elementary erupted and burned half the children in an overcrowded second-grade classroom. There were also the murderous fires, the ones that spread from black household to black household, fires ignited by the Christian torches of God-loving racists. There was something menacingly familiar about fire and black life in America.

The theater fire was an abstraction to me. It represented the destruction of the insured property of a racist. Its only significance lay in the message it may have burned into the cold heart of the theater owner and his brothers.

He had reneged on our contract. Our lease, the lease of Oakland & the World Entertainment, Inc., a subsidiary of the Stronghold Corporation, was valid. After the theater owner discovered the party was the actual lessee, he had tried to back out of the lease.

Huey had bolted into the man's office in a rage. He had

demanded the lease be honored. He had even pleaded. He had warned. The income from the movie runs at the theater paid for supplies and services at the Intercommunal Youth Institute, paid for sickle-cell-anemia tests and other treatments at our free clinics. But that was not the point. The point was that a promise to the Black Panther Party had to be respected. We would not go to a court of law to argue the point. The point was that, in Oakland, a higher law was emerging, outside the established order.

It had been a mistake of the ultraleft *and* the right to presume that the "legitimacy" we had exhibited in our recent electoral campaign characterized our party. We had no respect for the laws of the United States, a cloak of fork-tongued legal idiom that disguised the most iniquitous acts. It had always galled me, personally, how much faith black people placed in the law and the so-called judicial system.

Blacks and liberals had spent nearly a century simply trying to overturn the racist "separate-but-equal" doctrine expressed in the case of *Plessy* v. *Ferguson*. Had no one noticed that no one had been able to truly enforce the meager dictates of *Brown* v. *Board of Education*? Thousands of blacks had, in the meantime, lived and died under the disgrace of Jim Crow laws in the South, and under the deplorable conditions created by legal discrimination in the North. We Black Panthers disregarded the law. We were, indeed, as newspaper headlines frequently suggested, outlaws.

The newspapers' implications that the party had set fire to the theater to extort money from the owner were beyond my field of concern. Like the legal system, the fourth estate was but a tentacle of the powerbrokers' octopus. In the American press, feeding the poor was condemned as communism. The priority of profit was deemed democracy. Thus, we ignored their characterizations of the incident and focused on our own losses from the fire.

The movie theater had provided income of a couple of thousand dollars a week. We needed the regularity of that money. Without it, we would have little ability to keep our promises to our people. We would not be able to serve their basic needs. We would have difficulty demonstrating the merit of our vision.

Fortunately, the Lamp Post was beginning to show a profit. The Lamp Post was a cocktail lounge and restaurant Huey had leased not very long before. The owner, though a distant relative of Huey's, had been a reluctant lessor. Huey had asked him to rent to us at a reduced price, so that we could realize enough income to support our Survival Programs. The owner had challenged Huey's reasoning that blacks like him who had gained an economic foothold in America had a duty to assist in elevating their Brothers and Sisters. He told Huey that he had earned "his" and owed nothing to anyone. He had clung to that position until faced with the prospect of having nothing. His survival was dependent on the support of the black community. It was bad business, Huey had explained to the Lamp Post owner, to turn his back on that community. Showing at least business acumen, he had capitulated and finally leased the Lamp Post to us on favorable terms, along with an option to buy. Only Panthers worked there now.

Panthers were assigned work according to their abilities. There being no such thing as private income, a party member's labor was rewarded through the redistribution of our collective resources in the form of food, clothing, housing, medical care, transportation, and personal expense money. We thought of this system as a model socialistic arrangement by which each member, our party, and our people were all served.

Panthers worked as cooks, waiters, and managers of food distribution for our breakfast programs. Panthers worked in our clinics as maintenance people, records clerks, drivers, and liaisons with medical professionals. Panthers sold the party's newspaper on the streets and distributed batches of newspapers to the various stores and businesses that stocked them. Panthers provided necessary security for all our facilities. Panthers worked at our day-care centers and school. Panthers worked at the Lamp Post.

We had assigned pretty women as cocktail waitresses. We had placed good cooks in the kitchen. We had trained bartenders. We had outlined posts and schedules for security men. The Lamp Post was a complete Black Panther Party operation.

Everybody who came to the Lamp Post seemed to like that. Blacks were proud of it. There was really no place for blacks in Oakland as attractive; the better restaurants and clubs catered exclusively to whites. The thick red carpeting at the Lamp Post was always vacuumed. There were immaculate cocktail and dining tables, adorned with bright red tablecloths, starched and pressed, and candles flickering inside red, beveled glass holders. The soft couches and chairs were of tufted red leather. Disciplined Panthers provided excellent service. The highest-quality food was offered at prices far below average. More important, however, the Lamp Post *represented* something: a black community place, where profit was shared, returned to the same community. That was why the Lamp Post was becoming so profitable—that, and the fact that Huey Newton was usually there.

It had become the only place outside the penthouse where Huey felt at ease. He went there for dinner nearly every night. He dressed himself meticulously for these outings, usually in a silk shirt, a rich blazer, sharply pressed pants tight on his narrow hips, shined Italian loafers. He would take a big car, often accompanied by two of the strongest of the special security squads, Larry and Big Bob, along with me.

Ignoring the unmarked police cars that sat outside the Lamp Post, waiting to make notes about Huey or to photograph him, we would enter the dark cocktail lounge. Women would virtually surround Huey when we entered. Dark chocolate and nearly white black women would be there in their best clothes, with and without their boyfriends, to see him. He would buy them rounds of cognac at the bar or invite one or two to join us, in the sunken dining room, for a soul-food meal of smothered pork chops, greens, and cornbread. He would kiss cheeks and shake hands, spending an entire night in an admiring crush.

The increase in our income from the Lamp Post was not enough, however. We still consumed most of our loosely organized Central Committee meeting time with discussions of how to obtain more money.

Of course, in addition to our other income, there were the regular contributions we received from various wealthy people. Primary among them was Bert Schneider. There were also other stalwarts who gave or lent us large sums of money: couples like Tom and Flora Gladwin and Herb and Shirley Magidson; and a new generation of rich kids like Molly Dougherty and her brother Chris. There were the cherished contributions of professional services by people like Arlene Slaughter, a progressive realtor, doctors like Bert Small and Richard Fine, and lawyers like Tony Kline and Fred Hiestand. We knew, however, that our party could not continue to be dependent on the goodwill of our friends. We needed an independent mechanism to maintain our operations.

Memories of the Bill Boyett boycott spawned the idea. Boyett was a black liquor-store owner who a few years before had refused to take a certain product off his shelves.

We had wanted to strip the liquor-store shelves in the black community in Oakland of a particular brand of cognac. The U.S. distributor had rejected outright the idea of sharing any of his profits with the impoverished community that consumed so much of his product. He had turned a deaf ear to the mild appeals of several local black businessmen to make contributions to scholarship funds or sports and recreational programs for children in West and East Oakland. He had flatly refused to discuss his racially discriminatory employment and business practices. The businessmen had appealed to the party. Together, we had decided that a halt to all distribution of his product in black Oakland would change his mind. Boyett and several other black liquor-store owners refused to cooperate. Sales of that cognac were too profitable.

We thought it would be easy to isolate Boyett with a little boycott of his two stores. We would make an example of him, after which the rest would fall in line, after which the distributor would be forced to address our request. The boycott was a fiasco. We spent months picketing Boyett's stores to convince him to unite with his community. We put Panthers on picket lines in front of his stores from opening to closing, nearly sixteen hours every day. We held rallies and gave away food in front of his stores. We drove customers to other stores, to put added pressure on him. We reduced his sales to nil. Miraculously, he kept his doors open. Supportive money came to him at first from other black liquor-store owners, but they eventually became too drained to help him. After that, only the distributor's money could keep Boyett alive.

It was not enough. Boyett was facing financial ruin. The fight was so drawn out, however, it hardly mattered when he finally removed the cognac from his shelves. The distributor, floating through the storm of those months untouched, avoided having to pay his dues that day. He set up negotiating meetings that would take years to bear fruit.

The one noteworthy yield from the Boyett boycott was that the publicity accompanying the effort contained a strong message. Black merchants and businessmen—not only in Oakland, but in every locale where there was a party chapter or branch—were on notice that it was not profitable to defy the party. Some resented that. Others, like the black business leaders who had instigated the strike against the distributor, welcomed the strength of the party in uniting black business interests with those of the entire community. Carl Washington, one of only three black liquor distributors in the United States, and Nelson Fields, owner of a bar and several liquor stores in Oakland, envisioned a black community empowered by the development of an independent economy. That was not incompatible with our goals.

It was in this spirit that Huey instructed men from the special security squads to begin visiting Oakland's "after-hours" clubs. The question of black unity sat begging outside the doors of those popular cabarets, where liquor was sold after hours, and drugs and gambling were offered all the time. The owners were rogue businessmen who paid off police to maintain themselves, drained the pockets of their poor patrons, and slapped around anybody who did not like it. We decided that they would have to become part of the solution or be deemed part of the problem. We offered them liberation for the former and damnation for the latter.

They resisted. We explained that we would be their conduit to redemption, coming for regular tribute or collecting a terrible tax. In the beginning, the resistance of those we targeted was formidable. They were always prepared for trouble, in the form of robbery or takeover attempts or attacks by overzealous police not on their payrolls. Whatever resistance they attempted in regard to us, however, was insufficient. In very little time, we were regularly collecting a percentage of profits from some, then from all of them.

Inevitably, rumors began circulating that the party was no longer engaged in the business of social change, revolutionary or otherwise. The party was certainly not the legitimate political organization it had claimed to be during the recent electoral campaign, the stories went. We were a new kind of criminal organization, the police-promoted rumors suggested. We were operating a nightclub *and* extorting payoffs from petty criminals and legitimate businessmen, solely to make a profit for ourselves.

Bobby Seale and I remained, however, examples of a new, more moderate Panther. It was generally believed that we had no knowledge of or relationship to the kicked-in doors or shot-up facilities of reluctant after-hours-club contributors. Indeed, our electoral campaign had created the illusion that Bobby and I were so separate from such rough activity, it was as though there were two arms of the party: the militant, dark side and the more moderate, reformist side. I felt we had achieved a state of perfection. Bobby was confused.

The truth was, Bobby had no real knowledge of the after-hours operations, as they might have been called, while I endorsed them for the contribution they provided to our programs. Bobby was usually not privy to information about this kind of activity because he was incapable of placing it in perspective. At least, that was how Huey felt. It was one of the reasons he rarely invited Bobby to the penthouse, and it was also why he rarely discussed anything substantive with Bobby, despite his nominal leadership. Bobby's superficial role left an unfortunate gap in the party, however. The electoral campaign having ended, the chairman of the Black Panther Party had nothing to do.

Actually, after the campaign, it had been hard to suddenly shift our energies. Most of us, especially Bobby and I, had been absorbed in the process in anticipation of Election Day, finding exhilaration in gaining on the resolution of *something*. With the campaign banners folded, tedium suffused the days and weeks.

From the inception of the party in 1966 until the decision in 1972 to seek political office, the party had operated largely on an emergency basis. We had always been beset by assassinations, jailings, long legal trials, and had always had to rally our forces around one crisis or another. Now, primarily because of our election campaign, we were faced with the prospect of the long haul. We were faced with the unfamiliar arduousness of building the revolution without being directly confronted by police attacks and arrests, heavy bails, or funerals. Our campaign had seemed a first step toward institutionalizing the idea of revolution. Paradoxically, it had created the present dilemma.

I was able to resume managing and editing our newspaper. That provided me with a valuable routine. Huey was, of course, embroiled in his various ventures to raise money, as well as in drafting the next steps in our long-range goals. Most other Panthers were busy in their thousand duties, enhancing and expanding our Survival Programs. Bobby seemed to have neither a function nor an interest.

Publicly, Bobby was Huey's other half and partner. In reality, nothing was further from the truth. Huey was the creative thinker, the dynamic personality that invigorated and directed the party. Bobby had gone to Sacramento because Huey had ordered him to go. He had held on through his Chicago and Connecticut trials because Huey had demanded it. Bobby had spit out the speeches that echoed Huey's ideas.

Bobby had sparkled when he had been charged by the public spotlight and the challenges of the past several years. He had thrived in boosting the Survival Programs and excelled on the campaign stage. Now, with the lights of the campaign turned out, and no crisis around which to rally, Bobby was a puppet at rest.

He could have forged ahead with the Survival Programs, there now being over thirty of them, including a new free ambulance program, a senior-escort program, as well as dental and optometry programs. But Bobby's facility for rallying seemed to fizzle in the long haul.

He could have developed the New Oakland Democratic Organizing Committee, the mass mechanism created as a result of the campaign. Over 1,500 people, black and white, had come to the first postelection dinner, to sustain the campaign's momentum, to organize around the local disparities between the people and the power. Our newspaper was headlining those disparities in a new supplement, *Oakland, Base of Operation*. Most glaring among them was Oakland's new revitalization project.

The proposed City Center was a sprawling, forty-one-acre development in downtown Oakland initiated by the progeny of the founding fathers. While investment packages were being negotiated to reshape Oakland's downtown area, blacks in adjacent West Oakland were being moved out by the city government to make way for "progress"—spelled p-r-o-f-i-t-s. Major nonlocal investors had pledged to join the locals in transfusing blood into the decrepit heart of the city if a proposed freeway extension was constructed to lift prospective white suburban consumers over the unsightly blight of blacks in West Oakland and into the City Center. Over four hundred people and nearly one hundred families, occupying 600 apartments and houses, were being uprooted for that freeway. Week after week, our newspaper supplement denounced the mass displacement, and called for a halt to the City Center project or a community share in its profits. Bobby did nothing about this issue or anything else. He said not a word about Johnny Spain's San Quentin Six trial, as we headlined it in the newspaper, failing even to use his impressive voice to bridge the widening gap between the prison guerrillas and the party. He offered no program for solidifying our relations with the various organizations around the world that supported the party, in Germany, France, Japan, even Israel; nothing to build support for the other revolutionary causes to which we were pledged, in Mozambique or Angola, or especially in South Africa—where we were giving meager support to the PAC (Pan-African Congress) through our close ties with its U.N. mission representative, David Sibeko. Bobby was idling away that postcampaign period, mostly moping over our electoral loss. He had really believed he would be mayor of Oakland.

It was that idleness that eventually gave birth to what Bobby termed a brainstorm. He authored a plan of so-called internal improvement. It was to be a kind of cathartic program to purify the party membership, top to bottom. Inexplicably, Bobby suggested that his idea tied in with the theories on which the party had based the creation of our new image and promulgated our Survival Programs. Through his program, Bobby claimed, "the people" would move even closer to the party. Panthers would become role models for the people.

To put his idea into action, he appealed directly to Huey, in a rare visit to the penthouse. Dismissing him quickly, Huey gave his blessing to Bobby's program of internal improvement.

Huey was preoccupied with raising money. We were resurrecting Oakland & the World Entertainment, for the potentially lucrative business of concert promotion. We would, Huey assured the Central Committee as he outlined his new project, eventually become the sole concert promoters in Oakland.

Many concerts had been performed for our benefit. Artists and entertainers from Leonard Bernstein to Richard Pryor to the Grateful Dead had helped raise money for the Black Panther Party over the years, donating both their time and their talents. Those benefits had unfortunately yielded little money once production costs had been covered. Besides, the number of artists lining up to offer us such benefits had dwindled to almost nil. Now, Huey promised, we would be the beneficiaries of our own productions.

In seemingly no time at all, Huey announced that he had negotiated our first contract: a concert featuring the Ike and Tina Turner Revue. It would be a one-night performance, opened by the singing of Larry Graham and his Graham Central Station band. A few weeks before the concert, Huey added me to the show, tying a thin political thread to the affair. Ticket sales went very well, and the Oakland Auditorium performance was virtually sold out by the day of the concert.

Late afternoon on concert day, security teams were making a last sweep of the huge auditorium. Panthers who were ushers were reviewing their positions. Panthers handling tickets were getting instructions.

I tested the microphones with Larry Graham's people and the Turners' road manager. I scanned the dressing rooms of Ike and Tina, as well as those of their band members and singers, to make sure the flowers, champagne, and fruit we had contracted to provide were there. We were also providing transportation, security, and $12,000 for their one-hour performance. With the exception of Ike and Tina, everything seemed in place as the hour to open the doors approached.

As concertgoers trickled in, a crisis began to unfold. Norma Armour, a transfer from L.A. and another of my old and dear comrades from those long-ago days, explained the trouble to me. She was afraid to speak to anyone else. As she was assigned to handle the ticket and concession money and other financial business of the concert, she had been the recipient of a nasty note from the Turners, who had finally arrived. Despite our having paid them $6,000 the week before, and despite Norma's having tendered their road manager $5,500 in cash when he arrived, the Turners were refusing our $500 check for the remainder due them. If every dime was not paid in cash, their nasty note threatened, they would not perform.

The unfairness of it hit me hard. It was impossible to pay the $500 in cash. We needed the cash for concessions and the banks were now closed. It was simply absurd to suggest that we would offer them a bad check for such a small amount. It was outrageous that they would accept $11,500 from us, having sung not one note, and then haggle over $500. I tried to find June when I ran into Bobby coming into the auditorium with his bodyguard Karl and others. I told him about the problem. Whatever I thought about Bobby's shortcomings, he was the chairman of the party. It was his decision as to what should be done.

Bobby grabbed Karl and the rest and followed me to the backstage dressing-room areas. The musicians who opened the first door on which we knocked told us we had to see Ike Turner personally, indicating his dressing room. Turner, a somewhat diminutive fellow, opened the door. Bobby flamboyantly introduced himself as Bobby Seale, chairman of the Black Panther Party. He reminded Turner of how the party was dedicated to serving black people, of how much the concert meant in doing that, of our recent electoral campaign, of the fact that we were all black people who could surely resolve a small problem. "Right on, 'Brother,' " Turner responded sarcastically, nastily, "but if I don't get my money, we ain't singing a note." Loud snickers and giggles erupted inside the room, coming from the members of the Ikettes, the Turners' singing group.

The rudeness of Turner's words paled when he slammed the

door in Bobby's face. The door remained closed despite Bobby's pounding on it, again and again, imploring Turner to reconsider. Bobby waved away Karl's offer to kick in the door. The continued banging made most of us uncomfortable and a little embarrassed: Panthers were not accustomed to suffering such disrespect. With relief, I followed Bobby down the hall after he finally decided to stop knocking on the door. He sought out Norma and began vehemently chastising her for not having enough cash at hand, demanding that she get more right away. It was theater of the absurd. I tried to give Norma some comfort by defending her, but time was our enemy. I had to leave her then and there, to open the program. The auditorium was full.

The small band with which I had rehearsed began its introduction to the one song I would sing. I stepped into the colorful lights that laced the stage. I could see my mother, who had come to Oakland from Los Angeles for the concert, seated in the front row with my daughter. Virtually all the faces I could see were black people, who were now cheering and stomping.

I started my song on cue, despite the distractions. I had difficulty moving across the stage in the long, fitted pink gown and matching high-heeled suede shoes I was wearing. More distracting, however, were my thoughts of what would happen when Ike and Tina Turner failed to appear on stage. I did the best I could. Then Larry Graham and his band stood the audience on its feet. Graham was very popular in the Bay Area of California. His was a native San Francisco sound, a driving beat that he had brought from his Sly & The Family Stone days, the product of the genre and era of Jimi Hendrix. The crowd remained on its feet throughout his entire dazzling performance.

A half hour after Graham finished, they were back on their feet when there was no appearance by Ike and Tina Turner. They were whistling and clapping their hands and stomping their demand for Ike and Tina. Norma was breathlessly waiting for the return of the people she had sent to get a series of small checks cashed at local stores.

Huey was furious. He had just arrived with Big Bob, and I had rushed to tell him why there was so much commotion. He found Karl, criticized him for allowing Turner to close a door in the chairman's face, ordered June to organize Larry and other security men to follow him, and started toward Turner's door. I was at his heels.

The small, roachlike man opened the door again. On seeing

Huey, he launched into a tirade about "his" money, against the vibrations of the crowd's cries.

Huey kicked back the door completely. He let Turner see his entourage.

"Motherfucker, you have one minute to start the show. If you're not on stage in one minute, we're going to break up all your instruments and kick your motherfucking ass. Is that clear!"

Huey stationed a few men at the door, which he ordered to remain open. He had June post a large ring of security people around the floor area below the elevated stage. Once the show started, no one was to leave the stage, they were instructed, until a one-hour performance had been delivered.

Within a flash, the band was onstage playing the recognizable, fast-stepping overture sounds of the Ike and Tina Turner Revue. The glittery Ikettes were warming up the audience with their complicated, fast-paced dancing, the fringes and sequins on their short, tight dresses bouncing wildly.

Dressed like her singers, Tina danced out, frenzied and sensual as ever. The crowd went wild. They were thrilled. When Tina finished her opening song, she introduced Ike. He was standing behind her with the band, his big electric bass guitar hanging low on his little body. He stepped forward to applause. With a wave of his hand, he silenced the audience and stopped the music. He proclaimed in a loud voice that he and his company were under threat from the Black Panthers to perform, even though they had not been paid. They could not go on under such conditions, he appealed to the audience to understand.

With that, he and his band began gathering up their instruments and heading toward the offstage areas. Tina and the Ikettes followed. The audience was unsympathetic. They began booing. It all seemed to happen in seconds. I had hardly been able to drink in Turner's announcement when I saw his face connect with the full force of the karate-trained foot of a Panther standing guard on the stage steps. From my seat next to my mother and daughter, I began to feel I had entered somebody's hallucination. A melee was under way.

Ike's band members scurried, leaping en masse the eight feet or so from the stage to the auditorium floor. They might as well have leaped into the jaws of Satan. They realized that too late. They had not understood that the security people provided by the concert promoter, like the promoter, like the men encircling the stage, were all the same: Black Panthers.

Panther security teams were pulverizing the musicians. Ike's body seemed to be lost, having been slammed to the floor with that first blow. Soon the band members' weak attempts to defend themselves turned into desperate attempts to flee. I sat stupefied, watching Tina Turner crouching a few feet from me, crying over a small figure that seemed to be Ike. When someone ripped a clump of her false hair from her head, she abandoned the little man and ran off screaming.

I watched it all until I saw the three Ikettes escaping. Something propelled me to act, though I was sure it was just a desire to show support for Huey, who was somewhere in the fray. Handing my purse to my mother, I kicked off my high-heeled shoes, raised my floor-length dress, and dashed up the stage stairs on the other side of the main scene of the fighting. I followed the Ikettes running down the cavernous backstage hallways toward the dressing rooms. As I gained ground on the slowest one, I caught her by the hair of her sewn-on wig. I trained my fist directly onto her jaw. Stunned, she tearfully wriggled herself free from me and scrambled through a door out of sight.

I gave up my search for them after a bit and returned to my mother and daughter. In the main hall, the Oakland Auditorium's regular security guards were simply standing around in their uniforms watching. The audience was standing, too, observing the continuing brawl as though it were a boxing match. Catcalls and jeers spat out from them, amid laughter. They were satisfied, it seemed, as crowds are when their turned-down thumbs have an effect. As the one-sided fight subsided, the audience began filing out of the auditorium. I could hear small conversations among various clusters of them, bantering back and forth about who saw what part of the clash. I guided my mother and daughter outside, where I commandeered a Panther car to take us to the Lamp Post.

All of black Oakland seemed to be crowded into the Lamp Post. The spirit inside was festive. Everybody was drinking and eating and buzzing about the fight at the Oakland Auditorium. People were congratulating us. Even Huey had to laugh when my baby girl told him how she saw Tina "Tuna" trying to fight. And the press laughed as well, the next day, at the hastily called press conference I held to respond to the charges Ike and Tina had filed with the police. Their complaint had singled out Huey and me for assault and sundry other claims.

"No, I did not have a gun," I responded with a smile to the newspaper and television reporters, who seemed to be enjoying the repartee with me. Since the campaign, I had become something of a darling of the Bay Area press.

"Can you imagine me actually pistol-whipping somebody?" I asked them rhetorically.

They all laughed.

The assassination months later threatened to change everything. It was certainly counterrevolutionary. The focus our campaign had brought to bear on the failures of Oakland's school system had surely inspired it. Not surprisingly, everyone suspected us of the murder of the Oakland superintendent of schools, Marcus Foster.

We were busy expanding our own school. Despite setbacks like the Turner business, Huey had found the money to buy a large building in the heart of East Oakland. Some of the money had come from friends like Bert Schneider. Some of it had come from the streets, the after-hours streets that Huey's special security forces marauded. Some of it had come from the Lamp Post.

Good or bad money, it had opened the doors to more than Huey's dream. The new building, which had once been a church, had a large auditorium that could seat nearly five hundred people. There was a well-equipped kitchen and cafeteria to feed around two hundred, a good-sized parking lot, a lovely courtyard, and two floors containing some thirty-five offices and rooms. If the school was a direct benefit to black children in Oakland, if it contained the indirect political benefit of building a model for something better, it also promised a better life for our own Panther children.

The reports of Marcus Foster being gunned down that November morning outside the Oakland school-board building sent a seismic shock throughout Oakland that shook our new school and sullied our new image. The telephones in our school and offices were jangling with journalists asking how we felt about the death of a man we had denounced. We had not denounced Foster, Bobby and I told a press conference the afternoon of the assassination. Foster was not our enemy. Our campaign had criticized a system, not a man, certainly not a black man. We were developing an alternative model now, we said. Over and over, we swore that the party had had nothing to do with Foster's murder. Over and over, we assured the community that we denounced the assassination and the assassins. We accepted without comment the instant elevation of Foster to martyrdom. Bobby and I attended his funeral.

Foster was clearly a pawn in a game. What we privately tried to determine was what game had been played, and who the players were. Had the post-Hoover FBI gone completely mad, we wondered, and resorted to murdering Foster only to make a rear attack on the party? Even the insinuation that the Panthers had carried out the brutal assassination of an innocent, middle-class black man would be enough. The party would be isolated or, better, denounced by their own people. Foster was a pawn in an FBI game. It was the only explanation for the assassination.

Just as we reached our conclusion, it seemed to be affirmed. Audio tapes were sent to radio stations in and around Oakland and San Francisco announcing the formation of the Symbionese Liberation Army, the SLA. The name had more of a CIA ring to it, we decided.

Its leader referred to himself as "Cinque," after the African hero of the uprising on board the slave ship *Amistad*. He announced that the SLA had "offed the pig Foster," an enemy of black people. He dressed up his announcement with sentences lifted from our campaign rhetoric about Oakland schools, with words from our *Oakland, Base of Operation* newspaper supplement. We immediately made another public statement and specifically denounced the SLA.

The machinations of the SLA thereafter claimed the daily headlines. Led by the black Cinque, or Donald DeFreeze, the SLA was in fact a mostly white group. DeFreeze claimed he had, wondrously, escaped from California's maximum-security prison at Vacaville. He had then formed the SLA.

DeFreeze asserted that the SLA's first "revolutionary act," the murder of Marcus Foster, was only a beginning. Soon, in fact, another ugly SLA drama was claiming new headlines: the kidnapping of newspaper heiress Patty Hearst. Their demands regarding her kidnapping distorted the party line: in exchange for her release, they were demanding that the wealthy Hearst family provide a free-food program for "the people."

At that point, we believed not only that the FBI had assisted DeFreeze out of prison but that the SLA was an FBI invention. We considered the Patty Hearst kidnapping a staged event. Numerous pieces of information were filtering in to us that indeed constructed another story about the kidnapping. The implication was that Patty Hearst was a willing victim. As that was no more farfetched than the SLA itself, it only bolstered our conclusions.

The same rumor mill soon produced what we considered the laughable prospect that the SLA had created a hit list. For publicly denouncing the SLA and "backsliding" on Foster, Bobby and I were purportedly at the top of that list. While that was laughable, what the SLA was accomplishing was not. It had taken very little time for the SLA, through its murder of Marcus Foster and the Patty Hearst kidnapping, to establish the illusion that it was a revolutionary organization, one that was operating inside the boundaries of our base.

We did everything we could to unearth DeFreeze from his hiding place and struggled to otherwise overcome the SLA's tainting of the word "revolutionary." After a dramatic Patty Hearst–SLA bank robbery, the media became disenchanted with the SLA. The SLA slid from the headlines, as the group itself eventually slid into nonexistence. Some would say it was because DeFreeze turned on his masters.

In the shadow of the Foster assassination, we stayed on course. The school was flourishing in its new habitat. The Survival Programs were still effective. The newspaper was being improved. We had reached the point of self-sufficiency in its production and printing, and had recently installed a wonderful new coeditor: David Du Bois, son of W. E. B. Du Bois. Thus, it was a jolt when I was called to a meeting for the launching of Bobby Seale's new internal improvement program. I had actually forgotten about Bobby and his idea.

I was mostly bored listening to him describe his program to the leadership cadres and the rank and file gathered in the school's auditorium. And I was wondering why Huey had agreed to it. Bobby was telling everybody that the party was initiating a new campaign, which he had ordained with a sloganized name: Away with All Pests.

Bobby was explaining that he had designed the Away with All Pests campaign to clean up our image. He added that the emphasis was on the word "clean." It was at this point that whatever minor merit his scheme possessed now vanished for me. I felt ashamed watching him prance on our stage before his captive audience of befuddled Panthers. He was informing them that every Panther work and living area was to be immediately made "spic and span!" Everything was to be maintained so, he continued, subject at all times to the meticulous examinations of his "inspection squads."

"You know, Brothers and Sisters," he said, arms flailing in imitation of a Baptist preacher, "when I was in the army, our sergeants would wear a white glove to inspect our bunks and lockers. If they touched anything and their white gloves showed one speck of dirt, we were in trouble. We'd be disciplined!

"Well, we're an army, ain't we?! We got to get it together, don't we? Set an example for the people. Well, that's why we're goin' on this here cleansiness campaign.

"From now on, your Central Committee members and our brand-new squads are gonna be inspecting your houses and rooms and everywhere you work or sleep to make sure everything is *clean*. This is what the Servant and I want for you, Brothers and Sisters. Away with All Pests!"

The weak applause reflected the audience's apprehension. I was outraged. It was not just the absurdity of it. It was not just Bobby's comparison of our party to the army of the very U.S. government we were pledged to destroy. It was the imposition upon dedicated party members of a crazy scheme that would serve no revolutionary goal. It was the prospect of being weighed down by a project that was nonproductive. It was that Away with All Pests existed solely to pacify Bobby.

I had the power to exempt myself from Bobby's program, and I did. All the other Central Committee members, however, and lower-level leaders were organized into Bobby's squads. Within weeks, those squads were arriving at houses and facilities, bursting in at midnight or later. Exhausted Panthers, who had to rise early for breakfast programs or newspaper distribution, were roused and told to stand at attention. Windowsills and blinds were rubbed by the white-gloved fingers of his Central Committee recruits and their squads. Bed linens were exposed for inspection. Dresser drawers and medicine cabinets were flung open. Bathrooms and kitchens were thoroughly examined. Any untidiness or dirt discovered subjected the entire household or facility to some sort of discipline—one time because a Sister had an unclean device for douching. It was hard to judge how high the level of alienation of the members became after the inspections began.

Bobby was oblivious to the grumblings. Indeed, he ordered that his "cleansiness" program to get rid of "all pests" be foisted upon the entire party, beyond Oakland. The reduced Panther membership that was maintaining our remaining chapters and

branches, from Philadelphia to Houston, was now burdened by
the enforcement of the same nonsense by local despots imitating
the chairman.

With the work under way toward cleaning up the appearance
of our facilities, Bobby decided it was time to turn inward. He
introduced a health and fitness aspect, a "personally designed"
exercise program. At sunrise every morning his inspection squad
leaders were to have all local Panthers standing at attention at an
Oakland park, to begin their day with physical exercise.

Once the troops were gathered, Bobby gave them a little
speech. Alongside him would be Emory and June and John Seale
and other members of the Central Committee, as well as most of
the more notorious members of the security squads. Then the
rank-and-file members would line up in various configurations to
begin exercising. This was eventually extended to include jogging,
three and a half miles around Lake Merritt. I was told that while
hundreds of Panthers made the run, Bobby was "overseeing" them
from his cruising car, driven by his bodyguard.

I went to see Huey.

"How long are you going to allow this?" I asked him point-
blank.

"Look how beautifully the sun dances on the lake," he responded, peering through his giant telescope from his twenty-
fifth-floor vantage point.

I was not prepared to drop the subject, no matter how lofty
he wanted life to be.

"I can see my 'cage' from this angle," he continued, referring
to the Soul Breaker, and making a point of ignoring me. "I shall
will myself to fly one day," he went on.

I listened in silence.

"That's the problem. We have no vision. We do not want to
fly. The shackles are no longer on our bodies. Our minds are
shackled." Then, abruptly, he said, "You want me to deal with
Bobby because he's ridiculous. Bobby is Bobby. Don't you see? If
we want to fly, to become part of the universe, we need Bobby.
We need all the Bobbys. The issue is not to stop Bobby but to
elevate him. He won't become a Buddhist overnight. We must
make him one . . . Anyway, I hate this bullshit. It drains me. I
want to get on with the revolution. Let it be done with. If we die,
we'll be freer than this."

He turned to hold me, tightly, and spoke almost desperately.
"I need you to stick it out. If you don't understand me, who will?"

He had, of course, made my anger pedestrian.

Then he broke the spell of the moment he had created. "You know, it's not a question of Bobby. We've got to crawl over a wall of shit and blood, with pigs and fools and time pushing us back. There's no time to be free—and that's all I want. I just want some pussy and some sky above my head."

He smiled to himself, looking out into space without his telescope.

"And maybe beneath my feet," he finished, laughing.

He looked through the telescope again, down at Lake Merritt. "Why does everybody bring me problems? I need solutions. I know the problems. Do you really expect me to solve all of them?"

He started laughing again. "I cannot believe Bobby has those people running around like that."

All my ideas for Bobby's role suddenly seemed irrelevant, or at least unworkable. I pressed on, though, and made some suggestions, about black prisoners, Oakland's local issues, African struggles. Huey rejected everything by pointing out that almost any project involving Bobby would require careful overseeing. Now the chairman's work was at least innocuous enough to keep him busy and not put the party in harm's way.

"How come you don't have your ass down there jogging?" he eventually said, turning away finally from his giant lens to pat my rear end. "I bet you could jog like a motherfucker. Be a fine example to all those comrades."

"I could ask you the same thing about your ass *and* your example."

"All right. Let's examine this. What's Bobby trying to do? There's nothing wrong with cleaning up the houses. There's nothing wrong with a fitness program for the body. A revolutionary mind in a revolutionized body. What's wrong with that?"

"We have to stop kidding about this, Huey. Bobby is wasting not only time but money. Do you know how much we've spent on white towels, paint, jogging outfits? And people are getting pissed off. Most of the comrades are too tired to do their assigned work after two hours of morning exercise, and after being pushed out of bed in the middle of the night for Bobby's fucking inspections."

"Bobby inspects fucking, too?"

"Seriously. People are going to start leaving."

"I don't give a fuck who leaves. I hope they all leave. I'll make this revolution with one hand tied behind my back."

"Yes, Huey."

"Okay, okay. Seriously, I really don't know what to do with Bobby right now. Bobby can't make speeches twenty-four hours a day. You tell me."

I realized later that there was an abiding reason I, too, rejected all the ideas about Bobby's work. I felt, sadly, that Bobby was incompetent.

"Come up immediately! I've resolved everything," Huey said to me over the telephone several months later.

As I entered the penthouse, I noted Gwen glaring at me, signaling that something new was under way.

Bobby Seale was seated at the dining table with Huey. That was certainly something new. Moreover, the sleeves of Bobby's white shirt were rolled up, as though he had settled in for serious work.

Big Bob and Larry were seated on Huey's dark leather couches, barely noticeable in the dim light of the adjoining living-room area. They were sipping cognac. A small hill of cocaine was perched on a Johnnie Taylor album cover near the head of the glossily polished dining table, where Huey was seated. Some of the contents of a bottle of cognac on the table filled Huey's glass. In the middle of the table was a magazine article and a clump of paper and pens.

Huey stood to kiss me. He gestured to me to sit next to him. Gwen placed a cognac glass before me. Huey poured.

In between sips of cognac and an occasional snort of cocaine, Huey elaborated on what he characterized as a brilliant idea. Bobby could only be described as ecstatic over it, nodding again and again in agreement with Huey.

"Yeah, man," Bobby repeated, "I know I can play this part . . ."

It was incredible. It was all about a *Newsweek* magazine article Huey had recently read. The article centered on the life and death of a black man from a Midwestern city. The man had been identified by the police as some sort of gangster. He was, on the other hand, a kind of antihero figure to the local black community. On account of a flimsy legal infraction, the man had been confronted by a battalion of police come to arrest him. He had first stood them off, but had been finally killed in a hail of bullets, his own guns blazing his last lonely retort. The bravado of that moment was the central theme of the article, and of Huey's plan.

Huey decreed that Bert Schneider could produce a film canonizing the man and his dramatic battle and finale. The film would elevate the ideal and image of the black man, a man fighting back, seizing his own liberty, and accepting death, as life, on his own terms. It was, Huey felt, a profound message, one that would, in addition, counterbalance the negativity of the disgusting genre of so-called blax-ploitation films that Hollywood was profitably vomiting forth at the time. Of course, the point also was that the party could make significant money from the venture. Another point was that it created, finally, a useful role for the chairman. Huey was actually suggesting that Bobby Seale star in the film.

There was something bizarrely brilliant in it, I thought, lighting the first cigarette of the several packs I would smoke before leaving. It could not hurt us, I mused, shamefully elated over the prospect of halting Bobby's obnoxious "cleansiness" program. Nevertheless, I was still appalled by Bobby's fantasizing over the film and his life as a movie star.

"And you know, man, this is perfect for me," Bobby was saying, " 'cause you know I used to be a stand-up comic. . . ."

I took a gulp of cognac.

"Yes, Bobby," Huey said, "and you can take Leslie and the baby and move to L.A. for the shooting. You can leave as soon as we set things up with Bert, while Elaine writes the story."

Huey handed me a sheaf of blank paper. I was to read the story and begin developing what he referred to as an outline for a script. While I perused the magazine article, I did my best to avoid looking at Bobby's performances.

He was up on his feet demonstrating how he would play certain scenes. Huey was spurring him on with requests to see him reel to the ground from gunshot wounds or show rage over racism and injustice.

Over the next twenty-four hours of uninterrupted discussion about the film, only Gwen's small Greek repast brought relief. Larry and Big Bob, dutifully remaining separate from the discussion, had at least the benefit of whispered chats with each other. No one dared mention the idea of being exhausted. Huey never noticed, of course; the cocaine and cognac were firing him.

I suppose it was sheer exhaustion that kept me from noticing the flash point. I was concentrating on keeping my eyes open and trying to conclude the marathon with suggestions about having food, or at least more cigarettes, sent up to the apartment from the Lamp Post. Huey seemed to hear nothing, unless it had to do with the film, the financial independence it would provide for us, the national consciousness it would spark, the positive image of the black man and the party it would produce via the role of Bobby Seale.

Too exuberant, Bobby also did not notice. He was offering to move to L.A. immediately and live with his cousin there. In that way, he was excitedly telling Huey, he could save the party money. The party would not have to pay for his housing and could even make some money renting his place in Oakland, or make it a collective house for some of the party members trickling in from our other chapters.

"And I don't have no problem with my cousin no more, man," Bobby was saying, as an afterthought to that point. "I set him straight about you."

Those words had not yet registered with me when I saw Huey return abruptly to the table. He had been pacing near the wide-open sliding doors that led to the balconies of the living-room area. He had taken off his shirt, and his muscles were gleaming with sweat. He became a tiger.

"What do you mean, *Bobby*, that you 'set' your cousin 'straight' about me?" he said, slamming his palms down onto the ebony surface in front of Bobby.

"Aw, man, you know. I thought I told you about him. It ain't nothin'."

"Then tell me what is 'nothin'.' "

"Aw, man, he just said that ever since you got out the joint, you've been takin' all the credit for the party and everything. But I told him he was wrong, man. I told him: 'Hey! Huey's been good to me. He's treated me right.' "

"You did, huh?" Huey said, his brown, almond-shaped eyes glaring into Bobby's. "And then what did you do, *Bobby*?"

"Nothin', man. Like I said, I set him straight. I told him how we started this thing *together* and we didn't care who was in charge. And he told me he could see where he was wrong."

I was wondering how even Bobby could fail to recognize the obvious signs of danger, but he plowed on, bragging about how he had defended Huey, elaborating on his cousin's ill-conceived comments, even quoting his cousin's treasonous statement that the head of the party should have been him, Bobby, not Huey.

"Just a minute, motherfucker!" Huey interrupted, bent over the table, his hands gripping its sides. "I asked you a question! I asked you what did you *do!*"

Bobby was lost in his soliloquy. "I don't understand what you mean, man," he stuttered. "I told you, I took care of him. He won't talk like that again."

"Big Bob!" Huey called out, still staring at Bobby.

Bob rose, startled from his cognac-stupefied state.

"Big Bob!" Huey repeated.

Blinking hurriedly to waken his brain, Bob walked over to Huey. "Yes, Servant," he said.

"Can you believe this motherfucker?" Turning to Bobby, Huey continued: "Bobby, you should be telling me how you kicked your stupid cousin's ass. You should be dancing around here showing me how you stomped him . . . Isn't that right, Big Bob!"

"That's right, Servant."

There was silence. Bobby's eyes finally registered fear, filling with tears. He said nothing.

"You know why you didn't kick your cousin's ass, Bobby," Huey began again, " 'cause you're a punk, Bobby, 'cause you let little assholes like Ike Turner slam doors in your face, 'cause you wouldn't have pointed a finger at a pig, much less a gun, if I hadn't made you.

"You're a punk, Bobby, and you can tell your motherfucking cousin I said *that*. You've been believing your own lies too long, Bobby, running around telling people you're the *cofounder* of the Black Panther Party. And I made the mistake of letting that slide because I owed you something for all the time I spent running down my idea at your house and eating up all your mama's food. But you are *not* the cofounder of the Black Panther Party! Are you! Did you mention *that* to your cousin?!"

He actually waited for a response. Nothing was said. The room was electrified.

"No, you didn't tell him that, and that's why he thought you deserved some kind of better treatment. Can you imagine your ass as head of this party?! Did you tell your cousin how I dressed you up in a beret and put a shotgun in your hand and told you what to say and who to say it to—knowing you didn't know a pig from pussy! It's *my* party, and you don't have one claim on it! Do you, motherfucker?!"

Bobby was too terrified to open his mouth. I lit a cigarette.

"Big Bob!"

"I'm right here, Servant."

Huey turned away from the table and spoke to Big Bob,

standing behind him. "Get my bullwhip!" he ordered, pointing toward his den.

Larry got up.

Huey turned to Bobby again. "Bobby Seale, you have violated the trust of this party. You have failed to defend this party in word *and* deed. The party will discipline you."

Bob returned with a large black bullwhip.

"Take off your shirt and stand against that wall, Bobby. Do you accept the discipline of this party?"

"Yes, Huey. You know I love you, man," Bobby said, so terribly pathetically, unbuttoning his shirt.

"You should have told that to your cousin."

Bobby walked across the living-room floor to the designated spot. He put his shirt on the floor and waited for his punishment. My moment of pity for him lapsed as I recalled the lashes on my own back, the numerous comrades he had ordered disciplined in the past months of craziness.

When Bobby was situated, facing the wall at a thirty-degree angle, Big Bob delivered the first of the twenty lashes Huey had ordered. With the ferocity of his four hundred pounds, Bob brought the tail of the whip down onto Bobby's back. Though a relatively thin man, Bobby bent only slightly with each lash, his head down, eyes tight, braced for the next crack. I remained at the table, smoking. Gwen was glancing at me from the kitchen, where she was busying herself with dishwashing and cleaning. Larry, his face a stone, was standing near Big Bob, waiting for an instruction from Huey. Huey was walking furiously back and forth near Bobby.

"Give Bobby his shirt," Huey ordered Larry when it was over.

"Bobby, you are no longer the chairman of this party. I am here and now removing you from office."

"Right on, man—thank you, Larry," Bobby said, accepting his shirt and slipping into it. He was standing there without his shoes, having removed them in a more comfortable moment.

"As a matter of fact, Bobby, I no longer want you in this party."

It was a deadly serious moment. To leave the party voluntarily was to be deemed a counterrevolutionary. To be ousted from the party meant there had been a renunciation of principle so severe that the actor effectively *became* a counterrevolutionary. Under either circumstance, one had shifted sides.

Even Bobby saw the danger in that. He quickly grabbed his coat from the back of a dining-room chair. Starting toward the front door, he said, "Okay, Huey, man, I accept that."

"Okay?!" Huey hollered after him. He stomped toward Bobby. "What do you mean, 'Okay'? I built this party with my life, and I brought you along for the ride. I even saved your fucking soul in the meantime. And now you have the nerve to walk away from me?!"

Bobby stood petrified with confusion near the door, only steps away from escape.

"Fine, fine, motherfucker!" Huey spat out. "Be out of your house—*my* house—by morning. Matter of fact, be out of Oakland by morning. I don't want you in my party or in my city. Do you understand!"

Bobby mumbled in panic. Urgently, he opened the door, leaving his shoes and saving himself with a brisk, barefooted walk down the wide carpeted hallway to the elevator.

Huey was not finished. He raged on. Finally, he ordered Bob and Larry to go to Bobby's house immediately. They were to move the chairman out of that house within the hour. If he did not comply, they were to get rid of the chairman by any means.

Two days later, I was named chairman of the Black Panther Party. It was an oppressive charge. I was inheriting the mantle of a dead man.

Bobby had survived that night and was now living with his wife, Leslie, at the home of her family in Philadelphia. I was left to create something out of his empty post.

Few people were trusted by Huey now. The exceptions included Big Bob and Larry, the others who made up the special security squads, and, I presumed, me.

Now David Hilliard was expelled, for an alleged infraction of newly invented rules involving his wife, Pat, and his girlfriend, Brenda. David had been Huey's staunchest advocate and his close friend since he was thirteen years old. He was still serving out his prison sentence with revolutionary stoicism. Now he was doubly condemned.

Next came the expulsion of June Hilliard, David's brother, whose devotion was slighter but deadlier. He was charged with having drawn a gun on Huey over the expulsion of David.

Then came the expulsion of John Seale, Bobby's brother, untrustworthy as a blood relative of a counterrevolutionary.

Now came the brutal attacks on the after-hours clubs. Teams of armed men were sent out every night to demand larger homages. One resistant club owner found himself and his patrons confronted by a virtual platoon of Panthers wielding automatic rifles and leaping from a truck platform that supported an M-60 machine gun mounted on a tripod.

And now there were other expulsions, of other men and women who could not swim in the crosscurrents of those days. Men were pistol-whipped for alleged stealing, lying, or lying about stealing, and anything else imagined by the now-paranoid mind of Huey, which cocaine and circumstance seemed to be destroying.

By the time Huey was arrested in August 1974, I had braced myself for what seemed the inevitability of an accusation against me.

During that first month of my tenure as chairman of the Black Panther Party, I began to lose the thread that connected me to what I had become.

Whatever I thought about Bobby Seale, it was certainly never that he was an enemy of our people or party. Bobby's condemnation had nothing to do with his competence or commitment. There was no justification for it. It had to do with a cocaine-boosted rage. I had to admit that all of Huey's subsequent heavy-handed acts had the same foundation. I had to reckon with my own role in all of it, and wonder whether I could continue to have a role in any of it. I was not losing the thread as much as the faith.

Faith was all there was. If I did not believe in the ultimate rightness of our goals and our party, then what we did, what Huey was doing, what he was, what *I* was, was horrible. If the party had no humane and lasting value, that would nullify the loss of so many precious lives: of John and Bunchy and George and Jonathan and Fred. It would mean a disastrous mistake had been made in a Faustian bargain.

I had to face the question of whether to go or to bide. I had to accept the consequences of the answer. And I had to face it alone. I could no longer hide behind Huey.

I had remained above the fray of that last month of terror, as I had my whole life in the party. Now I was compelled to confront what my participation in the party really meant. Was my loyalty determined by personal aggrandizement? Was my commitment rooted only in my private dreams? Were the songs and words I wrote simply embellishments of deeds that could be measured more by caprice than by principle? Was I duplicitous— something far worse than anything Bobby had ever really been— ready to foster what was an illusion of revolution?

Alone, thinking, rocking, I began to hear the sounds of the old, repetitive piano scales that had filled my youth. Like the other pieces of my childhood, they were morsels of life scavenged by my mother, trying to drown out the sound of scurrying gutter rats and escape the despair. I began to taste the salt air of Atlantic City, remembering how my mother had squeezed her sweatshop salary to dress up my childhood with vacations there; to pay for a decent hotel room, even if it was not one close to the beach where hotel rooms were for "whites only." I felt the cold of New Year's Day, when we watched Philadelphia's Mummers' Parade, where whites wore blackface and blacks were not allowed to participate. I could smell the soap and talcum powder of summer baths on York Street, throughout which my mother sat with me to keep the roaches from falling into the tub.

It was strange that such little remembrances would shock me into finally recognizing that my mother had carried me on her back all those years. With her coarse lessons and hard ways, she had tried to steal a life for me. Nevertheless, I had felt the weight of our poverty, the indignity of our lives.

I had experienced the pathetic bustling joy of everybody in our neighborhood when somebody "hit the number." I had heard the sorrow in the sound of bongos and "do-waps" on North Philly streets produced by gangs of wine-drinking youngbloods angry at all the wrong people. I had felt the degradation in the impossibility Nita and Barbara and the rest of us girls had known trying to see beauty in our dark skin or our full lips or the texture of our African hair or even in the size and shape of our feet and derrieres.

I had come to know that York Street was as American for black people as baseball at Connie Mack Stadium was for whites. I knew that millions of black mothers had tried, like my own, to gloss over the pain with piano lessons and stolen new dresses, the way they smoothed Vaseline onto patent-leather Easter shoes. I knew that millions of blacks had been forced to find hope in playing numbers and relief in Scotch or heroin. I knew that millions had found comfort in the strength of the Joe Louises and

Jackie Robinsons and Marian Andersons and Josephine Bakers who had clawed their way out of our degradation. I knew that millions had found salvation in the name of Jesus.

I had become mad. Huey had surely become mad. Perhaps that was really our bond. Perhaps it was the bond of all of us, really, our rage.

Huey had hated the senseless cycles of life on the streets of West Oakland. He had wanted more for his friends, more for his family, more for his father, even more for his dear Armelia Newton, who had, like my own mother, tried to hold the head of her seventh son high above the stench of being black in America.

Huey had seized a moment in the historical chain to make another bid for our humanity. From the first Africans who had leaped from slave ships in suicidal rejection of slavery, we had struggled for freedom. A thousand slaves had slit the throats and poisoned the food of their masters, living with the singular desire to live free or find freedom in hell. A thousand blacks had run for freedom, dodging bullets and "nigger dogs," riding the third rail of the Underground Railroad to freedom. A million blacks had linked themselves to the Harriet Tubmans and Frederick Douglasses and Sojourner Truths and Marcus Garveys and W. E. B. Du Boises and Martin Luther Kings and El Haj Malik El-Shabazzes. Still, we were not free.

Huey had created his Black Panther Party with both his brilliance and his madness. Now he had made me chairman of that party, calling me out. I was afraid. The question was whether I held a scepter of terror or a sword of freedom. The question was whether to go or to bide.

The answer came in the echoing cries of Mrs. Huggins and Mrs. Carter and Mrs. Jackson and the other hurting mothers who had given their sons to our struggle. It was in seeing the sum of the bits and pieces of my thirty-one years.

The answer was love—the love that was inside the madness. It was about not forgetting. It was about living and about dying for freedom. This was all we could do if the Dorothy Clarks and Armelia Newtons were ever to see the other side of the mountain. I had to hold on.

CHAPTER 17

A WOMAN'S REVOLUTION

HUEY'S RAGE WAS REPLACED BY SILENCE. He had been arrested on serious charges. Despite my fear of Huey after he had slapped me a short time before, despite my despair over his cocaine-fueled self-destruction, he still appeared magnificent to me standing inside his cell. I wished I believed in the healing of hands. I wished I could dispel whatever demons were robbing him and me and, I believed, many others of his best. Looking into those almond eyes, I felt ashamed of my fear of him.

I would take care of the blood, I told him. He shrugged. Callins, the tailor, had taken the brunt of his raging anguish. Callins's blood now stained the penthouse ceilings and carpets and walls and plants, and Gwen's clothes, even the fluffy blue-and-white towels in the bathroom. I assured Huey the blood would be washed away and his apartment renewed in time for his return. The bail had been paid, I continued, and he would be out soon.

That was before I knew of the second charge: attempted murder. Waiting to be released on the Callins charge, Huey was rearrested—charged with the shooting of a seventeen-year-old prostitute several nights earlier.

Kathleen Smith had been working the corners near the California Hotel, where petty criminals and traders in women and drugs were welcome. She had, of course, been a victim all her life. It was the sad culmination of her existence that somebody put a bullet in her head, placing her young and empty life on hold.

There was a bitter paradox in that accusation. I knew that Huey Newton could not have shot an unknown girl from the streets.

Huey had been on the streets of Oakland most of his life. He identified with the women that worked those streets. He was one of them, he often said, locked in America's ugly reality, a world where the strong devoured the weak and everyone was on the "block." And those lost black girls saw in Huey's strength, in his leadership of the Black Panthers, someone who might free them from the block. They were his Sisters, and he had no stones to cast at them.

But the black community would not forgive the Huey Newton the press began to invent. *We told you he was a killer*, the morning press proclaimed. "Oh!" the people cried. *We told you he was a gangster, not a revolutionary.* "Ah!" the people responded. *He's no hero!* "No!" the crowd would begin to roar. *He's crazy, don't you see?* "Yes."

Knowing what all of it meant, Huey did the only sane thing: he relieved the party of the burden of his presence. He tried to throw off his own burdens. He left us.

Now it was a matter of saving his party, Huey's explicit request to me in the whispered telephone conversation during the first days of his exile. The task was to salvage the shreds of what had been abandoned.

A woman in the Black Power movement was considered, at best, irrelevant. A woman asserting herself was a pariah. A woman attempting the role of leadership was, to my proud black Brothers, making an alliance with the "counter-revolutionary, man-hating, lesbian, feminist white bitches." It was a violation of some Black Power principle that was left undefined. If a black woman assumed a role of leadership, she was said to be eroding black manhood, to be hindering the progress of the black race. She was an enemy of black people.

I knew I would have to muster something mighty to manage the Black Panther Party. My quick decision to get Huey to ordain Larry Henson as the new chief of staff had been the most important step in that direction. Larry's own male chauvinism would, I concluded, be held in check by his serious commitment to the dictates of the party. Whatever problems it presented would be outweighed by his fearlessness, and by the relentlessness and even savagery with which he always carried out orders. He was capable of hoisting me above the battlefield of men who might resist or challenge my leadership.

During the critical two weeks after Huey's departure, before I announced my new role to the membership, Larry proved he would tolerate no disrespect of me or the orders that flowed from the Central Committee that I was quickly reconstituting. He proved he could and would put down usurpers, that he could manage the military arm of the party and would unquestioningly support all party decisions with the force of that arm. With Larry behind me, I was unfaltering when I announced to the entire party that Huey Newton was in exile and that I was taking his place.

In those early weeks, I did everything possible to demonstrate to Larry that his loyalty was treasured. I introduced him to the expensive suits at the Tailored Man shop in San Francisco. I turned over Huey's Lincoln town car to him. I rented a beautiful apartment for him in the stylish Lake area. I guaranteed him unlimited access to the party coffers for his personal use. Eventually, I sealed our bargain, as it seemed to be, with a kiss.

Larry was a sensual man. His bedroom eyes were alternately hazel-colored and gray. His large hands were at once soft and strong, usually held at his side. His thighs and arms, like his entire body, were brawny. His skin was smooth and dark. It was not difficult to be attracted to him, but there was no way to determine exactly why I became his lover. Perhaps it was the simple pleasure of being with him. Perhaps it was because of what I recognized as my recurring fascination with dangerous men. I was sure I needed him as copilot. Above all, I loved his loyalty.

His was a toughness not molded on murderous urban ghetto streets. Larry had been raised by a hardworking father and adoring mother in Flint, Michigan, a small town that could only claim distinction as being not too far from Detroit. There he had been raised in semirural, working-class poverty.

Flint was a place where black families clung together mainly out of necessity. It was where black fathers were the sole supporters of their families, through a lifetime's work in automobile manufacturing plants, and where black mothers were in the kitchen all day long. Flint was a world where black men ruled their women —and said they never struck their wives with a closed hand. It was a universe in which black men spent their weekends in small bars, if their paychecks included overtime, brandishing knives in brawls, drinking Four Roses whiskey straight, and dancing "nasty" to honky-tonk music with girls in tight red dresses. Flint was a town where everything hinged on one industry and black life hinged

on getting past racism and into that industry. Larry had vowed
he would die before having to work for that industry.

Larry had watched his father leave home for work around
midnight for thirty years, never missing one shift. His father often
plowed through Flint's brutal winter storms to reach work. Finally,
Mr. Henson retired with a gift of a blanket and a commendation
in the company newsletter. Larry's bitterness over that life was as
fierce as his love for his father.

The work ethic he inherited from his father had driven him.
From the moment he came to "the base" in Oakland from the
Michigan chapter's Detroit branch, he demonstrated his willing-
ness and ability to execute any task.

Like most new arrivals from other chapters, Larry had been
assigned menial work. He worked in the party's day-care facilities,
where he had as carefully and conscientiously washed babies and
cooked their food as he had taken his turn on the overnight security watch. He cleaned the child-care facilities during the day
as diligently as he cleaned the guns June Hilliard gave him at
night. He was reliable, loyal to the point of killing or dying. His
record earned him a place in the special security ranks. Now he
was chief of staff of a party that could survive only, I believed,
under his sure hand.

Within a month of Huey's exile, Larry had shaped our strag-
gling army. He had ordered the guns and asserted authority over
the hardest of the men, aboveground and underground. He was
carefully reorganizing the next link in his chain of command,
elevating the toughest and truest men, like Perkins and Ricardo
and Big Bob. He also had put down a series of disruptions on the
Oakland streets that came as news of Huey's exile spread.

In the month before his exile, Huey had provoked a vicious
hostility toward the party on the streets of Oakland. After-hours
club owners, as well as drug dealers and assorted petty criminals,
had bonded together in their hatred of him. They had tried to
put together a contract murder of Huey. With Huey's flight, they
saw an opportunity to reinstate themselves as "men." Little groups
of gangsters, and others with personal grudges, began frequenting
the Lamp Post, loudly denouncing Huey. One man actually tore
down the framed painting of Huey that hung there. After-hours
club owners were responding with guns to Panthers at their doors.
Expertly, Larry tamed their rebellion.

◄ ►

The symmetry of it was lyrical, I thought. Three months after I took on the leadership of the party, Jerry Brown became governor of California. The Black Panther Party had supported Brown, though that support had come only at the eleventh hour.

A small, vociferous collection of local black Democrats had been threatening to denounce Brown. He was making no specific campaign commitments to black people. Neither their opposition nor Brown's candidacy had concerned me inside the whirlwind created by Huey's sudden exile. It was Percy Pinkney, a black community organizer from San Francisco, who brought those affairs to my attention. He called to urge me, first, to have the party endorse Brown. Since I could see no reason not to support the very liberal Brown against a Republican, I agreed immediately. Then came the main item on Percy's agenda. He implored me to join him at an upcoming meeting that was being demanded of the Brown campaign by the local malcontents. He did not want to be Brown's sole representative there.

My enthusiasm over attending that meeting had little to do with Percy or Brown. I was looking forward to thwarting the aims of the Negroes involved. They were the same clique who had extracted small grants and favors from whites in business and government with the invocation of the "black community" and the implication that it was better to deal with them than with the Panthers. There was no question in my mind that they were now trying to bargain for personal advancement, perhaps even a Cabinet post. The prospect of the election of a liberal governor had apparently aroused their greedy fantasies.

Though the party had not been officially invited, I strolled into the meeting as if we had been. I shook everyone's hand as I walked through the room. Only Percy smiled when Larry and I took seats in the front row of folding chairs. It took no time to identify the worst of the opportunists, who shouted insults at Percy, calling him a lackey. If Brown did not stop "bullshitting," they claimed, they would make sure he lost the black vote in Oakland and the whole Bay Area.

When Percy granted my request to speak, I reminded the group of Ronald Reagan, the racist, outgoing governor, of whom they had made *no* demands, as I recalled. I reminded them that Brown was inherently better than his Republican opponent. I reminded them also that I had seen none of their black faces of late in the "community" in whose name they were speaking. Fi-

nally, I announced that the party was not only supporting Brown
but committing troops and workers to his campaign.

They began deserting each other and their position. "Oh,"
they cried, "if the party supports Brown, then . . ."

The black vote in Oakland was very strong for Jerry Brown.
It was part of the sweeping majority that made him governor of
California. In replacing the right-wing Ronald Reagan, Jerry
Brown was a breath of fresh air for poor people and working
people *and* people of color. Moreover, Brown had not locked
himself into the established Democratic machine, which fed on
itself. Free to act on his own moral principles, he could be expected
to lean well to the left of his party.

For our party an invaluable asset fell into place with Brown's
first act as governor. Brown named Tony Kline his appointments
secretary. Kline's role was to structure the apparatus by which the
governor would appoint his Cabinet. This made him one of the
most politically influential men in the state. Up until that moment,
Tony Kline had been a lawyer for the Black Panther Party.

J. Anthony Kline had been Brown's close friend since their
law-school days together. That was after Brown left his studies as
a Jesuit, and after he distanced himself from the philosophies of
his father, Edmund "Pat" Brown, California's tough governor before Reagan. The practice of law did not suit Jerry Brown's temperament. After an uneventful stint as California's secretary of
state, he decided to make a bid for the state's highest office. Before
that, he had remained sequestered from the pulsations of California politics. That was in great contrast to his close friend now
seated across the table from me.

Tony had been immersed in the social dynamic of the times,
using the law to fight the impositions of the rich and powerful
upon everyone else. He was currently the leading attorney in the
San Francisco–based public-interest law group Public Advocates.
Before Public Advocates, Tony had been engaged in the fight for
the legal rights of California's very large and very poor community
of farmworkers. Somewhere in between, he became involved with
the Black Panther Party.

It was at a time when party facilities were the regular targets
of police assaults. Police would raid a party facility with guns
drawn, waving a search warrant. Tony and a few other young
white lawyers in the Bay Area decided they could offer the party
a safeguard against such assaults, at least at our national head-

quarters. They began taking turns staying at national headquarters twenty-four hours a day. Their aim was to provide immediate legal representation to the party when the police arrived in their customary fashion. Their hope was that the very presence of a member of the bar would eliminate the possibility of violent confrontation, forcing the police to operate within the letter of the law. Tony Kline had been a close friend and legal advisor to the party ever since.

Tony and I were laughing over those memories during dinner. Each of us was now standing on higher ground. We had the potential, through the union of our forces, to create conditions for fundamental change.

By the time Tony moved to Sacramento, he had been elevated to the Cabinet post of legal affairs secretary to the governor, and I had announced my candidacy for a seat on the City Council of Oakland. My candidacy had been on our agenda since the last campaign. Huey had talked with me about it a great deal. It was more important now than ever to pursue this goal, he advised me over the telephone from Cuba, where he had settled into exile.

There was very little time left before the election in April 1975. I had no idea how I could at once run for office and steer the Black Panther Party, but there was too little time to waste worrying.

I installed Beth Meador, a black law student, as my campaign manager. Impressively, I was able to get black businessman Otho Green to be finance manager of the campaign. Green had been Bobby Seale's only black opponent for the mayor's seat. Inside the party, I placed Phyllis Jackson, who had been one of the mainstays of the previous campaign, as coordinator of party campaign workers. I positioned Ericka Huggins to fill the vacancy of administrator of our school and its affiliate programs and projects. I had already appointed Joan Kelley administrator of our nonmilitary apparatus, such as the Survival Programs and legal matters, and Norma Armour, coordinator of the ministry of finance. I made Michael Fultz, from the Boston branch, coeditor of the newspaper with David Du Bois. The pieces were in place.

There was one result of all this I had failed to think through: I had introduced a number of women in the party's administration. There were too many women in command of the affairs of the Black Panther Party, numerous men were grumbling.

"I hear we can't call them bitches no more," one Brother actually stated to me in the middle of an extraordinarily hectic day.

"No, motherfucker," I responded unendearingly, "you may not call *them* bitches 'no more.'" I turned brusquely to Bill, my bodyguard, and told him to make a note for Larry to deal with "my Brother here."

It was a given that the entire Black Power movement was handicapped by the limited roles the Brothers allowed the Sisters and by the outright oppressive behavior of men toward women. This had meant little to me personally, however. The party was so far to the left of the civil rights and black nationalist men, nothing in their philosophies was dreamt of in ours. And because of Huey—and now Larry—I had been able to deflect most of the chauvinism of Black Panther men. My leadership was secure. Thus, in installing Sisters in key positions, I had not considered this business. I had only considered the issue of merit, which had no gender.

The grumbling over the elevation of women grew louder. I had to call upon Larry to shut all mouths.

Soon, however, the party's esprit de corps was jeopardized by a different set of problems. A group of organized drug dealers emerging in black Oakland threatened to "move on" the party if it made any attempt to fuck with them the way it had fucked with the after-hours clubs. Party funds were being drained at the rate of more than $10,000 per week because of improvements to our school. Campaign expenses were tugging at our other accounts. However, none of it seemed to compare to the sudden assaults on my name and image.

The body of Betty Van Patter had just been found in San Francisco Bay. She had been reported missing for some time, during which, through Charles Garry's office, I had had to answer police questions about her disappearance. I had had no idea where she was. In early January, three months before the election, Garry advised me to meet with the Berkeley police about her murder.

I had fired Betty Van Patter shortly after hiring her. She had come to work for the party at the behest of David Horowitz, who had been editor of *Ramparts* magazine and a onetime close friend of Eldridge Cleaver. He was also nominally on the board of our school. I had called Horowitz and other board members about our growing financial problems and how those problems were being exacerbated by intensified Internal Revenue Service surveillance of our bank accounts. I had also mentioned a related problem.

In the manic moments before Huey's departure, the manager of our financial records, Gwen Goodloe, had run away. She left her books and other paraphernalia intact, but we were left without her knowledge. Norma could not possibly fill the gap given the added pressure of increased government scrutiny of our finances.

A few days after I spoke with Horowitz, he called me about Betty, a friend of his who had been a bookkeeper at *Ramparts*. She was having trouble finding work because of her arrest record. If I did not mind that she was white, he felt I should hire her. She was a wizard at maintaining financial records, having been educated and trained as an accountant. She would certainly be able to put things in order, Horowitz assured me.

I rented an office for her where she could attack the party's complicated bookkeeping operation in privacy. Norma worked with her, to learn and to keep watch over our documents.

Immediately Betty began asking Norma, and every other Panther with whom she had contact, about the sources of our cash, or the exact nature of this or that expenditure. Her job was to order and balance our books and records, not to investigate them. I ordered her to cease her interrogations. She continued. I knew that I had made a mistake in hiring her.

Under the various definitions of U.S. criminal and tax codes, there was no question that many of our money transactions could be ruled illegal. There was also no question that our only concern over legalities was the possibility of the arrests of our people and the destruction of our programs. We knew that it was all a matter of form. Despite the diligence of its efforts, the IRS had found it virtually impossible to drag us into a legal quagmire without itself getting very muddied.

Our accountants and tax lawyers could hold off the IRS. It was for the party to keep our affairs in order. Betty Van Patter was showing herself useless in that endeavor, her nose in our business more than our books. Moreover, I had learned after hiring her that Betty's arrest record was a prison record—on charges related to drug trafficking. Her prison record would weaken our position in any appearance we might have to make before a government body inquiring into our finances. Given her actions and her record, she was not, to say the least, an asset. I fired Betty without notice.

Now I was being questioned in Charles Garry's office about her murder. The Berkeley detective opened the interview by stating that I was suspected as an accomplice or conspirator in her murder. My angry response to his false accusation was that if he uttered it again, I would sue him for slander. I knew now that the real purpose of his interview was to defame me and my candidacy for office. There were no more police questions. The innuendo was enough. That investigation instigated the flurry of rumors that spread through the streets.

It was difficult for me to allay the anxiety of many of our white supporters, who wondered, in numerous telephone calls, whether it was possible that some element in the party, "perhaps" unknown to me, might have done it. I could not dispel the fear I saw in Beth Meador and Otho Green and other non-Panthers working in my campaign over what might happen to them. One state assemblyman pledged to endorse me said he was reconsidering because he had heard I was under investigation for murder. All I could do was say, over and over, that while it was true that I had come to dislike Betty Van Patter, I had fired her, not killed her.

I began wondering where Betty Van Patter might have really come from, with her strange prison record, and why she had been killed. I began reevaluating Horowitz and his old Eldridge alliance, particularly after I discovered he was adding grist to the rumor mill. I tried to dismiss these odd connections as I had always refused to allow myself to be distracted by dwelling on the possible specifics of government sabotage of the party.

There was no question that the FBI was geared to destroy us, no matter the present disarray in the White House over the Watergate affair. I knew that even the CIA was part of that effort to eliminate the party. But I also knew that we would lose perspective if we looked behind every closet door.

Now, however, I was frightened by the vastness of the possibilities. I could create a magnificent thing or I could create a disaster with my party leadership, my electoral campaign, my friends in the governor's office. I realized that Huey had borne such a weight all along. Was this what had driven him nearly mad? I wondered how long it would be before my back was broken.

I moved into a more secure apartment with Ericka Huggins. Thinking about the apartment was calming. It was in a large, tree-studded, guarded complex where there was a bedroom for each of us and one for our children to share whenever they stayed the night. We had a party of sorts the night before I moved, laughing while we reviewed old photographs and other mementoes found in closets and drawers. Larry was there. He was relaxed, snorting some cocaine he had brought—a sporadic habit he had acquired before Huey left. In the morning light, when the moving company people were knocking at the door and Larry had gone, I discovered a small amount of his cocaine remaining on a dressertop. I quickly brushed it into a piece of aluminum foil and stored the small packet in my wallet, intending to return it to Larry.

I forgot about the packet entirely over the next two days, until Ericka Huggins and I arrived at San Quentin prison. I bounced into the visitors' entrance agitated because I was late for my scheduled weekly appointment with Johnny Spain. I was thinking about time, and about Johnny's next court appearance in the San Quentin Six case, when there before me, in the hands of a black female guard at the first metal detector of San Quentin's two security check points, was the small quantity of cocaine I had stupidly salvaged.

Confusion reigned. The guard was not sure what substance was in the packet, whether she should talk with me about it, what she ought to do with it. Even the lieutenant and captain who soon joined her were unsure. In the turmoil, I left, vowing loudly that I would rather not visit than be questioned like a criminal.

Two weeks later, Garry's office called to inform me that a warrant for my arrest had been issued in Marin County, on charges of "possession of narcotics in a place where prisoners are kept," a felony.

I tried to face the next days with bravado. I invited the press to my bail procedure. When I was bound over for trial, I held firmly to my not-guilty plea. I dismissed a plea-bargain offer, under which I would plead guilty to a simple charge of possession of the drug in exchange for a dismissal of the felony count and no prison time. I did not care that the offer was being guaranteed by Bruce Bales, the D.A. in Marin County who was slated to prosecute the San Quentin Six case. I demanded a trial. There was nothing over which to bargain, I insisted, knowing it was a bargain that would, at the very least, cost me the election. I held on until faced with the facts.

In a pretrial conference in his chambers, the judge and Garry summarized the situation for me: it was unlikely I would prevail, innocent or not, in a trial in Marin County. I could only be tried by a jury panel selected from the white, affluent residents of the area, residents whose opinions about blacks and Black Panthers were drifting from bad to worse. Adverse publicity over the San

Quentin Six case was monumental. If I was convicted, I faced a maximum of fourteen years in prison. I "pleaded and bargained" on the spot.

Choked by the Betty Van Patter accusation and the albatross of the "cocaine plea," I mustered all the energy I had to struggle through the last two months of the campaign. Aggravating the situation like a gnat was one of my lesser opponents, an unknown young Negro.

He was suggesting to little gatherings of prospective supporters that I had an unsalutary lifestyle, as exhibited by my cocaine case and by what he labeled as my secret sexual life. "Those in the know," he stated, were sure I was a "man-hating lesbian." He pointed to the number of women who had suddenly "taken over" the party, especially now that the great Huey P. Newton was out of sight.

Oddly, I had never thought of myself as a feminist. I had even been denounced by certain radical feminist collectives as a "lackey" for men. That charge was based on my having written and sung two albums of songs that my female accusers claimed elevated and praised men. Resenting that label, I had joined the majority of black women in America in denouncing feminism. It was an idea reserved for white women, I said, assailing the women's movement, wholesale, as either racist or inconsequential to black people.

Sexism was a secondary problem. Capitalism and racism were primary. I had maintained that position even in the face of my exasperation with the chauvinism of Black Power men in general and Black Panther men in particular.

Now hearing the ugly intent of my opponent's words, I trembled with a fury long buried. I recognized the true meaning of his words. He was not talking about making love with women— he was attacking me for *valuing* women.

The feminists were right. The value of my life had been obliterated as much by being female as by being black and poor. Racism and sexism in America were equal partners in my oppression.

Even men who were themselves oppressed wanted power over women. Whatever social stigma had been intended by the label "lesbian"—always invoked when men felt threatened, I observed with the benefit of hindsight—did not concern me. It was simply the rattle of a man terrorized by a social order dominated by other men. It was a social order I was bent on destroying. But his accusations did wake me.

There would be no further impositions on me by men, including black men, including Black Panther men. I would support every assertion of human rights by women—from the right to abortion to the right of equality with men as laborers and leaders. I would declare that the agenda of the Black Panther Party and our revolution to free black people from oppression specifically included black women.

I would denounce loudly the philosophies of the Karengas, who raised the name of Africa to justify the suppression of black women. I would lambaste the civil-rights men who had dismissed the importance of women like Fannie Lou Hamer and Ella Baker and Daisy Bates and even Kathleen Cleaver. I would not tolerate any raised fists in my face or any Black Power handshakes, or even the phrase "Black Power," for all of it now symbolized to me the denial of black women in favor of the freedom of "the black man."

I would claim my womanhood and my place. If that gave rise to my being labeled a "man-hating lesbian, feminist bitch," I would be the most radical of them.

I made it clear that no more discussion would be had regarding my personnel decisions. The women I had positioned would be accepted for what they were: the most capable. I would be very hard on those who questioned me on the basis of my genitalia.

It was with this attitude that I insisted on attending the disciplinary session I ordered for a Brother who had blackened the eye of the Sister with whom he was "relating," because she had not properly cooked his greens. It was with this attitude that I had Larry and Perkins accompany me to a meeting with my accusatory campaign opponent, in which we threatened him with bodily harm if he ever so much as spoke my name again in public. Before the campaign was over, it was this attitude that pushed me to lance a festering sore.

I had not intended committing an act of vengeance. Despite my memory of the fists that had brutalized my body a few years before, there were larger issues involved when I ordered Steve to Oakland.

I called him from his Los Angeles underground because he had become a blatant transgressor of party rules. I ordered him to Oakland to put him and his violent band on notice. He had shown open contempt toward my leadership in an incident at the Lamp Post during the early days after Huey's departure. While he had remained quiet over the months since, his hostile disrespect was rising again. Opposition from him would be hard to put down. I had to rein him in. Those reasons alone, Larry agreed, provided good cause to confront him.

Larry had decided that we would meet Steve at one of our various "safe" apartments. I was not there to greet him, waiting for Larry's signal that Steve and his two lieutenants, Al and Simba, had been "settled in." They were first stripped of their weapons at the point of shotguns. Once "undressed," they were seated to wait for me.

"This is how you treat me, after all we had," Steve said to me as I entered the apartment. He was smiling, seated on the living-room sofa with his head back, his legs apart.

Al and Simba had stood up when I opened the door.

"Get up, Brother, when the chairman enters the room," Larry said, indicating to Big Bob to put him on his feet. I waved my hand to Bob not to bother forcing his respect.

I told Steve what the problem was. Al had been in Oakland a few days before. I had wanted to see Al one of those days, but my schedule had not allowed it. I had told Al to stay in Oakland one more night, in order to meet with me the next day. He had left that same night, however, leaving a message that Steve had ordered him back to L.A. Steve knew I had asked Al to remain in Oakland. He had deliberately countermanded my order.

Al agreed. I turned to Steve and asked him if that description represented the situation fairly.

"What's your point?" he said, smirking, relaxed, his head tilted to the side in a lordly gesture.

"Smack this out-of-line motherfucker, Bob!" Larry said.

Nobody moved, including Steve, until Bob's big hand stunned the side of his face. His head was tossed to the other side, Bob's hand wiping away his grin.

Simba and Al slid toward the arms of the couch at their respective ends, isolating Steve.

"I asked you if that was true," I continued, sitting forward on a small wooden chair directly in front of him, my legs crossed and with a cigarette in my hand. Larry was standing next to me.

"The only reason you're doing this is because I kicked your ass . . . Man, this is some personal bullshit," he said, appealing to Larry.

"Answer the question, Brother," Larry said, eyeing Big Bob.

"Look, man," he continued, ignoring me for Larry, "Huey made me a don. I told you that. I don't take orders from her, and my people don't take orders from her."

"And I told you then," Larry said, with a tight jaw, "and I'm telling you now, that you take orders from the Central Committee, motherfucker!"

"Naw, man. She knows different! She knows Huey told me to run my thing on my own, and . . ."

"Hold it!" I said, glaring at him.

He threw up his hands in exasperation. "Aw, man, I can't deal with this. It's personal. Can't you see that?!"

"I do *not* accept this attitude, Larry," I said. "If this Brother doesn't want to answer my questions, I'm finished talking."

A round of shells was forced into the chambers of the shotguns. Perkins and Big Bob moved forward from their places in the room toward Steve. Simba and Al leaned farther away from him. Steve looked ready to capitulate.

"You know, if you keep it up, motherfucker," I said to him, "you won't have any operation at all! This is one party—can you understand that—one party! All of it—aboveground *and* underground—is run by the Central Committee.

"I am the leading member of this party, and if I tell you or your daddy to come to Oakland, to stay in Oakland, to live and fucking die in Oakland, you will do it, or you will be gone from this party! Is that clear enough?! Now I'm going to ask you one more time. Did you tell Al to get back to L.A., and fuck what I said?"

He threw up his hands again.

"Brother, are you going to answer or not?" Larry said, his eyes on fire, his right hand reaching behind his back for his pistol.

"Come on, man, you know this is ridiculous . . . Call Huey. Yeah, that's it! Call the Servant. I know you can reach him. Ask him, man. He'll tell you. I'm not lying." His voice was quieter now.

If I had mentioned Steve's name to Huey at that moment, he would not have immediately recognized it. Huey did not know most of the members of the party by name or face, and he had made a particular effort to avoid knowing any of those in the underground.

While Huey appreciated the underground, he feared being too close to them, for a number of good reasons. He had developed his own special security forces and left the underground alone as a necessary evil. They could do whatever they wanted, provided nothing they did reflected detrimentally on the party or was in conflict with the party's orders. They could do what they willed until he called on them. That had allowed Steve tyrannical reign over his band. On one of the few occasions Steve had been called to Oakland, I was sure Huey had casually agreed that he could refer to himself however he liked. I was just as sure that Steve understood that that did not exclude him from the discipline of the party, because he always jumped when Huey called.

"We're not calling anybody right now," I responded coldly. "Right now, I'm going to give you an opportunity to apologize, and to acknowledge the leadership of this party—"

"You mean, to say I'm sorry I kicked your ass," he interrupted.

"I'm through, Larry," I said, getting up from my chair, scraping it along the floor with my foot as I rose.

Big Bob reached over, lifted Steve from the couch, and slammed his solid body to the floor. Simba and Al jumped up, only to be commanded by shotgun to sit down again. I moved to the side of the room as the coffee table was being taken out of the way.

Four men were upon him now. Larry stood icily by, supervising every blow. Steve struggled for survival under the many feet stomping him. Drawing out a hunting knife hidden in his boots, he only encouraged the disciplinarians. Their punishment became unmerciful. When he tried to protect his body by taking the fetal position, his head became the object of their feet. The floor was rumbling, as though a platoon of pneumatic drills were breaking through its foundation. Blood was everywhere. Steve's face disappeared.

The Alameda County Central Labor Council endorsement was the one I wanted most. The labor vote represented the majority of people in the Oakland electorate, black, white, or other. Historically, union workers voted in a block according to the recommendations of their union leaders. As an umbrella organization composed of twenty-one major labor unions, the Alameda County Central Labor Council was the key to the labor vote. Repeatedly, only candidates endorsed by the council had won elections in Oakland, which was the hub of Alameda County.

The rumors swirling around my candidacy did not disturb the president of the council. He was a man toughened on the docks of Oakland when labor bosses were carving out union territory with harsh measures. As head of the council, he reputedly determined the member unions' endorsements for electoral candidates. True or not, a winning candidate always felt a duty to him and his council.

As I entered the council's meeting room, the president greeted me effusively and showed me to a seat at the head of the long conference table. Each council member asked a prepared question about my position on various issues affecting labor. I showed them the depth of my personal commitment to labor by recalling my mother's painful experiences, through which she evolved to become a union organizer for pressers in clothing factories. The council members nodded their heads and spoke of their own memories of the hard old days.

Within a short time, I received the council's endorsement. I saw that endorsement as more than a campaign victory: it placed the party in an alliance with organized labor. However loose, that alliance was a medium to synthesize the interests of the black men and women in organized labor with those of the black working poor—domestic workers and itinerant and part-time laborers— who were the heart of our constituency. The endorsement seemed to signal that the working-class backbone of the Oakland electorate could join forces with Oakland's poor underclasses.

The council's endorsement was, I knew, a severe blow to the upper-class Republicans. They had always been able to rely on the council to slide their candidates into office. By supporting my candidacy, the council had shifted the very foundation of Oakland politics.

The others fell in line. I won the endorsement of the United Auto Workers (UAW). An influential number of the automobile workers were black men who liked the idea of the Black Panther Party. Indeed, the local tended to be more progressive than other unions, but they had shied away from the party in the past. My candidacy seemed to offer them a chance to express their radicalism. In addition, it seemed to me that they genuinely liked what I had to say, particularly when I responded to their query as to what I would do as head of the UAW.

I told them I would call for an immediate halt to automobile production in the United States. No cars would be manufactured until each auto maker had contracted for a minimum, twenty-year income guarantee to all its current workers as a safeguard against an inevitable future of massive labor reduction. The crux of what

I told them was based on Huey's intercommunalism theory, relating to the rapid growth of American technology and specifically to the fact that a car could be manufactured from start to finish without human hands.

An automobile manufacturer could now produce a car through robotics, I asserted. The manufacturer's dilemma was that although he could make a million cars with very little labor cost, his supply of cars would overwhelm a diminished demand. The elimination of automobile workers and their consumer dollars would cause a domino effect in the entire marketplace, triggering further unemployment. There would be fewer and fewer car consumers. Thus, the American automobile worker was worth his weight in labor, as a consumer of automobiles and other products.

It was, however, only a matter of time before the millions in the so-called developing world would have both the desire and the means to purchase automobiles. Those markets would be developed soon through World Bank and North American bank loans. When those markets were opened, the American automobile worker's purchasing power would become insignificant. Thus, I concluded, American automobile workers should strike now, while their consumer dollars still mattered. The UAW immediately endorsed my candidacy and made a financial contribution to my campaign.

Then came the surprising simultaneous endorsements of the United Farm Workers (UFW) and the Teamsters. UFW president Cesar Chavez and the UFW had long been friends of the party. Though Chavez led a nonviolent movement, the farmworkers had been victims of violent beatings, even shootings. Attacks on them were made with clubs and guns supplied by California's landed gentry and agri-industrial corporations. They were wielded by members of the Teamsters Union.

Theirs was a horrible war. The outcome of it would determine on whose interests the California sun would shine, a sun that produced the greatest agricultural output in the United States. It was a war which left both unions outside the Alameda County Central Labor Council. The Black Panther Party had unequivocally taken sides with the UFW. Chavez's support of my candidacy, then, was natural. What was stupefying was my receipt of the Teamsters' endorsement.

I had made only a token effort in seeking Teamster support. It was not merely their assaults on the UFW; I felt the Teamsters were the element of the American labor movement that was slipping into the clothing of the exploitative businessmen they were supposed to be challenging. I knew, too, that if Teamsters thought about Black Panthers at all, it was certainly not favorably.

Thus, I saw my appearance at the union's candidate selection meeting as a pro forma exercise. I made a few uninspired statements about my positions on organized labor. I acknowledged that I was certainly more of a Black Panther than a Democrat, and tossed out my now-standard line that the Democrats would become Panthers before Panthers became Democrats. After that, I walked away.

Suddenly, a big fellow from the local of the International Brotherhood of Teamsters was in my campaign office, pledging their endorsement, along with a financial contribution and workers for Election Day. I swallowed my surprise with a simple thank-you. Then I arranged our joint press conference.

Thereafter, I received the support of every elected Democrat in the area, including the party's longtime friend Congressman Ron Dellums and the influential California assemblyman Willie Brown. Then came the endorsements of middle-class professional and business organizations, among them the massive teachers' union and the black lawyers' association. The most astounding was the support of Cal-Pac. Cal-Pac was the organization of black liquor-store owners that had been at odds with the party for so long, due to our boycott of the stores of one of its leaders—Bill Boyett. Boyett himself actually joined me in a press conference to announce his organization's support of my candidacy.

During the crescendo of the campaign, spring arrived. The memory of my cocaine trial and the Betty Van Patter business had vanished with winter. I was looking like a winner.

My image or voice was constantly on television or radio, in advertisements and interviews. Billboards of the "Elect Elaine" campaign were everywhere. People were sporting my campaign buttons all over Oakland, their cars flashing campaign bumper stickers. Everywhere, I reminded voters that my campaign represented a new Oakland, a more egalitarian Oakland, an Oakland that would share its reservoir of wealth.

By Election Day, I stood as potentially the first non-Republican to be elected in Oakland since World War II, and the first black woman ever elected.

◄ ►

People were sobbing openly in my campaign headquarters. I was losing the election. Thousands had assembled in our downtown Oakland campaign offices to celebrate the moment the spirit of the people would prevail. Their chagrin deepened as it appeared that that moment would not come.

That was why, I presumed, they barely took notice of the details of the results: I had garnered 44 percent of the vote. That was only 6 percent short of forcing a runoff election with the opposing Republican. He had received *under* 51 percent of the vote—the balance having gone to write-in candidates. As the sense of defeat deepened at our election party, I was seized with elation. It *could* be done in five years.

That 44 percent was the sign of a new force in Oakland. Forty-four percent was a force to be reckoned with. It was a force that had rocked the city's power base. It positioned working people, poor people, and people of color on one side and the capitalist constituency on the other. Within five years, the equilibrium could be tilted.

As I embraced campaign workers, friends, and party comrades milling about the headquarters late into the night, I realized they actually did not see what we had done. Within five years, Oakland could become a base for black liberation. Within ten years, Oakland could become a base for revolution.

Oakland was not Detroit. Detroit was a city where the dominant black and working population had been economically abandoned. Detroit's economy had been dismantled and moved to the hinterlands by frightened whites fleeing from "black domination." Oakland was certainly not Newark, where blacks had prevailed in a fierce fight with racist Italians a few years before, only to inherit a city in the red. Oakland was not Washington, D.C., that nebulous geopolitical entity in which the majority black population could see but not touch the power.

Oakland was a city in which the near-majority black population had something to seize. Oakland had a durable economic base, one that was tied immutably to the city government. It had the port of Oakland.

The capitalist club in Oakland had revolutionized the port with new technology. It was one of a handful in the world that were fully containerized. Containerization provided for large cargo containers to be transferred directly from shipboard to rail. Those containers, the size of railway cars, could be shipped untouched to their final destinations. That allowed for a freer flow of trade. It permitted liberal interpretations of tariff regulations, favoring not only shippers and transport companies but also importers, exporters, suppliers, and manufacturers.

In addition, Oakland's port enjoyed a strategic location. It furnished access from the Pacific Ocean to all of America, and from all of America to the other side of the Pacific. As a result of the combination of containerization and natural position, the volume of Oakland's port business had increased phenomenally. It had become the second largest port in the world.

The port's business pumped billions of annual dollars into Oakland's economy, a euphemism for Oakland's private business community. That was why Oakland's economy was so strong. But to me the most significant aspect of Oakland's port was that it could never be relocated or sold to private interests. It was organically and legally part of the city of Oakland. And that was why no right-thinking capitalist even contemplated abandoning Oakland, no matter how many angry natives squatted there.

Now Oakland was a city in which new tides were rising. It was a city whose apparatus I felt the party could control by the end of the next five years.

In bed that election night, my mind awash with myriad ideas, I made a note to call Tony Kline. He would be busy with his duties as legal affairs secretary. Among those duties was recommending candidates for judicial appointments. Under the law, all municipal, superior, appellate, and supreme court judges, other than those elected under extraordinary circumstances, were appointed by the governor. In practice, the governor did not personally screen or review applicants. That was left to the legal affairs secretary.

I was wondering how many judicial slots were open in Alameda County and Oakland. I was thinking about a 44 percent voting base, about organized labor, about the port. I really needed to see Tony, I thought, as I drifted into sleep buoyed by dreams of the future.

CHAPTER 18

ALPHA AND OMEGA

I WOULD SEE HUEY IN TWO DAYS, the Cubans had said on my arrival in Havana. I was ambivalent about that. I was angry, too, about Huey's marriage to Gwen. It reawakened the pain of my father's rejection and of all the years of wanting men who never wanted me.

During my tour of revolutionary memorials the next morning, I began writing a script of bitter words for my first meeting with Huey. I was not thinking about how Fulgencio Batista y Zaldívar, former Cuban president, had been driven from his palace. I had no interest in the memorabilia of valor that were shown to me. I listened dispassionately to my Cuban-American Friendship Committee guide's depiction of the Cubans' successful defense against the 1961 U.S. attack on the Bay of Pigs. I was feeling sorry for myself, recalling Huey's weak explanation over the telephone about the "necessity" of marrying Gwen.

I spent the day wallowing in my tantrum, reviving my old desire to be his, to belong to him like a whore; ready to renounce my instincts to be a free being, to violate my pledge to be a feminist pillar—all over a band of gold. I could not stop hating his marriage to Gwen. I vowed to demean her, and to leave him to rot in the interiors of the lush island.

Bill Brent's story was instructive, I thought, during dinner the second night in Havana. I had not met him before. He was a member of the party from San Francisco. A huge, rugged man, Brent had spent some time in San Quentin prison, had later been involved in a police-Panther shoot-out in San Francisco, and after that had slipped through police nets and made his way to Cuba by hijacking an airplane.

The water pressure had been shut down in the area for several days, Bill told me when I asked to use the toilet in his two-room flat. As we sat down to dinner at what resembled a small card table, he explained that the weekly meat ration had been reduced. The meat was, in any event, a meager complement to the sticky rice his woman friend had cooked. Bill laughed about the various inconveniences. It was home now, he said simply.

Bill's story shattered the illusions harbored by criminals-cum-revolutionaries who sought out Havana with ideas of building private little armies to make ten thousand private assaults. Bill, with his impulses of revolutionary zeal, had not been welcome. Like the other hijackers landing on the shores of the island, Bill had been taken immediately to a jail cell.

There had been no light or water. Laughing in retrospect, he told how he had longed for the days and nights in San Quentin, for the arguments with guards over television hours or library books. There had not even been a piece of paper or the hope of a book in Havana. Havana was a place where carrying a knife was punished with five years in prison, where "fools" were always suspect, and where hijackers were automatically imprisoned, presumed to be pigs until proven otherwise.

After eighteen months in prison, Bill had been offered an opportunity to work in the sugarcane fields. Even his strapping body, he told me, had buckled under the hardship of the sunup-to-sundown cane-cutting with a giant machete, his fingers and palms bleeding and stinging with his own salty sweat. Nevertheless, he had worked like a mule, at the same time force-feeding himself Spanish, and had earned a chance to go to the university. Now he had become a trusted Cubano and was a member of the Cuban-American Friendship Committee.

Meat rations and faulty sewage systems were far better than life in his unheated cell and in the cane fields. It was all far better than life as a black man in America, he added.

He was happy there with his white American woman, who had joined him for life. Freedom meant more than comfort, and love was everything. He sent his regards to Huey, whom I would see the next day.

◄ ►

Huey would be uninterested, I thought, jolting along the roads to Santa Clara with my Cuban comrade in a fifties automobile. He would not really care about my ordeal in Jamaica, where I had had to stow in my underpants the $10,000 in cash he had commanded I bring to him, because nobody could explain its purpose in Jamaica, much less in Cuba. He would not want to hear about how I had gotten a wholesale price for the Patek Philippe gold watch he had insisted he needed, just so he could arrive on time to labor in a sweatshop—from which he had now resigned. He would just want to wear the new watch, try on the leather pants and silk shirts I had also brought, and look through the pornographic magazines I had hidden—the Cubans being very puritanical about sex. Huey would probably not even thank me for dragging those ten suitcases and two trunks of luxury items through two customs checkpoints. That was what I was thinking, riding through the Cuban countryside.

After a few hours, we arrived in Santa Clara, at what would be my housing for approximately the next month. Los Indios Hotel was a garden complex of thatch-roofed chambers, resembling tepees collected in an Indian village. I thankfully noted that there was a giant air conditioner in my room, which was partitioned by a half wall, on the other side of which was a tiled bathroom with a shower. It was far more comfortable than my hotel room in Havana. I turned on the straw-shaded bedside lamp, from which an enormous *cucaracha* leaped onto my hand.

I rummaged around in the trunks and plucked out one of the numerous cassette tapes and the small tape player I had brought Huey. Stevie Wonder sang me to sleep:

> You know, my papa disapproved it
> My mama "boo-hooed" it
> But I told them time and time again . . .
> I was made to love her
> Worship and adore her
> Yeah, yeah, yeah. . . .

Gwen would not be joining us, Huey said, his telephone voice waking me. She was working. He was not. He was simply the Cubans' guest now, reluctantly exiled, and somewhat reluctantly provided for as a comrade-in-arms.

He arrived still beautiful. His face was bronze, with a reddish glow. His striking eyes were clear, framed by the strong dark eyebrows. Entering my room at nine in the morning, he kissed me with an open mouth. He pressed me to his sinewy chest, with arms that subjugated me as in the beginning, when arms were all that mattered. So many telephone conversations had not held the connection. We had been separated and isolated for a very long time. I forfeited my lines and forgot everything else.

"You *are* the other part of me," he whispered, releasing me, looking into my eyes. "We'll die together, you know. I feel that. You'll go down with me, or I'll go down with you. It's impossible otherwise. We're one."

He held me at arm's length to look at me fully. I was not sure I would die with Huey. I was sure I would continue to live by him and love him.

We walked outside, arms locked, into the Cuban sunshine, among the gardens of Los Indios. It was a resort reserved for committed socialists. A circular, thatch-roofed white bar was an island in the center of the complex, facing a large swimming pool. There was a bartender on duty, and a few swimmers were in the pool. We plopped onto the barstools with the excited anticipation of lovers who had not yet made love.

Huey ordered a double crème de menthe on ice and an oyster cocktail. I drank a Bloody Mary. We had the whole day before us.

"How are the oysters?" the bartender asked.

"*Mejor*," Huey responded, with what turned out to be one of the only two or three Spanish words he had decided to learn.

"*May-hor* means the best," he explained to me. "I love to say it, because I always think: Whose whore? And answer: You know, *my* whore!" He pinched my backside.

We laughed about everything in the entire world, it seemed, and drank many more crème de menthes and Bloody Marys. The evening came suddenly. Now we would face Gwen.

Her beautiful brown face was thinner, but her expression was patient, as always. She had arrived home only seconds before us, she said. Their apartment was in a collection of two-story stone structures built for middle-level members of the governing socialist party. The apartments were located in a cul-de-sac, and were not unlike upgraded U.S. government housing. Despite the fact that it was small and sparse, their apartment was, by Santa Clara standards, quite luxurious, with two bedrooms, a bathroom and shower, and a kitchen that contained a working refrigerator. More important to me, it was theirs.

Gwen kissed me when I entered the apartment and showed

me her "trunk," where she kept her "wedding dress." She would have cooked a chicken, except that Huey had said we would be eating at a restaurant. The $10,000 I had brought would buy a lot in their new community.

Their arrival had been calamitous, Gwen said with a laugh. She had had to swim to the Havana shore, according to their excited storytelling. They jovially filled in each other's sentences as she changed clothes. Their boat had capsized, they sang out in unison from different rooms.

"I challenged death with a deep breath in the ocean, but Gwen dragged me to shore," Huey said overdramatically, and with too much love, I thought. But it was their story. I was out of the storm of their landing, and out of their loving.

Gwen seemed very fragile, though, as she told me about her life there. She had gotten a job as an English tutor for nurses and doctors at the local hospital; after which her routine was to return home and cook dinner. She was also muddling her way through Spanish lessons. Her children—whom Huey had unofficially adopted—had arrived sometime during that year and become quickly fluent in Spanish.

Listening to her, I began to contemplate what I lacked. She could certainly cook well, I thought childishly. She accepted Huey on a day-to-day basis, which I knew was a chore, at best. Gwen was a "real" woman. She *was* a woman, and *his* woman. I, on the other hand, was a politico, a partner, a comrade, notably with "pussy," which was sometimes relevant. It was maddening that my new eyes could not stop looking back.

In the restaurant, Gwen's children, Ronnie and Jessica, ten and eight, ordered our food in the clipped Spanish they had absorbed from their Cuban playmates. The menu offered mainly pork, some chicken dishes, no green vegetables. The Cubans' assiduous farm experiments had not reinvigorated the sugar-sterilized fields. Even fisheries were nonproductive. We ate fat-laden pork chops and drank *mucha cerveza* (beer), and laughed with relief that we were all present and accounted for.

We took the children for the creamiest vanilla ice cream, untainted by chemical agents. As we meandered through Santa Clara's lively streets, we were carefree, making our amends with each other and with life.

"An-gel-a Davis! An-gel-a Davis!" the children called out to Gwen. "An-gel-a Davis!" they called, as we strolled along unpaved walkways and under Spanish archways. Her large Afro reminded the Cuban children of the only black American woman about whom they had been told.

Huey suddenly erupted with a ridiculous show. He shooed away the innocently excited boys and girls following us, who wanted to touch Gwen's hair. In harsh, mean words, he told them to back off, as though they understood English, as though they understood the street rage he harbored.

As Gwen and I tried to quiet his shrieking at the children, I saw an apparition. I saw it with a clarity that astounded me. I had heard its growl in North Philadelphia, in the exchanges of gang members, where one member would threaten to stab another.

Whatchou lookin' at, motherfucker?

It must be yo' mama's ass 'cause it's black and shiny.

I had felt its breath there, when brother had killed brother and sister had assaulted sister. I had sensed its fingers clutching at brothers and sisters in West Oakland, and in Detroit, and in Watts, and on Chicago's West Side, and in all the other urban corners into which our lives and our ravaged hopes had been stuffed. It had set off a thousand family battles over such trivialities as skin that was too light or too dark, or the wearing of the wrong color, or the wrong type of coat or the wrong attitude.

The urban ghettos of America had imposed something more severe than poverty. They did more than stamp out African roots and history and a sense of community in Africans lost in America. The ghetto battered and defiled the very humanity of its inmates, driven mad by the mirage of America's promise sparkling just beyond impenetrable barriers.

Watching Huey challenge and taunt what had become a sizable crowd of Cuban teenagers, I saw the personification of this madness. Huey knew this monster. He hated it. Yet he had been unable to rearrange the genetics of the ghetto which had been socialized into his chromosomes. Gwen and I simply tried to exorcise the spell.

He laughed at us on the return to my room. It was the laugh of "the Nigger" who tells his street partners that if somebody had not stopped him, he would have "killed that motherfucker"—the one who laughed at him.

When they left me alone, I clicked on the tape I would keep until I left: "*I was made to love [him] / Worship and adore [him] / Yeah, yeah, yeah. . . .*"

◀ ▶

Sometime in the next days, Huey and I violated the beer bar that was for men only. We talked about Kathleen Smith.

She had died after six months in a coma. Exile might be permanent now. There was no statute of limitations on Huey's new charge of murder. Her death punished him in more ways than that.

"I don't even know her face," he said quietly in the beer bistro.

The ghetto snatches most lives, I wanted to say, holding his hand.

"Our investigator, David Feccheimer, Hal Lipset's man, seems to be very good," I reported brightly. "He's discovered some important things about the shooting." It was my attempt to be comforting.

"For example," I said to a blank face, "the so-called eyewitness, Crystal Gray, was not only Smith's pimp and lover, she's blind in one eye and she's a heroin addict. She'll never stand up to cross-examination."

He was not even looking at me.

"She's very dirty," I continued. "Gray has a thousand names, and a bunch of penny-ante criminal charges the prosecutor has recently wiped off the books. But we'll know more about the whole thing soon. There's a man in it, some nigger who seems to be connected to the niggers who put the contract out on you."

"I don't give a shit. I don't want to hear about it. You deal with it." He closed the subject.

He touched his new gold watch. "I'm not learning any Spanish. I'm coming home. Make it possible. That's all."

There were more days of crème de menthes and sometimes Triple Secs—and no cocaine at all in Cuba. I had tried the white powder once, in the early days before it became his habit. My heart had pounded, and the hollows inside my head, between my eyebrows and forehead, had burned. Mostly, I had been scared, I remembered, watching him drink away those days.

We cashed in more U.S. money and went to a beach resort one day. The children were in school, and Gwen was working.

"Castro won't see me," he complained. "I don't know who that son-of-a-bitch thinks he is. I've been here a whole year. I finally told them I don't give a fuck. I'm leaving this place. That's why they don't mess with me. They know I don't want to do a damn thing here but leave—as soon as you make it right."

"I'm working hard, Huey. You know that," I responded, unsure of my sincerity.

"They don't have jack shit here," he continued, looking around. "And they're trying to bring in tourists. It's stupid. Whatever they get from tourism won't be worth it. Castro won't be able to keep 'em down in the sugar fields after they see the Parisians."

He had a point, I thought in passing. The outsiders would bring the Cubans *muchos dineros*, but they would also bring capitalist cupidity.

"In Havana," I noted, "I gave my natural comb to a maid in the hotel, and she damn near got down on her knees to thank me for that low-grade piece of plastic I had bought for about ninety-eight cents."

"You gotta watch these motherfuckers," he said, eyeing his new watch, and then a Cuban eyeing him. "They want shit and they don't have it. The more they see, the more they want . . . Hey! Keep your eyes off my watch!" he suddenly shouted to the man, who did not understand.

"You better calm down, Huey, before they arrest you."

"I've been arrested before."

"Not in Cuba. Ask Bill Brent."

"Then I hope he keeps away from me," he said excitedly of the Cuban.

"Or what? You'll kick his ass here in Santa Clara and go to the Havana Soul Breaker, where even the rats don't speak English and Charlie Garry can't get to you, much less get you out."

He was annoying, I thought, presenting his "street nigger" to men who had stood up to CIA assaults. Strangely, he calmed down. But I was worried about his explosiveness. Mostly, I was worried about the prospect of his returning with it.

"Huey, you know I can't predict how long it will be before we settle the Smith investigation," I blurted out. "I'm not sure when it will be right . . . Until then, you've *got* to make this work."

"I'm not working," he answered, purposely misunderstanding.

"So you're going to drink your way—and fight your way—through the next two years or so?" I offered bluntly, though cautiously.

"That's what you think? I'll be here two more years? Bullshit! I have to get back."

"And do what? Go to prison? . . . Your party's well. Ride it out," I said, wondering whether my urging was necessary for him or for me.

"All right, all right. I don't want to talk about it . . . Why don't you tell me about what's-his-name," he said, ordering another round from the formally dressed waiter. "Tell me about the nigger you told me was a problem that you'd resolved."

"You mean Steve from L.A.?"

"Whoever."

"It was a simple matter of having to establish order. You know about that; you left me without it. Steve wanted to challenge me to a duel, saying you made him a 'don,' whatever that was supposed to mean."

"You know," he said, nearly spitting out a swallow of his Triple Sec onto our table. "I think I might have told him some shit like that." He laughed.

"I cannot believe you!" I said, as to a child. "If it hadn't been for Larry, that fool would've run with that and taken over *your* party. Or destroyed it. Did you consider that?"

"But you dealt with it. That's why I hired you." He laughed again. "So, what'd you do? Give him the whip?"

"No. I sent him to the hospital with a variety of broken bones and a very bloody face. Actually, he never made it to the hospital. He was so scared the Brothers driving him there were going to dump him somewhere along the way with a few bullets in his head, he jumped out of the car in the middle of the street and ran away. We haven't seen the motherfucker since."

"Looks like you settled that old score." he said with a conspiratorial smile.

"Don't put that on me. It was business, that's all. All in the name of saving your party. The Brothers out of L.A. understood the problem. Ricardo even pushed for it. They knew his ass."

"Relax. . . . I really don't care why you did it. You did it. That's enough. We've got the same blood."

I resented his implications, though I knew the truth was somewhere in between.

Later that night, he said good night for an hour, coming inside to kiss me ferociously. He wanted guarantees, I thought; he wanted to taste and touch his ticket back home.

◄ ►

On another of his long-goodbye nights, I asked him, "Why did you marry her?"

He pushed me away from him and leaned against the door of my room. "Because she's got some good pussy." He smiled.

"It's not a funny question," I retorted, tears welling in my eyes.

"You can't be serious. You know Gwen is my 'little hot dog.' And I *need* a wife. Matter of fact, *you* need a wife. Think about it. If we both had wives, we could be lovers forever."

His flippancy hurt me. He told me how he had thought of getting married in Mexico while waiting for the Cubans to authorize his entry. He suggested Mexican marriages did not matter anyway. Besides, he finished, he did it mainly because he thought it would increase his credibility to his hosts; how the strict socialists would give him better treatment if he were legitimized by a wife and family—her children that had become his children.

"Wait a minute," he interrupted himself, now propped up on my bed. The generator blew out for a few seconds and we were in the dark.

"Don't you *have* a wife?" he whispered. "Aren't you giving Larry some pussy—you must think I can't read between the telephone lines."

The lights returned.

"That's not an issue. If it wasn't for Larry, you wouldn't have anything left. He's cleaning up the streets and keeping all the assholes out of my face."

"So you say that to say what? You love him?"

"In many ways, I do," I said hesitatingly.

"I don't care who you think you love. You're still mine," he said, beckoning me with cocksure, open arms.

I remained still for a minute and then moved to the edge of the bed. He pulled me down to him.

"You're mine, I said, even if you fuck the whole world. Accept it. The fact is, I need Gwen. She's good to me—'better than I been to myself,'" he added, quoting the old blues line with a certain smile. "You need Larry. What the hell. We need Gwen and we need Larry. It's *our* party."

He left me wanting, and he knew it. I was still bonded to him, my other self, my male self, with whom I was united in a place not tainted by the conflicts of men, or by time.

◄ ►

We spent the days drinking and going over events since his departure, filling in the blanks left in our telephone conversations.

"So Tony Kline does what now, exactly?" he asked during one of those long days of walking and wading through a variety of nearby bars.

"I told you: he appoints judges, among other things. Titularly, he's the legal affairs secretary to the governor, which means he coordinates all the legal matters that fall under the governor's direct jurisdiction. So, he appoints judges and represents the state in things like extradition, and in relations with other states and the federal government. He also deals with other legal departments of the state, such as your favorite: the Department of Corrections. Since Tony and Jerry have been in, the world is just a better goddamned place.

"Jerry Brown knows he's the big chief over the fifth largest economy in the world. And he knows California's economy is so strong, it's an independent little kingdom. From where I'm sitting," I asserted, "Jerry seems to be trying to use his position to institute a better *world*."

"He's become some sort of socialist?"

"Not exactly—but I'll give you an example. Tony, at Jerry's behest, is battling the federal government to disallow its leasing of three miles of Pacific Ocean off California's shore for the drilling of oil. In other words, he's working to stop the president and Standard Oil from stealing the oil under California's ocean and from screwing up the coastline. Tony has them entangled in a thousand environmental webs."

"I love it! That's right, Tony, keep their hands off *our* port."

We found ourselves near a pleasant-looking restaurant and decided to have lunch. It was late in the day and we were virtually alone there, in an atrium that seemed carved for lovers. It was an old and beautiful place with floors and walls of handmade tiles.

"Go on," he urged when we sat down to eat.

"There're a million things happening on the Kline-Brown front, a little note about which I'm sure you'll enjoy. Brown is a former Jesuit, you know. His Jesuit studies apparently left him overly analytical about everything. I've talked with him enough about his brave new society ideas to know he won't make the smallest decision without weighing fifty million possible outcomes. The point is, with such a mind, he fell under the charm of one of your very best friends. Your personal San Francisco Zen master."

"Richard Baker? You're kidding."

"Not at all. Brown sees merit in the path to sudden enlightenment, and has become something of a follower of Richard. He and Kline and their pack often mull over their thoughts at the old Zen Center. In fact, Jerry's becoming known as the 'Zen governor.' "

"No shit. Give me a rest."

"If you think that's too much, let's talk about Kline's appointments to the bench. He's put Ben Travis on the Alameda Superior Court. You know, *our* John George's law partner."

"Who else?"

"Well, it's only just begun, but there's also Clinton White, now a Superior Court judge in San Francisco. Every vacancy in the state is being filled with black men, women, or somebody of color. White men need not apply, unless they're like Tony's first appointment to the municipal court bench in Oakland, Rod Duncan, who's married to a black woman *and* who endorsed me for City Council."

"When do I come home?"

"Not so fast, kemosabe. There's still the big bad FBI. I mean I just found out the FBI has ordered the guards where I'm living to turn over a weekly list of the car license numbers of all my visitors. They're still on us like white on rice, even if they have become more sophisticated."

"So have we, apparently."

We nearly made love that day, except for our unwritten rule.

"What do you think about the possibility of receiving diplomatic pouches from, say—oh, let's see—North Korea, through our port, once it's ours?" Huey asked as we sat down in another bar on another day.

What he was proposing was frightening to me. I looked around to see if anybody had heard him, as though anybody hearing would understand.

"With the port tied to the city government in Oakland," he went on, "it's possible for us to control the port by controlling the city—including the containers. Think about it, *diplomatic* containers are *never* opened."

"Except that the North Koreans have no diplomatic relations with the U.S."

"They have with China. And China does with our neighbor to the north. I'd love to have my hands on a couple of thousand AK-47's."

We both looked shocked at the incredible possibilities, which did not seem fantastic at that moment.

"Anyway," he said, "it's a bright picture you paint. But where's the dirty stuff?"

"I suppose the dirtiest stuff has to do with a new band of junior-flip but well-armed drug dealers."

"Somebody's got some drugs?"

"It's serious, Huey. Cocaine in Oakland is cheap now, no longer the drug of choice reserved for the rich and famous. It's coming into Oakland at low prices from I don't know where. But can you imagine a white boy in a Rolls riding through the Projects? Well, it's happening. Big-time dealers are establishing turf in Oakland through the use of upstart local distributors.

"Some women from the East Oakland projects—too close to our school for comfort—came to tell me what was happening. The white boys are rolling in there and the youngbloods are scrambling for the distribution. It's becoming a wide-open business, though nobody speaks about it.

"It seems to be limited for now to those projects because even the pigs don't fuck around in there, though you know they're in the shit on the outside. The system is almost in place. A welfare mother will be given, say, fifty dollars a day to hold a significant quantity of cocaine in her apartment. What welfare mother can resist fifty unreported bucks a day? Since damn near everybody in the Projects is a mother on welfare, that's several hundred places to stash the stuff.

"The only thing they have to do is vow to keep visitors out of their safe houses unless they have clearance from the controlling dealers. One woman had an unauthorized visit from her brother one day and was later publicly—can you believe it?—*publicly* stomped by the little dealers for it. They broke her pelvic bone. After a few more similar examples, everyone was in line. So nobody speaks, and nearly everybody participates. Except the ladies who came to me personally at the school to ask for our help."

"Wait a minute, wait a minute. Who *are* these niggers anyway? And *how* do some niggers get that much stuff into Oakland?"

"I don't know all of that now. Larry sent Simba with his Vietnam vet reconnaissance skills to head a squad to go inside to review the situation. Young niggers—sixteen and seventeen years old—were perched on the rooftops with automatic rifles, with scopes yet! Guarding the two entrances to that six-square block of a shithole. They had the nerve to ask Simba and his squad what their business was."

"Aw no, motherfuckers!" Huey exclaimed. "They don't ask us. *We* ask the questions. *We* make the rules in Oakland!"

"Exactly. So, within that week, I held a press conference in the community center that is right in the middle of the Projects. Larry stationed several squads in there to emphasize the point. I announced that the Black Panther Party was initiating a *daily* food giveaway program right there in the most impoverished corner of Oakland. The mothers who joined me at the press conference squeezed my hand under the table afterward. So we have people in the middle of the shit every day."

"It's not enough."

"I know."

Gwen always came dressed beautifully for dinner, which we ate together in a restaurant. She could transform some simple cotton thing into a classic ensemble. I was amazed at her.

Her face showed no worry or weariness, despite the hardships of her life with Huey. I thought about the stone floors she washed by hand, having learned from the Cuban women how to give them a high gloss without polish. I recalled the scrub board she had shown me, on which she half-beat and washed their clothes, including towels and sheets, with something like Lava bar soap that could not issue one smidgen of suds. She had learned to pluck the feathers from chickens to make their dinner, she told me one day while she was boiling huge pots of drinking water. In addition to keeping Huey's house in order, she worked—a concept as foreign to Huey as Spanish would remain. *She* worked to keep their Cuban comrades satisfied that their "family" was participating in the revolution. And she allowed for me, in silence.

Sitting next to her, I caught the scent of one of the numerous bottles of cologne I had managed to transport there. Her hair was in place, framing her Grecian features, which were complemented with a bit of makeup. Her nails were perfectly filed, and lightly polished. She was talking to her children about minding their manners at the table. As I watched her, it occurred to me that she had banished the terrible confusion of life in exile and created something calming—which seemed to me charming at that moment. It was hard to remain competitive with her, I thought, despite her constant fondling of the gold band on her finger.

"Ronnie," she said to her son, in her high-pitched Chicago accent, "I would really like you to sit up at the table and finish your rice and beans . . . Well, Elaine," she said, turning to me, "you haven't really told us much about the school and how it's going . . . Ronnie and Jessica, wouldn't you like to hear about your comrades back in America?"

The children unresponsively played with a cat that was meandering in and out of the Los Indios restaurant. Huey gazed happily and possessively at the two of us women and distanced himself from the discussion with a few beers.

"The school's going quite well, Gwen," I said, speaking somewhat patronizingly to her. "I think you'd be interested in what we've done to its appearance," I said, becoming conscious of my tone.

Watching Huey appraising both of us as I spoke, I began to feel dizzy. If she was his woman, I was thinking, she was not mine. Whatever the relationship between him and her, or him and me, there was another deep relationship among us I had never acknowledged. It was between her and me. Gwen was my Sister.

"That is, Gwen," I started over, "we've made some improvements to the physical plant. And this has increased the value of the school phenomenally. For whatever that's worth in the final analysis."

"How many students are there now?" she asked.

"About two hundred, with four hundred on the waiting list."

"Incredible!"

"Who's handling the school again?" Huey asked.

"Ericka Huggins is the director. Regina Davis, out of Boston, handles the day-to-day administration of the classrooms, kitchen, children's needs, and everything else.

"We've really improved everything in the school," I continued, speaking directly to Gwen with my new appreciation of her. "The curriculum has been rewritten so that we now place children by ability, not by age. That is, we don't have grades anymore, only levels of classes, according to subject matter. This was Ericka's idea. So, one child can be in a fourth-level math class, for example, and at the same time in a first-level English or reading class. This has made it possible for us to guarantee that our students will graduate at about the standard ninth-grade level. In fact, the first graduating class since you left, Gwen, was skipped over the junior-high level. Ericka forced the board to test them and they were placed immediately in public high schools at twelve and thirteen years old."

"That's absolutely fabulous!" she responded. "It's like the Cuban schools, which are far superior to the public schools in the U.S. And there's a higher literacy rate here, too, even though, before Castro, ninety percent of the people were illiterate . . . But tell me about our school's interiors."

"My favorite touch," I said, echoing her enthusiasm, "is that every classroom is carpeted with thick, colorful wools, which makes the rooms very peaceful. And we've bought new dishes and bright-colored tablecloths for the dining-room tables. I had the concrete parking lot pulled up and replaced with grass, and enclosed by a redwood fence; it's a play and sports area now, kind of idyllic. In the auditorium, all the seats have been recovered, and we've installed professional sound and lighting systems. We've also bought a grand piano for the auditorium, for the kids' assemblies and weekly performances. They're really proud of their school. I want to buy the lot next door, to put in a swimming pool."

"So buy it," Huey intruded, his voice making both of our heads turn.

"Thank you, Your Generousness," I responded, immediately resuming my conversation with Gwen. "What I think we've finally created is an environment that is actually opening up the kids' minds and imaginations, despite all the anxieties they live with . . . Which reminds me about the English class I decided to teach myself . . .

"My class is considered special, because the ten- and eleven-year-olds in it were classified by the system as uneducable. I took it on because I wanted to personally prove that these children could learn to read and write. But the saddest thing was when I asked them to try to write something about the best and worst things that had ever happened to them. One boy struggled to write that the best moment in his life was when he stopped a man from beating up his mother."

Gwen's eyes became teary. I imagined the story touched something in her own history. She had lived pretty much on her own after the birth of her first child when she was fourteen.

"The thing is, Gwen, we might be trying to build a model

school, provide a *real* education to black kids, but right now, I think, we're mostly saving a bunch of lives . . .

"I mean, we've got a six-year-old girl whose entire right leg is marred by third-degree burns. She said her 'uncle' had dropped a pan of hot grease onto her leg—her whole leg? There's a nine-year-old boy who'd been shooting heroin into his mother's veins before school every morning. Three kids from one family came to us with no shoes—only thongs—and when we went to their house, we couldn't find a single toothbrush. One of my own student's back was imprinted with permanent welts from being beaten so much, which we discovered when we took her to the children's hospital for a checkup. A mother brought her two children to school one morning pleading for us to keep her kids because her crazy-ass husband was after all of them with his Vietnam-salvaged M-16."

Ronnie and Jessica had run outside to play. Gwen and Huey were still and silent as I spoke. It was hard to reckon with the fact that life for black children locked in America's ghettos had become worse than what any of us had ever experienced.

"How are we teaching them anything?" Gwen asked softly.

"I think by building this protected space for them, and keeping anybody from doing any more damage than has already been done. That seems to clear the way to teach them the skills.

"We have new buses to get them safely through the snake pits of their neighborhoods. They get breakfast, lunch, and dinner at school. We buy their books and school supplies. We take them for medical and dental checkups. The school is so much a part of their lives now that most of them are there even on weekends— to play and eat. Some kids are even spending the night with our Panther kids—in the dorms we're renovating. Also, we're buying new clothes for a lot of them. Joan and Norma set up a bunch of bullshit accounts at various department stores, under just as many names. When the credit under one name becomes bad, we simply switch."

They both chuckled.

"Finally," I told Gwen, "we're getting into their family life, trying to help with money, housing, and other problems. For instance, we had people on the school rooftops to look out for the fool with the M-16. He showed up after school. No M-16, but he had a handgun under his coat. The Brothers dealt with him and ordered his ass out of Oakland. We put the mother and her kids into a shelter for battered women."

"It may be more than we can continue to take on," Huey said heavy-heartedly.

"Actually, I don't think so," I told him. "It's working."

I turned back to Gwen. "Anyway, we're finding it *is* easy to teach the kids with all of that. Plus we've got the very best equipment, including computers, now."

"It's become like a private school," Gwen said, excited to find herself included in something larger than her life with Huey.

"This is exactly why I oppose busing," Huey said, musing aloud. "It's a diversionary tactic, which is why the Nelson Rockefellers support busing, not that one of their offspring will be run through a public school. Rockefellers are trained in private places, where they're taught to take over the world, while the rest of the suckers—niggers at the bottom—are trained to work for them— if you can get a job. So they created this busing game to keep us running around for years trying to be integrated into bullshit, and to keep all the poor whites from seeing the truth by making them think they have something to lose if blacks are in the same classrooms with them. The fact is, *no* child, black or white, in the American education maze is going to learn the truth. The ruling class has no intention of letting anybody in on its secrets, the true history of America or the real purpose of its mass education, to turn out good little soldier-workers to grease the wheels of capitalism."

The three of us walked outside to find the children, our arms linked together.

"I can't understand why all these Negroes think," Huey continued, "that busing has a goddamned thing to do with solving the black-child–white-doll identity problem. Are the capitalists going to desegregate school curriculums, wipe out poverty, eliminate ghettos, institute social *and* economic equality? Because that's what it's going to take for black children to find the value in themselves. Fuck no! *We* have to give our children a sense of their value. *We* have to create new institutions—like our school. Not bus our kids into a setup!"

All the Triple Secs in the world had not deadened the passion I saw reemerging.

Gwen and the children left us. Huey walked me back to my room.

"And they have the nerve enough to do studies on why so many black children grow up with so few skills," he said bitterly, closing the door to my room. "As if somebody can think growing up in the ghetto."

"You just grow up."

"Who said we grew up?"

I reflected on that. "I guess I really haven't . . . I'm still running around looking for Daddy," I said softly, surprising myself.

Letting a smile play across his thin lips, Huey said, "Why? You've got one now." He laughed and flipped himself onto the bed in my room. "Come to Papa."

The last days slipped away. The month was nearly over, and I would surely leave.

"There's still a lot to talk about. Let's not go to the bars today, Huey," I said when he arrived for our routine rendezvous. "Let's stay here."

"So you're ready to break your vow of chastity?"

"When will you stop making jokes when I'm serious?"

"When you learn to be a laughing Buddha." He sat down in the wicker armchair, the only chair in the room. "Okay. I hate to have cocktails before noon, anyway."

"Do I save the best for last?"

"You always do," he said, leaning back and closing his eyes, folding his muscular arms across his chest.

"What if I say that LEAA money is the best?"

"What's that," he said, eyes still closed.

"Stands for Law Enforcement Assistance Act. Congress created it to subsidize local police departments."

"Thompson submachine-gun funding."

"Precisely."

"What's that got to do with the party? Other than it gives the pigs more firepower to use on us."

"Well, operating under the corporate name we use for the school, we submitted a proposal to the Alameda County administrators of the local LEAA funding to get some of their money. Joan Kelley picked up on the game, theoretically open to any organization that could assist law enforcement. So we proposed a comprehensive juvenile crime *prevention* program for East Oakland

—which we identified as *the* highest crime area in America."

"America. That's deep." He smiled, opening his eyes.

"Our main competitors were a coalition of the Oakland PD, the Unified School District, and the Parks and Recreation Department. The county couldn't just dismiss our brilliant proposal, so they cleverly placed us among the leading contenders. They held a whittling-down meeting in a hotel near San Leandro."

"Whitesville."

"Joan and I showed up with about fifty teenagers from our teen program. All of them were looking surly, young Brothers with no shirts, reeking of Old English 800 and weed; young Sisters with big earrings, popping gum."

"Scared the shit out of them."

"The teens were beautiful. And they loved the theater of it. We introduced them as our target group, those we intended *diverting* from a life of crime."

"Sounds good to me."

"The Alameda County sheriff jumped up and said it was nothing but a Black Panther Party game. I resented that, with drama, and stated that I was there as executive director of our school board and a member of the crime-infested community in which neither the sheriff's department nor the police department had invested one dime of their previously granted LEAA money to preventing the problems of crime among our youth!"

"Right on!" he enthused.

"That's what our kids said, up on their feet stomping and whistling. We turned the place out *and* got all the money."

"Fantastic. So where else are you stealing money from?"

"We've got a few other funding proposals out under the same corporate name. We've already gotten some state money for the school. Of course, we're still getting donations from our friends. There's the Lamp Post. The rest we're doing the hard way, turning bad money into good. And Norma's great. Maintaining at least fifteen sets of perfect books . . .

"But I didn't get the money I really wanted. Thanks to Ruth Love, the new Negro superintendent of schools. After I met with *Ms.* Love, she toured the school. She told me we were doing a fine job and that she'd see what could be done."

"About what?"

"I wanted her to make the school an experimental arm of the Oakland School District, so we could get the almighty ADA dollar.

Average Daily Attendance funds are shelled out from the state to the local schools to encourage maximum daily attendance. It's eight dollars per day per child. With our two hundred kids, we'd receive sixteen hundred per day. That's thirty-two thousand dollars per month."

"And she won't help, even though we've got the best school in town?!"

"No. She's so damned scared of Black Panthers *and* competition—Oakland's district being one of the worst, as you know, if not *the* worst—she's refused to budge. I'm not finished with her, but I do have other irons in the fire. Remember Huey Johnson, from Trust for the Public Land, who wanted us to work with him on putting vegetable gardens in the ghetto? Johnson's now head of the state's interior department."

"It's a new old-boy club."

"It's time. Well, when Johnson headed Trust for the Public Land, he was funded via a $10 million line of credit from the Bank of America."

"Later for ADA money."

"Tony told me about it. Johnson's line of credit and a problem at the school gave me an idea. The garbage collectors—"

"Wait a minute now."

"Listen for a second. Oakland's garbage is collected by a private company, Scavenger, under a thirty-five-year contract with the city. Scavenger called the school about our bill—five hundred bucks or something. They threatened to stop collecting and take away our big dumpsters. I called Scavenger and told them I would not tolerate threats. And that the first motherfucker who touched those dumpsters would be blown away."

"I've trained you well. Let's walk outside."

"I got some Brother's uncle," I continued, "to let us rent his truck to pick up our own garbage, from the school and everywhere else. Only to learn it was illegal to haul one's own garbage."

"What's this got to do with Huey Johnson's ten mill?" he said as we sat down at the bar outside.

"Patience . . . Scavenger had a lock on the thing. I talked to Fred Hiestand, and he put together another corporation."

"I need to see Fred. He should come to Havana."

"All right, I'll arrange it, but let me finish . . . Turns out Scavenger is a little Mafia-run operation. After Fred found there was a way to get their contract nullified, I decided we'd buy our own trucks and we'd become the garbage collectors in Oakland, at least black Oakland. We'd have another steady flow of money and build another model: what I called 'cooperative corporations'—*profit* with a socialistic touch. Now here's the Huey Johnson stuff . . . I knew we could outgun Scavenger in Oakland and eventually replace them. We just needed a jump start. And why not the Huey Johnson Bank of America deal, I thought."

"And why not?"

"Have you ever seen a white boy's face when a nigger speaks the word 'million' in reference to dollars? Tony Kline set up a meeting for me with Bill Coblentz, a San Francisco attorney whose most noteworthy client is R. W. Clausen, *the* president of *the* Bank of America, worldwide. Tony, Coblentz, and I sat down for lunch, and after a few white wines, I made the pitch. Invoking the Johnson arrangement, I asked Coblentz to assist me in convincing his main client to do the same for us. Surely a community-oriented, *cooperative* business was worth a paltry five-million-dollar line of credit. He started stammering about what he could really do. So I invited him to the school. He took the tour and fell in love with the kids and our operation. Even made a small personal donation to the school—and said he'd think of something, even though five million was a lot."

"Has he?"

"Not yet. But I intend to convince Coblentz to introduce me to Clausen himself. That ought to be interesting."

"You're late." I was anxious. It was my last day with Huey. "I'm leaving in the morning, you know."

"Don't leave me." He kissed me on the cheek.

"Don't be flip with me. I'm the one who loves you."

"But why do you love me?"

"Because you've got some good pussy."

"Don't I, though." He laughed.

We spent all of that last night together. We convinced the hotel bartender to sell us a bottle of liquor. We lay next to each other on the bed.

"You think I don't realize that it's not helpful to the Cubans to have me here," he said, sitting up. "And it certainly doesn't mean anything to me to be here. I'm a no-man in a no-man's land. That's why I'm ready to come home. But I'm *not* crazy. I'll wait for your signal. You really have saved the party."

"I would say thank you, but the last time I said that to you, you hit me."

"Did I?" he said, actually thinking about it. "My hand must've slipped, 'cause there were always so many motherfuckers that needed slapping. We need each other. You've put us in position." He got up from the bed and started pacing.

Huey had reclaimed himself in Cuba, despite his whining over its industrial inadequacies, its heat, its foreignness. It was not just a detoxification from cocaine. It was removal from the violent diversions of the FBI and the local police and the streets of Oakland.

He sat down in the wicker chair and drew a cigarette from my pack on the nightstand.

"I don't know what I ever wanted to do with my life," he said very quietly. "This is all I can do . . . Fuck it . . .

"Elaine, there're some things about the immediate future I have to say to you now. Whatever becomes of me, the Black Panther Party will have to be dismantled sooner or later. Everything changes, and we have to change, or else we'd become stagnant and self-perpetuating like the Russians.

"We have to take revolution out of the abstract by expanding the revolutionary apparatus in the United States, develop a mechanism that embraces more blacks as well as whites and others. Sooner will be better than later for me, because I'm tired of being the central figure in a structure I created. I'm tired of the paramilitary regimentation—even though I know they would've killed us off by now without it.

"Perhaps we can build a mass, multiracial organization *and* keep the vanguard apparatus as a dominant force. We have to clear a common ground where the interests of black people can coexist with those of the great majority of people in America suffering under capitalism.

"I'm still not in agreement with Marx's dismissal of the lumpen, because there are too many black people who fall into that class. Marx dismissed the peasant class, too; but Mao dealt with the realities in China and organized the peasants, who became the backbone of revolution. We have to bring in the so-called middle class, the white-collar workers, lawyers, teachers, writers, artists, what-have-you, the 'facilitators' of capitalism, who can be facilitators of our revolution. Marx failed to foresee the rise of this group and its potential significance to revolution. They can and must be aligned. Of course, there's the working class, though the

American worker is not as trustworthy as Marx predicted. Can you imagine a Hughes Aircraft worker making double time agreeing to bite the hand that feeds him? Naturally, there're the other people of color. The poor of all colors."

"Tell me what I need to do."

"What you've put us in position to do is actually establish the base. But it has to be a revolutionary base, not a Black Panther base. If we can align these groups into a revolutionary framework in Oakland, we'll not only establish the base, we'll establish a model for expansion.

"Originally, I thought this could be accomplished if you ran for office again—for mayor. But that would be too costly for us, especially if you won. You'd be unable to run the party. I have someone else in mind. You can think of him as our Sun Yat-sen," he said, referring to the progressive Chinese leader who was president of a provisional government before the success of the revolution. "Lionel Wilson is his name. I've been informed he wants to be mayor. His appeal can be very broad-based. With the party behind him, it'll be the correct appeal. And I think he can win.

"Lionel's no revolutionary. Matter of fact, he's a judge. First black on the Alameda Superior Court, appointed by Pat Brown. But Lionel's not tied into the system. He's angry, and not afraid. I think I understand him because I know his youngest son, Stevie. It always seemed to me that Stevie was tortured by the fact that the family barely looks black. So he started running around Oakland acting like the 'blackest nigger' on the street. Stevie is Lionel's heart. The point is, Lionel's the piece that can link together the potential revolutionary force in Oakland. I want you to put him in office. If you do that, we'll have the setup to make the base for revolution in the United States."

"We'll take Oakland. Port, stock, and barrel."

"Put Lionel in, and maybe I'll be back for the rest."

CHAPTER 19

FRIENDS AND ENEMIES

LIONEL WILSON WAS AN ATTRACTIVE MAN, around sixty, with gray-stranded brown hair, straight and silken. His skin color was vanilla caramel. His smile was broad, and his handshake was firm. His step was firm, too, I saw, when he escorted me from the entrance of his chambers to a seat before his large desk. His speech had the measured gravity of his office.

He was not the kind of black who was friendly to Black Panthers, I was thinking, as I sat down opposite him. He was the kind I thought of as "colored," born and steeped in bourgeois ideals. He reminded me of my father in many ways.

He wanted to retire from the bench. It had become an ungratifying role, he said, though he was gratified to have extended some measure of justice to a people for whom justice in America had always been in short supply. He appreciated the credentials and prestige his judgeship had accorded him. That status would be helpful in the future, he said, a future he openly acknowledged he wanted to build alongside the Black Panther Party, in the interest of black people. He did, as Huey had said, want to be mayor of Oakland.

Though we did not speak about Stevie, I felt Lionel's passion for the rights of black people, and the change in consciousness I suspected he had made in his life, had a lot to do with his son. I suspected that Huey's characterization of the son's black-and-white frustrations had forced the father to look beyond the safe world of middle-class black life.

Privileged blacks like Lionel typically steered their lives away from sociopolitical questions that might disturb the delicate balance required of blacks who walked in the white man's world. Very few blacks in America had been so privileged as Lionel. He had been able to move into the guarded world of white academia and emerge a lawyer despite the obstacles he had faced. He had become a fine prospect for a white governor to place in a middle-level judgeship to "disprove" the realities of racism. I mused on that as I sat across from him.

He would not announce his candidacy, he said, for some time—at least six months, which would allow him a year of campaigning for the next city election in April 1977. He would have to wind down, finish his immediate judicial tasks. Moreover, he had to organize a campaign strategy.

That six months would, I assured him, permit me time to adjust the party apparatus in order to be able to put sufficient people in the field to register blacks to vote, and to walk the precincts of the large black populace. It would also give me time to set aside the support money the party would donate to his campaign.

In summary, I told him, I believed we could deliver the majority of the black vote; and the labor vote would not be difficult to secure. His primary job, in the end, I suggested, would be to sway the liberal and middle-class whites, and bring home the "bourgeois" black vote. The difficult task before us, we agreed, was to neutralize the strength of the white Republican vote.

Lionel would be a fine Sun Yat-sen, I reported to Larry later. Larry and I were experiencing a kind of honeymoon together. I had returned to Oakland from Havana only days before.

"Don't worry 'bout a thing, Edie," he said that night. Edie was the sweet appellation, a combination of my first two initials, that he had conferred on me not long after we became lovers.

His toughness was tender, I thought, enveloped in his body, which was full and fit and dark and sweet. He made love with fire, a smoldering, satisfying heat. I caressed his muscular buttocks as we lay in the dark and dreamed out loud.

"Everything's pretty cool, Edie," he was saying. "The main problem we have to deal with on the streets, besides the pigs, is the drug-dealer thing. We've got some names now . . . but"—he hesitated—"the thing is, they're so young. We don't know of one of them past twenty-one or so. It's hard for me to deal with, Edie. Brothers turned out so early, all because they don't have shit else."

"I know. But I don't think we can afford to be sentimental here, Larry. I've never known you to be sentimental."

He eased me out of his arms and picked up his glass of cognac from the floor next to the bed. The lights that lit up Lake Merritt below were flickering through the water's reflection onto his bedroom windows.

"You know, I'm really not scared of dying," he resumed, adjusting his pillows and swallowing a gulp of his drink. "And I really can't think of too many motherfuckers I'm scared of."

"And I can think of a whole bunch that're scared of you."

"Yeah, a lot of people are scared of me, Edie. And most of the time, I think that's good. Motherfuckers have to be taught to respect us, and that's one of my jobs—to enforce the respect. But shit, for me, it's not who I wanted to be. I'm not some low-life . . ."

"And nobody thinks that. You're a revolutionary."

"We're revolutionaries. But I'm the one who's hurt a lot of people, people I didn't even know. I might've even cared about some of them. Hell, I don't really care about them, 'cause they've been in the way. It's something in me. I just don't feel good about going down with a record of hurting young Brothers."

"Don't tell me you became a born-again Christian while I was away," I said to interrupt the heaviness and push back the forlorn feelings we shared about the price of our freedom.

"Don't be ridiculous," he answered. Then, "Okay. That's it. I've said what's on my mind. I'll do what's necessary. Whatever you say."

"I say, don't get involved. The deal is for you *not* to get involved. And I don't want you involved directly, because I really can't do this thing if you get arrested or killed."

"Me either." He laughed.

"Then just stay by my side, and close. But deal with this. You've got to. I don't have the ability—or the balls."

He laughed and poured himself another cognac.

"The fact is," I continued, "we can't let these coke dealers move into Oakland. I think we've got to stop them now or else they'll grow to be more than we can handle. I'm only saying we need to stunt the growth. Is that possible?"

"I can make them disappear."

"Before the election? That's what we need. A clean slate in Oakland. They're fucking up everything."

"I'm clear on that."

"Well, that's what you have to keep in mind, and forget about their ages. Forget yourself. I know I don't have to convince you, but I'm saying that if we don't put them down, the Mafia, or whoever they're getting the coke from, will be here in a minute —in full force, and not with some small-time garbage-collection business. Oakland's ripe for them. But if we take care of this problem now, we can concentrate on putting Lionel in. Then Huey can return and it'll be a brand-new world.

"I think we've got to eliminate this in one strike. Maybe call a meeting with the ones you know about. Tell them the facts of life in Oakland: they can go to L.A. or somewhere. If not, then I say put an end to the thing—at once. It'll be a long time before the next gang of motherfuckers tries to organize in Oakland. If nothing else, we'll buy time till Huey gets back."

"I want to think about it. You know, talk to the Brothers. What you want to do won't be easy, no matter how you cut it."

"Of course. You have to think about it. But tell me something better. Tell me anything that'll deal with this sooner than later."

"It'll be dealt with—one way or another. I promise you that, Edie—with my life."

Words were important to him, and those words were not the empty pledge of a sweetheart.

"There's something we've got to do right away, though," he said a few minutes later.

"On the drug thing?"

"No. It's about Ricardo. He's coming to trial in the next few months on his case, the one he caught in the club that night with the Servant and Big Bob."

"We've got good lawyers. He'll beat it."

"Maybe he'll beat the assault on the pigs. But the gun possession is straight up. The pigs that came up on him took the .45 right out of his holster. The case is clean, and gun possession in California is two years now. I can't go two years without R.J. It's bad enough with Big Bob down on the Callins case. R.J. keeps the inventory straight and keeps the Brothers right on my orders. He's my main man."

"I know he can't do time. He and I go way back. I've known Ricardo since he was only sixteen or seventeen when he came into the Southern California chapter out of Watts. Sometimes I think the party stole his life."

"You're wrong about that. R.J. is proud of himself, and he's a bad motherfucker . . ."

"Yes, but I mean, it seems like we took his youth away."

"The pigs did that."

"Yes they did. They really did . . . You know, Richardo always reminds me of Jonathan Jackson. No, we definitely can't let the pigs snatch any more of his life. I'm going to be in his lawyer's face tomorrow and find out what the fuck is going on."

"I love you, Edie."

"Me, too, Larry."

Our tide was rising, I thought, as I watched Lionel at the bench.

Tom Orloff, the Alameda County D.A.—who was slated to prosecute Huey on the murder charge—was sitting with his deputy, who was formally arguing for the state. Orloff had become obsessed with a need to personally be involved with even the most minute prosecution of Panthers. The deputy prosecutor insisted that the court understand that even though Ricardo had pleaded out to the assault charge, the sentence for gun possession was two years in prison. He presented Ricardo's extensive arrest record to bolster his argument, and reiterated that Ricardo was not only a member of the Black Panther Party, he was a known gunslinger for the party.

Our lawyer argued that, given that Mr. Jones had conceded guilt, in exchange for which the prosecution had dropped the more serious charge of assault, he should not be so severely punished on the lesser count. He urged the court to impose the legal option of community service.

Larry and I watched impatiently from the rear of the courtroom. Lionel studied the papers before him. From time to time, he looked over his glasses, a gesture that indicated he was digesting some legal point. The issue was the law of sentencing. The question of guilt or innocence was a foregone conclusion based on Ricardo's plea.

When the lawyers sat down, Lionel made his considerations. It was true that Ricardo had been arrested numerous times, Lionel noted, referring to the prosecution's argument. That arrest record included several charges of gun possession. It was also noteworthy that Mr. Jones had never, as the defense had pointed up, been convicted. Thus, Lionel stated, in the eyes of the court, the defendant's legal record was clean.

For the record, Lionel continued, he did want to state his position on the question of possession of handguns, which the state had raised so forcefully. The illegal (unregistered) possession of handguns by citizens of California was offensive to the public interest. He wanted the record to reflect that the court prayed that a body of law would be enacted by the legislature to ban all private possession of handguns.

The record in the instant matter had to be taken on its face, however. The facts had to be viewed with an independent and impartial eye.

Lionel then ruled. Given Ricardo's record and plea, he would set punishment with a fine of $1,000 and suspend the prison term in lieu of one year of mandatory community service.

As Larry and I—and surely Ricardo—tried to restrain ourselves from whistling and stomping, Lionel added that he had a specific recommendation as to such community service. Ricardo was to work at the Oakland Community Learning Center (which Orloff, his deputy, and everybody else knew was the party facility that housed our school), in accordance with the directives and requirements of the administration of that center. The entire courtroom was rendered speechless—except me, whispering to Larry: "A really fine Sun Yat-sen."

I decided I deserved another visit to Los Angeles at that point. From time to time, I stole away there, to my mother's place or to visit Suzanne de Passe. Usually, I went alone; sometimes I took my daughter. I thought of those short, infrequent jaunts as pastoral. At my mother's apartment, I could be spoiled with hoe cakes and sausages in bed in the morning, and relish apolitical books, magazines, and television programs, and the momentary relief of being out of gunsights. I had been able to convince Larry that it was the one place I did not really need a bodyguard. My visits to L.A. were secret, unscheduled, and I was safely harbored for those short periods under my mother's roof—or Suzanne's, which I did not mention.

As she had come to fully support my party membership, my mother supported my need for these forays to L.A. Whatever frustrations I had had with her, which fluctuated over the years; whatever fears she concealed about my membership in the party; whatever my moods and neuroses, and hers, I knew that she always kept my flame. Her love for me had real strength, though I sensed it had as much to do with her own needs as mine.

I had just arrived at my mother's apartment late that night

when Tony Kline called. She handed the telephone to me as I walked through the door, then left the room.

"Tony! How'd you find me?"

"Don't ask. Got a minute? . . . Okay. Here's the question. Who do you know in Maryland?"

"I don't know. Well, the party's still got some people there, but . . ."

"Listen. This is important. The governor's here with me. Just tell me who and what you know in Maryland. There's a presidential primary there next month . . ."

"Shit, Tony! Jerry wants to be president?"

"Maybe. We have to test the water . . . But here's the governor. He wants to talk to you."

The governor said he had a million possibilities to weigh, not the least of which was whether he could actually beat the Democratic front runner, Jimmy Carter. He felt his father could get the support of the AFL-CIO voters in that industrial citadel, and he could undoubtedly finesse the support of the Catholic Church. My senses were suddenly alerted to the Kennedyesque quality in him, feeling in the next second that it had less to do with his Catholicism than his poetic intellectualism. He was vital—in his forties—handsome, and certainly charming. His heart carried the idealism that Kennedy's image portrayed, envisioning a better America, a better planet.

He wanted names. He wanted to know what percentage of the black vote I could help him garner. He acknowledged that he could not, even with the entire labor and Church vote, win Maryland without Baltimore, and he could not win Baltimore without the black vote.

There was no possibility of sleeping. Jerry Brown had been virtually unknown when he won election to the highest office in the most powerful state in America. I was calculating. While the presidential nominating convention was only four months away, Brown's gubernatorial victory had been accomplished via a less-than-six-month television campaign. The possibility of his actually becoming president of the United States was real, I thought, nearly hyperventilating.

Tony, as well as Fred Hiestand—who was not only a party lawyer but had become the governor's key advisor on various legislative issues—would go with him to the White House. Our agenda would not be far behind. I began to envision black federal court appointments, the dismantling of the CIA, the seizing of all

FBI files, new ambassadors to China and other important places, diplomatic relations with Cuba and such countries, massive disruptions in federal budgets, millions shifted from defense spending to social programs. My mother's eyes became heavy listening to me articulate my thoughts, pacing, smoking, and, mostly, trying to piece together a package for Baltimore, to tie a Black Panther ribbon around the whole wide world.

The next morning I took the first flight to Oakland. I thought my news would excite Ericka Huggins as I rushed into her room to tell her everything. She responded with a sleepy recollection about having told Tony I was in L.A. visiting my mother and wondering why his call had been so urgent. She seemed to have no interest in my plans.

I took a shower while waiting for a decent hour to begin calling people I thought could help. Shampooing my hair, I thought about Ericka's response and what I considered her loss of passion. I wondered if this had been driven out of her in 1969, when John was assassinated, or during those two years of isolation she had later endured in a Connecticut jail. I loved her so, I had named my daughter in her honor. Her emotional fire was surely gone though, and I found myself more and more frustrated by that. It seemed to take something away from all of us, especially me.

My secretary, Janice, was tracing down every relevant name on my Rolodex. The responses to my telephone calls were leading nowhere. Black folks I knew seemed to know black folks with a modicum of political clout in every city on the Eastern Seaboard except Baltimore. I began to long for the days when the party's Maryland chapter was thriving, the days before we called most of the troops home. I began formulating desperate plans: I would order a hundred Panthers back to Baltimore immediately, or perhaps I would go to Baltimore myself, plow through the city until I reaped something. I was considering all of this when Paul Cobb, head of a local black community group, rather casually mentioned over the telephone that he knew someone in Congressman Parren Mitchell's office. Then he added that perhaps I knew him, as he was the brother of Rap Brown.

I canceled all my plans for Baltimore. Dialing the operator, I thought about Rap's silence. He was, I believed, still serving out a very long prison sentence arising from his work with SNCC. He had virtually disappeared from the front lines, and somewhat from memory. His fiery voice had been silenced by the pigs. We no longer heard his words, words that had given him his nickname and an international reputation—"Burn, baby, burn!"

Within the day, I made the link with Parren Mitchell; and not much later I had squeezed support from Ron Dellums as well.

Dellums had a radical spirit which he consistently expressed—with little effect—in the tired forum of the U.S. Congress. He had gone to Congress in the late sixties as a progressive, representing a significant piece of politically radicalized Berkeley along with a section of black Oakland. At the time of his first election, most people had believed he was actually a Black Panther. It was an image he did little to dispel, as it suited his ideals and ambitions—"radical" being synonymous with Northern California.

Dellums initially scoffed at a Brown presidency. He was supporting Fred Harris, a senator from Oklahoma. Dellums claimed Harris was a true liberal—though it seemed to me that this claim to liberal fame had to do with little more than Harris's being married to a Native American woman. The question was whether Harris could win. Since the onset of the state presidential primaries, Harris had made what could only be described as a pathetic showing, coming in behind even Jesse Jackson. The black question was that, since we could safely predict no black would be marching into the White House anytime soon, was there any "white boy" whose shoulders could carry our load to the most powerful position in the world. The answer was, I insisted, a "home boy" who happened to be governor.

I imposed upon Ron the wisdom I had gleaned from a recent conversation with his congressional colleague from Georgia, Andrew Young, a leader in the civil-rights movement and a very close comrade-in-arms of Dr. Martin Luther King, Jr. In a brief conversation at a Democratic dinner in Oakland, I had asked Young why he was supporting Jimmy Carter for president. I relayed to Dellums that I told Andy I thought of Carter as a racist redneck. Andy had said I was probably right that Carter was a redneck and a racist. However, I quoted to Dellums, Andy had added: "But he's *my* racist redneck."

Dellums was bowled over with laughter. Brown was, he finally decided, a most qualified candidate for our white man in the White House.

In the Maryland Democratic primary, Brown prevailed over Carter hands down. It was Brown's first primary, and he had trounced the front-runner. Ron had personally joined the forces, along with Mitchell, in Maryland. With the greatest enthusiasm, Ron testified to me about the glory of the victory. He offered, moreover, that when he saw black ladies in a Baltimore church nearly knock down chairs to shake Brown's hand after his speech, he had become convinced he had done the right thing. His political eye saw that Brown had the charisma, along with the "liberal" fiber, to become our president of the United States of America.

With the results of the subsequent Democratic presidential primaries that Jerry Brown entered, I became nearly orgasmic: outside the Deep South, Brown was beating Carter.

I tried to convey my euphoria to Huey through the telephone lines to Havana. Brown was winning. Lionel could win. Things were moving.

Except for the festering organized drug problem, Larry and his lieutenants had rendered the streets of Oakland safe for Black Panthers. That was true despite the recent tragic murder of Deacon. An organizer of our teen program, Deacon was shot down by a West Oakland gang member as he tried to negotiate peace between opposing gangs. In retribution, West Oakland had been combed, however, and cleaned.

Joan Kelley was deftly weaving a financial blanket from the yields of her proposal writing which was sheltering our social programs. Michael Fultz was editing the newspaper with savvy and polish, David Du Bois having gone out of the country indefinitely to attend his aging mother. Phyllis's structuring of the political apparatus for Lionel's campaign allowed me to believe he could win.

Phyllis Jackson's presence in the party had always seemed funny to me. Mostly, it had to do with the fact that she had been born and raised in Tacoma, Washington, the black population of which (I regularly taunted her) had surely been reduced 25 percent when she left. I joked about her having not so much as heard of Malcolm X until she left Tacoma, and about her participation, as a token-Negro majorette, in events like the Tacoma Daffodil Parade. But Phyllis was a serious soldier. I thought of her more as a friend than a comrade, and I admired her perhaps more than anyone else in the party.

She was the fastest-talking person I knew other than myself. She was passionate and intense, often neurotically so, a trait with which I identified. She was droll and extremely quick-witted, and, I always hated to admit, rarely wrong in her rapid-fire analyses.

When I first assumed leadership of the party, I had desperately wanted Phyllis to be my secretary. It was, I came to agree, a position in which her talents were wasted. Although she reluctantly took on the task, she fought with me daily. Once I realized that she could organize and orchestrate any project on her own, I stopped fighting her and let her fly. Now she coordinated a variety of projects, not the least of which was the party connection to the next election in Oakland.

As for the management of the party's increasing income, Norma Armour was maintaining a tight rein. She meticulously accounted for every penny we raised or spent. She was so solid and trustworthy, I no longer reviewed our books.

She was responsible only to me. Since her lips were as tight as her purse strings, only she and I knew the precise status of the party's financial situation: the real sources of all our funds, how much there was and how it was actually spent. Only she authorized expenditures, and only I authorized her. Recently, however, she had allowed her niggardly nature to threaten our accord.

Norma had told Larry that she did not have on hand the thousand or so dollars in cash he had demanded she bring to him immediately. He was with the Brothers at an after-hours club, and supposedly needed the money to prove some point. Norma decided his request represented a foolish expenditure and lied to him. He arrived at her door with the Brothers and smacked her around.

The problem was not Norma, I reflected, after she called to tell me what had happened. I had to admit to myself that it was becoming difficult for Larry to subject himself to the dictates of any woman—including me, in spite of our relationship and his commitment to the party's discipline and order. I had been giving him almost everything he wanted, including the authority to make his own rules within very wide parameters. He could not reach our pocketbooks, however. Any arrangement looser than the one with Norma, I believed, might have resulted in a swift dissipation of the millions of dollars we were now generating.

I tried to smooth Larry's ruffled feathers about Norma with a mild admonition that focused on the internal affairs of the party. I had certainly laid down the law that no comrade could physically abuse another. Violators were subject to severe punishment. He had enforced that law, I argued. Now he had violated it. It was an intolerable example.

Larry retorted that the issue was his authority. While he was supposedly second-in-command, he had no sway over Norma—implying that he had no access to the money Norma controlled. He was not a "boy," and she was not his mother. It was then I knew we had reached a serious impasse. The problem was neither money nor Norma's authority over it. It was "manhood."

This was not the only time that Larry's rage over threats to his maleness had erupted. In a hotel room in Chicago, he had ripped the nightgown I was wearing. He had had a fit over my "contradiction" of him in front of Flint Taylor, the lawyer we had met there earlier, in connection with my testimony in the civil case against the government for the murder of Fred Hampton. On another occasion, during a regrettable weekend I spent with him, he violently swept bottles of cologne and other bureau-top paraphernalia from his dresser in response to my refusal to pick up the clothes he had left lying around his apartment.

Each time, I had achieved peace with fluttering eyes and the surrender of ego. In this same way, I finally effected a tenuous truce between Larry and Norma.

Machismo aside, the machine was rolling perfectly, I reported to Huey, on tracks that were being laid from City Hall to Washington. I wanted him to know that it seemed, truly, the best of times for all of us.

The threat came from a direction I had not anticipated. I learned that my name was now on the top of a prison guerrilla gang's hit list—given, it was said, the absence of Huey Newton, the primary target. My chief fear, however, was that the knife raised against me would end up in the back of Johnny Spain.

Over and over from the beginning of the long San Quentin Six trial, the prosecutor had singled out Spain as the only Black Panther in the group. Though all of the Six were branded "comrades," the others did not have the taint of the Panther. The prosecutor stressed to the jury that Johnny Spain had been under Black Panther George Jackson's leadership on the murderous day. That was demonstrated, the district attorney asserted, by the fact that Johnny was the only one at George's side during the melee, and even at the end, outside San Quentin's Adjustment Center when George was slain.

Having attributed most of the violence of that day to George Jackson—specifically the death of two guards—the prosecutor emphasized that the legal connection between Spain and Jackson as Panther comrades was conspiratorial. This, he concluded, proved that Johnny was liable for the conspiracy murder of the two guards.

The prosecutor possessed a critical piece of information that Spain's lawyer, Charles Garry, did not have. One woman on the jury had privately confessed to the judge—in mid-trial—that the man convicted of the murder of one of her close friends was a Black Panther. She could not find it in her heart, she confided to the judge—in the presence of the prosecutor—to be impartial about Black Panthers. The judge had asked her if she could try.

Even without that knowledge, we all felt as the trial closed that Johnny's conviction was inevitable. I was frantic. I was certain that if he were convicted, he would be placed in the gravest jeopardy. He would surely be killed, either by prison guards or some member of one of the anti-Panther guerrilla gangs, particularly the one that had now targeted me.

When Brown defeated Carter in the California primary by a margin of two to one, we began to see the Presidential Seal emblazoned on our walls. It was nearly the last and certainly the most significant primary—California representing one-fifth of the electoral college. Only the Democratic Convention stood between Brown and the White House.

Nobody believed the Republican nominee, Gerald Ford, could struggle to reelection. Thus, if Jerry could take the nomination as he had taken the California and other state primaries he had entered, he would surely be the next president of the United States.

I had become a delegate to the Democratic National Convention. In the weeks before the California primary I had concluded that I needed to be at the convention and had entered my name on a caucus ballot. Within each political party delegates to a presidential nominating convention were determined in local caucuses, established by congressional district lines.

The process was, I learned, more selective than elective. Only

Democratic organizations were informed of the dates, times, and places of the delegate caucuses, and those via small, typed bulletins mailed by state party officials supporting a particular presidential candidate. Each candidate was to take to the convention a percentage of the caucus elected delegates—the exact percentage to be determined by the primary election. The major caucuses were for Brown and Carter.

It had been a mystery to me how the few people in attendance at the Brown caucus I attended found their way there. The school auditorium in Dellums' district where we met was empty of almost anybody except other prospective delegates—and our people.

Since I had no real understanding of how such caucuses operated, I had overloaded my odds of winning a delegate seat. We organized a small food giveaway for that day. Our announcement fliers offered a free lunch, along with balloons and toys for children, to all registered Democrats who came to my caucus with their fliers.

The few hundred West Oakland blacks our fliers conjured up, mostly mothers and their children, made a fine Saturday of the affair. They enjoyed the box lunches and soft drinks as much as the little piece of community theater into which they had been recruited. Most of them had marked ballots for me in other times, and willingly voted for me again. They were just as willing to endorse Tony Kline (a resident of the district who, like every delegate, had to be elected). The same scenario was being repeated in East Oakland, where we had positioned Ericka Huggins to run for a delegate seat in Congressman Pete Stark's district. Both Ericka and I—as well as Tony—were elected.

Immediately after the caucuses, Assemblyman Howard Berman called me from Sacramento. He was a stalwart on Jerry's team in the legislature. A man named Jack Brooks really wanted the number-one delegate seat that Ericka held, Howard advised me. "Everybody" really felt Brooks should have it, given his multithousand-dollar personal contribution to Jerry's gubernatorial campaign. I was certainly willing to accommodate "everyone," I explained to Howard. That seat was, however, a very dear thing to me. We agreed I would try to make such an accommodation if he arranged for Brooks to meet with me at our financially strapped school.

Jack Brooks liked me as spontaneously as I liked him. He had retained the mentality of the construction worker he had once been, though he now owned a major construction company, in addition to a bank. Brooks told me he admired the conscientious-ness and adroitness with which the Black Panthers operated. Deal-ing with us, one knew what to expect, and had to respect that we "did not bullshit." What I liked most about Brooks was his un-derlying *Mr. Smith Goes to Washington* attitude about American politics, and the fact that he shed tears after he toured our school and visited with the children. The other thing I liked was that he had a commonsense philosophy about life. He donated several thousand dollars to our school and went to the convention as the number-one Brown delegate from his congressional district.

Larry and Perkins traveled with me to the convention in New York in July. Larry was taking no chances with my security. Darron Perkins, a security chief for the party, was a steadfast soldier; so much so, that I had come to see him as Larry's successor, if such a thing ever became necessary. Before joining the party, he had been in Vietnam, leading search-and-destroy missions for which he was commended many times. I spent a lot of private time with Perkins because he always made me laugh. He was a short, sturdy man who had brilliant white teeth that gleamed often as he uttered countless witty commentaries about life. Perkins's wry sense of humor always irritated Larry, as did my friendship with Perkins.

Since neither Larry nor Perkins had the necessary credentials as a delegate, neither could accompany me into the convention arena. I had restrained their belligerent reaction to that by simply pointing out that everyone entering the convention floor was searched. The notable exceptions were the army of FBI and Secret Service agents there. Thus, I was left alone to concentrate on deciphering and manipulating the action in the three rings.

The convention unfolded with a spectacle of balloons, plac-ards, and badge-wearing, costumed conventioneers. (The Carter people actually strutted about in the dress of the Planter's Peanut advertising figure.) Then the rules of the game were revealed.

By the end of the second of the four convention days, a massive number of Brown delegates had already been sold over to the Carter machine, which was well organized and funded. Specific promises of freeways and such had been made to delegates who were mayors and governors; support for reelection went to senatorial and congressional delegates; federal judicial appoint-ments went to judges and lawyers; and legislation to certain so-called special-interest delegates—with the blatant exception of black people, there being only a handful of black delegates among the thousands. Brown was not a man who operated with a machine. A dreamer and an intellectual who detested expedient politics, he had no idea how to dike the swelling tide.

Brown was overwhelmed on the first ballot. Jack Brooks and I were two of the handful of California delegates who refused to go with the flow. Since that was an empty gesture, I began to concentrate on what could be salvaged.

The Puerto Rican Socialist Party had been trying to get the convention to address the question of the independence of Puerto Rico, the U.S. territory whose delegates held symbolic seats. They had appealed to me, among others. I used the opportunity as an official delegate to try to get the issue introduced. It was, after all, a just cause, and had been articulated cogently in the paper they wished to present, as drafted by their lawyer in the United States, Arthur Kinoy.

Ron Dellums wanted to make the one and only statement that would be made about the plight of black and oppressed people in the United States, in an attempt to inject humanity into the otherwise reactionary Democratic platform. He felt he could do that via a nomination for the vice presidency. If he could manipulate such a token nomination, I felt I could persuade Ron to incorporate the Puerto Rican business into his acceptance address to the convention. Thus, I spent the rest of the hours during and after the convention program helping Ron bargain for support.

Ron was not the sort of black that the small black caucus of delegates wanted to put forward. He was a "radical," around whom they did not want to rally to present their united black front to the powers that were to address issues pertinent to black people. Nevertheless, accompanied by Larry and Perkins, I joined Ron's people in badgering and cajoling the black delegates at their various private caucuses to endorse Ron's nomination. It was a small coup—smaller still in light of Carter's nomination for president. Ron made a stirring statement to the convention, though, which included support for the independence of Puerto Rico.

We would have to free the port of Oakland without presidential help.

CHAPTER 20

ENEMIES AND FRIENDS

LIONEL WILSON ANNOUNCED he was running for mayor of Oakland. The first stage of Phyllis's organizing operation for Lionel's campaign was ready. It was based on a concept developed by the SNCC organization when they were furiously registering black voters in the South. We referred to it in the party as the "10-10-10 program." It involved one person organizing ten people around a political goal. Each of the ten would then be educated to organize another ten, and so on.

Despite vigorous voting campaigns, blacks still believed that the act of voting in America was futile. The voting record of Oakland blacks reflected this belief; even the registration percentage was still very low. Registering Oakland blacks to vote had made the difference in terms of whatever success we had enjoyed in our last two Panther campaigns. Massive black registration was critical to Lionel's campaign.

Phyllis had decided that if only ten Panthers were dispersed daily to each register 100 prospective supporters of Lionel, within one month we would have registered 30,000 people. In three months, we could have 90,000 *qualified* registrations: black Oakland residents who were Democrats. In a city whose total population was approximately 400,000, that number would overwhelm the white Republican vote. In the next phase of the campaign, Panthers would organize one in ten of those registered who could each bring ten others to the polls.

Phyllis had identified around twenty Panthers in Oakland who had the potential to work hard enough to register the number we required. She would whittle down those twenty talented ones to ten. Those selected would be those who proved they could deliver. We offered incentives to all of them.

Panthers worked for long hours, most finishing the day after midnight, a seven-day-per-week obligation. Those selected to be our ten registrants, however, would be relieved of that regimen for the next few months. Whenever anyone turned in the required hundred registrations, his or her workday was ended. To this incentive was added the promise that a car would be available to each one selected. Other incentives included money and personal items. Within a few weeks, Phyllis had her ten.

During those first registration weeks, I received a call from Michael Berman, the brother of Assemblyman Howard Berman. Michael was known as a political whiz kid. He said he had heard the party was supporting Lionel for mayor and had a proposition that might be helpful. He urged me to use my influence to solicit the governor to fund the controversial Grove-Shafter Freeway extension.

It was a strange request given his brother's close relation to Jerry Brown. Moreover, I saw no apparent connection between that freeway and the election. I responded that the party had for years endorsed the court-ordered injunction that had halted construction of the Grove-Shafter. Our newspaper had lambasted the city for uprooting and displacing black people to make way for the freeway. I wondered if he was mad.

I reminded him that when Fred Hiestand uncovered an old law requiring the city to build replacement housing, we had forced the city to do that. The Oakland Community Housing Corporation had been developed to handle the city's $12 million capitulation allocation for three hundred new replacement houses. I was chairman of that board. The injunction was then lifted, and I no longer concerned myself with the freeway.

Berman explained that the problem was Jerry Brown. Jerry was refusing to release the funds for the freeway. The freeway would lay the groundwork for the long-delayed Oakland City Center project.

From my point of view, Jerry's action was to be applauded. It was the City Center project that had been the root cause of the homelessness of so many West Oakland blacks. As Oakland was being abandoned by middle-class whites, the Grove-Shafter Freeway was designed as a conduit for returning their consumer dollars to Oakland businessmen, a design of Oakland mayor Reading and then-governor Ronald Reagan. The City Center project was to be the receptacle. The party was doing everything possible to destroy that capitalist dream, I told Berman.

He plowed on. The construction of the Grove-Shafter extension was in fact the condition on which the Hyatt Corporation, Wells Fargo Bank, and the Bullocks and Sears department stores had made commitments to locate in Oakland's deteriorated downtown area. Their millions of investment dollars would build the City Center and also trigger the revitalization of Oakland's economy. Without the freeway, there was nothing.

I listened as Berman explained that the City Center project would generate at least ten thousand new jobs. In a city the size of Oakland, where so many residents, especially the blacks, were presently unemployed, that was a serious number. It was certainly an incentive to urge the governor to approve the freeway.

The benefits of the City Center project would not reach black people, I commented. The jobs *and* the City Center could be ours, Berman replied calmly, if our man for mayor could be credited with untangling the girders of the freeway. I began to hear Berman.

If Lionel could be associated with bringing ten thousand new jobs into Oakland, blacks would run to the polls to vote for him. The middle-class and liberal vote, too, would surely be his. More important, white Republican businessmen would have to acknowledge that Lionel, not their Mayor Reading, had opened the floodgates to millions of new dollars.

There were tactical questions to consider, however. First, blacks had to be convinced that the freeway would deliver the City Center jobs to them. If Lionel was elected mayor, we could point out, that question would be settled. He would be able to control the outcome and do the right thing. The city government was already situated to manage the freeway and City Center construction, having long ago allocated millions of its federal urban-renewal dollars to the downtown development. Secondly, Lionel would have to show that *he* overcame the state obstacle to the freeway that would build the City Center. I felt certain I could manage this for him.

When I called Lionel, he was at once excited and wary. He feared he would be denounced by blacks for supporting the freeway. It was still a thorn in the community side, despite the new housing. I told him the black voters could be shown that the ten thousand City Center jobs were part of the freeway project. I would take care of the few blacks who might protest. I could not imagine any of them challenging him if the Black Panther Party was behind him. The point was, I insisted, that we could not reject a plan that could propel him into office.

The blacks I contacted needed little convincing. By the end of the week, community leaders Elijah Turner, Paul Cobb, and John George (a former party lawyer who had just been elected to the Alameda County Board of Supervisors), and I were united.

Tony thought it was a splendid idea. At present, the governor was burdened by his failure to comply with his tacit preelection agreement to release the funds for the unfinished Grove-Shafter Freeway. Funds for local freeways came from a combined pot of money, 90 percent of which was federal and 10 percent state. It was the state, however, which determined the specific allocation. If Jerry was publicly pressed by the black community of Oakland to keep his promise, he would feel justified in doing so.

The problem Jerry faced, Tony explained, was his new transportation secretary, Adriana Gianturco. It was her department that authorized freeway expenditures. She was vehemently opposed to the Oakland project and had refused to release the funds. Jerry had brought her into his Cabinet because she was an environmentalist whose priority was to reduce California's massive air pollution problems by limiting the number of freeways. That idea was based on her model in Boston, from which Brown had stolen her. On the other hand, Oakland's businessmen had been bombarding Jerry with complaints about his reneging on his election promise.

Jerry was thus in a quandary over his obligation to support his own Cabinet member and his obligation to keep a political promise. In his heart, Jerry agreed with Gianturco, but he was distraught over the businessmen's pressure.

I suddenly deciphered the Michael Berman call. The Republicans had gone mad! Unable to move the governor, they had appealed to the moderate state Democratic Party leadership to prevail upon him. Jerry was so disassociated from the formal workings of his party, however, he might as well have been the Zen governor some snidely suggested he was. Berman had apparently offered to handle the matter for the downstate Democrats—for a political price. In effect, the Republican businessmen in Oakland had been reduced to consorting with the Black Panther Party.

Cobb and the others agreed that I would make the formal

appeal to the governor for the freeway. Tony arranged the meeting. I told the governor that I represented a coalition of black community groups that was spearheaded by Lionel Wilson. We had concluded that it was in our community's interest for the state to release the $33 million for the Grove-Shafter Freeway extension. Sufficiently primed, Brown agreed. The governor also agreed to endorse Lionel Wilson for mayor.

In a matter of days, the newspapers shouted that black community groups led by mayoral candidate Lionel Wilson had saved the day. Oakland would finally get its freeway. Wilson and the community had prevailed upon the governor, because the freeway would open the way for the new City Center and ten thousand new jobs for Oaklanders. The incumbent mayor—Lionel's opponent—was overcome with gratitude, the stories went.

Within a week of Jerry's announcement, several Oakland businessmen announced the formation of a business consortium: the Oakland Council for Economic Development, or the OCED. The purpose of the OCED, they declared through the press, was to develop the city's long-stalled City Center project. The mayor was thrilled that Oakland's businessmen had moved so swiftly. He gave the OCED his public blessing.

Cobb and the rest were tying up my telephone lines grumbling that the OCED was a conspiracy to steal the fruits of our labor. Not one black person had been so much as contacted about the formation of the OCED. Whitey, Cobb and the others lamented, had snatched our victory.

I reminded them that Lionel could soon be mayor. Our team would be in position to manipulate the City Center, as we had discussed. Our primary interest in the freeway was to build a bridge to Lionel's election. We had to keep focused.

Privately, I conceded that they were right. White conservative Oakland could do business as usual, and with our help. They would forget Lionel at the polls. The black community would feel that he and the rest of us had traded off our principles for an illusion. It stuck in my throat as I called Lionel.

We figured that if he publicly denounced the OCED, the blacks would feel better about him. On the other hand, he would lose his moderate appeal. The answer was somewhere in between. It was obvious, I mused aloud. Lionel would simply have to become a member of the OCED or, better yet, its chairman. As OCED chairman he could assure the black community he was safeguarding its interests while the conservatives would end up having to deal with a "nigger in the woodpile." Before he stopped laughing, I told him I would make all the arrangements.

The chairman of the OCED, Robert Shetterly, was also the president of the Clorox Company. He was glad I had called, he said, because he had heard so many nice things about me, particularly about the work I was doing with the community school.

I said that I was sure he had also heard that I was the head of the Black Panther Party, which had helped save the Grove-Shafter Freeway. I told him that I had supported the freeway only because it would open the door to the City Center project, which would mean jobs for black people. The very formation of the OCED in the aftermath was an insult to that effort. But I was most upset that not even one black was on the OCED.

He assured me his interests were the same as mine. He conceded that the freeway approval had assisted him in making the decision to organize the OCED. He felt, however, that the OCED would serve the best interests of *all* Oakland residents.

I told him I was pleased to hear that. I was looking to him to demonstrate it. My friends and I expected, therefore, his enthusiastic endorsement for the placement of a black on the OCED. I was recommending Lionel Wilson, whom I was certain I could convince to share the OCED chair with him, Robert Shetterly. With Lionel as cochair, I offered, not only would the community feel assured of the OCED's concerns, but he, Shetterly, would be assured of assistance in steering the goals of the OCED.

Stuttering, he said that he was part of a team and that, while he might welcome Lionel's input, he could not dictate to the others.

I was sorry he felt so impotent, I said. It rendered me impotent, too. I felt powerless to stop the Black Panther Party and other black community organizations from unleashing the same energy which supported the Grove-Shafter to now discourage its construction.

There was a long pause. Shetterly finally responded that he would like to consider the matter, to mull it over with the OCED. "Think long. Think wrong," I said, quoting my mother. He chuckled.

Gianturco was furious, Tony told me. She remained adamantly opposed to the Oakland project; she thought it benefited no one but a few rich businessmen. She felt the governor had overridden her because he was a male chauvinist, and she was threatening to resign. Tony said the governor would probably be relieved to have an excuse to rescind his pledge. Tony agreed then that if Shetterly did not place a member of the black community—Lionel—on the OCED forthwith, the governor would withdraw from the freeway fray.

I called the Clorox offices. Shetterly explained he was having difficulty discussing the matter with his peers; most of them were out of town on business. He asked for another week to try to confirm Lionel as a member of the OCED. He hoped I could understand, however, how untenable it would be to make Lionel cochair.

I interrupted. Since he was unwilling to take the correct course, I said the state pledge to fund the freeway would be rescinded. Arguing that that would serve no good purpose, he held his ground on the implausibility of that possibility.

A week later, the governor's office informed the Oakland mayor's office that the state's commitment to Oakland's freeway extension was canceled. The governor's press release stated that the city of Oakland had violated the good faith on which the freeway funds had been released.

The stated purpose of the new OCED, the governor's press release continued, was to develop the City Center project. However, although the development interests of the OCED could only be realized because of the work of the black community, blacks themselves were starkly absent from its membership. This had opened Brown's eyes. The OCED was using the state's gift to the community of Oakland to serve narrow business interests. As that was contrary to the spirit of Governor Brown's commitment, that commitment was revoked.

I waited in my office at the school for the telephone calls. I refused Shetterly's. I talked with Cobb and George and the others about the morning newspapers' front-page stories. Mayor Reading was in a state of considerable rage. J. Anthony Kline had called him from the governor's office, he stated, to inform him that the governor was "deserting" the city of Oakland. Reading was "shocked." The mayor denounced the governor's decision as a political ploy.

I told the press ringing me that I endorsed the governor's decision, that in fact I had appealed to him for justice.

Lionel's elation was tempered. If he was now placed on the OCED, it might appear that the wrong kind of political bargain had been made. Moreover, he reasoned, if he was elected, he would be unable to justify having his feet in two camps. He had thought about how to salvage the situation. He concluded that *I* should be on the OCED. As he saw it, Oakland was in economic shambles and would remain so even if he became mayor. We needed the power of the OCED to pull it up as much as they needed the freeway. If I were on the council, it would underwrite everything. We had to "seize the time," Lionel laughed, quoting the title of my first record album.

I needed the support, as well as the consensus, of the others. I called them. They thought it was a perfect plan. I accepted Shetterly's call late in the day.

Shetterly wondered if I realized that the Hyatt executives and others, waiting in the wings with their millions of City Center investment dollars, had become thoroughly discouraged. They were ready to close off all discussion. He could calm the troubled waters, I told him, and without haggling over Lionel's membership. The black community would be satisfied with *my* membership on the council, I offered, and added, in his silence, that I felt certain the governor could be convinced to recommit the freeway funds upon my appointment to the council.

Shetterly laughed. It was the laugh of the losing poker player who had had the best hand. We agreed to meet for lunch in the next few days.

We met at an elegant restaurant atop the Kaiser Center, overlooking Lake Merritt. Having arrived early, Robert Shetterly greeted me at the entrance to the restaurant. I had never seen his face, but he knew mine—moreover, I was the only black woman there.

Shetterly looked me over with the subtlety of well-bred white men. I did not need to consider him so carefully. He was everything I opposed. We were meeting in his world, but we were at that moment standing on common ground, face to face with what we each detested most about America. We reviewed our menus, chatting pleasantly about the flowers planted in the rooftop garden outside the window adjacent to our table.

"It's a very interesting bunch in Sacramento now," Shetterly ventured. "Are you planning to run for the City Council again?"

"Not at all. I think I serve my interests best in other capacities."

"As to your interests, Elaine—if I may—I've spoken, as I

promised, with everyone on the council. We're all in complete agreement that you'd be a fine addition to our membership."

"I think that's best for all concerned. And I've spoken with Tony Kline. He's sure that under the circumstances the governor can be persuaded to reinstate the freeway funds."

"It's such a small amount of money," he said in a dry tone.

We ordered crab salads and wine.

I looked directly into his eyes. "I'll be going back to Sacramento this week and will let you know the outcome of things. So you can notify the council and the investors—and, naturally, the mayor."

He did not appreciate my sarcasm.

"John Reading is really a fine man, once you get to know him."

"Though that's highly unlikely, of course."

"Well, the mayor is a nonvoting member of the council, you know."

I tried not to rush from my chair to the telephone to call Lionel. "Actually, I'm not specifically aware of who sits on the OCED."

As he listed the fifteen or so members of the OCED, an understanding came to me. Kaiser Industries (which included Kaiser Aluminum, Kaiser Steel, and Kaiser Health Plan) was on the council, as were the chief executives of Safeway Stores (the largest food outlet in the world), Pacific Bell (the California affiliate of AT&T), the *Oakland Tribune*, and others of the same ilk. It was a *cartel*. The form was local, but its substance was global.

What became clear to me was not so much *what* Shetterly and his men had built as *why* they had built it. It was not a simple matter of developing the City Center. Unlike other capitalists of the day, who had spirited away their operations to lily-white hinterlands when their industrial centers became crowded with black and poor people, Shetterly had organized the OCED to wrest Oakland from the encroaching, hostile natives. For he intended to seize the *future*, as it sparkled on the waters of the second-largest port in the world.

That port's business was confined by the city of Oakland, even though the billions of dollars it was currently pumping had never belonged to the city. They had always belonged to the progeny of the founding fathers, distributed at the discretion of the private, independent port board. Now the port's billions had the potential to be exponentially increased through trade agreements with the rising economies in Japan, South Korea, Hong Kong—in all of the Pacific Rim and Asian countries.

The three-quarter-mile piece of concrete called the Grove-Shafter freeway extension was the tie to the harbor for those international billions. As the foundation for the City Center, that freeway would do more than reintroduce into Oakland the lost middle-class millions ferreted away in the surrounding white townships. It would be the keystone of a new, global economic community. And such communities would surely supplant nations by the onset of the twenty-first century.

It was a very big game. Shetterly had recently lost a bid to merge Clorox with Colgate-Palmolive. All that was left now was his twenty-two-story edifice built to sanitize the still-black heart of downtown Oakland and be a foundation for the economic community of Oakland that he and Reagan and Reading and their club had envisioned. Shetterly and his men had the same agenda as the Black Panther Party: to claim Oakland.

"We meet monthly, early in the morning," he was saying. I noted his insinuation that black people were known to be too sluggardly to rise at the start of the day. "Right here, at the Kaiser Center, in a breakfast meeting. My secretary will call you to inform you of the next meeting and tell you exactly how to get to the meeting room."

I said, "I think it's premature to resume your meetings until I've gotten confirmation of the governor's change of heart."

I lit a cigarette. There seemed to be nothing else to say.

But Shetterly began again. "I'm curious, Elaine—what is it you *really* want?"

"Do you mean what do I want as the head of the Black Panther Party, Shetterly? What do I want as a black person, or what do I want as a black woman?

He smiled. "I mean whatever you'd like."

"It was your question."

"Well, you see, I believe that in America we have to allow for all kinds of philosophies."

"That's very generous of America, assuming you're speaking for America."

"What I'm trying to say is that while my own life has not permitted me a great deal of contact with black people, I believe America must open its doors to blacks . . ."

"Or you get Black Panthers?"

"Perhaps. At Clorox, though, we've been very serious about enforcing the federal guidelines for affirmative action in employment."

"It certainly makes good business sense," I said.

"Yes, but also, I've been sensitized, you might say, to the problems of those outside of the mainstream. My son is doing volunteer work at a free clinic in San Francisco, in the Haight-Ashbury district. The stories he's told me about the poor health and the lives of so many of the clinic's clients are, well, quite appalling. I've come to truly believe that something must be done to assist blacks and poor people. But I'm not sure what that is."

I refrained from responding.

Finally, I said, "I'm glad you told me about your son. It broadens my understanding of you, and of your question, as to what I want . . . When I was a little girl, I wanted to be white. My mother sent me to schools dominated by rich white children where I learned that I was a 'nigger.' Oh, it wasn't because anybody called me that, but because I saw that I was poor and black.

"So I came to believe that if I could be white, or as white as my color permitted, I could be elevated from the degradation of being a 'nigger.' I trained myself to talk like white people, to act like white people, to walk and dress and eat like white people. I made every effort possible to belong to white people."

"You've had a very difficult life," he said, now attempting to end the meeting.

"The point is not about my life, Shetterly. It's about what I want. And I think you should know exactly what that is and how much I want it . . . By the time I realized there was no place in America for a black girl, I discovered another trick. Even if I had been able to be white, there were no paths out of the powerlessness. The keys to the kingdom were gripped in the hands of a few white men—and *only* men. I could work for those men, if I 'behaved,' but I could never *be* them, have what they had, be master of my own ship . . . What I saw was that my oppression and my freedom were *umbilically* tied to the oppression and freedom of all my people. So I became a Black Panther."

"I think you should've tried harder. You're very bright and you could have done more. There *are* opportunities."

"Before you give me the standard statement about how I could have personally persevered and entered the mainstream, I want to finish the point. I also knew that I could never walk over the bodies of black girls like me. For that's one of the entrance fees. I mean, even if I had found a loophole—some way to get out of poverty and ease past racism—I could not do to *anyone* what had been done to me. So it's not a personal matter anymore."

"It's a sacrifice, though, don't you think?"

"For whom? Me? There's no sacrifice at all, because in the end I get everything I really want."

"And what is that?" he asked, with raised eyebrows.

"I want a new arrangement between you and me. I want to change the situation—*equalize* it.

"What I want, as the mother of Ericka Brown, is to keep her from having to dream about a job at Clorox, any Clorox. I want to make a place for her to have her own dreams. And to live out those dreams.

"As a black person, I want to see my people free from all oppression, to be able to develop into a proud and independent people.

"As a leading member of the Black Panther Party, I want to initiate that new arrangement. What the Black Panther Party wants is a new America. We want to diminish the power of you and yours over so many of us through the institution of a humane and egalitarian society—we could call it socialism. I hope the word's not too scary."

"I'm not sure of its precise definition, but I think you're talking about communism, and that system is not just scary, it can destroy the world."

"Well, whatever may come of my revolution, Shetterly, there's nothing for you to fear. None of it will come to pass in either of our lifetimes. Right now, all Elaine Brown actually wants is very little: every one of the ten thousand jobs at the City Center. And I want your guarantee to deliver them."

"Of course, I'd be delighted to help unemployed people get jobs," he said, sidestepping everything.

"I'm not talking about an affirmative-action program or anything like that, Shetterly. I intend to create an entity that the Black Panther Party will operate and control, through which I want each and every one of those City Center jobs funneled. I want you, under whatever title, to sign an exclusive agreement with this nonprofit corporation to act as the sole contractor of City Center personnel."

"May I ask why you want to do that?"

"Certainly. I'd think you'd find it interesting. And I don't mind sharing this with you because it won't affect what either of us has to do. As it's turned out, you need me to get what *you* want—perhaps more than I need you.

"Before I explain, you should know that I'm not overly concerned about the temporary freeway construction jobs. The so-called minorities will get a fair share of them, because my friends in the state will handle that. And if Lionel Wilson is elected mayor, he'll make sure the city's urban-renewal antidiscrimination guidelines are enforced as to construction of the City Center. By the way, I know you're a Republican, but I'm banking on your tacit underwriting of Lionel."

"But you must realize, Elaine, that while Lionel Wilson may be a fine candidate, I could not support him."

"I'm not trying to push this thing that far, Shetterly. I really want to work with you. I'm just suggesting you use your influence to influence others not to attack him. You know, assail his image for having Black Panther support."

"I think you give me too much credit."

"I don't think so. But I'm sure you appreciate that such a thing would undermine what each of us wants to accomplish."

We were now the only diners in the restaurant.

"As to my new City Center Employment Corporation, I intend to make it a political undertaking, to organize and educate the ten thousand mostly black persons that will be hired. Each of them can be organized around individual employment interests and *group* interests. Soon, those ten thousand, and the many thousands more among their families and friends, will have developed the consciousness and the will to act as one. They will be a force to bring about more *fundamental* changes in their collective interest. You see the point? The development of a socialistic model right here in Oakland.

"In any case, the bottom line is the ten thousand City Center jobs that you'll have control of. If I don't get a signed agreement by ground-breaking time, I don't see the freeway rolling."

"I think we understand each other, though I might have said it differently."

"I'm sure you would have." I laughed.

He laughed, too.

"But there's one other thing I've got, Shetterly. Besides the freeway. I've got the ability to take down this entire city if you and I fail to see this thing to completion. I mean the City Center, the port, and all twenty-two stories of the Clorox building."

"Despite your passion, Elaine, I think you're far too intelligent and sophisticated to mean everything you say."

He smiled the admonishing smile of a father. I smiled back, though I considered reaching across the table and slapping him.

I called Lionel. Whatever would come of the Shetterly business, I told him, I had certain expectations about his role in the future of Oakland.

I was guaranteeing him our party's support in becoming mayor of Oakland. I had only three requests.

I wanted to replace the police chief of Oakland with a black who would assume that position with the clear understanding that I—in the Panther sense—had put him in office. Secondly, I wanted to be a silent partner in his selection of a new city manager. Finally, I wanted him over the years to support my recommendations for vacancies on the port board.

He said it was the least he could do.

Adriana Gianturco operated in a man's world and seemed to know exactly how to do that. Under other circumstances, I might have held her iron will in high esteem. At the moment, it was infuriating.

As long as she was transportation secretary of the state of California, she was saying, her refusal to release the Grove-Shafter Freeway funds would remain firm. She was not interested in my arguments, though she said she was glad to meet me.

She did not care about construction contracts and jobs for blacks in the building of the freeway. Her main concern was the environmental impact of building another freeway. She was aware that black people had been displaced by the freeway land allocation. She reminded me that the Reagan people had done that and suggested that I might spend my energy on developing the new housing. She was absolutely unconcerned about the political aspirations of Lionel Wilson, or the blacks who wanted a black mayor.

I told her that her environmentalism was a charade for her racism.

"Don't give me that shit, Elaine," she said in her non-Boston, Southern-rooted accent.

I informed her that the Black Panther Party would publicly denounce her, spurring the entire black community to assail her with ugly epithets. She had been called names before, she said, by profit-seeking "pigs" demanding highways from Massachusetts to California. I pounded my fist on her desk. "Who in the fuck do you think you are?" She was not intimidated.

I had gone to Sacramento to see her the day after Tony called to tell me that even though the governor knew the businessmen had placed me on the OCED, Gianturco was so furious about the freeway that neither the governor nor anybody else felt a fight with her over it was worth the havoc it would wreak. Tony told me he was making every effort to resolve the issue, but that it could take months. I knew how to change Gianturco's mind, I had told him.

Now I was ready to hurl her out of the window of her office. Shetterly's millions was not the point, I reiterated. It was that a socially committed black man could become mayor. It was that the "people's" Oakland, not "their" Oakland, could be rejuvenated— the Oakland that was also the headquarters of the Black Panther Party. Ten thousand permanent jobs would be made available to poor and black people. She remained unaffected. In desperation, I changed strategy and pleaded with her.

I asked her to weigh the value of an only slightly improved environment against the lives of poor people who had little hope of employment without the fruits of the freeway. I urged her to think about what clean air meant to people who were too op-pressed to lift their heads and breathe it. I implored her to imagine life as a black person, what it felt like to be denied one more time, by one more white person.

I knew I had the freeway when she suggested that there was no way to enforce the promises of the businessmen. She had heard their promises before. Her laughter filled the room when I told her that none of those promises had been made to the Black Panther Party. She actually howled as I summarized my conver-sation with Shetterly, in which I had promised to destroy "his" City Center if he reneged. I told her about the new employment corporation, and that Fred Hiestand was registering it to do business.

She finally said, "I'll do it, Elaine, but not because I believe the businessmen will do the right thing. If the Panthers think you can control the thing and benefit somebody, it's worth a try. I have to tell you the truth, though. I don't fucking think you can do it."

"I'm not sure either, Adriana, but the thing is, we may never have such a moment again. In addition to the jobs, this freeway can get our man elected. That'll put us in position to transfer power and money into the hands of the people. Not only from the City Center, but from Coliseum revenues and the like, and, most important, from the port of Oakland. The environment won't be saved or damaged by this. And black people won't be freed by it. I just think we can make some change in the arrangement that's damaged both my people and this planet."

"All right. I told you I'm convinced you believe in what you say. Take the freeway. Try to use it for something good. You've got my commitment. But I'm still warning you, they'll stab you in the back. And I won't open my mouth, except to say 'I told you so.' "

I had a strange feeling when I shook Adriana's hand. For the first time in my life, I felt a white woman was my Sister.

Shetterly was in command as usual. He suggested I sit next to him in the back of the chauffeured car. He arranged the others, the head of Kaiser Health Plan to sit on my right, with Pacific Bell facing us. We had made our adjustments with each other after the first few OCED meetings I attended. I nestled comfortably into the soft dark velour of the limousine seat. Everything was clear now: our "partnership" and our present business, which was to meet with the governor.

I knew Shetterly was trying to eliminate the middle man—me. He remarked to the others how impressed he was that I had so quickly arranged the meeting with the governor. The other club members parroted his appreciation.

Shetterly ostensibly wanted to meet the governor to shore up the City Center project. Based on Adriana's change of position, Bullocks Department Store, the Hyatt Regency, Sears, and the others had reactivated their pledges to locate in downtown Oakland. But Shetterly also wanted to shore up his relationship with the popular Democratic governor for the broader OCED agenda. This was a move in his constant manipulation of the pecking order of his club that could guarantee his leadership in the future. Of equal importance, he was trying to free himself from the Black Panther connection.

I enjoyed watching his anxiety about the meeting. I enjoyed watching him attempt to use me. Mostly, I relished looking at his face once he realized the Sacramento connection would remain in my hands.

As we rode to Sacramento, I thanked Shetterly for applauding me for so little, though it was true, I added, that the governor was not prone to holding personal meetings with special-interest groups. Everyone chuckled on cue. And as I listened to Shetterly once again decry how terribly small that three-quarter-mile free-way extension was in relation to everything that hinged on it, I silently agreed.

The governor told Shetterly that Oakland could rely on him to keep his word on the freeway. As for the other concerns, he would welcome opening a channel to his office for the OCED, as long as the community's interests remained a priority. He concluded that he hoped Shetterly would relay his sentiments to the City Center investors.

It was a very quiet ride back to Oakland.

Despite the excitement of the party's progress, I felt a sense of doom—my doom.

It was connected to death. I was feeling not so much a fear of death as an awareness of the loneliness of dying. These thoughts had consumed me since the abortion.

A week after another of the numerous ruptures in our personal relationship, Larry and I had resumed our part-time love affair. When we argued the week before, I had decided never to have another affair with any man, and to underscore my determination, I had put away my birth-control pills. Seven days later, I anxiously prepared for a night of celebration with Larry by swallowing one week's supply of pills. I actually believed the accumulated dosage would be effective. I was shocked by my stupidity the next month.

There was no doubt that I would have an abortion. My life in the party had no space for another child, a child I did not desire. There was nothing to discuss with Larry. My body was mine.

It would be a very simple operation, the doctor explained to me. The fetus would be aborted in minutes; I would be able to return home in half an hour.

Legs apart, I listened to the soft whirring sound of the instrument that quickly emptied my uterus. I felt nothing—except sorrow.

I did not know what was being removed from my womb. But I felt it was something, somebody, who had tried to live—as I had tried for so long. And it was I who had broken the connection. I had destroyed the potential.

The immorality of it stung something deep in me. It was not in thinking that I had killed someone. I had done something worse. I had prevented someone from coming into being. I wanted to grab that being and say that I was sorry. I wanted to push it into some other womb, some other time, some other life. There was no god or man or woman, though, who could alter what I had done.

It was fitting that I live alone. When I moved into the new apartment, the doom filled all the empty spaces. It eclipsed the pride I felt in how well Lionel's campaign was progressing. It muted the pleasure of the press conference in which the governor, Shetterly, and I announced that ground would soon be broken for the new City Center bringing ten thousand new jobs to Oakland. Representatives of the Hyatt Corporation and Bullocks et al. had stood with us before the television cameras. Everything had been confirmed in writing. Nevertheless, I was sullen.

Ericka Huggins had been my close friend and comrade for nearly ten years. It had been painful to leave her. But I had to. I had become angry with her. Hardly a day passed when I did not chastise her over the decisions she made, accusing her of abandoning her post at the school to Regina Davis, her assistant. Recently, I had attacked her for absentmindedly leaving her key in our apartment door, for preparing "organic" meals, for burning candles and incense. The truth was her unburdened sorrow had begun to heighten my sense of doom. The truth was I brought every rage of the day to our door, and she never responded, her sorrowful eyes accusing and accepting. I had to live alone. It was best I live alone. She agreed, in her languid voice.

It was best, I repeated to Larry, though I knew there would be the same kind of resentment in the ranks as there had been when Huey moved into his penthouse.

The grumbling was mild and short-lived, however. Panthers were enjoying a highly upgraded standard of living at that point, and most credited my leadership with having produced it. Moreover, Larry had pointed out to the members that the expense of my new housing arrangement was also justified by the need for absolute security for the party's leader.

It was an all-white refuge, built before the Crash, when crystal doorknobs and handmade tiles and polished-brass fixtures were in vogue. I began to wonder if moving into that isolated security palace, with its cold parquet floors and lakeside luxury, had caused my sense of doom. Perhaps it arose from the second bedroom, reserved for my Ericka, my daughter, who, at seven years old, had never lived with her mother. There was a disturbing unfamiliarity in having her close. I had been a Black Panther all the years of her life—not her mother, in any meaningful way. Perhaps it was that in the apartment there was space to finally look at myself after thirty-four years of living with others. All of it seemed strange and uncomfortable.

I had no patience to deal with the distribution of damaging leaflets in the hills of Oakland three days before the election. A photo-reproduction of the front page of a Panther newspaper announcing the party's endorsement of Lionel was being circulated in Republican strongholds. Under the headline was a large photograph of Lionel, Cesar Chavez, and me.

I called Shetterly. It was after ten o'clock at night. He was asleep. We were at the brink, I shouted. I could not manage the party, the election, the freeway business, the Oakland Community Housing, the OCED, and also have to contend with his backstabbing. Of course, he knew nothing about it. Of course, he could not control what everybody did. I silenced him with a variety of reminders about the freeway, the City Center project, the existence of the Clorox building. I told him I knew he had tried to orchestrate a takeover of Colgate-Palmolive, but if he felt that had been a defeat, he could not imagine how defeated he would be if another piece of paper or word was issued connecting Lionel to the Black Panther Party. He told me he would look into the problem. I slammed down the telephone.

We rode out those next two days on the hope of the pollsters' accuracy. Lionel was projected to win.

Phyllis had registered over 90,000 black Democrats. She had had their registration cards copied before they were sent to the office of the county voter registrar. Now administering all of Lionel's campaign workers, she had commanded them to contact every one of those 90,000, to determine when they would vote, whether they needed transportation to the polls, baby-sitters, or anything else to assist them in voting.

On Election Day, Phyllis fielded every Panther and every

other campaign worker, on foot, in cars, and on buses, to drag those black registrants to the polls. The streets of Oakland were being harvested.

At the Alameda County Central Labor Council offices, Panthers were working with labor leaders to squeeze out the maximum labor vote. I saw the excitement on the faces of the mostly black workers at the voter registrar's office: black precincts were, atypically, voting early in the day. I passed Panther cars going in and out of the most dilapidated areas, including the government housing projects in West and East Oakland, taking mothers and their children to the polls. Panthers were virtually tearing people away from card and dice games and all-day drug parties to vote. The excitement of the day was so intoxicating, it immunized me against the still-clinging dread, temporarily.

Finally, the television reports proclaimed that Lionel Wilson had become the first black mayor of Oakland, the first Democrat elected to office since World War II. I stood at Lionel's side while the cameras recorded his victory and thousands cheered.

I did not tell Huey how all the pieces had fallen into place. I told him Lionel had won. I told him to come home. I said nothing at all about my sense of doom.

C H A P T E R 21

"I'LL CHANGE
THE WORLD
FOR YOU"

IF JOHN COULD JUST TOUCH ME, *like before, before he died. I need to feel his hands—even from the grave . . . Sit in the chair. This madness is only temporary. No. I have to move and not think. No. Think of John . . . John, John, remember when you came to me in Watts? Come now, please. This is the longest spell.*

I slept. For three days I did not move from the couch in Ericka Huggins's apartment. I ate some of Ericka's macrobiotic food and took the megadoses of Thorazine Dr. Shapiro had prescribed. I did not wash or change my clothes. I spoke only with Larry and Ericka—there for me as I had not been for her. They kept vigil over me. I was afraid to be alone in my own apartment. I was ashamed to see my daughter. Then Huey came.

He came with Big Bob and Gwen. They sat in a group, away from me. They looked ridiculous.

Huey had returned in July. "I didn't come back to replace you," he had said. "We'll run this thing as partners." He had no desire to disturb the organization that was now unrecognizable to him.

Larry was the strongest chief of staff Huey had ever seen. He thought Norma was "out of sight" in the way she had managed the millions of new dollars in cash and other things he had been awed to find we had accumulated. The Lamp Post, the school, all the programs and projects were being smoothly administered. My membership on the OCED he thought of as a powerful thing, though he showed little enthusiasm for it. He was proud the Oakland Community Housing Corporation had started the design for the three hundred new houses for the freeway "victims," suggesting I might, as chair, push to have the new complex named for Bobby Hutton—"the first to fall." He was gratified, he said, that he would be able to spend the next months concentrating on his upcoming murder trial.

Thousands had greeted him at the airport. They had gone away to wait for him, to do something dynamic or dramatic again. But he had settled into the beautiful new house we had gotten for him in the Oakland hills, at first content to just focus on his trial.

He had been pleased with his new trial attorney, Sheldon Otis. Fred Hiestand had found the right lawyer for him, he said. Otis was an experienced criminal defense attorney and far ahead of most in his class. He had built a machine to win the cases he defended. Otis's savvy, Huey had agreed, left little room to doubt that he would win.

I was looking at him across the room in Ericka's apartment, smartly dressed in his new vicuña sports jacket. He had space to develop his ideas and to create new ones, and time to write and live. I wanted to ask him why he had chosen the most destructive course instead. I was too afraid, because I sensed that *he* was afraid. He did not want to hear one more chorus of the same song, "We Need Our Leader to Guide Us." He had returned to the familiar ghetto instinct. I had watched him rely on that instinct more and more in the past several weeks. And I had begun to realize I was losing him to a world he himself knew was self-destructive.

Now he was suspicious of everything. He was suspicious of Otis. He was suspicious of Lionel. Since he really did not know Phyllis or Norma, they became suspect, too . . . *But you know me, Huey*, I wanted to say to him, in the calm of three days of Thorazine.

Big Bob smiled, as though he understood my thoughts. It was a smug, satisfied smile that suggested he knew "they" had won something. I looked at Larry, who had seated himself in a chair on the side, between them and me. His eyes said nothing.

Bob had, I believed, resented my leadership from the beginning. I assumed it had as much to do with his jealousy of my having placed Larry in the position he felt should have been his as with the fact that I was a woman. After he was released from prison, I felt that he had resented me even more, particularly for putting a rein on his violent tendencies. He had checked his frustrations with me until the moment Huey stepped back into Oakland. He was not alone, however. I had heard the male mantra with which he and others taunted Huey about how "weak" the party had become, meaning women in leadership positions.

Within a month of his return, Huey was riding the streets again with various security squad members, and Bob and Larry —whom Bob was nudging out of place next to Huey.

They would start with dinner at the Lamp Post. Afterward, the brotherhood would commence all-night rounds of drinking at numerous bars. Soon, Huey and his entourage of restless gunmen were prowling the after-hours clubs nightly with no purpose other than to intimidate.

Huey's house had become headquarters for the men, a sanctuary for machismo, where I envisioned the conclave of Brothers spending their days and nights shaking their penises at each other, wallowing in the absence of "bitches."

Huey was trapped between the burden of responsibility for an organism that had created him more than he had created it, as he told me so often, and the irresponsible ease of floating inside a world of angry men which he at once understood and detested. Huey's duality, the party's duality, crystallized the day our school was to receive its highest tribute.

Several lawmakers from the Bay Area, steered by black assemblyman John Miller, had urged the legislature to issue a commendation to the Oakland Community School for having set the standard for the highest level of elementary education in the state. The presentation would be made in Sacramento. Ericka Huggins accompanied about twenty-five of our children in several of our school vans. Aaron Dixon, my bodyguard, drove me there. Huey, who would come in his own car, was to receive the award on behalf of the school. That would clarify any ambiguity about his postexile role and buttress his character references for his upcoming trial.

State assemblyman Tom Bates would make the formal presentation. He greeted Ericka and the children and me in the morning sunshine of August on the capitol steps. The children glowed in their brand-new dresses and little suits. We had a brief lunch together; then the children toured the capitol. We waited for Huey. We delayed the presentation for two hours, waiting. The other legislators in attendance left. The press corps dwindled.

Huey and Big Bob finally arrived, disheveled and unseemly. I realized then that Huey had returned to cocaine.

He and Ericka and I stood on the capitol steps in the late afternoon. Bates handed him our official proclamation certificate. Huey's body shivered. His eyes bulged, and he could hardly accept the parchment for wiping his nose and sniffing. Ericka and I acknowledged our embarrassment with a glance.

Ericka had the good fortune of having to leave immediately, to take the children back to Oakland. I had to wait with Huey to arrange his transportation. In a drunken stupor, Bob had fallen asleep at the wheel of their car en route to Sacramento. The car had been abandoned on the highway, where they had commandeered a ride from a stranger, reportedly after offering him several hundred dollars.

Bob's eyes had been smug then, as they were now, looking into mine, knowing that I had retreated, not knowing it was back into the familiarity of my own madness. I had escaped to the sick bed of my youth. Huey glanced guiltily at me from time to time. He knew exactly what was happening. He knew, too, that I alone was aware of how he really felt about the men. His eyes pleaded with me to appreciate how hard they were biting at him, testing him.

Did I not remember, his eyes said, that we had acknowledged to each other how both of us had been at the center of our mother's lives, only to be tossed terrified onto the streets outside, where we became objects of derision. For him, it had been worse. The ghetto could be deadly for male children: knives brandished, then guns, then gang warfare. He had carried his ice pick inside a paper bag and gained a reputation as "crazy Huey," to ward off the attacks on the "yellow nigger," the "pretty boy," the "punk" that he would have been otherwise.

They look like my shoes, motherfucker.

They might be, 'cause yo' mama gave 'em to me last night.

He wanted to retreat from both worlds. But he knew how to deal with the men. He reverted to the instinct that always saved him when fear was all he knew. He turned his eyes away from me.

I looked at Bob and Larry, hearing echoes of the men's accusations that Huey had let some bitch run their shit, intrude upon their world, where aggression and violence defined manhood. I could hear the "signifying," which had ignited the macho instincts in the others—perhaps even in Perkins and Ricardo—displayed in night after night of carousing, and then cocaine all around. Larry was surely part of it, torn as he was by his turmoil over my leadership, by Huey's increasing deference to Bob, by our history over the past three years, by the respect I had given him.

As I gazed at Bob, I saw that both of us knew a line had been drawn somewhere along the way since Huey's return. The party's armed men had accepted on faith the femaleness that had burdened them since Huey left. Or they had satisfied themselves with the temporariness of it. In the softness of those times, most had held in check their sense of manly disgrace. Huey's postexile pronouncements that he was not climbing back into his poster image, and that the party leadership shared equally between men and women would remain as it had during his exile, enraged them. A gang had formed at Huey's door and called him out. Nobody said it, but it was understood that the Panther was a man.

Rising, Huey finally said that he and Bob and Gwen were only passing through on their way to dinner, to see how I was doing.

"I'm fine, Huey" was all I could manage.

He averted his eyes again. Bob stood. Gwen, having nothing to decipher, because her life belonged to him wherever it took her, rose with feline grace.

As Bob and Gwen waited at the door, Huey kissed me on the cheek and whispered to me, "Get well. Buy yourself some new things. Maybe take a little vacation. A few days with Suzanne de Passe, or something."

He was trying to signal me to step away from what he could neither leave nor save for me.

I returned to my apartment that night with Phyllis. She talked to me while I showered for the first time in days. She would stay with me and drive me the next day to do some shopping—as instructed. I laughed.

At the I. Magnin store in San Francisco, I was giddy. Over the years in the party, I had never imagined buying anything for anybody that did not have a purpose—our clothing, our homes, our cars, all of which belonged to the party, were properties of our political theater, selected to make impressions, to do one or another thing. I looked at the racks of clothing and mounds of sparkling jewelry and things, wondering what it felt like to wear something just for the pleasure of wearing it. I touched coats in the fur shop and tried them on, insisting Phyllis do the same. She laughed at me.

Impulsively, I called Norma from the fur shop telephone and told her to bring me $10,000 in cash. She was appalled, until I reminded her that most of the money she protected had been raised by Phyllis and me and we had never abused one dime of it. I bought a silver fox jacket for Phyllis and a red fox one for myself. Giddy, I went on to buy leather boots and silk blouses and other trinkets until the entire $10,000 was gone.

I called Suzanne. She seemed to hear what I did not say, for she said that I could stay with her as long as I wanted, or needed, to.

The friendship Suzanne and I had found in each other was outside "her" Berry Gordy and "my" Huey Newton, beyond her Harlem and my North Philly. In the seven years since we had met, our friendship had evolved, as we had in our respective spheres, she emerging as a vice president of Motown Records.

She had personally signed for Motown the Jackson 5, as well as Lionel Richie and the Commodores, carrying Motown past the sixties. She had done it through years of struggle with the million relatives Motown's chief, Berry Gordy, brought into his fold. She had survived being road manager for the Supremes, survived the sadness that had emptied her at nineteen, when her groom-to-be left her at the church door to marry another girl. She had done it while enduring racism and antiwoman attacks, and the kinds of insults in Detroit that I had suffered in L.A., when "bourgois bitches" like us were castigated by Detroit street singers and ex-gang members called Panthers. I really needed to see Suzanne. She was more than a friend. She was my sister-hero.

In the two days I spent with her, Suzanne never asked why I was there or how long I intended to stay. I slept well, without Thorazine, disturbed only by a nagging desire to remain. The difference between Huey and me, I thought as I kissed Suzanne goodbye, was that he was a man and I was not—gods always being men, or perhaps the other way around.

I survived the next weeks in Oakland on dwindling doses of Thorazine and little contact with anyone in the party.

Ericka Brown was a patient child, I thought, as I looked at her each night. At seven years old, she had a witty humor that was always filled with double entendres. She was tough, too, ready to stand her ground with children and adults alike, particularly in cases where she perceived an injustice.

Watching her now, I began to wonder what I represented to her. I began to think of what I really was, without the pseudonyms of revolutionary, black, or woman. I had made myself into this or that, according to the tune and the time. I was terrified by what

I was—a nasty nothing. My life had been a charade of imitating other people who, unlike me, were real.

The Black Panther Party had given me a definition. I had learned that racism and other oppressions bore down deep into the fabric of lives like mine and crippled them. And I had found peace in this knowing. I had found strength in the party's commitment to fight oppression. Now the barricades the party had erected against oppression seemed to be eroding. There would be *no* defenses for my daughter. Ericka, like me, would be estranged from all worlds.

I kept her close to me, hoping for the best.

The telephone rang. Big Bob had been arrested, Norma told me with a sigh.

He had been drinking all night at the Lamp Post. He had walked out into the early light with half a bottle of bar whiskey in one hand and a Sister in the other. The police assigned to watch our club had stopped him the moment he started to drive away. He had fought them and lost. He was beaten severely and arrested for assault. Sundry additional charges were attached to his arrest, including possession of a handgun and driving under the influence of alcohol.

Norma asked if his bail should be paid. I told her not right away.

Within a half hour, I heard from Huey. Bob was "his man." He had to be freed immediately. "Big Bob would die for me," he exhorted.

I could not support that position, I said, but it was his party. If he commanded me, I would have Bob's bail paid immediately.

Bob had violated every rule of party discipline, I said. He forced the Lamp Post to remain open for him and then confiscated a bottle of alcohol; he was drunk in public; he was unnecessarily armed. He had flagrantly jeopardized us. In nearly three years, not one such incident had been tolerated. I could not understand why the rules should now be abandoned.

Huey did not speak. I added that I felt Bob needed disciplining. He should wait a few days for his bail to be paid, to learn that the party could not be manipulated whenever he fancied violating its rules.

My jaw tightened as Huey implored me to pay the bail immediately. I would do so only, I said, if he issued me an order. Huey's order that Bob be gotten out of jail forthwith was incidental. What I heard was the bond breaking.

This was not about Bob. I recalled a conversation I had had with several of the Brothers one night, including Bob and Larry. Chortling, they had suggested that "if all else failed" the party had the ability to become a kind of black version of the Mafia. We have the guns and the men, they had boasted. We could take what we want from the Establishment. I had not considered what they said worthy of argument.

They wanted so little from our revolution, they had lost sight of it. Too many of them seemed satisfied to appropriate for themselves the power the party was gaining, measured by the shiny illusion of cars and clothes and guns. They were even willing to cash in their revolutionary principles for a self-serving "Mafia." If a Mafia was what they wanted, I would not be part of it.

A week later, Ericka Huggins called me. It was the first time I had known her to really cry. I always assumed all her tears had been left on John's grave. Regina Davis, her assistant, had been hospitalized as the result of a severe beating, her jaw broken. The Brothers had done it. Ericka was sobbing, begging me to tell her what was happening. I assured her that I would take care of everything.

I called Huey. His response was not that of my lover or leader. It was a bland acknowledgment that he had indeed given his authorization for Regina's discipline. I explained to Huey exactly who Regina Davis was, as I was sure he had no idea. Regina held together the proudest of our programs, our school. Without the recognition of Central Committee membership, she had worked more than fifteen hours of every day of every week for the past two years.

I emphasized that Regina managed the teachers, cooks, maintenance people, and other personnel at the school. Regina planned the children's daily activities, weekly field trips, health checkups. Regina oversaw menus, and food and materials purchases. Regina communicated with parents and other schools as to the status of current students, former students, and prospective students. "She *is* the fucking school," I said.

If she had told a Brother to do an assigned task at the school and he had refused, she had had every legitimate reason on earth to reprimand him. If she had verbally abused him by referring to him as a punk, and further commented that only the women in the party did any real work, she should have been, at most, verbally reprimanded. I added that there had not been one woman—indeed, not one comrade—so severely disciplined in two years. I had stamped out that kind of brutishness. Finally, I asked why I had not been consulted.

Huey was listening, I thought. To me, his silence did not convey anything except confusion. I felt the moment had come when he might return to me and seized upon it. I said that I felt something very damaging was occurring inside the party ranks, exemplified starkly by two recent incidents. On the one hand, Bob, who had violated nearly every party disciplinary rule, had been virtually lauded for his behavior. On the other, a stalwart like Regina had been actually hospitalized on account of a verbal indiscretion.

The women were feeling the change, I noted. The beating of Regina would be taken as a clear signal that the words "Panther" and "comrade" had taken on gender connotations, denoting an inferiority in the female half of us. Something awful was not only driving a dangerous wedge between Sisters and Brothers, it was attacking the very foundation of the party.

He did not respond for a long time.

"You know, of course, that I know all that," he said finally, softly, thoughtfully. "But what do you want me to do about it? The Brothers came to me. I had to give them something."

"You gave them Regina?"

"Stop it. She took a hard line. She brought that on herself. Stop acting like a child. It doesn't affect you. And you know the deal as much as I do now. I just want to keep motherfuckers out of my face. Yours, too, for that matter."

I said nothing.

"They know I won't tolerate disrespect of you. And you know it. I can't worry about everything. Right now I've got to deal with my trial, or have you forgotten about that?"

"Me? The one who brought you back? The one who's always loved you, and especially because you said you were 'not a man, not a woman' and all that? The Brothers didn't make a way for you. I did!"

"Of course," he said with a sigh. "But I don't think you can get around the fact that you couldn't have done it without them."

"Who? The Brothers? The Sisters?"

"Without the guns! Don't make me angry with you. I want to move past this bullshit! Stop whining. You don't have anything to worry about."

"Except the party, Huey."

"And what? You think this party's life?"

"It's been my life."

"Not mine. That's the difference between you and me. I don't want to save the world. I just want to be Huey."

"I know that. I've always known it. But you *are* this party. You started it."

"And I'll finish it."

"Like this? Really? You just don't want to deal with the details. I'm here, as always. But I need you to put your foot on this rampant machoism—and that's all it is. You know I can't do it. Only you can. If you let this slide, you won't have a party, and . . ."

"And there'll just be Huey . . ."

"Who *is* the party . . ."

"I want a new role."

"Have it. Finish your trial and get your Ph.D. like you said. I'm a strategist. You're a dreamer. That's who Huey is. And I can make a dream happen. Just put the Brothers in line and keep this thing alive. I'm not just talking about Regina. I'm talking about all the women. They're critical. And all of them are scared. I'm scared. They'll run."

"Let the motherfuckers run, then. Let all of them run!"

"I just want to talk about it, Huey," I said, feeling myself slipping away.

"You want to talk?! Talk, then. Let's have a Central Committee meeting about it!"

As you and I are the Central Committee, I thought, without responding.

"You're not talking!" he confronted me, using the violence of his voice to slap me.

"Is that what you really want?" I mumbled to the man on the other end of the telephone line.

"That's exactly what I really want. I want *all* the bullshit stopped. Set it up. I mean it. Tomorrow. Can you do that?"

"Yes."

He did not see that he was making a suicidal decision. He did not see the mayor's office. He did not see the governor's office. He did not look back at the years of struggle that had brought us so far. He was refusing to look at the magnitude of the future. The City Center, the new housing, the school were being built. The police and the drug dealers had been pushed back. Our bank accounts were swelling. Everything was behind us. Everything was before us. He did not look.

Worse, he was opening a door through which history might come to define him not for his genius but for his weakness. He was opening a door through which history might come to define the party for its worst, not its best—John and Bunchy and Fred and George and so many others, our food and other programs that provided a concrete means for our people to survive and develop the will to make revolutionary change in America. I knew then that I could not step through with him.

As I contacted each so-called Central Committee member, establishing the meeting for the next afternoon, I could not construct another plan. There were no more arguments left in me. I just wanted to go to my corner and catch my breath.

Ericka Huggins actually believed an open discussion would be constructive. Norma tried to absent herself on the grounds of an important bank meeting. Phyllis was ready to fight. The rest of the women did not fully appreciate the situation. As for the men, I had Janice call them, without mentioning the subject matter.

I knew the women, even Phyllis and especially Ericka, would collapse under the rage of the men. Big Bob would hold sway, with Larry following suit. Michael Fultz and Emory Douglas would be too intimidated to even add to the discussion. Perkins might have defied the trend, but he had just been sent to Chicago to hold together what was left of the chapter. Even if Ricardo supported me out of old friendship, he would be overwhelmed in the end. I would be isolated and deemed a disrupter. Huey would chastise me openly, and maybe *offer* "something" to the Brothers.

I settled into the calmness of careful action. I sent Janice home. I waited until classes at the school ended to contact Aaron to bring my daughter to me. In the interim, I called Suzanne and told her my plan—which was to leave Oakland that very night.

I feared Suzanne did not understand the seriousness of what I was saying. Perhaps the party's guns had really been an abstraction to her. She said she would help me in any way she could: a place to stay, a job at Motown.

When Aaron called to say he was leaving the school with Ericka, I told him to have another car follow him. I would be keeping my car. When he arrived with Ericka and handed me the car keys, there was a strange sadness in his eyes. He left without asking what I wanted him to do in the morning.

I called my mother, and in short, crying phrases told her that Ericka and I were on our way there to live. She asked no questions. She told me she would be waiting for my call when I arrived. I made an airline reservation out of San Francisco, the Oakland airport presenting too many risks of discovery by too many people who would recognize my face. I realized I had to call Norma again, to get enough money to pay our fares. I had to pack only what I could carry.

Norma came immediately with the $250 I had asked her to bring. I implored her to leave with me in the same sentence I told her I was leaving. Tomorrow would be terrible, I said, explaining everything I knew and felt. She would keep my secret, she swore, and would not be far behind. She felt, however, that she would have to stay on another week or so—something about getting her signature removed from bank cards. I thought that was insane.

We called Phyllis and Ericka Huggins and Joan, advising them of what we characterized as impending doom. I told only Phyllis that I was leaving. I wished Norma luck. She left me with a kiss.

The telephone rang. It was Huey. He wanted to talk over dinner at his house. His voice was placid, sorrowfully needy. I had no suspicion that his offer was disingenuous. If he meant to do me harm, I knew he would have knocked down the door of my apartment with some of the men, no discussion.

It's not you, Huey, don't you see. I have really loved you hard. And I shall go on loving you.

I blurted out to him that I could not come because I had a meeting already scheduled with Fred Hiestand. In that case, he said, he would see me at the meeting the next day.

I reached near-hysteria when Fred Hiestand did not answer his telephone immediately. I confided all of it to him in brief sentences once he answered, begging him to support my lie if necessary, begging him to give me a few hours. I knew Fred adored Huey. He was my friend as well. I hoped he would not have to sort out his friendships.

Ericka clutched her brown-faced Raggedy Ann doll as the doorman took $10 of my $250 to carry our baggage to the car. On the elevator down to the street, I calculated my response if Huey or anybody else arrived as we were leaving. I would say I was taking Ericka to the airport for a visit to her grandmother. It sounded sufficient, but I could not stop shaking as the doorman meticulously placed our bags in the trunk of the car.

I was the best driver in the party, I thought, fantasizing a Hollywood car chase if anyone spotted me on the way to the Bay Bridge. Ericka and I sang songs with the radio, across the bridge and into the airport.

We were late. The plane was almost due to take off. We ran through the airport. My valise crashed into a wall support and spilled my songs. I bundled the papers I could not stuff quickly back into the briefcase under my arm, told Ericka to cling to my jacket, and we kept running. I had always made Ericka hold on to something I was wearing whenever we were in crowds. "Are you holding on to Mommy, Ericka?" I would say. She held on to me automatically now.

Freedom. That was all I could feel in those first seconds away from the Black Panther Party.

The pain of leaving came swiftly. There were dreams we all held for our people and for each other, and we had begun to forge those dreams. I remembered the voice of Father Earl Neil, the black Episcopalian priest who had opened his church to our breakfast program in the early, unpopular days. He had told a large Panther food-giveaway rally that, while Jesus had fed five thousand with His miracle of fishes and loaves, the Black Panthers fed tens of thousands.

The party had held on through the turbulence, the betrayals and the bloodletting of the times. We had held on past the era of mass rallies and demonstrations; after the Eldridge Cleavers were born again in other guises and the SLAs were entombed in police rubble; after peace activists retired when the Vietnam War ended; after Attica was forgotten, or desecrated by counterrevolutionaries; after Black Power advocates became quieted by police guns and prison bars; even as the progressive movement itself was becoming a casualty of police assaults and battle fatigue. The party had held on, and moved forward.

Now I was flying away, abandoning what I had sworn to die for, leaving comrades and friends, and so much work undone. Yet I could not be so arrogant as to imagine I was indispensable. I could not be so mad as to sacrifice my life to a dream that was dying. The pain was entwined in the complexity, for I loved the Black Panther Party.

My child was sleeping. I looked at her brown face, so inordinately innocent. I was abandoning something, but I was saving something. It was the hope, that had been my hope, and my mother's hope, and her mother's hope, and the hope of each of my people—mothers, aunts, brothers, fathers, children. If my life had any meaning left, this hope in one black child would live.

We began to circle the lights of Los Angeles. I touched my sleeping baby and thought of the song I had written for her.

> One night just before bed
> She shocked me when she said,
> What would happen if I died
> 'Cause no one cared
> When black girls cried—
> Oh, Ericka, my little baby,
> Ericka, my little child,
> Ericka, there is no maybe,
> I'll change the world for you
> In just a little while . . .

451

ILLUSTRATION
CREDITS